From

GROWING UP UNDERGROUND

We didn't think of ourselves as libertines seeking new thrills. We were much too serious for that. For my part, I came to think of the four of us as a family. At times we seemed a single consciousness, divided randomly into four bodies, four biographies, but sharing a vision to which we had implicitly sworn loyalty. We believed that the world could be cleansed of all domination and submission, that perception itself could be purified of the division into subject and object, that power playing between nations, sexes, races, ages, between animals and humans, individuals and groups, could be brought to an end. Our revolution would create a universe in which all consciousness was cosmic, in which everyone would share the bliss we knew from acid, but untainted by fear, possessiveness, sickness, hunger, or the need for a drug to bring happiness. The left had taught us that what we learned in school, in newspapers, on television, and from political leaders was suspect. Acid had given us the idea that by merging into the cosmos, we would transcend our own deaths. We found it difficult to put our ideas into words for the benefit of those who did not start by sharing them. With each other, we needed no words. Once, I formulated my idea of revolution like this: I said I wanted to smash a hole in the wall of imperialism, through which the liberated armies of the world would march.

GROWING UP UNDERGROUND

by

Jane Alpert

CITADEL PRESS
Published by Carol Publishing Group
New York

First Citadel Underground edition, November 1990

A Citadel Press Book. Published by Carol Publishing Group. Editorial Offices, 600 Madison Avenue, New York, NY 10022. Sales & Distribution Offices, 120 Enterprise Avenue, Secaucus, NJ 07094. In Canada: Musson Book Company, A division of General Publishing Co. Limited, Don Mills, Ontario. Manufactured in the United States of America. ISBN 0-8065-1196-6

Originally published by William Morrow and Company, New York, 1981. The Citadel Underground Edition is published by arrangement with the author.

1 2 3 4 5 6 7 8 9 10

BOOK DESIGN BY MICHAEL MAUCERI

This book is for my parents,
who never stopped helping

Contents

Foreword
to the Citadel Underground edition

I AM A NINETEEN-YEAR-OLD NEW York City resident. And despite the fact that I was raised in a liberal, single-parent household, and all that that implies, my knowledge of the Sixties results from the media's efforts to romanticize and thus commercialize the era. My generation is deprived of the true picture, having been forcefed the media image of peace, love, and LSD. Until reading *Growing Up Underground,* I was unaware of the reality of the Sixties—an authentic, contradictory and diverse era.

This book is incredibly important, because while Jane Alpert relates her story in a truly personal way, she does so without succumbing to sentimentality. She demystifies the time, recounting her experience more rationally and honestly than anything my generation is used to. Her story is fascinating and vital reading for anyone distressed or unsatisfied with the media's commodification of the late Sixties and early Seventies.

Before reading *Growing Up Underground,* I had already made up my mind about the radical politics of the Vietnam War era. I have always believed in achieving political change nonviolently. I still do. But as a member of the MTV generation, my education has been somewhat stunted. In the Eighties, our awareness of social issues was defined by the mass media—the cover of *Time* magazine or whatever cause was the center of the music industry's attention.

What the media leads my generation to believe is that the Sixties radicals were honest, pure of heart, unconventional and unified in their ideas of how to bring about an end to the war. And this is an intimidating image, considering my confusion about politics and methods of protest. It's as if a person isn't worthy of having political views if they are at all ambivalent over what to do about them. Despite the profit motive behind the image, there are personal ramifications.

In her book, Jane Alpert admits to being confused with the ways of political protest. As firm as she had been in her beliefs, she had doubts about her motivations. It is difficult not to respect her candor. She brings to light the fact that the actions those in the left took were not all purely motivated. It was not a matter of the Good Hippies fighting the Bad Establishment. Not only did those in the left disagree as to the methods of protest, but they had unwittingly created their own establishment with its own rigid rules. Alpert also makes us aware of the sexism prevalent in the movement.

To read *Growing Up Underground* is somewhat liberating. To know that there is more available to us than what has been constructed by the media is a tremendous relief. In its own beguiling way, the media has stripped us of our history and put in its place a picture that is as paltry as the lies we were systematically fed about the Vietnam War. To read this book is to begin to understand the girth of its power.

Martha Plimpton
New York City
May, 1990

Martha Plimpton was born and raised in Manhattan where she continues to live. Though she makes her living as an actress, she plans to be a rock star when she grows up.

Introduction to the Citadel Underground Edition

I FIRST MET JANE ALPERT IN THE winter of 1970, on an occasion when neither of us cared to reveal the sum total of our intentions. *The New York Times Magazine* had given me a plum assignment, to write a piece about some restless, angry females who were calling themselves, with the brashness of that hectic age, the Women's Liberation Movement.*

Something was happening out there, and the magazine's editors, a little slow on the uptake, had confused the nascent feminist movement, of which I was a part, with the radical women of the extreme male left—some of whom, like Alpert, had been driven by their rage against America's war in Vietnam to desperate acts of homegrown terrorism that I found psychologically scary, personally threatening, and politically appalling.

Jane had recently appeared on the front page of the *Times*, her fist raised in a clenched salute, after her dragnet arrest with three others in a bomb plot. She was currently out on bail, and my editor had suggested that I might want to begin my piece with her—make her the lead, use her as a symbol of the surprising new militance among women.

"Nothing doing," I had responded. Jane Alpert represented a siren call that terrified me: an emotional, extremist, poorly thought out, "revolutionary" response to a war that was making everyone crazy. Her way was wrong, bombing was wrong, Weatherman was wrong. Her philosophy, and that of Bernardine Dohrn and others, was wreaking havoc and consuming good energy inside the fragile women's movement, and I was doing

*My piece, when it appeared in March 1970, was titled "The Women's Liberation Movement Is Out to Prove That Sisterhood Is Powerful."

everything I could to fight it. *We* were struggling to free ourselves of the male left. Jane and her male-left-identified friends, as we and they frequently said, were our enemies. But when I learned that Alpert would be at a press conference called by the women of *Rat* to announce their takeover of that counterculture newspaper, I couldn't resist a look-see at this radical bomber of the hour.

She was unsmiling, slighter and more reticent than I had imagined, and so much younger—by twelve years—than I. Clearly she was proud of her own piece of journalism for *Rat*'s premier all-women's issue, an interview with Afeni Shakur of the Panther 21 conducted inside the Women's House of Detention.

I stared at the dense page of type under Jane's byline and gave up in disgust. Trying for a militant artistic statement, the *Rat* women had superimposed a black fist over the copy, effectively rendering the words illegible. Wondering how she'd respond, I told Jane her interview was unreadable because of the fist. Her eyes narrowed as she backed away, betraying a small amount of uncertainty.

That was the extent of our encounter. Within a few months, Jane Alpert jumped bail and went underground. *Rat* announced her departure with a truly arresting graphic: a dripping faucet and the words, "Jane, you left the water running." Once again I felt deeply threatened on a psychological level by this woman whose every action implied that she was the light and the truth and the way.

Two eventful years later, while visiting the offices of *The Village Voice*, I saw a typed manuscript by the fugitive Jane Alpert lying in Dan Wolf's outbox. Five minutes of reading told me it was political dynamite. Jane had repudiated her previous revolutionary positions, admitted the failure of the underground radical left, and produced a lengthy theoretical statement of her newfound feminism.

"You gonna print this?" I asked my old editor and friend.

"Nah. ———[his deputy of the moment for radical political affairs] thinks it's too unkind to Sam Melville."

I won't belabor the feminist point. Jane's piece was eventually published in *Ms.*, where the effect was hardly as astounding as it would have been in the *Voice*.

When Jane made the decision to resurface late in 1974, Robin Morgan called some of us together to counteract a nasty smear campaign conducted by Pat Swinton and her lawyer with help from Flo Kennedy the activist and Bob Fass of WBAI, among others. I named our group the Circle of Support for Jane Alpert; Florence Rush and Barbara Mehrhof did most of the work.

Jane was sentenced on two counts, the bombing conspiracy and bail jumping, and went to prison for two years. After she was released we met for the second time. To our mutual surprise and delight, we became good friends. Friendship is based on complicated emotional factors. One factor for me, as I've told Jane many times, is that I've always believed that if I'd been her contemporary in age, my rebellion might have taken a similar turn.

The Jane I know today bears little resemblance to the grim-faced, implacable young revolutionist I first saw in the offices of *Rat.* In terms of appearance, she's thinner than she used to be, is very chic, and has a ready, engaging smile. Like most other New Yorkers, she works long hours to earn a living and would like a larger apartment. She reads widely and is always up for a good political or literary discussion, and we usually end an evening by complimenting each other on our eclectic, sagacious views. She hasn't lost a jot of her intensity, but she has channelled it most determinedly into writing and editing, strenuous amateur swimming competitions, and vegetarianism. It is with the vegetables that I occasionally catch a glimpse of the old, holier-than-thou Jane of the certainties.

When *Growing Up Underground* was published in 1981, some of the reviews were unduly harsh. In the intervening years, as memories of the Vietnam War faded, people had grown irrationally angry at the Sixties. Jane's autobiography presented some critics with an opportunity to vent their rage against those siren calls of extremism that had once disturbed their sleep. Her report of the effects of acid and mix-and-match sex upon a generation of activists was turned against her, as was her careful attempt to explain Sam Melville's mesmerizing influence on her state of mind. Jane was misunderstood by some who should have known better or given her a more careful reading.

The cynicism and somnambulism of America in the Eighties will have to give way to something else, and the sooner the better! I admit to a bad case of nostalgia for the idealistic aspects of the Sixties (and for the Thirties as well, although I wasn't there). Dreams about a radical transformation of society are always appealing; the trick is not to sentimentalize, or to gloss over a previous generation's mistakes. Jane Alpert's autobiography, which captures the fervor and sickness of impatient, would-be revolutionaries in a nonrevolutionary time, is utterly unsentimental. In fact, it is merciless in its self-examination. And therein lies its greatest strength.

Susan Brownmiller
New York City
March, 1990

Susan Brownmiller is the author of *Against Our Will: Men, Women and Rape* (1975) and other books. She worked in the civil rights movement in the Sixties and helped to organize the feminist movement.

PROLOGUE
A Meeting-1968

SQUEEZED IN A CORNER OF THE DILAPidated sofa, my feet tucked under me, I kept staring surreptitiously at the earnest radicals crowded into the storefront office. The time was early September 1968, almost four years since President Johnson's bombings of Vietnam had transformed the New Left into "the movement"—a hodgepodge of politicos, working people, students, hippies, and drug-and-rock freaks united by their opposition to the war. The dingy storefront on Tiemann Place—a street between the Upper West Side of New York, where I lived, and black and Spanish Harlem—was festooned with the by-now-familiar symbols: posters of Huey Newton, Mao Tse-tung, and Che Guevara; bookshelves crammed with *Revolution in the Revolution?* and *White Skin, Black Masks;* stacks of *Monthly Review,* the *Guardian,* and *Liberation.* Half the men and women around me (all of them white) wore tiny NLF flag pins or Black Panther buttons. All wore the movement uniform of faded work shirt, jeans, and sneakers or lace-up boots. I felt out of place.

I had to remind myself that I too had been actively opposed to the war from its beginning. Since 1965, my sophomore year in college, I had argued that the bombings should stop, the troops come home, and the Vietnamese people be left free to determine their own form of government—even if they turned out to prefer communism to Western-style democracy. I had signed petitions opposing the draft and calling for a permanent bombing halt and had been to the mass antiwar marches in New York and Washington. The year before, at the Pentagon my roommate Jean and I had escaped by only hours being tear-gassed by the National Guard. Yet in the past twelve months, the movement and I had been going in different directions. While I was concentrating on my graduate school grades and a promotion at work, Martin Luther King and Robert Kennedy had been assassinated, prompting furious disillusionment among black people and formerly idealistic whites. Last April students had seized five buildings at Columbia and openly declared war on the university's corporate trustees. Last month the Chicago police had assaulted thousands of protesters at the Democratic convention. Now, at my first movement gathering since the Pentagon, I was torn between the feeling that I had walked into someone else's movie and my childhood-old ache to belong. I wondered if my uncertainty was visible beneath my bourgeois appearance.

Actually, I looked as inconspicuous as the couch. At twenty-one I was still more girl than woman: an inch or two shorter than average; a sturdy, not glamorous, figure; dark brown hair which wouldn't grow long; pale skin; a broad Jewish peasant's nose; wide-set hazel eyes, extremely nearsighted but still my best feature; contact lenses; only passably straight teeth, in spite of orthodontia when I was twelve. I was wearing an old corduroy skirt and pullover, chosen so that I wouldn't look overdressed. Still, I was the only woman in the room wearing a skirt. In a more ironical mood, I might have joked about the conformity of these supposed noncomformists. In my current crisis of doubt, I could not afford such glibness. The larger question was not my dress but how I was living my life, which I would have had to answer, "Unproductively, unhappily, and with narcissistic self-absorption."

Not that I couldn't make a good account of myself on paper. I had graduated from Swarthmore in June 1967 (two years younger than most of my classmates because of grades skipped in grammar school) and in a year had become a full editor at Cambridge University Press, with particular responsibility for books on Greek and Latin subjects, my college major. I was taking graduate courses in classics at Columbia, where my grades were good enough to make an academic career a plausible alternative to publishing work. I had used the money from my last raise to move out of the apartment I had shared with Jean and another college friend into a high-ceilinged studio of my own on Riverside Drive. I was getting along well enough with my parents so that my monthly trips to their Queens apartment were almost pleasurable. They were proud of my new career and satisfied at how well I had "straightened myself out" after a troubled adolescence. But I suspected my own collaboration with their values. I loved them, yet it had been clear to me since I was thirteen that I would never be happy living as they did. Now the only difference I could see between my life and theirs was that I was lonelier. They at least had each other.

A year out of college and into the business world—I could already see the next forty years marching on. Having climbed the promotion ladder at Cambridge, I would move on to a larger publishing firm, finally becoming the trusted assistant to a top male executive at a major house. I would have an affair with my boss or perhaps with a vice-president at a rival company, recognizing that my lover would never divorce his wife while I turned to emotional putty in his hands. I would hate my job but would work until nine every night, then swallow two pills and go to sleep. I would read *Glamour* and *Mademoiselle* on airplanes, looking for clues to contentment, and would gossip nastily about the new twenty-year-old girl at the office who thought she had the answers. How did other women survive decades at jobs where they were not only relatively underpaid and powerless but unlikely ever to meet a reliable, loving, unattached man? Nor was graduate school—once my hedge against the future—any more promising an alternative. During the protests at Columbia the only students I respected were polarized to the left, the ones I despised to the right, which left me floundering in the middle, feeling like a coward.

I glanced down at the leaflet in my hand. This afternoon, before the first course meeting of Greek Orators, I had stopped at the Students for a Democratic Society booth outside the Columbia gates. The skinny, long-haired recruiter had the bulging eyes of a speed addict and looked barely old enough to have graduated from high school. When I said I wanted to join SDS, he laughed. "Nobody *joins* SDS," he told me, with an air of superiority. "That'll just get your name on an FBI list." My self-doubt must have shown in my face. The SDSer dropped his sneer and flashed me a sympathetic smile. "If you want to get involved, why don't you go to this meeting?" he said, handing me a leaflet. I grabbed at it gratefully, remembering to return his clenched-fist salute, and then just skimmed the printed sheet as I dashed to class.

Now, reading the leaflet for the first time, I realized I had come not to an SDS gathering, as I had assumed, but to a group called the

Community Action Committee (CAC). Last spring, while SDS was mobilizing the Columbia campus, the CACers (the majority of whom were over thirty and lived, like me, on the Upper West Side) had held a sit-in of their own at a university-owned tenement on West 114th Street, protesting Columbia's plan to raze the building for a school of social work. Most of them had been arrested at the sit-in, and this group arrest (I gathered from their conversation) had been a kind of communal baptism, binding them all in their commitment to each other and to CAC. At the present meeting they were discussing whether to hold a similar protest at a single-room-occupancy (SRO) residence called the St. Mark's Arms, which was owned by the Episcopal church of St. John the Divine. St. John's was about to evict the tenants in order to build a modern nursing home on the site; the view of the CAC members was that the church, whose parishioners included a few Columbia trustees, was interested only in making more money, not in the tenants' welfare. A sufficiently militant demonstration might stop the marshals from carrying out the evictions, at least temporarily.

I knew the conditions in buildings like the St. Mark's Arms. I had accidentally visited one or two SROs while I was looking for my current apartment. The radicals' angry descriptions of them as rat-infested slum dwellings were not in the least exaggerated. Yet I was disappointed to hear their plans. I had come to this meeting because I wanted something cataclysmic to happen in my life. I wanted to respond to the emergencies created by the Vietnam War, the assassination of Bobby Kennedy, the police stampede against protesters at the Democratic convention. The poverty that distressed the CACers had been part of the world long before I was born and would go on after I was dead. Was this very resistance of mine only a sign of how profoundly I had sold out?

Greg Rosen, the chairman of the group, gave a sigh. "We can't pull a demonstration together in a week," he said. "If we're going to be there when the marshals come, we'll have to be on the street from six A.M. until three P.M. That means calling five, six hundred people. How are we going to do that before the weekend?"

I had resolved to say nothing, but the temptation was giving me a headache. These CACers were not, after all, so very different from me. They had jobs and went to graduate school. They lived alone or in couples. They had been arrested once or perhaps twice, and they were trying, as I was, to hold on to the commitment they had once felt to social change, not to yield to the fear and apathy of an older generation. I raised my hand.

"I've got the whole weekend free," I said. "I can call a hundred people by Saturday. Will that help?"

My contribution turned the meeting around (or so I flattered myself). In a few minutes the entire phone list had been spoken for. Small knots of people gathered around Rosen to discuss printing leaflets, notifying the news stations, convincing the radical newspapers to print announcements. I had to wait some minutes until Greg was free and could tell me where to find a copy of the list and suggest what I should say to the people I called. By the time I left the storefront it was nearly midnight.

Usually I was afraid of this borderline neighborhood after dark. The way to my apartment was along a narrow part of Riverside Drive, elevated above the river and so quiet that footsteps behind me sounded like echoing tomtoms. When I started living alone here, I had promised my parents that I would always take a taxi to my door. The idea of such precautions now left a sour taste. I would not hail a cab—perhaps in full view of a CACer coming up behind me—and slam the door against imagined dangers. I turned the corner on foot and with my back to taxi-land, began the twenty-block walk home.

Once out of sight of the CAC office, I was hugging myself with delight. I was looking forward not just to the demonstration but to the telephoning this weekend. Already it was beginning: a sense of purpose, of hope, was coming back. The CAC meeting had been the first step in what I thought of as a radical cure.

The commitment I made that night led me eventually, through a circuitous route, to forms of protest more dramatic than picket lines. In November 1969, after I had helped to set off bombs at eight government and corporate buildings in New York, I was arrested, pleaded guilty, and went underground, where I spent more than four years. I still don't understand all the forces that drew me into the conspiracy or the underground—any more than I understand exactly why I raised my hand at that CAC meeting. But I am certain that politics was only one part of what inspired me. While I am proud to have moved decisively against the Vietnam War, I also know that my motivations stemmed as much from a longing for acceptance as from a passion to rebel, as much from the kinds of relationships I formed in childhood as from my outrage at the United States government. How I came to believe and act as I did—and later, in a spirit of renunciation, to surrender and go to prison—is the core of this autobiography.

Highly qualified criminal attorneys have advised me that the statute of limitations has expired on all the illegal acts described in these pages. To protect the privacy of those involved, I have changed many names and identifying details. I have also taken some liberties with minor aspects of settings that are impossible to recall or verify after so long a time. However, all the characters are real, all the events took place, and dialogue has been re-created as nearly as I can remember it. I offer this book not in the service of any particular ideology or with the intention of discrediting any persons or movements but rather to set the record straight on my own role in a turbulent period of American history.

ONE

Origins

I wish there were somewhere
actual we could stand
handing the power-glasses back and forth
looking at the earth, the wildwood
where the split began

—Adrienne Rich

I

Childhood

SOMETIME BEFORE 1900, WHEN THEY were still children, my grandmother Freda Cohen and my grandfather Abraham Kahane came to the United States from Russia, refugees from the pogroms. They met about fifteen years later in Baltimore, where my grandmother had been brought up and where my grandfather had come from Boston to open a men's clothing store. They married, and soon after, the new business folded. They moved then—with two children of their own—to the Lower East Side of New York, where, my mother told me, they lived in the only apartment building in the neighborhood that had an elevator. This background of failure spiced by extravagant new starts was a dominant theme of my childhood, too.

In the 1930's Abraham Kahane rejected the Orthodox Judaism of his youth and became a socialist. On Friday nights, while Freda still observed the Jewish Sabbath, he met in a storefront to discuss Stalin, Trotsky, and the latest developments in the revolution in the old country, with other Jews who had also turned away from the tradition. Freda grew closer to her own family. With their three children (of whom my mother, born in 1920, was the second) she spent up to six months of every year in Baltimore. My mother regarded that city as her second home until she was in college, when she came to prefer the company of the more educated and cosmopolitan Boston Kahanes.

Abraham Kahane died suddenly of a heart attack when I was less than a year old, a tragedy Freda believed was a punishment from

God. Descriptions of Abraham always reminded me of my own father: loving, generous to a fault, a keen sense of humor, and a tendency toward bad luck in business combined with a dogged ambition to do well. In the photograph on my grandmother's desk he even looked like my father, a short, rather plump man, trying to smile in spite of the blinding sun. I suspected I would have preferred him to my stately, undemonstrative grandmother.

My mother was the only girl in the family. Her responsibilities began early. When she was nine, her older brother, Morris, became ill with a brain tumor. For the next six or eight years he was mostly in the hospital or in bed at home. He lost part of his sight and hearing and developed a bad stutter. Leon, the youngest, was a baby during Morris's illness. While Freda cared for her eldest, the babysitting fell to my mother. I never heard her complain about this, although it did make it difficult for her to appreciate that most children spent their time playing. She was extremely capable, not only helping to manage the household but also graduating from Hunter High School at fourteen and from Hunter College at eighteen. Her interests, for a girl in the 1930's, were unusual. She was mechanically gifted and thought she might become an inventor or a research engineer. Instead, she majored in statistics and married an engineer—my father, whom she met on a boating party the year after she graduated.

My father came from a much less stable background. His father, Henry, had emigrated from Russia as an adult, under mysterious circumstances—in the absence of information, I guessed he had run up debts. He took the name Alpert at Ellis Island, while his brother, who came over at a different time, took the name Schwenkerman. No relative I knew had the slightest idea of the original family name. In New York, Henry married Chava Bronstein from Odessa, twenty years his junior. They had three children, Gladys, Ira and, in 1916, my father. A year later Chava died of influenza. The three children were farmed out to aunts and uncles.

My father had four different homes before he was ten. Then he settled in with his maternal uncle, Jake Bronstein, and Jake's wife, Ida. Uncle Jake—whom I always called simply Uncle, as my father did—was a bony, yellowish man with decaying teeth and a fierce temper. I used to shrink in fear when he pinched my cheek. Aunt Ida, whom we called Tan (short for the Yiddish *Tanta*), was a sweet, self-effacing woman, whom my mother half-contemptuously called the saint.

I hated visiting the Brooklyn tenement where they lived: narrow, stuffy rooms smelling of onions and old floor wax. I associated their poverty with the cruelty and anger that reverberated through the apartment and couldn't understand how my father, who made rooms glow when he entered, could have been raised in such a place.

My father, despite his disadvantages, was an excellent student and earned high marks on the entrance exams for Cooper Union's prestigious tuition-free engineering school. For seven years he worked as a draftsman during the day while attending classes at night. He was twenty-two when he met my mother. She was slender with auburn hair and a tiny, heart-shaped face, pretty enough to have worked part time as a floor model at Saks. He was blond, not tall, but well muscled, a good dancer and swimmer, with a high forehead (like Henry Fonda's, my mother said) and candid green eyes. My mother hinted that her mother had not been enthusiastic about their engagement, but when I asked why, she brushed the question aside. "Your father's the kindest man in the world," she always said when I had brought her to the verge of criticism. (The preservation of image at the expense of honesty was also a theme of my childhood.) They were married in June 1941, the same month in which my father graduated.

Six months later the Japanese bombed Pearl Harbor and the United States was in the war. My father was working in a division of a company exploring ways to produce artificial rubber and had an automatic essential-job deferment. But after the company underwent a reorganization, he became dissatisfied and started looking for a better opportunity. Eventually he found a position at an international corporation making equipment for the army signal corps. His job change created some confusion at the selective service board, and he temporarily lost his deferment, causing some consternation in the family. In time, however, the board determined that his new job also entitled him to a deferment, and so he was able to avoid combat duty after all. This is, I think now, close to how it really happened. The version I was told when I was growing up was different. I was told, from about the age of five, that my father had longed to join the Navy and had gone so far as to enlist when the selective service office positively forbade him to leave his crucially important job. The reason for this, my mother said, was that my father, although he didn't know it at the time, was working on the atom bomb. She didn't know it then either—but she concluded that must have been what he was doing when the mushroom cloud blossomed over Hiroshima and Nagasaki and finally ended the war.

I was born two years after the war was over (and one year after my mother's first pregnancy ended in miscarriage) in May 1947, a healthy, much fussed-over child. My mother quit her job and the family moved from Manhattan to a one-bedroom apartment in Forest Hills, Queens, with a dinette my parents converted to a nursery. My earliest memory is of going to sleep there to the comforting murmur of their voices in the kitchen. The family album is filled with pictures of me crawling across my parents' bed, playing on the beach, practicing standing up before an admiring crowd of relatives and neighbors. In those early years of my life my father took a new job, in a company owned by a relative.

In the summer of 1949 a series of accidents began. Playing with silverware on the dining room table, I tipped over an electric percolator full of coffee. My mother rushed me to the hospital for what proved to be third-degree burns over most of my left side. While I was still in the hospital, my father broke his leg in a household accident. My parents were out for a drive with my father's sister and her husband when a third mishap occurred. A car rammed into theirs while my mother was behind the wheel, waiting for the light to change. Only my aunt was seriously injured, but the accident had repercussions. My mother, then two months pregnant, gave birth in April 1950 to a child with severe birth defects. My brother, Skip, had several operations to help him breathe and to repair his damaged mouth and nose, and my mother became a round-the-clock nurse to a child the extent of whose impairment could not be known.

Skip survived, with above-average intelligence, but almost blind, with respiratory difficulties and permanently stunted physical growth. I remember him as a large, inert lump who took all my mother's time and attention. My mother's place in my life was taken by Helen Williams, a black woman exactly my father's age whose mother had worked for Tan and Uncle in Brooklyn. Helen had baby-sat for me since I was born and was with me at the time my brother was delivered. From the time I was three, she was the person who fed, bathed, and played with me and sometimes put me to sleep. She treated me as though I were the personification of grace. Every new achievement of mine, from turning a somersault to singing the alphabet, drew exclamations of astonishment from her. I came to prefer her company to any except my father's.

My father adored me and I basked in his attention. He told me stories of midgets who lived on top of my stomach in regions he called Ackle-backle-stan, Baluki-stan, and In-the-middle-of-stan. He invented a family of monkeys—Zobo, Dufar, and their two children —and improvised adventures for them corresponding to the pages of a picture book about the jungle. He made up nonsense lyrics to the "Battle Hymn of the Republic" (one began "Pickles sleeping in the icebox"), repeating the words until I had them memorized. When I was eight, he taught me chess, starting with a four-piece handicap, reducing it then to a queen and finally to a rook, praising and encouraging me when I learned to guess his next moves. He gave me a book of math problems which my uncle Ben had won as a high school prize and beamed when I came to him for help in solving one. "I couldn't do that when I was your age," he loved to say. Every few weeks he would designate Sunday as "Fun-day," which meant a breakfast-to-bedtime day of favorite games and piggyback rides. I would desert any friend or children's outing for one of those Sundays with my father.

My mother kept her distance from this frolicking. "Your father's the one who's good with kids," she used to say. "He ought to publish those stories he tells you." I remember her, perhaps unfairly, as a disapproving figure. Sometimes she would sing me to sleep in her gentle soprano. One line in her repertoire went "And if I ever lost you/How much would I cry?" It always made me intensely sad and happy to hear her hit the high notes on that because it seemed as if she were singing directly to me and that she really did love me. More often, it seemed, she was scolding me for my clumsiness (I was the only child she ever heard of, she said, who tripped over plain linoleum), for wanting her attention, or for liking children who weren't as "good" as I was. I loved to play with her jewelry box and to rub my cheek on the fur lining of her winter coat. When she saw me doing that, she would call me a strange child and declare that she didn't understand me.

We moved from the Forest Hills apartment to a new tract house in Wantagh, Long Island. I went to kindergarten and first grade there, learned (with some difficulty) to swing and ride a two-wheeled bike, and became best friends with Cynthia, a girl in my class who lived down the block. My favorite games were School, in which I pretended to be a teacher, and Make-Believe, an ongoing drama I directed and starred in, featuring my favorite characters from Greek myths, fairy tales, comic strips, and television. Skip showed steady improvement, learning to walk and talk and proving beyond any doubt that he was not mentally retarded. By the time he was four he was nearly as big as I was and able to hold his own in our physical fights. My parents helped build the first synagogue in Wantagh, where my father served as vice-president and my mother as a Sunday school teacher. After three years of relative contentment my father decided to take a job with a manufacturer of advertising displays in New Jersey.

During the summer before I started second grade, we moved to Englewood, New Jersey, where my parents had rented half of a two-family frame house. I was dimly aware that the move was a source of tension between my parents, but they didn't talk to me about it. I didn't mind it myself. I soon became best friends with the girl next door who was as willing an actress in my dramas as Cynthia had been. Skip began nursery school and seemed not to have many difficulties, although he didn't have friends either. I liked my new school, where I soon acquired a reputation as precocious and was given special advanced reading and arithmetic assignments. Two years later we moved again.

My father's new job was as vice-president of the Linz Glass Company, a factory in the Blue Ridge Mountains of southwestern Pennsylvania. The Linz family, which had started the company, had just sold it to a Chicago multimillionaire named Alan Welch who wanted my father to run it for him. This was more executive responsibility than my father had ever had, an enormous salary increase, and prestige. But it was a drastic change in our lives. In the summer of 1956, when we moved into the handsome old house in Point Marion, Pennsylvania, which the company had provided, we were in an isolated section of Appalachia, four hundred miles from everything familiar to my parents: theaters, subways, museums, bustling streets, skyscrapers, *The New York Times,* and other Jews. My mother discovered that the elementary school Skip and I would both attend in Point Marion was little more than a one-room schoolhouse whose teacher spoke an Appalachian dialect incomprehensible to a New Yorker's ears. She made up her mind that we would move to Uniontown, the county seat and a town of perhaps 30,000, forty minutes away. It took her six months to find a house she wanted to rent there. Meanwhile, rather than let us go to the

Point Marion school, she drove us to Uniontown every day, waited in town to give us lunch, and waited again until the end of the school day, when she drove us back home.

I first became conscious of myself as an outsider in Uniontown. For the first time in my life I nearly flunked a spelling test because I couldn't understand the teacher's pronunciation. One classmate asked me if my father gave me money for using "long words." My mother warned me that we were in anti-Semitic territory, where people might call us names and shun our company just because we were Jewish. This never happened to me, although I was occasionally told that I didn't "look Jewish." But I did feel different. I was the only child in the fourth grade who ate lunch with her mother and brother in the classroom, the only one who was late at least once a week when my mother had to drive the winding roads behind a coal truck. I was also the only one who hadn't grown up calling black people "niggers." (I hadn't known any black people except Helen and her children.) In the Uniontown school there were twenty or so black children, who kept rigorously to themselves and were the butt of the white children's jokes. I tried to make friends with one, a sixth grader named Dolores who was often alone at recess, but when she invited me to her house, my mother wouldn't let me go, saying she didn't know Dolores's family. My experiences, both with Dolores and with the white children in my class, made me curious about the school integration battles in the South I heard grown-ups discussing. I fantasized that the next time my family moved, it might be to the Deep South. There I would be one of the heroic white children who welcomed black children to her school.

My favorite book was Frances Hodgson Burnett's *A Little Princess,* about nine-year-old Sara Crewes who has lost her mother at birth but is the chief joy of her handsome young father's life. As the book opens, Sara is going off to boarding school in London while her father is leaving for Africa to manage his investment in diamond mines. A year later her father dies of malaria, penniless and raving in the African jungle. Sara is forced to become a drudge for the evil boarding school mistress. She starves in an attic, tutors young students for long hours, is teased mercilessly by her former classmates. Finally her plight is discovered by her father's business partner, who, it turns out, has been looking for her all over London. The diamond mines were a success after all, and Sara, now richer than before, is rescued from the boarding school into the business partner's home.

The Linz Glass Company was, to me, the reality for which the diamond mines served as metaphor, a marvelous place where red-hot furnaces turned sand into glass and rubber-clothed men blew the molten stuff into bowls, multifaceted ashtrays, and paperweights that shattered light into a million rainbows. It was the exciting highlight of a class trip that made me briefly a school celebrity when I was in fourth grade. The bad part was that I hardly ever saw my father after he started to work there. He left for work before breakfast, came home after I went to bed, and even on weekends was rarely in the house. I knew things were going badly because I heard him quarreling with my mother late at night, when I was supposed to be asleep. Like Sara Crewes, I never blamed my father for deserting me. I kept quiet, practicing my princess behavior. This gave me a case of chronic gastritis and, at the end of a year, landed me in a hospital with a bladder infection.

I skipped fifth grade and started sixth at the age of ten. A few children in the sixth grade went out of their way to befriend me. In the middle of the year I was elected editor of the school newspaper. My confidence soared. Uniontown seemed less lonely when I had someone to walk to school with every day and a teacher who praised my schoolwork and character. And then the diamond mines failed; Alan Welch fired my father for having made poor investments.

On a bitter New Year's Day 1959 we moved again, back to Forest Hills, to an apartment two blocks from the one I was born in. From the time I had to part with my cat in Uniontown until the morning, two days later, when we reached Forest Hills I alternately sulked and vented my hostility on Skip, who was still too young to understand what a state we were in. After the spacious Uniontown house, which had backed onto the extensive grounds of a friary, the two-bedroom city apartment felt miserably cramped. For months, we tripped over hundreds of boxes my mother couldn't find room for and didn't want to throw out. My parents hired a carpenter to build a partition in the room Skip and I were to share. I had the inner, more private half, with both the windows, but still felt as though I were in an attic. Listening to Skip's heavy breathing on the other side of the partition made me feel as though I were suffocating. Meanwhile, my father, who had a new job but at half the salary he had earned at Linz, was home less than ever and was hard to talk to. Helen came back to work for us, but now that I was eleven, we no longer had the rapport we had shared when I was small.

School was a nightmare. In the eyes of the sophisticated New York seventh graders I was a country hick who wore plaid-framed glasses, homemade clothes, and a frizzy Toni that made my hair bunch up on top of my head and around my ears. In a gym class of a hundred girls, I was the only one who still wore an undershirt. There was a code for what was cool and what was creepy, and I was unable to crack it. The teachers complimented me on my recitations and gave me A's, but my classmates hooted and mocked my phrases and intonations. After a five-minute speech on dog breeds, I was given the nickname Doggie, which stuck for the rest of the school year. Nor did I have the excuse that their cruelty was related to anti-Semitism. Ninety percent of them were Jewish.

Nearly all the bright students in the school were in a special accelerated class which finished the three years of junior high in two. Since I had skipped fifth grade in Pennsylvania, my mother was reluctant to see me placed in this advanced class. After two months in the new school I was so unhappy that she relented and let me transfer, hoping the change would boost my spirits. It made little difference. All through junior high school I never had a friend.

I came home every day fighting back tears and venting my hurt on my mother, not because it was her fault but because she was there. I told her she was stupid and backwards and that when I grew up, I would never speak to her. I threatened to run away from home and thought that I meant it, while all I wanted was to see her cry. I deliberately kept my room a mess. I accused her of preferring Skip—who was having as hellish a time as I was in his new school and may have needed her help more. I think if she had seen through my rage and simply taken me in her arms, she could have dissipated most of my temper, but she was too proud to risk rejection and was not naturally demonstrative. Every move she made seemed part of a plot to make me miserable.

As I finished seventh grade, my father quit his new job and used the family savings to open his own consulting business. He rented an office on Forty-second Street, bought office machinery, hired an answering service, had stationery and circulars printed. He was home more often than he had been in years, and I was briefly happy again. I loved going to his office on weekends and playing with the big

Rolodex and the IBM typewriters. I helped him type thousands of file cards and stuff envelopes with advertisements. We had lunch at Tad's Steak House and fed the pigeons at the New York Public Library. Sometimes on the way home, we stopped at the Forty-second Street Chess Club, where I loved to watch him hunch over a chessboard for a silent game with a stranger. The new business lasted six months. Then, with no customers and no money to pay the rent, the utilities, or IBM, my father closed the office and came home for good.

This last disappointment appeared to overwhelm him. My father was a good man who had brains and ability, had cheated no one, and had worked sixty- and seventy-hour weeks for nearly ten years. Although what had happened was mostly the result of misfortune and not his fault, it cost him his self-confidence. Instead of job hunting, he stayed at home, unable to face the possibility of another rejection. And the blow to his dignity caused a temporary change in his personality. Always a gentle and compassionate man, he became unpredictably abusive, and would hurt and startle me with his sudden outbursts. But I also found a kind of sweetness in the violence, since when the storms were over, he would hug and comfort me, and weep over what had become of us.

After some months of this his pride led him to announce that he had found a job with a company called ABC. He wrote the phone number on a pad over the telephone. Once again he was gone every morning when I got up and came home after I went to sleep. This pattern lasted until the night before my ninth-grade graduation when he failed to come home at all.

I was on my way out the door to a graduation rehearsal when my mother accused me of not noticing his absence. She may have been right. I had grown accustomed to not seeing and, more, to not asking. As soon as she challenged me, I caught her anxiety. I was distracted through the rehearsal. When I came home, my mother, tight-lipped, told me my father had been found. He was in a hospital in Harlem. We would see him tomorrow, after the graduation ceremony. Her ashen face told me that we had reached the bottom at last.

We drove through Harlem with the windows of the car tightly rolled and the doors locked. It was like visiting another civilization: soul food restaurants, children playing stickball, women in tight, flounced dresses, men lounging on the corners as though they had nowhere else to go. My grandmother, who had arrived from Washington, murmured that New York had a lot of *shvartzehs* but that

Washington had more. I had heard the word before but didn't know what it meant. I asked my mother if this was where the ABC Company was.

"There's no ABC Company," my mother snapped. "Couldn't you figure that out?"

I might have, but I didn't.

When I saw my father in the hospital bed, it was all I could do not to bolt the room. His face was very white and lined. His eyes were bloodshot. His arm was attached to an intravenous feeding machine. His voice was so weak that I had to put my head on the pillow to hear him. I kissed his cheeks again and again, and he hugged me, but without much strength or enthusiasm. He had always been a muscular, vigorous man. In the hospital bed he seemed diminished and old. He was barely aware that he had missed my graduation. When I told him about the ceremony, he didn't seem to be listening.

When he came home, still tired and listless, my mother accepted an invitation for the four of us to spend a weekend with the Silvers, family friends who had a house on the ocean in Massapequa, Long Island. It was the first trip we had made in many years that I enjoyed. Sam and Yetta Silvers lived in a rambling two-story house bordering a canal. They had a huge yard, two boats, and three kids who instantly accepted me. Paul, the oldest, was fourteen, a year older than I, tall, ruddy, athletic. Tommy was twelve, sweet-natured and bookish. Fat little Sally was ten, exactly Skip's age. She preferred my company to Skip's or to any of the neighborhood girls. This flattered me, especially after the long months of rejection. At the end of the weekend my mother told me that the Silvers had invited me to stay on until the end of July. I ended up remaining until the end of August, when I had to return to Forest Hills to start high school.

The Silvers children seemed to live in their own world, undisturbed by adult invasions. They spent their days swimming or boating in the canal, making projects in the garage, or playing in their friends' yards. They came in the house only to sleep or eat, getting up from meals with a mumbled "Scuse me" ten minutes after sitting down. After two years of the cramped Forest Hills apartment, overwhelmed by loneliness and by my parents' problems, I was in a children's paradise. I learned to swim, turn cartwheels, and steer a motorboat. Poorly coordinated as I was, I even managed to balance on water skis. I played dolls and house with Sally, who assured me

I was the best friend she ever had. I talked about books with Tommy, who never made me self-conscious about being a girl. And I was physically attracted both to Paul and to his best friend, Chuckie.

After a long day of play I would go off after dinner with Paul and Chuckie, into the woods behind the Silvers' house. We sat on an abandoned trunk surrounded by maples and willows, and in the fading summer light I took off my blouse and bra and allowed them to kiss and touch my breasts. During the day they mostly ignored me, but at night they regarded my body with awe. I knew I was going beyond Ann Landers's guidelines and that my father would be apoplectic if he found out, but I could have stayed on that trunk with Paul and Chuckie until the snow came. I was frightened only once. One August night the three of us misjudged the time of sunset and came back to the house after dark. Sam Silvers was waiting for us on the porch, his face reddened from drink. He was a tough, sinewy man with barking voice and a short temper. I was afraid of a thrashing or, worse, of being sent back to Forest Hills in disgrace. But he only stared coldly and ordered Paul and me upstairs while Chuckie made a dash for his own house.

I didn't think of myself as a sexual rebel; I had no intention of outraging anyone by my behavior. I was doing what came most naturally to me, creating a private world, safe from intruders, where I could play with my friends and feel that I was loved. Sally, who confided in me, and Tommy, who treated me as an equal, were as important to my universe as Paul and Chuckie, who gave me the physical affection I got nowhere else. From the security of that made-up family, I felt capable of taking on the world. The game I was playing was essential to my stability, but it was also more dangerous than I dared admit. I was dreading the return to Forest Hills as though it were a prison.

II
High School

WHEN I RETURNED TO FOREST HILLS AT the end of August, I discovered that my mother had taken power in the family. While my father was recuperating from what my mother now called, sotto voce, his nervous breakdown, she had gone to work for the World Book Company, selling encyclopedias from door to door, "just to tide us over," she explained. She had also registered for education courses, starting in September, and intended to get a teacher's license within a year. Ill at ease with the changes in her, I resisted her attempts to befriend me. I didn't want curtains in my room or a new wardrobe, especially not if it meant a day discussing color schemes with my mother. I didn't care about the family's financial stability. I just wanted my father back—my *father,* not the remote figure who now haunted my mother's home.

My mother, recognizing my discomfort, told me stories meant to win me to her side. One day, she said, she had come home from selling encyclopedias to find my father sitting in the bedroom, a notebook in his lap. "He said he was 'writing,' " my mother reported, in a tone of disgust. "I said I wouldn't have him indulging his fantasies while I was ringing doorbells." A few days after that she had my father attending training classes at the World Book Company. Then she persuaded him to join an organization for out-of-work executives. By the end of the summer he was diligently seeking employment again. I could forgive him for giving up the dream of owning a business, but not for his allegiance to my mother, whom I viewed as a usurper. If only he had left her and taken me with him!

I would have helped him without ever inflicting the humiliation on him that my mother did.

My mother had always been bright and capable. She was earning her own living by the time she was eighteen and, if she hadn't quit her job to have children, would by now have been established in a career. When she went back to school, she earned straight A's in graduate math and education courses, at the same time selling encyclopedias, substitute teaching in the public schools, and running the household. She had always read widely, could solve math problems in her head and knew how to rewire lamps and fix leaky faucets in a snap. "I'm more intuitive than your father," she liked to say, "but he's deeper than I am. Skip's impatient, like me, but you've got your father's mind." I felt put-down and suspected that her assignment of family traits reflected the alignments more than it explained them.

I came to believe that she hated me. If I made the mistake of confiding in her about a book or a person I liked, she would interrupt to tell me my blouse was stained or my hair was in my eyes. If I accused her of not listening, she retorted with an uncanny insight that made me more resentful. "You run after people who are unworthy of you," she would tell me, seeming to detect each new crush before I knew it myself. "When I was your age, I had a crowd of friends. I never cared about one particular person over others—until I met your father." How did she know that I had my heart broken again every month, by either a boy I wanted to touch me or a girl I wanted for a friend? When I did bring acquaintances home, my mother—I suppose from loneliness—would waylay them in the kitchen and ply them with tea, cookies, and conversation before releasing them to my room. Unable to see her pain, I accused her of trying to steal them from me, a charge she dismissed as absurd. I had no privacy; even my half a bedroom, behind the plywood partition that divided me from Skip, was suffused with her presence. Between homework assignments, I wrote out my hatred of her on scraps of notebook paper, then tore them carefully to shreds before going to sleep, half fearing, half longing for discovery.

Forest Hills High School, where I became a student in September 1960, was considered by parents and educators one of the better schools in the public system. Its enrollment had tripled in the fifteen years since it was built. Classes were overcrowded, and the halls, between bells, were as jammed as a rush-hour subway. I often squeezed from one end of the two-block-long building to another without seeing a friendly face. Coming from a home in which I was now isolated, the school, regimented and impersonal, heightened my loneliness.

Academically Forest Hills was still dominated by cold war post-Sputnik attitudes. In American history we studied the Monroe Doctrine as a symbol of the United States' benevolence toward Latin America. We discussed the Kennedy-Nixon presidential race without once mentioning the civil rights issue—perhaps because the school administration felt threatened by black community demands to bus non-Forest-Hills children to the high school. In English we worked on pronunciation and read *Silas Marner* as though it were a morality play. The administration's mistrust of students was very nearly paranoid. We were required to carry huge wooden passes if we left class to go to the bathroom. Fifteen-year-old monitors patrolled the halls, sending to the dean's office anyone caught loitering. Smoking was forbidden within a block of the school building, not because it was unhealthy but because it was considered unseemly behavior for teenagers. Consequently, the bathrooms were always crowded with smoking students and cutting classes without getting caught was an art nearly everyone attempted.

I was assigned to the honors program, in which all of us were white and mostly from middle-class Jewish homes. I was also one of forty honors sophomores assigned to a noncredit experimental course called Preparation for College in which we studied college catalogs and learned how to make good impressions at admissions interviews. Although I was glad to be away from the junior high school students who had taunted me for a year and a half, I wasn't comfortable in my high school classes either. I felt guilty over my sexual experiments in Massapequa and was sure that no other honors student had ever behaved so disreputably. But I had no chance of making friends with the nonhonors students, who were mostly Greeks, Italians, and blacks. Once or twice I tried to start conversations with them in the bathrooms or on the way home. My efforts were rewarded with blank stares, sometimes with laughter, as though I were speaking a foreign language. I admired their insolent, independent style, but I couldn't make it my own.

The first friend I made in Forest Hills was Adele, an honors sophomore whose plain, earnest face was so like my own she was sometimes mistaken for my sister. Adele's parents, Polish survivors of the Holocaust, owned a candy and tobacco store on a block between the wealthy WASP section of Forest Hills and a working-class Greek and Italian neighborhood. The family lived in four crowded rooms in the back of the store. Ashamed of their poverty, Adele rarely invited friends home. The first time we met (through a mutual acquaintance in the honors program) we shared complaints about the competitiveness of our fellow students and the shallowness of our teachers. Soon we were talking on the telephone every night and lending one another books. Adele's favorite when I met her was *The Fountainhead.* I devoured its seven hundred pages in a few nights and became devoted to Ayn Rand.

The Fountainhead was one of the first adult books I was allowed to read, and its ideas influenced me strongly for a year or two. Ayn Rand hated weak-minded conformists who had no faith in themselves. Adele and I were insecure and not very popular, so we responded powerfully to that, assuring each other we were not so much misfits as independent spirits. Rand complained about people's shallow tastes in art—their preference for the sentimental and accessible over the transcendent and difficult. Dutifully Adele and I read the *New Yorker* and *Partisan Review,* went to the Guggenheim, *Last Year at Marienbad,* and *The Blacks.* Our comprehension was slight, but we were very serious and held long, earnest discussions meant to persuade each other that we had caught on. Rand's view that religion was irrational and an insult to man's intelligence captivated me. A year after I first read her books, I announced to my parents that I would not participate in our temple's confirmation ceremony. I capitulated—after many tears and implied threats that I might not be allowed to attend college out of town—but not before I had made my point by insisting, for several weeks, that I was going to declare my atheism from the pulpit.

Ayn Rand's heroes and heroines moved me even more than her ideas. The women were strong and sexually independent. They slept with any men they wished and fell in love with men who were even more ruthless than they. The heroine of *The Fountainhead,* Dominique Francon, is a wealthy, beautiful journalist who is cold to men until she meets Howard Roark, an architect so uncompromising that he cannot hold a job in any established firm. At the end of the book she helps Roark blow up a housing project after a committee of inferior architects botches the design. Dominique, in an attempt to look like an innocent victim of the explosion rather than a conspirator, slashes her arteries with broken glass and nearly bleeds to death. She recovers in time to watch Roark win acquittal in a passionate defense of individual rights. Adele and I argued for weeks over the moral implications of the bombing and the acquittal, but we never doubted that if Howard Roark had asked us to blow up a building, we would have counted it an honor.

In *Atlas Shrugged*, which I read soon after *The Fountainhead*, the inventors and industrialists of the world go on strike by withdrawing to a Shangri-la founded by John Galt, philosopher-king of the laissez-faire right. Galt's organization is no ordinary labor union. Its members are the men who run the copper mines and steel industries, who write great music and literature, and one woman, Dagny Taggart, an engineer in charge of the country's leading railroad company. Dagny, who combines a "masculine" mind with an elegant feminine appearance, falls in love with Galt but is reluctant to sacrifice her railroad to his strike. Finally she recognizes that the strike and ensuing collapse of industry and essential services are the only hope for a world renaissance. She joins him, and the two other men who have loved her willingly give her up to John Galt, recognizing him as their better and an ideal match for Dagny.

Although I rejected Rand's right-wing economics and political philosophy by the time I was fifteen, certain elements of the novels, which had more to do with psychology than with social ideology, stayed with me for many years. *The Fountainhead* had planted in me the idea that bombing a building could be a morally legitimate form of protest. *Atlas Shrugged* portrayed the social revolutionary as hero. And Dominique and Dagny, brilliant, powerful, yet sexually passive heroines who submit to the men they love, remained my role models long after I had forgotten where I first heard their names.

In June 1961 my father ended a year of job hunting by signing a partnership agreement with a college friend, Leonard Schor, a manufacturer of electronic parts. Thoroughly alienated from both my parents and my brother by this time, I would have preferred to skip the family celebration at a Long Island restaurant, but since both Schor children, who were the same age as Skip and I, were going, I couldn't. I managed to excuse myself from shopping for a new dress, but not from the trip to the beauty parlor which was supposed to make me presentable for the evening. As soon as I came home from the beautician, I soaked my hairbrush in water and furiously attacked every puff and curl, then teased my hair into the Tuesday Weld look I considered chic.

The photograph taken on the restaurant steps is an embarrassing reminder of my adolescence. The other seven are wearing fashionable clothes that fit. Their hair is in place, and they are smiling dutifully, even happily, at the camera. My father's arm is around my mother's shoulders, and Skip, short and overweight, looks reasonably content. My dress is three inches too short and tight, exaggerating my overblown fourteen-year-old curves. My hair, raised stiffly at the crown, limps down the frames of my glasses like a fallen soufflé. The sun is not in my eyes, but I am scowling, obviously attempting to spoil the occasion for the rest. Like some congenital monster, impossible to dispose of or to love, I am fixedly ignored by both families.

In May 1961 a group of black and white youths sponsored by the Congress of Racial Equality (CORE) set out by bus from Washington to test the southern states' compliance with desegregation rulings. The questions posed by their trip—whether we lived in a just society, by what methods change could be accomplished, when violence might be acceptable—were the very ones raised in Ayn Rand's novels. And racism had been a subject of some interest to me ever since my experience in the Uniontown elementary school. I was gripped by the freedom riders' progress through the South.

On May 20, my fourteenth birthday, a crowd of two hundred whites in Montgomery, Alabama, attacked the freedom riders with baseball bats, sticks, metal bars, and knuckle-dusters. The next day a larger mob attempted to attack a church where Martin Luther King was speaking. The segregationist governor was finally forced to call in the National Guard. The numbers of the freedom riders swelled in response to the violence. Their confrontations with segregationists in Alabama, Louisiana, and Mississippi captured national headlines through the month of June until, in September, the Interstate Commerce Commission affirmed its prohibition of discrimination in transportation.

I wanted to be a freedom rider. I pictured myself in a knot of black and white students, singing freedom songs as we rode into the South, facing down armed mobs as we disembarked. I imagined myself explaining my commitment to TV journalists, then graciously stepping aside so that my black friends could speak in their own behalf. (It was years before I realized that my fantasy relied on the same patronizing attitudes the civil rights movement wanted to eradicate.) The idea that I might be beaten or spend weeks in a southern jail made my vision more romantic. In my imagination, I was fearless.

When my parents spoke admiringly of Martin Luther King and the freedom riders, I wanted to scream at their hypocrisy. They lived in an all-white neighborhood, employed a black maid, and knew no black people as friends. How dared they claim the civil rights activists as their own? At times I feared that their racism had been passed on to me like a genetic trait and that it was already too late for me to prove that I was different.

In the second semester of my junior year I was transferred to a section of the honors English program taught by Marilyn Brandee. A recent graduate of Forest Hills High School and Queens College, Miss Brandee was one of the youngest and most intellectual teachers at Forest Hills. She was also sexy. She wore narrow skirts and bright nail polish and taught her classes sitting at the edge of her desk, looking unselfconsciously casual as she shot questions at us. It was the first high school class I didn't devote to watching the clock.

At a time when open discussion of personal experience was still considered unseemly, Miss Brandee's psychic intuitiveness allowed us to relate literature to our daily lives. She also taught us how to uncover hidden meanings in great works of art. When we read *The Scarlet Letter,* she asked us to tell her how Hawthorne used light and dark. No one knew what she meant. She told us to read the novel again, this time with a stack of index cards on which we were to note each word describing a color or shade. When we were finished, we were to go through the cards and decide what the descriptive words added to each scene. In the process, we discovered the uses of symbolism, imagery, and metaphor. After *The Scarlet Letter,* we eagerly asked Miss Brandee for more novels we could read in the same detective fashion. She gave us *Moby Dick.*

We went on to poetry. Adele and I had read Rilke, Thomas, cummings, and Stevens with pleasure but little understanding. Miss Brandee taught us to trace patterns of language in a poem as a clue to its meaning. After reading several poems by Yeats and Eliot in class, we were required to write short papers analyzing poems of our own choosing. I selected Dylan Thomas's "If I Were Tickled by the Rub of Love" because I loved his sonorous reading of it on the Caedmon record and because its meaning had always eluded me. But I had no idea what his references to "sea of scums" breaking "on the sweethearts' toes" meant, even after several works of criticism had helped me figure out the rest. I took the line to Miss Brandee in the English department office where she and a few male colleagues were smoking on their break. She blushed, for the first time that I could remember. "You may be too young to understand this poem," she said. Then she corrected herself. "No. It's just that I can't explain it to you. It's a sexual image." I hadn't meant to embarrass her and was sorry that I had asked, especially in front of her male colleagues. Everyone to whom I told the story was convinced that if I'd found Miss Brandee alone, she would have talked to me as an equal, but in the office she had to maintain appearances for the fifty-year-old traditionalist chairman. This may not have been true, but it was a sign of our great affection for her that we all believed it.

My junior year was marked by controversy over the newly organized United Federation of Teachers, which was threatening to strike in the spring if the city failed to meet its contract demands. My mother, who was then substitute teaching, refused to join the union. Like many older, conservative teachers, who thought of themselves as professional educators, not as employees, she spoke of the union organizers as rabble-rousers who were demeaning the calling. Naturally I was on Miss Brandee's side, not my mother's.

Miss Brandee, as rumor had it, was one of Forest Hills High School's union representatives. As the semester went on and strike talk grew more heated, her absences became more frequent. Union business? we wondered. Or perhaps—even more exciting—she had a lover? I took to spending most of my free afternoons in the English department office, pretending to help the chairman type program cards but actually listening to the teachers' gossip for inside news on the strike. They never spoke of it in my presence.

On April 11, 1962, the teachers walked out. There were reports of violence on the picket lines, and my mother insisted that Skip and I stay home for the day. Even though I was aching to know if Miss Brandee was on the picket line, I stayed home but that evening called all my friends to find out if anyone had seen her.

The next day the school board won an injunction forbidding the strike and all teachers came back to work. We studied Miss Brandee carefully. I thought of Hawthorne's lines about Hester Prynne on the scaffold, whom the Puritans expected to see "dimmed and obscured by a disastrous cloud" but whose "beauty shone out and made a halo of the misfortune and ignominy in which she was enveloped." In fact, I saw no change. She was dressed, as always, in a straight skirt and sheer, flawless stockings; her nail polish was unchipped, her manner crisp. Just before the class ended, a boy in the back raised his hand and asked her what we all wanted to know.

"Miss Brandee, would you please say something about the strike?"

There was a brief silence.

"I'm sorry, I can't do that," she said.

It was never mentioned again.

As I spent more time in the English department office, I came to know other students who frequented the office—the Forest Hills bohemian crowd, girls who wore black tights and sandals, sprinkled their speech with "man" and "cool," and appeared contemptuous of school authorities while maintaining high scholastic averages. Adele and I had always mocked students who attached themselves to cliques; but by my junior year the two of us had drifted apart, and I was once again hungry for companionship. I shared with the bohemian crowd admiration for Miss Brandee, a growing interest in literature, adulation of "hip" Greenwich Village, and disdain for bourgeois Forest Hills. And I was fascinated to hear those girls talk about sex without giggling or feigning disinterest—unlike the other honors students.

The girl in this crowd I admired most was Beatrice Caplan, a tiny sixteen-year-old with a sharp-boned, expressive face and a rebellious temperament. Beatrice eventually graduated tenth in a class of nearly 1,300 and won scholarships to three major universities, but never bothered to study what didn't interest her. She charmed her way to high grades in science and math, at which she wasn't very good, and concentrated on English and foreign languages, which she picked up with astonishing speed. A gifted actress, she had appeared in several school plays, learning her lines only hours before dress rehearsals. She replayed her favorite roles at dull moments in conversation, convulsing her friends by the lift of an eyebrow or a sudden eloquent shrug of her shoulders. She was alternately affectionate and imperious, snubbing anyone who dared to call her Bea and treating her best friends with genial tolerance. She rarely telephoned me but almost never refused when I wanted to come over to her apartment. Her sister, Joanne, was away at college and I spent many nights sprawled on her vacant bed, across the room from Beatrice, changing the blues records on the stereo and talking until dawn about poetry, music, and boys.

In spite of my consuming interest in sex, I was inexperienced. At the end of my sophomore year I had gone out for a few months with Don, a boy who was considered fast because he had smoked cigarettes and was flunking honors biology. I used to go to his house after school and roll around with him on the kitchen linoleum, where we groped under each others' clothes until we heard his mother's car pull into the driveway. Although we never thought of going further, I still felt guilty. I had nothing to say to him and was convinced that my indulgence with him was going to ruin my reputation. Beatrice made me feel that my fears about Don had been childish.

She was the first girl I knew who claimed not to be a virgin. In our senior year she told me she had had an affair the previous summer with a camp counselor named Bernie who worked at the camp where she was a counselor in training. They played tennis together two or three times a week and made love afterward in an empty cabin while the rest of the campers were swimming. "I don't see him anymore," Beatrice sighed. "I could have gotten pregnant, and you know what my father's like. He would throw me out of the house."

Beatrice told me that with Bernie she'd had vaginal orgasms, which were the best kind. "I never heard of them," I said skeptically.

Beatrice rolled over on the bed and gave me one of her knowing looks. "It *happened* to me before I read about it," she answered loftily. "I found a name for it in a book by a psychiatrist. He said only mature women have vaginal orgasms. Women who remain childish either are frigid or have a different kind." She sounded so authoritative, and I respected her so much, that I couldn't help believing her.

On Saturday nights we usually went to Rienzi's coffeehouse in Greenwich Village, where we sipped espresso, smoked forbidden cigarettes, and fantasized that the men at the next table would ask to join us. One night, as Beatrice, our friend Ellen, and I were trying on earrings in the mirror in Beatrice's bedroom, preparing to leave for the Village, Beatrice suggested that we bring a bottle of liquor with us. Her parents' liquor cabinet was locked, and none of us was old enough to buy alcohol; but Beatrice had a plan. She would call the local liquor store and give the order in an imitation of her mother's voice. Then she would duck into the shower while I answered the bell. "If you take off those earrings, you'll look about eleven," Beatrice teased. "Just say your mother's busy and give him the money." The charade worked perfectly. But we made the mistake of ordering Gallo's cream sherry, which Beatrice had remembered liking at a party of her sister's friends and which made us all violently ill. At twelve-thirty, staggering home from the Village, I called my parents and said I was spending the night with Beatrice. There I tossed on the floor until dawn, unable to vomit up the stuff (as Beatrice and Ellen promptly did), clutching my stomach while Beatrice said, with exaggerated sympathy, "I guess you just shouldn't drink, Jane-i-fy."

I never could resist her mischief. Once, in the Eighth Street Bookstore, Beatrice challenged me to help her steal a few volumes of poetry. Although the store was nearly sacred to me—I had spent many Saturday afternoons on the floor cushions, reading Levertov, Rexroth, Olson, Baldwin, Hentoff—I couldn't tell her no. "We'll just write our names on the flyleaves," Beatrice said merrily. "If we get stopped, we'll say we brought the books with us." Later we graduated to libraries. "Why should we bother standing on line to check out our books?" Beatrice demanded. "We can always bring the books back when we're finished."

I forgot about the stolen library books until my mother found them on the top shelf of my closet. "But why would you steal library books?" she kept asking me, obviously troubled. I couldn't think of an answer. As long as I had Beatrice's approval, my mother's hardly mattered to me.

In the fall of my senior year, a notice on the bulletin board listed my name among the school's six National Merit Scholarship semifinalists. My high score assured me a full-tuition scholarship from the World Book Company, which gave twenty awards each year to the children of employees based on the National Merit exams. I was eligible for the award since the company had retained my mother on its books as an employee during her first year of teaching. Reaching the national semifinals also virtually guaranteed my admission to any college in the country. When the first happy shock subsided, I read the other five names again. Four were familiar, from my honors classes. The fifth, Anita Safire, I had never heard of.

When the six of us were called down to the principal's office to shake his hand and pose for photographs, I met Anita for the first time. She had the sexual maturity and self-confidence of a grown woman and wore miniskirts four inches shorter than the current fashion. The principal did a double take when he shook her hand. Anita returned his stare with a gaze of amused contempt.

I sidled next to her and murmured a joke about the principal as the pictures were snapped. Anita rewarded me with a chuckle. Then she accepted my suggestion that we walk home together after school.

Anita had grown up in California and moved to Forest Hills the summer before I met her with her father and her new stepmother, her father's third wife. She was planning to return to California in the fall and live with her mother while she attended college. Ethan, Anita's father, was a computer designer and a former Communist who, although he had quit the party in the forties and mellowed into a liberal, was still far to the left of anyone I had ever met. Joan, his new wife, emptied ashtrays a lot and seemed eager to make Anita like her. Anita was allowed to smoke, to call her parents by their first names, and to stay out as late as she pleased. She was intelligent but not ambitious, preferring crocheting to homework and seeming indifferent to the fact that her classes were all with slower students. Her main interest was her boyfriend, Saul. She had met him one fall afternoon at the fountain at Washington Square, where he was playing guitar with a group of friends. The two of them told me the story as if it were a legend each knew in a slightly different version. Anita had been standing off to the side of the fountain, watching Saul's pick flutter against the steel strings. Saul met her eyes and missed a chord. Anita smiled enigmatically (in Saul's version; in Anita's, she blushed) and turned to go. Saul put down his guitar—to the hoots of his friends—and ran after her. They had been together since.

I met Saul one day after school, when I joined Anita and him at his job in the garment district. His jeans were molded to his buttocks, and he wore a wide ring of Mexican silver on his finger. He squeezed Anita's waist, one hand lightly brushing her breast, and I understood that they were lovers. I felt like an astronomer who had, after years of looking through a telescope, finally observed the sought-for planet. I made an assiduous study of the two of them.

Saul was not an intellectual—he had dropped out of Bronx Community College in the middle of his freshman year—but he was thoughtful, and radical politics seemed to run in his blood. He had demonstrated against segregation at Woolworth's when he was a high school student and, through acquaintances in the civil rights movement, had become interested in the theory and practice of nonviolent resistance. He spoke of the World War II pacifists—Dave Dellinger, A. J. Muste, Bayard Rustin—who were heroes to him and of the newly founded Village Peace Center on Third Street, an organization advocating nuclear disarmament and conscientious objection, years before the Vietnam War made the position popular. I had once read, in Daniel Wolf's introduction to a collection of *Village Voice* articles, the phrase "those of us who . . . had long since been left cold by the dull pieties of official liberalism with its dreary, if unspoken drive to put every family in a housing development and give each child his own social worker." Saul intrigued me not only because he played the guitar and walked like a cowboy but because he was one of those oppositionists Daniel Wolf had described. He was as much a rebel as Beatrice, but his outsider quality had an ideological basis; he lived by a moral and political code different from my parents' and in every way more appealing to me.

My parents were threatened by Saul as they had never been by any of my other friends. The offspring of working-class Jewish immigrants, Saul had rejected his own parents' middle-class aspirations. He had no interest in returning to college or in becoming a business success. He spoke with a Brooklyn accent, had dirt under his fingernails, wore boots and denim jackets and neckerchiefs, and projected an animalistic sexuality that hypnotized me and was more than my parents could tolerate. When Saul and Anita presented me with an enameled cigarette lighter as a sixteenth-birthday gift—unaware that my parents had forbidden me to smoke—my father ordered Saul out of the apartment. He told me that Anita, but not her boyfriend, would be permitted to return. Saul, he said, was filth; and I was not to mention his name again. My friends and I left together. From then on I cultivated my relationship with them in secret.

By this time my father's new partnership with Leonard Schor was flourishing, my mother had a teaching assignment she liked, and my brother was in a private school, where he was getting the extra attention he needed. The one remaining family problem was me. I had fallen in with people my parents thought of as bad influences. I lied; I stole for pleasure; I appeared to be sexually unrestrained; I was enamored of radicalism in any form. My first choice college was left-wing, progressive Antioch, which I visited the summer before senior year with my father and Adele. I was especially drawn to the work-study program, under which students spent six months of each year on their own, working in cities or in rural areas other than their homes. My parents resisted, suspecting that I wasn't ready to live away from home, let alone away from dormitory supervision.

Although I failed to advance to the National Merit finals, I was accepted at all the colleges to which I applied—Antioch, Barnard, and Swarthmore—and the World Book scholarship took care of tuition fees. Swarthmore was the compromise my parents and I arrived at. Although not quite so free-spirited as Antioch, it was better than staying home, while my parents thought it so prestigious that they couldn't say no. Flattered as I was to have been accepted, I wondered whether I would be happy at so academic a place. I imagined an institution where all the students were like the honor-class grinds at Forest Hills, studying fifteen hours a day and disapproving of anyone whose thoughts wandered outside the confines of a library.

Anita had been accepted at Berkeley. Saul, reluctant to spend a year across the continent from her, registered for a term at the Brooks Institute of Photography in Santa Barbara. He bought a motorcycle and planned to make the trip cross-country in September. Beatrice, who had accepted a scholarship offer from the University of Chicago, lied about her age to win a camp counselor's job in Vermont. "I told them I was twenty," she said. "If I said eighteen or nineteen, they might be suspicious because it was so close to the minimum, but they wouldn't expect someone to add three whole years to her age."

To keep me busy over the summer, my mother found me a job as a clerk typist in the inventory department of Robert Hall Clothes, where her cousin worked as an executive secretary. I was supposed to be grateful since summer positions were difficult to obtain, especially for under-eighteen-year-olds, who needed work permits from the city. It felt more like punishment than privilege. From eight until four-thirty, with exactly forty-five minutes for lunch and two ten-minute coffee breaks, along with thirty other women, I sorted pink, blue, yellow, and green cards into piles under the inspection of a neurotically suspicious supervisor. Employees weren't permitted to talk to each other or go to the bathroom without permission from the supervisor. The dress code was stricter than in Forest Hills—we had to wear stockings, even on ninety-degree days, and were reprimanded if our clothes looked wrinkled or our hair uncombed. It took me an hour and a half each day to commute from Forest Hills to the West Thirty-third Street office, mashed against thousands of file clerks who, I thought, would work at the same jobs the rest of their lives. If I had doubted whether I wanted to go to college, the summer at Robert Hall convinced me.

In August 1963, Saul and Anita went to a civil rights gathering at the Lincoln Monument in Washington, where Martin Luther King, Jr., was to be the featured speaker. I thought of quitting my job a week early so that I could go, but my parents refused, guessing, perhaps, who my companions would be. As usual, I had my revenge. They wouldn't let me go to Washington, so I wouldn't let them drive me to Swarthmore on the first day of orientation week. I would take the train, with one or two suitcases, and they could come the next week, if they wished, with the rest of my books and belongings. My mother was in tears, but I was adamant—especially after Saul offered to take me to lunch and walk me to the train station on the day of departure.

During my last week in Forest Hills I was awake until dawn every night, leaning out the window in my half of the bedroom, blowing cigarette smoke out on the silent street. When I left this time, I promised myself, I would not come back.

III

Leaving Home

I MET SAUL AT SMITH'S BAR AND GRILL across the street from Pennsylvania Station on the day of my departure for Swarthmore.

He didn't share my enthusiasm over finally leaving home. "That's an egghead place you're going to," he announced over a lunch I was too excited to eat. "You'd better take something to cheer you up those nights when other folks are buried in their books."

"Like what?" I asked.

"Ever had Three-Star Hennessy?"

I had never drunk anything except the unforgettable Gallo's cream sherry at Beatrice's but was too embarrassed to admit that to Saul.

"I'll give you a pint for a going-away present." He grinned, apparently enjoying my discomfort.

A paragraph in the college catalog had stated that the town of Swarthmore was dry and that liquor was forbidden in the dormitories. If I told Saul that, it would confirm his harsh opinion of the school. Besides, wouldn't arriving on campus with a pint of liquor in my suitcase help establish me as a sophisticated New Yorker and no ordinary college freshman? Since I would be two years younger than most people in the class of '67, I felt I needed the extra credentials.

In a dusty liquor store next to the station Saul pointed to the bottle he wanted and produced his wallet to prove that he had turned nineteen.

"Sorry it's not gift-wrapped," he said as he reached around me to stick the package in my tote bag. He let his hand rest on my hip. I stood very still to avoid shaking him off. Then I concentrated so as not to trip as we walked together to Penn Station, Saul's arm still tight around my waist.

Was it silly of me to feel more than friendship in his grip on my waist? I had always been attracted to him, but he had always seemed so in love with Anita, whom in a few days he would be following to Berkeley. Meanwhile, his touch was making the blood pound in my ears.

At the platform, next to the waiting train, I tried to think of some clever, casual way to say good-bye. Saul put down my bags, wrapped both arms around me, and pulled me against his groin. "You're the second woman in my life who's leaving town this week," he said mournfully. Then he thrust his tongue deep inside my mouth. I put Anita out of my mind, closed my eyes, and surrendered to the sensation.

"Wanna go to a hotel?" he murmured.

"I'll miss my train," I whispered, in a tone that I hoped matched his.

"There'll be lots of trains."

I was sure he meant the invitation. I also knew that I could go to a hotel with him, give up my virginity, arrive at Swarthmore six hours or six days late, and still not alter the basis of my relationship with him or affect his plans to go to California.

"I've got to go," I said firmly.

I stumbled on the train, not knowing how or why I had made the decision. I was still so absorbed in the memory of Saul's kiss that when the conductor called out "Ardmore," it sounded so much like "Swarthmore" to me that I scrambled from the car, dragging my bags with me. Ten minutes later, when the train had left me stranded in a strange town, I realized my mistake.

Swarthmore was idyllically lovely. An uphill path, shaded with velvety pines, led from the train station to Parrish Hall, the Victorian manor that served as the administration building. Maple leaves were turning red and ocher. Men and women, absorbed in conversation, walked together on the graveled paths or sprawled on the grass, playing guitars or reading. A garden bloomed in back of Parrish Hall, filling offices and classrooms with the fragrance of roses. The Crum, a hundred acres of woods and meadow adjoining the campus, was alive with squirrels and sparrows and leafy spots for sunbathing or talk. For the first few weeks of September the weather was golden, and college seemed more like summer camp than work. I made friends easily, went to movies and recitals and poetry readings, and floated from impromptu folk singing to picnics to introductory lectures, convinced I had arrived in paradise.

At the end of orientation week I signed up for an ambitious program: not only the standard freshman survey courses in English literature and political science but also physics, calculus, and first-year Greek. Greek was purely a whim. I remembered a Forest Hills English teacher who, when we read Book Nine of *The Odyssey* in his class, explained the "Nobody" pun by writing the Greek words *Odysseus* and *oudeis* on the blackboard. This had entranced me. So had the Swarthmore amphitheater, at the edge of the Crum, where I was told the classics students produced a play in ancient Greek each spring. I chose physics and calculus in spite of warnings from upper-class students and faculty that, as a prospective humanities or social science major, I should fill the one-year science requirement with one of the easier courses: biology, astronomy, or general science. I was determined to be different—and perhaps, too, to prove I was as smart as my mother, a straight A math student in both college and graduate school. Physics and calculus, unfortunately for me, were the toughest introductory courses in Swarthmore's science division. I fell behind after a few weeks and told myself I would make up the missed work, as I had in high school, by cramming before exams.

At first I compared myself favorably with other first-year students, especially the women. My roommate, Lissa, was a graduate of a New Orleans country day school. Like me, she was away from home for the first time. She was an excellent student. She had applied and been accepted to all the seven sister schools plus Swarthmore, Reed, and Oberlin and had been awarded scholarships at several. Her high school work was much more advanced than mine. She showed me a long term paper she had written on the theme of emancipated women in American literature. It was substantial enough to be a college thesis and required as much reading as I had done for all my high school courses together. Lissa was also extremely pretty, the same height that I was, but slim and graceful where I was chunky. Her shoulder-length hair waved into a smooth pageboy, while mine was stringy and wouldn't hold a curl. Yet she, too, was insecure, though she showed it in a different way. While I did most of my studying in the dark, chummy library smoker, where men and women could work together as late as midnight, Lissa would study alone in our room or in one of the concrete-walled rooms in the dormitory basement, where no men were allowed. She worried that her accent and her Peter Pan collars would typecast her as a southern debutante, in spite of the fact that she had been born in Boston, was half Jewish, and came from a family active in the civil rights movement. Since she made herself so invisible while I covered up my anxiety with gregariousness, for the first month or so, to my secret satisfaction, I had more dates than she did.

Once Lissa reluctantly agreed to go out with a crew-cut fraternity jock who told her she was the only "really nice" girl in the freshman class. She decided to spoil his image of her by dressing for the date in clothes and jewelry borrowed from my Greenwich Village wardrobe: two-inch-diameter hoop earrings, a shapeless sweater, tights, and thick strokes of eyeliner, which I applied to her lids in the style Beatrice had taught me. We called to the other women on our hall to look at her before she left. One by one, they burst out laughing. The trick worked. Lissa's bewildered date brought her home at ten o'clock and didn't ask her out again. But I kept wondering afterward if I looked as alien in my clothes as Lissa did and if others were laughing at me behind my back, as they had laughed that night to her face.

My own social life dwindled after a few weeks. My first crush, on Patch Dellinger, ended in disappointment. Patch, a blond, husky sophomore, was the eldest son of Dave Dellinger, who was the editor of *Liberation*, the left-wing magazine, and one of Saul's pacifist heroes. I loved the idea of going home to boast to my Forest Hills friends that I was dating the offspring of a famous radical. Patch and I went out only once, during orientation week. A few days later I made the mistake of trying to hold his hand as we walked across campus. He dropped it as though I had burned him. In the next weeks he was frostily polite and never asked me for another date.

It was then that I wrote to a boy I had met in Washington Square Park over the summer, suggesting that we get together in New York some Saturday night. Steve wrote poetry and could play "Malagueña" on the guitar. He had told me he was a sophomore at City College and lived with a friend in the Village. He wrote back at once a letter hinting he was more ready to relieve me of my virginity than anyone at Swarthmore. One October weekend, in a miserable walk-up on Thompson Street, while I tried to block out the incessant whining of four hungry cats and the piles of laundry and dishes, he got the job done with surprisingly little fuss. I went back to Swarthmore the next day feeling slimy and still unable to forget the meowing of the cats. When Lissa asked me about my date, I pretended I'd gotten too drunk to remember. I then found out that Lissa was dating Patch Dellinger.

I began to slide, imperceptibly at first, into depression.

It was my intention, when I came to Swarthmore, to join the Political Action Club (SPAC), an organization of campus New Left activists. Instead, I worked for the campus newspaper, the *Phoenix*, and the literary magazine, the *Roc*, and kept postponing my plans to attend a SPAC meeting. Editing, composing headlines, criticizing student poetry, and writing an occasional article on campus affairs came more easily to me than political discussions with the well-read social science majors who made up the membership of SPAC, whose arguments I had trouble following and whose arrogance intimidated me. Still, I admired the SPACers. Several of them had spent the summer working with SNCC in the integration movement in Cambridge, Maryland, where they had been tear-gassed by the National Guard and attacked by red-neck mobs. In October, when the administration invited a representative of the Union of South Africa, an advocate of apartheid, to speak on campus, SPAC members called for pickets around the lecture hall and organized a walkout in the middle of the speech. Nonradical students criticized the SPACers for their opposition to free speech, but I was proud to carry an "End Apartheid" placard in the demonstration.

Through the fall of 1963 SPAC members were devoting several days each week to work with a black mobilizing committee in Chester, a town three miles from Swarthmore. A community of about 60,000 on the Delaware River, Chester had been a major shipbuilding center during the war but had fallen on hard times in the fifties. Poverty and unemployment were especially severe in the black community. I saw the town several times on trips—not for political meetings but to eat cheese steak hoagies at Stacky's, an Italian-run sandwich shop in the black ghetto. The dilapidated houses and sleazy bars reminded me of the desolate inner city of Washington, D.C., where my grandmother and uncles operated their business, complaining constantly about the *shvartzehs*. When SPAC called for a demonstration to protest conditions at Franklin Elementary School, in the heart of the Chester ghetto, I was ready to go. It seemed an opportunity I'd been waiting for since I heard of the freedom riders.

Early Tuesday morning, November 12, nearly seventy-five students assembled next to Parrish Hall for the SPAC-chartered bus ride to Chester. Less than half were SPAC activists. The rest were freshmen like me who had not attended more than one SPAC meeting but had admired civil rights demonstrators for years and felt the time had come to take sides. Extra cars were pressed into service. A dozen students had to wait for the bus to return from Chester for a second trip. Lissa and I sat next to each other, too nervous to talk much, and looked out the window for our first glimpse of Franklin School.

Few of us realized that the militant tactics advocated by SPAC leaders differed from the civil disobedience methods employed in protests in the South. On the other hand, SPAC's publicity efforts had made the facts about Franklin School familiar to us. The school had been built in 1912 to accommodate five hundred students. It now held more than a thousand, all of them black. Classes were held in a former coalbin and in the boiler room of a housing project across the street. The school building had been declared a fire hazard by local building contractors. Children had been injured on broken stairs and worn-out playground equipment. The week before a group called the Chester Committee For Freedom Now (CFFN) had gone to court, seeking an injunction under state antisegregation statutes to close the school and transfer the students to safe (i.e., all-white) schools elsewhere in Chester. Our job was to make sure that the committee achieved its goal.

When we reached the school, two hundred Chester residents, overwhelmingly black, were guarding the entrances, arms linked as a symbol of unity. Others were milling about the yard. As children arrived, they were directed to the housing project across the street, where SPAC chairman Carl Wittman and other Swarthmore students were conducting children's classes in black history. Preferring the potential drama of the picket line to baby-sitting, I squeezed myself into the front line around the school and watched as our ranks continued to swell.

At nine-thirty official word came from the school board: we had succeeded in closing the school for the day. Loud cheers, hugs, and handshakes. Then Stanley Branche, the black founder and chairman of CFFN, announced he was going to the school board to present the community's demands. Did we want to go with him? The crowd responded with buoyant approval. A few minutes later we were advancing on Chester's business district.

On that brisk fall morning under a strong sun, linked on the left to a middle-aged black man in work clothes, on the right to a young Franklin School student, I glimpsed the utopia preached by Martin Luther King: a culture in which all were equal, in which no one was made to feel inferior because of skin color or poverty or age or disability, in which a neighbor was someone whose arm you could hold. As we sang freedom songs, tears came to my eyes from the wind and the emotion I felt.

At the school board Branche disappeared for a long time. The crowd grew restless. Some talked of picketing Larkin School, an all-white elementary school a few blocks from the school board, one of the institutions to which CFFN wanted the Franklin School children transferred. The idea, springing from the moment's frustration rather than from planning, made me uneasy. I was relieved when Branche emerged from his meeting. The school board members had refused to negotiate. We were to go home for the day but return to Franklin School tomorrow. We would continue the picketing until they were ready to talk.

Back at the college that evening, the day's demonstrations were the only subject of conversation. No one had been arrested yet, but Wednesday, said the experienced SPACers, would be different. If the school board continued intransigent, we should be prepared to fight. I didn't know quite what fighting meant in this context; neither did most of the participating freshmen. But I trusted the SPAC leaders and Stanley Branche and wanted to be part of their victory over an unjust school board. If that meant a day or two in jail, it didn't seem a heavy price to pay. Believing that my decision was rational and right (although still feeling a bit nervous over the outcome), I called my parents, hoping for their support.

My mother uttered a few incoherent phrases, then handed the receiver to my father. In tones he might have used to a recalcitrant employee, he ordered me to stay on campus and leave demonstrating to the others. Neither was interested in hearing about the conditions at Franklin School or about how I felt on the picket line and the march through Chester. Hurt and angry at their refusal to listen, I could only conclude that we had different political goals. I hung up with no intention of obeying them.

Wednesday morning, arriving once again at Franklin School, we found the crowd in a grim mood. Vandals had smashed 150 windows in the school building during the night. Seven young black children had been taken into custody for the crime, but most of the crowd seemed to think that segregationists were responsible. Still, the vandalism had accomplished the immediate goal of the demonstration: Franklin School was closed until the windows could be repaired. This would take at least the rest of the week.

Once again Stanley Branche proposed that we march behind him, this time to the mayor's office. Why the mayor? Someone explained that as the handpicked candidate of the Republican machine that controlled the town, the mayor was a symbol of the corruption and racism we were demonstrating against. We swept down the street, heading for the municipal building, a block or two from the end of yesterday's march.

What happened next had as much in common with the urban riots of the later part of the decade as with the pacifist resistance of the early civil rights movement. The crowd was angry and inclined toward anarchy and was led by a man who showed little disposition to moderate the tumult. We were nearly running through the streets of Chester, five hundred or more of us, singing "Turn Me 'Round" with such ferocity that reporters heard the words as "Burn It Down." At the doors of the municipal building the crowd hesitated only a few seconds before pushing through the double glass doors. The lobby resounded with our freedom songs. Branche was the last to enter. A husky ex-paratrooper who had once been a professional conga player, he timed his appearance perfectly, swaying his hips and shoulders in a sensuous two-step that mesmerized his audience. In a low, compelling voice, each syllable distinct, he led the chant. "Freedom! Now! Freedom! Now!" We picked it up in a frenzy.

I was prepared, or so I thought, for arrest, even for police brutality. But I was not prepared to find a wellspring of anger inside me, tapped by the chanting. As if hypnotized, I was frantically stamping my feet, cheering "Freedom! Now!" long after I was too hoarse to make a sound. I had stopped thinking about Franklin School, the citizens of Chester, the evils of racism and poverty. The utopian vision that had tugged at me yesterday was gone. In its place was something else, a fury that tore out of me with a life of its own, primitive as infancy. I was screaming against everyone and everything that had stood in my way—the boys who had rejected me, the man who had fired my father when I was nine, my absent father, my mother, my brother. I wasn't the only one in the crowd who temporarily lost control. When the police arrived, the entire mob sighed audibly, as at a long-awaited climax.

The men were taken to Broadmeadows State Prison. The rest of us, women and children, numbering about sixty altogether, were taken to a women's detention facility in Chester. We were all jammed into two large bare rooms, one the dining hall and the other a recreation room for sentenced inmates—from whom we political defendants were kept carefully separate for the duration of our stay. The children under sixteen were released a few hours after we were booked. The adults (over eighteen) were told that bail would be set the next morning. Lissa and I, seventeen and sixteen respectively, were in à special category. We could be released only in the custody of responsible adults—and so we would stay in the jail until the college decided what to do about us.

I stayed up most of that first night, sitting at a long wooden table with a group of Chester women who played cards and talked. For me, these were the most illuminating hours in the Chester jail. All the women around the table had been born and brought up in Chester. Most had children in the Chester school system. They lived near each other and were neighbors for years before CFFN was started. As I heard them talk about the problems of their neighborhood—not only the schools but their landlords and jobs and the illnesses of their children and parents—I began to realize that I knew pitifully little about their lives. For the first time I asked the questions I should have tried to answer before joining the demonstration in the morning. Was it good to have achieved the closing of Franklin School for an entire week, or would it only make the children suffer? Was Stanley Branche a selfless leader who had the community's interests at heart, or was he out for power for himself? Would the white college-student contingent in the jails ultimately help or hurt the civil rights cause with the voters of Chester? Was the school board really as intransigent and racist as Wittman and Branche wanted us to believe?

Thursday afternoon all the woman except Lissa and me were released. In the few hours we spent alone in the jail, we shared our anxiety over the classes and homework we were missing, the mid-term exams we would be unprepared for. Already far behind in three of my five courses, I was in worse difficulty than Lissa. Just as I was coming to regret my impulsive decision to join the demonstration on Wednesday, another two hundred demonstrators were ushered into the jail, singing as lustily as we had the day before. This group had not bothered to go to Franklin School, which was still closed because of the broken windows. Instead, they had created havoc in the municipal building until the police came. The point was to overload the courts and flood the jails until the government was forced to give in out of sheer exhaustion. Cathy Wilkerson, a Swarthmore junior and SPAC activist, boasted of how militant the demonstrators had been. One SPACer, Peter Grant, had leaped on top of the switchboard in the municipal building and pulled out the plugs with such undisguised glee that the switchboard operator took refuge under the board. Hoping to impress Cathy with my own fortitude, I mentioned that Lissa and I had been in jail more than twenty-four hours already—and added that I was thinking of avoiding future arrests until I reached the legal age of eighteen. Cathy shot me a contemptuous look. Feeling reprimanded for having weakened so quickly, I kept my mouth shut around her afterward.

We stayed in jail until the following afternoon, at which point the school board, fearing yet a third day of militant demonstrations, yielded to virtually all the community demands. It agreed to transfer 165 students from Franklin School to other schools in the district, to eliminate classes in the coal bin and in the housing project boiler room, to improve the toilet facilities, repair the concrete steps, and clean the playground. Finally the government had agreed, in exchange for a promise from Branche to end the demonstrations, to drop all charges against the demonstrators. The problem of how Lissa and I, as juveniles, would be released into adult custody was solved. We hugged each other, more in relief at getting out of jail than at the CFFN victory.

On the way to the courthouse we were singing again, but I choked on the words when I saw my parents standing outside the courthouse. After receiving the news from the Swarthmore deans, my father had taken a day off from work and my mother from teaching school to fetch me from jail. In spite of the doubts that had disturbed me in the women's jail, the sight of my parents made me ready to affirm everything I had done: the demonstrations, the arrest, and prison. I couldn't appreciate the fact that they had come out of concern for me. When I had needed them to listen, they had been short-tempered. Now I could take care of myself, and I hated them for trying to interfere.

My parents drove Lissa and me back to the campus. Lissa thanked them courteously, promised them she would call her own parents in New Orleans, and headed for the dorm. My father turned to me.

"I don't want to hear a speech from you," he said. "I told you what I expected and you didn't listen. I'm not going to warn you again. Wait until you're old enough to pay your own bills; then you can do whatever you damn please."

Cretins, I screamed silently at the departing Oldsmobile. At least you could have asked me why I went.

One week later President Kennedy was killed.

I was in the smoker of the library when John Lewis came bursting in to deliver the news. John was not much taller than my brother, but he had freckles and flaming red hair, which was how I first recognized him when he dashed into the smoker, screaming that the President had been shot in the head. Then he ran from the room, horseless Paul Revere, racing toward the next community before any of us had quite absorbed the message.

The smoker emptied as I found myself thinking, stupidly, about Kennedy's hair. It looked blond on television, but I had seen him once during the 1960 campaign and knew it was red. Remembering his hair, I left the empty smoker and walked to my dormitory. In the hall outside our room, Lissa and Ann, who lived in the room next to ours, were holding each other and sobbing. Both of them were from southern liberal families to whom Kennedy represented a new hope for justice and equal rights for all races. I had never been as strong a supporter of the President as the two of them; I had already learned from Saul to think of electoral politics as beside the point. But I did feel shock and a fear I couldn't quite define. I moved on to the lounge. It was crowded with students, sitting on tables and on the floor, silently watching the television screen. A long-jawed commentator stood next to a hospital emergency entrance in Dallas. "The President of the United States is dead," he said. He seemed to have been saying the same words for a long time. No one spoke. Numbly I left the dorm and headed for the woods. Later, watching Lyndon Johnson on television, I felt betrayed. The words were right, but the face, the posture, the accent grated on me. I hated the Texas drawl, the age lines around his jaw and on his forehead. Some political science professors said we were lucky Kennedy had been forced to choose so experienced a vice-president. Johnson, they said, was a brilliant politician. If he chose to, he could carry out Kennedy's policies more effectively than Kennedy had. I found it easier to think that this ugly usurper, whose instantaneous swearing-in seemed an affront to the memory of his predecessor, had actually had a hand in Kennedy's death. A year and a half later, when Johnson began the uninterrupted bombing of Vietnam, I felt no surprise. I had never expected him to be other than evil.

After I had described to several SPAC activists the women I met in the Chester jail, they urged me to invite them to the campus to discuss their views with students. I was elated at the opportunity to be useful, even after as little experience as I'd had, and threw myself into arrangements for the meeting. In spite of all my planning, it went badly. The Chester women who had been so articulate in prison were tongue-tied in the staid parlor of Parrish Hall. The knowledgeable SPACers could hardly disguise their contempt when the Chester women proved ignorant of basic political and economic facts about the town. After the meeting Jack White, one of Swarthmore's few black students, criticized me sharply for having overestimated the Chester women. I had romanticized them merely because they were black and poor, he said, and had allowed fantasy to interfere with my judgment. Embarrassed after my failure, I mostly stopped attending SPAC meetings.

I wasn't alone in my disillusionment. While conservative students accused those of us who had gone to jail of enacting adolescent dramas and lacking a real commitment to the problems of the poor, the Chester community fell to wrangling. Stanley Branche called the Reverend D. G. Ming, sole black member of the Pennsylvania Human Relations Committee, an Uncle Tom. Ming charged Branche with libel. Other black leaders charged that Branche was hotheaded, politically inexperienced, and self-aggrandizing. The county commissioner addressed a large group of students, warning us that we had acquired a bad image in Chester since the militancy of the November demonstrations. We could be far more effective, he said, if we directed our efforts toward voter education and improved living conditions and against the control of the town government by absentee landlords. While Carl Wittman and a core of SPAC activists insisted that Chester had begun a new epoch in the civil rights movement, as significant as the first sit-in at a Greensboro, North Carolina, lunch counter, the tide of opinion on campus was turning against the SPACers. By spring, although Chester residents were demonstrating in increasing numbers, the SPACers who worked with them were isolated from the rest of the campus.

In March Peter Grant, the student who had pulled out the plugs from the municipal building switchboard, and Walter Jones, a young black from Chester, were arrested for vandalizing a Chester police car. Bail was $2,500 for each. Grant, who came from a wealthy family, refused to pay his bail until money was raised to free Jones, too. SPAC promptly plastered the campus and the Ville (as the town of Swarthmore was nicknamed) with signs appealing for funds to pay "freshman student Peter Grant's bail," as they put it. I contributed to the bail fund but was irked by the false publicity. Why wouldn't SPAC advertise that Walter Jones, too, was in jail and that Grant's stand was one of principle, not poverty? I went to a SPAC meeting to register my complaint.

When called on, I said that I personally supported Grant and was glad to contribute to the bail fund for Walter Jones. But if SPAC meant to win new adherents as well as raise money, it ought to tell the truth. Why not put both Grant's and Jones's names on the posters? No one agreed with me. No one even bothered to explain what was wrong with my objection. I was an outsider now; my views didn't count. The meeting went on as if I hadn't spoken. It was the last SPAC gathering I attended.

The long hours I put in at the library in the last months of the semester were not sufficient to make up for the work I'd missed earlier. At the end of the first semester I had failed both physics and calculus. I might have tried to make up the failures by working harder in those subjects during the spring, but I decided to drop them instead. I substituted courses in philosophy and English and began to consider majoring in Greek.

I had no more dates. The stillness of the dorm on Saturday nights sent me into depressions which lasted through Monday morning, when my eight o'clock class seemed too much of an ordeal to get up for. A clique of unpopular girls spent every Saturday night in front of the television in the lounge, eating potato chips and gossiping. I dreaded ending up like them. To avoid even the appearance of it, I stayed in my room or paced the halls, pretending to be absorbed in my work. I even looked forward to going home for Christmas vacation, when I could count on a date with Steve, the City College student who had relieved me of my virginity.

On New Year's Eve Steve took me to a party in Roslyn where the guests were oddly young and talked about high school affairs. When he saw the puzzlement on my face, Steve confessed to me that he had lied about his age. He was not a nineteen-year-old college sophomore but was a seventeen-year-old high school senior. I was the first girl he had ever slept with. I was appalled. I wanted to go home at once, but at exactly midnight the city buses had gone on strike. To compound my humiliation, Steve confessed that he didn't know how to drive. I was forced to call my father and entreat him to pick me up in Roslyn. Steve tried to convince me that we should continue seeing each other, but I was too angry at his deception—and too ashamed of my gullibility—to have anything more to do with him.

If the new semester had started off more happily, I might not have agreed to go out with Keith Hamilton. A gawky sophomore from Maryland, Keith was a civil engineering major, with a receding chin and a Marine Corps-type crew cut. His thick-lensed black-framed eyeglasses made his nose stick out and his pale eyes recess into his head. His skin was shiny pink, his political opinions dully middle-of-the-road. He told corny jokes, was proud that he could belch on cue, and lived in Wharton, the most socially conservative of the men's dorms, where the proctors actually checked rooms to make sure no women were sneaked in. But he was undeniably attentive. Even after I turned him down three Saturday nights in a row, he would seek me out in the dining hall and maneuver into the seat behind me at movies. Sometimes he ran after me between classes so that he could walk with me from one part of the campus to another. He was happy to listen to me and would look gratifyingly scandalized at cynicisms my high school friends would have taken for granted. When I couldn't put him off any longer without driving him away entirely, I accepted a date with him.

We went to a movie and then for a long walk through the snowy streets of the Ville. Keith talked to me of his home on the eastern shore of the Chesapeake Bay. He told me about fishing for soft-shell crabs and hunting without ammunition in his rifle, for the pleasure of watching the deer. He described the wild ponies on Chincoteague Island and the brilliance of the Milky Way seen from a sleeping bag in an open meadow. Involuntarily I looked up at the stars, a thousand times brighter in suburban Swarthmore than in New York. Keith laughed. "Much brighter than these," he said. And then, seeing that he was beginning to affect me, he added, "Maybe you'll come for a visit this summer."

I didn't say no. We kept walking and were more than a mile from campus when we heard the library clock chime 2:00 A.M. I had missed my curfew. "It's okay," said Keith. "I know a place we can wait until the dorms open in the morning." He led me to the side entrance of a church, then to the finished basement. "The rector's a friend of mine," he explained. "I was pretty unhappy my first year here, and he helped me out a lot." In the moonlight pouring in through the church windows, Keith looked subtly altered. His features became more regular, his eyes softer. I was touched by the picture of his freshman year, so lonely that he had to seek the friendship of a minister. My own defense was to cultivate a defiant bohemianism. But suppose I dropped that and accepted Keith's offer of friendship instead?

We spent the rest of the night in the church basement, talking and once, toward morning, dozing on the vinyl couches. The next week we returned to the church in the middle of the night and made love. It was Keith's first time. I waited a long time, until I was sure of him, before I told him that it wasn't mine.

One day, near the end of May, after I had finished the last of my finals, I was cleaning my room, playing *The Freewheelin' Bob Dylan* on the portable stereo, and waiting for Keith to pick me up for dinner. When I heard my name, I thought it was Keith, although he usually knocked on the window. I looked out and saw, instead of my lover, my old friend Saul.

I ran down to hug him. He had sent me a postcard saying he was going to stop here on his way back to New York from California, but I hadn't believed it until I saw him on the other side of the window. Even as I held his hand and laughed with nervous pleasure, the sight of him was unreal. Swarthmore was too manicured, too English-country-estate for Saul's earthiness. "How've you been?" Saul asked, gripping my waist as he had nine months ago in Penn Station. In another moment Keith was next to us. I made an effort to seem natural.

"Keith, this is an old friend of mine who's just come from California. Saul, my boyfriend Keith." They shook hands with no apparent tension. The uneasiness was mine. I wasn't quite used to receiving attention from one male. The presence of two made my pulse race as from too much black coffee. As the three of us went off to the cafeteria, I concocted a plan that reflected my anxiety to please more than my own preferences.

The question was where Saul would sleep. This should not have been a problem. Many dorm rooms were empty at year-end, and there were also on campus six attached houses known as the lodges, former sorority houses now reserved for the use of overnight guests. The lodges were cheap and comfortable, and I could easily have booked Saul into one of them. Instead, I suggested that we reserve the lodge in Saul's name but that Keith and I sleep in it while Saul slept in Keith's dormitory room. I proposed this with such confidence that neither of the two men was inclined to protest. Saul was good-humored about being consigned to the dormitory. Keith seemed gratifyingly touched at the rare treat of an entire night with me in a full-size bed. Later I wondered at Keith's failure to anticipate the obvious dangers. While it was common—though against the rules—for men and women to sneak into each other's dormitory rooms, neither of us had heard of students using the lodges illicitly. Besides, although my own final exams were over, Keith still had two to take, one of them at nine o'clock the next morning. He would have to hazard his way out of the lodge by a quarter of nine, with no time to retreat to safety if spies were lurking about.

Over the next few hours, while Keith studied for his exam and I gave Saul a tour of the campus, I realized it was not Keith I wanted to sleep with that night. Saul's presence, his touch, and his smell were a tangible reminder that in accepting Keith's affection, I had settled for less than I wanted. Looking at the college through Saul's eyes, I wondered if that were true of more than my affair with Keith. Suppose I had refused to go to this elite, protected college and had struck out on my own, as Saul had? Gone south to work full time for the civil rights cause? Or insisted to my parents that it was Antioch or nothing? I had had a contented few months, and my grades were up from the fall semester; but Saul implicitly raised my doubts as we strolled from the meetinghouse to the rose garden to the snack bar. At ten o'clock I left Saul at Keith's dorm and went to meet Keith at the lodge we had reserved.

If my first completely private night with my lover was an idyll of sensuous pleasure, I've managed to forget it since. My only clear memory is that in the morning Keith quietly dressed himself, kissed me, and let himself out the door in what must have been ample time for his nine o'clock exam. Saul was coming to pick me up for breakfast between ten and eleven, so I had no reason to get up. I rolled over for another hour's sleep.

I was awakened before ten by an unexpected noise on the stairs. I sat up abruptly. It was too early for Saul. Besides, he would certainly knock on the door, not loiter outside it. It must be a cleaning woman. I began to panic. The rule against cohabitation on campus was honored mostly in the breach, but discovery and punishment were not unheard of. The women on the maintenance staff recognized all of us students at sight. If I were caught here by one of them, I would certainly be reported to the deans. I pulled on my clothes and went to listen at the door. The cleaning woman seemed to be on the ground floor of the lodge, probably dusting the room for the afternoon's seminar. In five minutes she would be upstairs.

I opened the window of my second-story room and looked out. The rear of the lodge faced the highway at the edge of the campus, with a stretch of grass and white pines between. The asphalt roof in front of me slanted down so that its edge was no more than eight or nine feet from the ground. The grass below looked soft. If I crawled out the window and to the edge of the asphalt, I ought to be able to drop safely and noiselessly to the ground. Then I could come around to the front of the lodge and enter again by the ground-floor door, looking perfectly legal.

Making as little noise as possible, I let myself out on the roof.

The asphalt was slanted more steeply than it appeared from inside the window. I got my balance with difficulty, gripping the window frame with one hand as I inched toward the roof edge. Then I stood up and carefully slid my right foot down toward the gutter at the edge.

The moment I released my hand from the frame, the gutter bent under my foot. My ankle twisted. Losing my balance entirely, I fell, tried to right myself in midair, and managed only to twist my body as I landed on the hard ground, flat on my back.

Telling myself to be quiet was useless. The screams kept coming out of my throat while, from every direction, people ran toward me.

"What happened?" asked a maintenance man in overalls who was the first to reach my side. I remembered the pine trees in time.

"I was trying to climb a tree and I fell."

By that time a crowd was pushing in for a look at me. Someone who claimed to be a nurse ordered that no one touch me. I tried to sit up. A chorus ordered me to lie still. The nurse said someone should go for brandy. Meanwhile, the pain ebbed and I became convinced that the injury was trivial, a mild sprain perhaps. The real danger, that it would be discovered I had spent the night in the lodge, was only beginning. At last Saul ambled over.

"What the fuck happened to you?" he asked, kneeling next to me. He looked more amused than upset, although he told me later that the sight of me flat on my back had shocked him.

"I thought I heard the cleaning woman," I whispered. "I would have made it safely out the window, but I tripped on the damned gutter."

"You went out on the *roof*?"

He looked at the window and then again at me. His expression said he thought I had half lost my mind.

The doctor at Ridley Memorial Hospital (where I arrived in an ambulance, in which Saul drank most of the brandy that had been brought for me) said I was lucky. Only three vertebrae were broken and the spinal cord was intact. I would have to remain flat on my back in the hospital for ten days. Then he would apply a rigid body cast.

"How long will I have to wear the cast?"

"Three to six months."

The idea of walking around in plaster through all of June, July, and August and possibly through part of the school year made me frantic. So did the fear that the X-ray machine had detected my diaphragm, purchased at a Margaret Sanger clinic last spring under the name of Mrs. Hamilton. For the next ten days, while I lay in the hospital bed, confessing one-half of my worry, my parents and friends tried to cheer me up. Keith drew a series of dots and dashes on an enormous piece of poster board and taped it to my ceiling; he explained that it meant "I love you" in Morse code. Patch and Lissa brought flowers and books. So did other women in my dormitory. My parents booked a motel room near the hospital and brought in a consulting orthopedic surgeon from New York. Saul went back to New York—remembering his last encounter with my parents, we agreed it would be easier if they didn't meet—but he called me every few days. Only he and Keith knew for a fact that I hadn't fallen while climbing a pine tree, and though others must have been suspicious, no one questioned my story, and I began to feel better.

At the end of the ten days I was wheeled to a laboratory in the basement of the hospital. Four attendants rolled me around on a table, first winding me in gauze like a mummy, then wrapping me in sheets of plaster goo. It didn't hurt, but it was peculiarly depersonalizing because the attendants wouldn't answer my questions or explain their procedure. When they finished, I was allowed to stand up for the first time since the accident. The full-length mirror in the lab reflected a dismaying image. The cast extended from my collarbone to the tops of my thighs. For some reason—whether comic or serious, I had no idea—it had been molded to resemble a woman's body. Two mounds of plaster rose in the vicinity of my chest, the cast curved out next to my hips, and a belly button-sized indentation made by one of the attendant's fingers marked my navel. The entire cast stuck out nearly six inches from my body so that my arms lay not straight down but at an angle, as though I were trying to fly. I had just enough room around the hips to walk with robotlike mincing steps. When I added the hospital robe—required dress for returning to my hospital room, though I could not have been more concealed than I was by the cast—I looked like a mobile pup tent with tits.

I had been back in Forest Hills just over a week when a call came from Barbara Lang, dean of women at Swarthmore. If I were well and able to travel, she said pleasantly, she wanted to see me and either my mother or father at Swarthmore.

"My mother or father?" I repeated, surprised.

"Yes, when it's convenient for one of them."

For a few hours, I considered pretending the call had never come, but such a strategy seemed unlikely to work for long. My parents agreed to make the command appearance together on the first weekend in July when Skip was off in summer camp. Their alarm over the message added to my own anxiety.

Barbara Lang was the most conservative of the Swarthmore deans. She didn't believe in premarital sex, disapproved of alcohol, thought that women shouldn't smoke, and was hostile to SPAC. She had been the member of the Swarthmore administration most opposed to students organizing in Chester. A month ago she had upset me by refusing to grant my request for a single dormitory room for the following school year. I was convinced that this was because she knew I slept with Keith and wanted me to have a roommate who would keep an eye on me for her. When my parents pressured me to speculate on the reason for her summons, I guessed that it had to do with my rooming arrangements for September. In the back of my mind was a more alarming suspicion.

It was a scorching July day when I maneuvered out of the family car in my cast and lumbered up the hill to Parrish Hall, my mother and father on either side. Barbara Lang was waiting on the porch. She offered us lemonade, which my parents politely accepted and I declined. My mother complimented Dean Lang on her dress, and the administrator thanked my parents for making the trip. Seated uncomfortably on the edge of a white rocker, I began to feel that my cast was not only a physical encumbrance but a kind of scarlet A. The dean cleared her throat.

"I'll come to the point directly. When the story of Jane's fall from a tree came to our attention, we were suspicious. The tree nearest to the point where she fell has no branches lower than twenty feet from the ground. An expert climber would have difficulty scaling it. Frankly, we don't believe Jane was even attempting to climb it. A more obvious explanation of her fall is that she was spending the night in the lodge with a male, for some reason became frightened, and jumped from the window. As you may know, Mr. and Mrs. Alpert, such cohabitation is against the rules."

She paused for a few moments, letting her works sink in. Wildly, I thought of denying her version. Since she couldn't possibly prove it, if I stuck to my story, they might not be able to punish me. Then I reminded myself that she had not yet indicated any punishment. If the purpose of this trip was no more than a lecture from the dean, I would do better to keep my mouth shut.

"Since you make no attempt to deny it, Jane, I take it that my hypothesis is correct. Nor is this the first incident that has given us pause over your—ah, adjustment to campus life. In November you were arrested in Chester. In May you found it impossible to accept your room assignment for next year.

"Grades, I should point out, are not the issue here. Your end-of-the-year grades were more than satisfactory and your teachers describe you as a very capable student. But grades are not the only indicator of a student's welfare.

"In consideration of all the factors involved, including the fact that you're younger than most of your classmates, we are asking you to take a year's leave from the college.

"This is not a punishment, and I hope you don't see it in that light. There will be no indication on your record of the reason for your leaving. If you wish, you may let people think that the cause is medical." Here, she lowered her eyes in a gesture meant to indicate the cast, but which seemed more to condemn me for possessing a body. "You may wish to study for a year at a university in New York, NYU or Barnard, perhaps. Or you may want to work. Our only condition is that you live with your parents. If you accept those terms, there will be no problem readmitting you in 1965–66.

"We spent a great deal of time reaching this recommendation, and I hope you understand that it is for your own good."

I heard my father's voice before I could collect my thoughts. "It's most generous of you, Dean Lang. I'm sure Jane is grateful for your concern."

They were waiting for me to answer. What could I say? It would be useless to protest my innocence of any crime, and in the presence of both my parents and the dean, it was impossible to describe how the prospect of a year at home affected me.

"I'll think about it," I mumbled, conscious of sounding surly.

On the way back to the car, the weight of my cast seemed to have doubled. I was conscious of the odor of perspiration collected inside the plaster. I wriggled around inside the cast until I could pull out a tuft of padding. Surreptitiously I hid it behind the seat of the car.

On the turnpike my father spoke for the first time, without turning around to look at me.

"I have only one question," he said. "Did you gum up the rules?"

"Yes," I said, in a small voice.

We did not speak for the rest of the trip.

IV

A Very Good Girl

SUSPENSION FROM SWARTHMORE convinced my parents that I needed professional help. For four years they had been telling themselves that I would outgrow my hostility, my precocious sexuality, and my self-destructiveness, but it now appeared that a year of college had made me worse, not better. My body cast—initially a reason for them to treat me with special tenderness—became, after my expulsion, a symbol of my failure and theirs. Its crude imitation of a female form was a reminder that my transgression was sexual. This humiliated my parents as much as it did me, as though my injury were a revelation of the secret flaws in the family. They began to whisper that possibly the family's frequent moves during my childhood or my father's illness four years ago had led to my present troubles. (The more Freudian and threatening interpretation, that I had been deprived of necessary attention and affection at least since the birth of my handicapped brother, was never raised.) They decided to send me to a psychiatrist.

I have forgotten the name of the first doctor I saw, a stern white-haired man whose office was furnished with Oriental rugs, paintings, sculptures, and antique lamps. After asking my parents to leave the room, he suggested that I tell him why I wanted help. I did want to be healed, if possible, of my misery, and in the hope that this evidently powerful man could accomplish that, I was scrupulously truthful. I told him that I loved my parents but that I couldn't adhere to their outdated code of behavior. "They think I'm crazy because I sleep with my boyfriend," I explained. "I think I'd be crazy not to—but because I got caught and suspended from school for doing it, they think it proves they're right."

The doctor nodded reassuringly. He said that he couldn't take my case himself—only because he had too many patients already—but he would recommend someone skilled in dealing with family problems. It was evident, he said, that both my parents and I needed help in communicating with each other.

The doctor recommended a man with a degree in social work named Mr. Holmes. He wore round glasses on a round nose, and his face was perfectly expressionless. He asked me to lie on his couch, a vinyl daybed covered with a sheet. I hadn't expected this from a social worker. Lying down made me think of the psychotic patients in Robert Lindner's *The Fifty Minute Hour*, a book I had sneaked from my mother's night table when I was in junior high school. I asked Mr. Holmes if I was supposed to talk about my childhood. "Say whatever you like," he answered in his thin, toneless voice. I wished I could see his face. Obediently I told him my early memories—of losing my mother's hand on a crowded street and of my brother coming home from the hospital when I was three. I was beginning to get interested when he stopped me. "The session is over now," he said. "We shall continue next week." I left through a special patients' exit where I could not see or be seen by anyone in the waiting room.

Mr. Holmes, as I could tell from the scratching sound behind my head, took notes as I talked. I was sure he was writing down the least interesting comments I made and ignoring the significant ones. My growing conviction that this was the case led me to suspect that I suffered from a dangerous mental disease only an expert could recognize. I looked up books on psychiatric medicine in the library, trying to figure out the name of my illness. The descriptions of the symptoms overlapped, adding to my confusion. I left Mr. Holmes's office feeling as though I had flunked a crucial exam.

I asked Mr. Holmes when he was going to talk to my parents. He told me he wouldn't see them until he had something to say to them. I asked when that would be. He said about six months. I couldn't wait six months. He said my impatience indicated some underlying difficulty we should talk about. He had a pasty complexion and watery eyes. I disliked him heartily. When I lay down on the couch again, I could think of nothing to say. That evening I called his office and left a message that I was quitting.

He called my home in the evening, sounding agitated. I was pleased to discover that I had a modicum of power over him.

"You may not quit like this, Miss Alpert," he said. "You're supposed to come into the office and discuss it. If you still wish to leave therapy after we talk it over, that will be up to you."

I knew a trap when I heard one.

"I already tried to discuss it and your answers weren't satisfactory," I said, reveling in the sudden turning of tables.

"You didn't discuss it," he said. Although the voice he used would have been low-pitched for anyone else, for Holmes, it was a shriek.

"Well, you should have figured it out," I replied.

"But one doesn't quit therapy over the telephone. One simply doesn't."

How had he ever been licensed to work with adolescents? If he had learned nothing else after listening to me for a month, he should have realized that telling me a rule was a sure way to persuade me to do the opposite.

"I'm not coming back, Mr. Holmes," I said, and replaced the receiver.

When I told my father what I had done, he agreed with me.

"There's no point in your seeing the man if you can't trust him," he said. "The only thing that worries me is what the first doctor said to us."

"What was that?"

"He said you were severely disturbed, in need of competent help, and if you didn't get treatment now, you'd be in serious trouble before you were twenty."

I was shocked but tried not to show it.

"When did he tell you that?"

"When we walked to the elevator, after your appointment with him."

My father was surprisingly ready to drop the matter. Neither he nor my mother had ever had much faith in psychotherapy. They had sent me to Holmes only because they thought they should, and had never believed that I would be helped. But I was convinced that the regal-looking doctor had prophetic powers.

To pacify the fates, I made up my mind to be very good. Over the next four years I managed to convince my parents, my teachers, and sometimes myself that nothing was really wrong with me at all.

* * *

None of my high school friends came back to Forest Hills that summer. Beatrice registered for a course at Harvard summer school, sharing an apartment in Cambridge with her sister. Anita stayed at her mother's house in California. To insure that I had a regular escape from the oppressiveness of my parents' apartment, I signed up for a six weeks' intensive Latin course at Columbia, learning to negotiate my way on and off the subways in spite of my cast.

My mother was told that my grandmother was dying of stomach cancer. She was operated on in June, then moved from the hospital to a nursing home outside Washington, D.C. My mother spent the summer shuttling between New York and Washington as my grandmother shrank to a skeletal eighty pounds and gradually lost her faculties. My mother told us that she would die soon but maintained the pretense to her face that she would recover. This, she said, was the way my grandmother wanted it. The word "cancer" was never mentioned in the old woman's presence. A few days before Freda died, she profoundly upset my mother by insisting that I had converted to Christianity. My mother, who had avoided mention of either my broken back or my suspension, tried to tease her out of her conviction, but my grandmother would not be budged. Since in Freda's traditional Jewish code conversion to the *goyim* was the equivalent of death, the accusation chilled me. It was false, but there was no logical defense against it. And as a hallucinatory fantasy it did make sense. At the end of my junior year in high school, immersed in Ayn Rand's objectivist theories, I had declared myself an atheist and refused to go to temple with my parents. I was having an affair with a non-Jew; perhaps I would marry him and raise non-Jewish children. By the time I was brought down to Washington in August to see my grandmother I was hoping she would forgive me in advance for what I hadn't yet done. No forgiveness came. She had recognized no one in days.

After she died, I agreed with Keith that we should become engaged. He wanted this formality to pacify his parents, who had been affronted to learn we were having sex but whom Keith thought he could mollify by formalizing our intention to marry. I didn't understand his reasoning but rather liked the idea of an engagement. It sounded dignified, grown-up, and secure. Because Keith was still a Swarthmore student, I felt that becoming closer to him was becoming closer to Swarthmore, where I was determined to return at the end of my year of exile. At a jewelry shop in the Village we selected a ring, a heavy band of Florentine gold with a design of grapes and leaves. We had the initials "K.H. and J.A." engraved inside in an old-fashioned flowing script. When the ring was ready, Keith picked it up at the shop and presented it to me at my parents' dinner table. Their response was a chorus of silence—they didn't approve of Keith—but I had expected that. I kept the ring on my finger for all of the next year, my talisman, through the months at my parents' home, that I would someday leave again.

I settled for the simplest way out of the uncertainty into which Dean Lang's action had plunged me: I applied to Barnard as a temporary transfer student. I chose Barnard because I had a few high school friends in the sophomore class and because I thought I was more likely to win admission to the Swarthmore honors program as a junior from Barnard than from NYU or Queens College, the other local alternatives. My Merit scholarship was continued once I gave, as reason for the transfer, my back injury and need for medical attention in New York.

Barnard was not nearly so challenging or lively as Swarthmore. The graduate schools, the important campus newspaper, the political clubs, the well-known student theater and music groups were all across the street, on the Columbia campus, making Barnard women feel and act like second-rate students. Only my course in the nineteenth century English novel was as demanding as the average Swarthmore course, and that was taught to a packed lecture hall of nearly a hundred women with no opportunity for questions or discussion. By my second semester I learned to take advantage of the opportunities at Columbia and registered for a Virgil course across the street. But I had no social life on either campus. By five o'clock each evening I was back in Forest Hills studying. On weekends I was usually at Swarthmore, with Keith. Then, halfway through the year, Keith too was expelled from Swarthmore.

He accepted it stoically. His grades had been below average for three semesters in a row, and he had (unknown to me) been on academic probation for the past term. Possibly, too, some members of the administration felt it unfair that he continue at Swarthmore with a C minus average when I had been suspended with a B—since, although it could not be proven, no one doubted it had been Keith in the lodge with me. Keith didn't seem very upset. He had never felt comfortable at Swarthmore and had gone there only because he won a special scholarship awarded each year by an alumnus to a resident of the Eastern Shore. His talents were more practical than intellectual. He probably would have been happier at a state university, where training for a professional vocation wasn't considered a faintly suspicious pursuit. But instead of going home, he announced his intention to come to New York and look for a job and an apartment.

I tried to feel flattered by his wish to be closer to me. What I really wanted, though, was to return to Swarthmore. Keith's move to New York felt like pressure, and while I was outwardly compliant, I resented it. I did everything that I thought a woman was supposed to do when her man was in trouble. I encouraged Keith to pursue his casual interest in architecture by taking evening courses and finding work in an architect's office. I persuaded my father to arrange an interview for Keith with a professor of architecture at Cooper Union, his alma mater. The professor did help Keith find a job as an office assistant at a small architectural firm on Union Square, and Keith and I promptly celebrated his success. Yet I was already secretly making up my mind that Keith was a failure. I wanted to get away from him, but I didn't want to admit, while I was still living at my parents' home, that I had made a mistake.

At the end of my year at Barnard I saw my friend Beatrice for the last time. She called me at the start of her summer vacation and insisted that we see each other that night. She was leaving town the next day, but wouldn't discuss her plans on the phone. "You know I can't talk here," she said. "But come as soon as you can."

Physically Beatrice had changed very little in two years. Her eyes had the same amused, faraway look, and her tiny, lithe frame still seemed to be in perpetual motion. But she looked worn-out, as though she hadn't slept in a week or were recuperating from a long illness. When I came into her bedroom, she was playing Judy Collins on her stereo and trying to close suitcases by sitting on them.

"God, I can't believe how long it's been since I've seen you," she said, skipping over the letters of mine she'd never answered. "I thought of you about a million times last summer, but I was in Cambridge until the day I had to get back to school." She had shared an apartment there with her sister, she told me, while they both took summer courses at Harvard. It was there that she had met her current boyfriend, Jerry, who, she claimed, was a terrifically good-looking research scientist at MIT. Skeptically I asked how old he was.

"Twenty-five," said Beatrice proudly, and it did sound venerable. "He had just been separated from his wife when I met him. She's finally agreed to give him a divorce. So we may get married this year."

I twisted Keith's engagement ring on my finger. We had been through a difficult few months with each other, and there was nothing about Keith that gave me reason to boast. I asked Beatrice why she had been so mysterious about her summer plans.

Her eyes sparkled at the question, as they had in the old days when she invented stories to tell our parents so that we could sneak off to Greenwich Village for the evening.

"We've got an apartment together in Chicago for the summer," she said. "It's a great piece of luck—it's not even going to cost us anything. But I can't tell my parents that we're going to be living together. They think I'm going to Harvard summer school again."

I was mystified. Why couldn't she tell her parents she was going to summer school in Chicago? They wouldn't have to know that Jerry was living with her. Beatrice shook her head when I suggested it.

"You know how sharp my mother is. As soon as Jerry answered the phone, she'd know. This way there's a number in Cambridge they can call and friends will cover for me. I'll call back and they'll never know the difference."

By the time I left her apartment she had convinced me that only a few of her closest friends—among whom she still counted me—knew the truth. When we hugged good-bye, I was only sorry that we would once again be separated by hundreds of miles.

Two weeks later a mutual acquaintance called to tell me that Beatrice and her boyfriend had committed suicide together in a boardinghouse in Rome.

The tale about the apartment in Chicago for the summer had been pure fiction. Beatrice's friends in Chicago had been told exactly the reverse of what she told me: that she was going to be living in Cambridge with Jerry while her parents would be given a telephone number in Chicago. The day that I saw her in Forest Hills she had gone to her grandmother with yet a third story that had induced the old woman to give Beatrice $2,000. This money had paid for two one-way airline tickets from New York to Athens for Beatrice and Jerry, two boat trips from Athens to Rome, and the hotel, meal, and other expenses of their two-week stay abroad.

Had they actually planned the suicides before they left, bringing bottles of sleeping pills for that purpose? Beatrice's sister, Joanne, who had been vacationing in Greece when they died, was sure that they had.

"They took only enough clothes for two weeks and they spent every cent they had," Joanne said to me and a few cousins at the Caplans' kitchen table. "They were never going to buy return tickets. And do you know the name of the street they stayed on in Rome? In Italian it's the Street of Two Slaughterhouses." Someone said the street name was surely a coincidence. Joanne shook her head. "You don't know my sister. She was always onstage. She never called me when she was in Greece. She knew where I was; she had the address and the phone number. She knows I would have gone to her if she needed me. I would have gone around the world." At that Joanne broke down. It was the only time during the *shiva* I saw her lose control, and it made me feel as though I were preying on her tragedy. I didn't ask her for more details.

When the funeral was over, I persuaded Beatrice's Chicago roommate, Sarah, to have dinner with me at a Mexican restaurant in Brooklyn Heights, a few blocks from the office where I had a summer job. Sarah told me that Bernie, the famous summer-camp lover who had supposedly given Beatrice vaginal orgasms, had never existed. Beatrice was a virgin when she came to college, Sarah thought, and Bernie's name had come from a Jules Feiffer comic strip. After a month or two at Chicago, Beatrice was inventing stories of other lovers, one of whom was supposed to have hanged himself in a closet after she rejected him. Before long all her classmates knew about her deceptions, but Beatrice never admitted them. When caught in a contradiction, she would keep on inventing details until people laughed openly, at which point she would put on an offended look and grow quiet. At a party near the end of freshman year a brash young psychology major had confronted her. "Why don't you stop playing these games, Beatrice?" he had demanded. "We all know you're full of shit." She had clammed up then, Sarah said, and wouldn't open her mouth even to eat. The next day her women friends had taken her to a psychiatric hospital. She was diagnosed as a suicidal manic-depressive and stayed in treatment until midsummer. (This, I figured out, happened at the same time I was in a body cast, suspended from Swarthmore so that I could learn to "adjust.") In July she had made a sudden recovery and had gone to visit her sister in Cambridge, where she met Jerry, the first man who seemed genuinely to love her.

Sarah and I walked down Montague Street toward the promenade and the bay. We both wanted to relieve the tension of the dinner conversation but were unable to change the subject. Sarah asked me if I were the person who used to steal books with Beatrice.

"Yes, that was me," I admitted.

"I thought so. . . . She spoke of you often, especially in the first year."

"She was the most magnetic person I ever knew," I heard myself say. "I could never say no to her, no matter how ludicrous or risky her ideas. I suppose I wanted to believe all those crazy stories of hers. They made her seem so exciting . . . she fitted them somehow."

Sarah said nothing for a few moments, but I knew the same thought was in both our minds: that Jerry was the last of Beatrice's friends who couldn't say no.

Before I returned to Swarthmore, I received another shock, this one delivered by Saul. He had spent a second year in California, then returned to New York again in June, saying that this time he was home for good. He told me he had learned enough about photography to set himself up as a free-lancer and described his work in exuberant detail. But my questions about Anita went unanswered. Finally, after three months of merciless nagging, he told me what had happened.

In the fall—while the Berkeley campus was shaken by the Free Speech Movement—Anita had become pregnant. Saul was not the father, and if he knew who was, he wouldn't say. Anita had refused to have the abortion her father would gladly have paid for and had not married or moved in with the child's father. She had also refused Saul's offer to marry her. In the spring she gave birth to a son. She quit school to take care of him and, since her father had cut her off, was supporting herself and the child on welfare. Her health was good, Saul said, and she had not lost her senses. She was doing what she wanted to do. "I worried more about her than she worried about herself," he said. "She's a remarkable woman."

I took the news hard. Anita was the one person I knew in high school, besides Beatrice, whose approval had mattered most to me. I wanted to admire her courage in having the child, but like

Beatrice's suicide, it was too far outside the sphere of normal choices for me to take it in. Why would she want the social ostracism of an illegitimate pregnancy and birth? Why, gifted as Anita was, was she so willing to quit school and risk the possibility that she would never return? How could she take on the responsibility of child rearing without someone to give her support? Because these were the same questions my mother, who had always disliked her, would have asked, I didn't repeat them to Saul. Beatrice's suicide had shocked and saddened me; Anita's radical choice aroused as much envy in me as dismay. I wanted to write her a letter, but I couldn't think of what to put in it. I wasn't even sure she would want to hear from me. What I wanted most was to bridge the gulf between us—but that, I sensed, was going to require more than a letter.

Returning to Swarthmore as a junior classics major in honors, I found the college strikingly changed. Chester had not been a campus issue for a year. One of the reasons for that was growing hostility by blacks to white involvement in civil rights issues. Another was the confusion into which SPAC sympathizers were thrown when Stanley Branche, the firebrand of CFFN, appeared to reach a reconciliation with local Republican politicians. A third was the Vietnam War. Since early 1965, Johnson had been bombing North Vietnam. Draft calls had shot up, and SDS chapters around the country had helped mobilize protests against the draft and the war. SPACers (many of whom were also SDS members, although SDS had no official chapter at Swarthmore) were broadcasting antiwar teach-ins from other universities onto the Swarthmore campus, marching against germ warfare research at the University of Pennsylvania, and attending conventions aimed at "broadening the base of the antiwar movement" to include not only college students but factory and office workers, high school students, farmers, and housewives.

I agreed wholeheartedly with SPAC's antiwar position. I had resented Johnson from the day he inherited office and had not been converted to his side when he won the lesser-of-two-evils 1964 election against Goldwater. I only had to read the first two or three sentences of any of the I. F. Stone articles that were passed around the campus that year to feel convinced that Stone's analysis of the U.S. military was right. Once an otherwise-intelligent acquaintance shocked me by suggesting, over sloppy joes in the dining hall, that the Vietnamese communists did *not* deserve the support of the American left. To me it was obvious that the National Liberation Front was an indigenous revolutionary movement, while General Ky was a corrupt puppet of the United States. But my interest in a war so far from home was limited. I was much more gripped by the new grass-roots campus movement to eliminate curfews for women students.

The curfews were a remnant of Victorian paternalism. They had never been imposed on male students, while women had endured them since the college was founded in the 1860's. The controversy began during the spring of 1965, when I was at Barnard and Dean Lang attempted to move back the 2:00 A.M. weeknight curfew to 12:30 A.M. In the resistance to Dean Lang's new restrictions, both men and women students, whose views on civil rights demonstrations and the war ranged from conservative to radical, began to examine and openly criticize the unequal treatment of women on campus. Gradually not only the curfews but the rules against cohabitation and the regulations governing "open house"—the few hours each weekend when men and women could visit each other's dormitories—came under fierce attack. The deans, fearing the loss of alumni support if they abolished too many rules, tried to pacify the movement by token liberalizations of the curfew, but the movement had already gone too far to be stopped. Within a few years after my graduation, curfews were dead and a new era dawned: the dorms were almost completely co-ed.

Greater sexual permissiveness and the movement for equality we didn't yet call feminism went hand in hand on the Swarthmore campus. In my freshman year, of the twelve student government members only one had been female. In my senior year, there were five. A close friend was elected editor of the *Phoenix*, the first woman to hold the position in more than fifty years. We women still wore dresses to seminars and waited for men to call us for dates, but there was now as much talk of European travel, graduate school, or professional training after graduation as there was of marriage. The graduate degree jocularly referred to in the early sixties as PHT—Putting Hubby Through—was losing its air of noble martyrdom. A few years later, as women competed with men for admission to medical and law schools, for leadership positions in the antiwar movement, and for jobs, no friend of mine could remember what it had meant.

In this newly charged atmosphere, so different from humdrum

Barnard, I finally pulled myself together enough to break up with Keith. One Saturday morning at about eleven I returned to my dormitory after a night with a new lover to find Keith and his parents waiting for me. Keith gave me an armful of carnations, his parents took us to lunch, and covered with shame, I realized my situation was too hypocritical to continue. The next weekend I returned the engagement ring. Keith came to Swarthmore once more to beg me to come back to him, swearing he would always wait. A couple of months later I learned he was dating a black friend of mine from high school who had just left her husband. She and Keith were supposed to be very happy together.

Though I had been content for over a year with Keith, I had never really been in love with him. We had become involved only after I was convinced that the men to whom I was attracted would never reciprocate my feelings and that I was better off with the safety and security someone like Keith could offer me. But in the spring of my junior year I met someone to whom I was completely vulnerable, and for a few delirious months it seemed that he felt the same.

Marty was a boyish-looking sophomore, a writer for the *Phoenix*, who had grown up in Queens, not far from Forest Hills. He had a crooked Huck Finn smile and a birthmark that darkened the right side of his face like a permanently fading suntan. His father had died of a heart attack when he was thirteen, his mother of cancer when he was seventeen. The hungry-orphan look in his brown eyes melted my heart, and though I was moved by his tragedy, I secretly envied his independence of the adult world. He had his own money and could make decisions for himself, with only slight interference from an aunt and uncle, his legal guardians. I wished I had as much autonomy myself. We went to a concert together, then started meeting each other for meals. For a couple of weeks we spent every evening in the lounge of my dormitory gazing raptly into each other's eyes. "Who would have thought I'd come all the way here from Little Neck to go nuts for a Jewish girl from Forest Hills?" Marty would say, shaking his head. I thought our love was too pure to sully with sex—which, truthfully, I'd never much enjoyed once the foreplay was over. Finally Marty did ask me to come to his room and, when I hesitated, burst into tears. If he didn't love me, he said, he wouldn't care so much, but the way he felt now. . . . I offered not another word of protest.

With Keith, I had been scrupulous about using my diaphragm, but I didn't want such tedious details to intrude on my new romance. Marty and I made love whenever we could that spring and never discussed or used contraception. My period stopped in April, but a local doctor told me not to worry. In June, just after the school year ended, when I was back in Forest Hills, I took a pregnancy test at a clinic. It came back positive.

During the spring I had been accepted for a six weeks' summer course at the American School of Classical Studies at Athens, designed to introduce classics students and teachers to the rudiments of archaeology. My parents had agreed to pay for my plane fare and expenses. In ten days I was supposed to leave on a charter flight for Europe. I telephoned a Philadelphia abortionist whose name I had obtained before the academic year was over. (The women's student association president, who that semester was one of my best friends, kept a list of local abortionists—against state law as well as college rules, but part of a venerable Swarthmore tradition.) The abortionist gave me an appointment for a June morning four days before my flight was scheduled to leave. It was going to cost $300, of which I had not a cent. Marty took half the money from his monthly Social Security check and borrowed the rest from the liberal-minded mother of one of his friends, Brian Stone. He seemed more distraught than I was, and once burst into sobs, saying that if anything happened to me, he would kill himself. I kept my own apprehensions under wraps, cheered him as best I could, and hoped there would be no complications that would cause my parents to find out.

We left New York for Philadelphia early on the morning of the fourteenth. Marty drove and Lissa, who had been staying with me at my parents' apartment for the first week of the summer, came for company and moral support. They dropped me at the abortionist's office, a seedy brownstone in North Philadelphia, where a woman in a nurse's uniform said they couldn't wait but should return about three o'clock. After two or three hours downstairs in a roomful of black, Hispanic, and white women, some of them as old as forty and all of them silent with fear, I was summoned upstairs by the nurse. I met the doctor in the makeshift operating room on the second floor. The medical license on the wall had been issued in Puerto Rico, which made me uneasy, but I was reassured by the doctor's strong features, his large gentle hands, and his age, which must have been near fifty. I gave him the $300 in cash and asked if I could stay awake for the operation. "Too much pain," he said, shaking his head. He told me to lie down on the metal table. The nurse covered me with a stained sheet, and the doctor examined me. Then he stuck a needle in my vein. I felt my arm swell with liquid, grow cold. Then I lost consciousness.

The nurse slapped my hands to wake me. A strong smell of vomit assaulted me, and I felt too dizzy to move.

"You threw up on yourself," she said. "I've been cleaning you up for half an hour. Didn't I tell you not to eat before you came?"

The doctor was washing his hands at the other end of the room. "Your friends were in an accident," he said, ignoring the nurse as he approached the operating table. "They were supposed to be here by now, but they'll be an hour late."

"An accident?" The effort of speaking made me want to go back to sleep.

"Don't worry. No one was hurt. But we have to leave you here now. "They'll ring the bell downstairs when they come. Be sure to close the door behind you."

Marty was prone to careless driving, especially when he was upset. God, what if something had happened to him or Lissa?

"Was it a boy or a girl who called?"

The doctor looked at me pityingly.

"It's impossible to tell at this stage," he said. "It's just a tiny bloody thing."

It took me a moment to realize that he had misunderstood me and thought I was asking about the fetus. I had forgotten all about it until then—or had I never thought of it at all? A sudden image of a tiny, throbbing humanoid dangling from the doctor's forceps filled me with dread. Had he flushed it down the toilet? Wrapped it in newspapers and dumped it in the garbage? Is that why I couldn't be awake—so that I wouldn't see it?

They left me alone in the room. I got up and, moving as if in a dream, put on my underwear, skirt and blouse, shoes. I stuffed my stockings in my pocketbook, knowing I was too groggy to put them on straight. Then I made my way down the flight of narrow stairs, gripping the banister and moving one step at a time. I sat down to rest twice, and once I nearly fell. The doorbell rang when I was halfway down. I pictured Marty and Lissa bandaged, on crutches, on the other side of the door.

Lissa was there when I opened the door, looking concerned and loving and not at all hurt. She put her arm around my waist and helped me down the outside stairs to the street, where we got in a cab and went to meet Marty at Swarthmore.

Marty had collided with another car two blocks from the abortionist's. No one had been hurt; but the car needed minor repairs, and Marty had to file a police report on the accident. The three of us stayed in Swarthmore overnight, using the accident as an excuse to my parents for the extended visit. Late on the fifteenth we drove back to New York. From there, Lissa flew home to New Orleans, Marty went to San Francisco, where he was planning to spend the summer, and I made my flight to London, then Copenhagen and Athens, without further mishap.

The sun didn't set in Copenhagen that July. I met two friends from Reed College there: Jack, who was the hometown boyfriend of a Swarthmore classmate, and Jack's roommate, Roy, who was Jewish but looked Irish, wrote poetry, and was the nephew of one of America's most famous playwrights. In the two-day layover before my flight left for Athens, the three of us were inseparable, and until the last few hours of my stay none of us went to sleep. We passed the afternoons in the Ny Carlsberg Glyptotek or in the bohemian quarter, the sunny evenings in cafés, and the nights that looked like twilights in Tivoli Gardens. Finally, at 3:00 A.M., eight hours before my flight to Athens, Jack went off to his hotel, exhausted, and Roy and I went to mine. For another hour we sat on the porch until the gray sky turned to pearl, listening as the milk trucks came closer, then went upstairs, undressed, and fell into bed. We didn't want to make love, we agreed, since I was so involved with Marty and Roy was in love with a girl at Reed. We made love anyway. In the morning Roy saw me to the airport, where he kissed me lingeringly and scribbled his address in London for the rest of the summer on the back of an envelope.

For the first day or two in Athens I wondered how I had allowed myself to be unfaithful to Marty—was it the emotional aftereffect of my abortion? a spell put on me by the Copenhagen twenty-four-hour day?—and then stopped thinking about everything but Greece. At the American School, we lived in a cool white building at the foot of Mount Lykabettos, in the northern part of the city. We researched assigned papers in the small but highly selective *Ameri-*

kanikē Skolē library and ate our meals—homemade moussaka, fresh fish, retsina, cheese, and homemade tarts—on a wooden porch that looked out over the slopes of the city. When it was too hot to sleep at night, we took refuge in the lounge that opened onto the porch, where there was a record player and a small collection of American records, of which two by the Lovin' Spoonful were favorites of those of us under thirty. I played "Daydreamin'" so many times I could hum it all the way up the steps to the Acropolis.

On the Peloponnesos, we visited a remote Neolithic site where a half dozen foundation stones were the poignant, only remains of a civilization six thousand years old. We climbed to the peak of Acrocorinth at sunset, listened to a pin drop in the ancient amphitheater at Epidauros, and were led by George Mylonas, the great archaeologist, through the graves of Agamemnon's Mycenae.

At the Terrace of the Lions on the island of Delos, I delivered a paper I had prepared in the school's library, using the records from the French excavation of the site. Something happened to me when I actually saw that stark row of beasts, guardians of the once-holy precinct of Apollo and miraculously intact in the midst of two and a half millennia of rubble. I had studied photographs of the marble lions and could tell my fellow students all about their archaeological uniqueness, about the speculations as to their origin, and about the sacred lake they faced, now a hollow of dry sand. But the personal effect that living history had on me was beyond my ability to express. I felt the beginning of an obsession that could have turned me into a classicist.

In the last weekend of the summer session, Neil Perlmutter, a Swarthmore classmate, arrived on his motorcycle and took me to Sounion, at the tip of the Attic peninsula. We swam in the eerily calm Mediterranean and lay on the rocks, letting the sun bake our faces until long past the school's dinner hour, periodically squinting at the ruins of a temple to Apollo above us. I told Neil then that I had decided to become an archaeologist so that I could return to Greece to live. It was true, too. I had never been able to form a plan for any future; but Greece inspired me, and I knew I could spend my life immersed in its treasures.

When the school session ended, five weeks remained before my charter flight returned to New York from London. I went to Rome for two weeks, then met Ginny, a friend from Athens, in Venice.

Ginny was a Greek major at the University of Washington who had taken a year abroad to work for an archaeologist. Hitchhiking together through the lake country of northern Italy, the Swiss Alps, the Loire Valley, and finally Paris and across the channel to England, we talked of little except classics. At the Louvre we headed directly for the Greek vases. At Canterbury we took three days to study the medieval remains and learn the Roman history of the site. Ginny told me I should apply for a job with Oscar Broneer, an American archaeologist digging at Isthmia near the Gulf of Corinth. "Broneer hires a new female assistant from an American college each year," she said. "He only pays your expenses, and you'll probably do more typing than archaeology; but you make great connections." I drafted my letter to Dr. Broneer while I was still in London.

On the flight home I thought about Marty for the first time all summer. I had written him eight or ten letters but found it hard to know what to say when I was so happy and he seemed so far away. The only job he had been able to find in San Francisco was pumping gas. His letters sounded lonely and sometimes self-pitying. "Stop your tourist bulletins," he complained in one. "I want to hear how much you love me, not about the goddamned Parthenon." Another time he wrote he had gone to bed with a woman he met at a party. Although I was jealous, I was relieved, too. It would make it easier to tell him about Roy, who already seemed a foolish but long-ago mistake.

My parents, my brother, Marty, and Patch and Lissa (who had become engaged that summer) met me at the airport. Marty hugged me as hard as when we first knew each other, and I felt reassured that nothing had changed between us. We could not stop smiling at each other. My parents were fond of him and seemed, for once, not to mind our open displays of affection.

On our second night together, sitting on a couch in the Little Neck house Marty shared with his two brothers, I told him about Roy. The scene that followed was straight out of *Tess of the D'Urbervilles.* He jerked his arm away from my shoulders and stood up, his lips trembling. "I'll take you home now," he said. I thought he was joking. He wasn't. On the way home in the car, I asked him how my one night with Roy was different from his sleeping with a woman he met at a party. "You're not the girl I thought you were, that's all," he said. I began to cry. I couldn't decide whether I hated myself more for having slept with Roy or for having been so stupid as to tell Marty the truth.

He didn't call me until the day before the semester started. "I'm still very angry at you," he said. "But I'll drive you back to school if you want." I was glad that I could save face for my parents and hoped for a chance to repair the damage. But Marty seemed to have wanted me back only to punish me further. For the next month he treated me like hand-me-down clothes. He wouldn't call or come by my dorm for days. He broke dates to play poker with his male friends. He was becoming popular now in his junior year, with his own off-campus apartment (a major status symbol) and more frequent appearances in the *Phoenix*. A coterie of freshman girls followed him from meals to class to the library. When I told him how unhappy he made me, he shrugged. I held on to the idea that he would learn to love me again if only I kept on being faithful to him. One night he took me to his apartment to tell me he wanted to break up. Soon after, he began dating a beautiful freshman whose complexion and long, glossy hair could have made a *Seventeen* cover.

After Marty left me, the idea of becoming an archaeologist returned with almost the vividness of the summer. I registered for a graduate course in Greek pottery in the archaeology department of the University of Pennsylvania. I sent in applications to graduate schools that had departments of archaeology as well as departments of classics—Berkeley, Harvard, and Columbia. In my classics seminars, I volunteered for the assignments related to archaeological finds: the origins of Rome, the historical basis of Homer. Late in the fall a letter came from Oscar Broneer in Isthmia, answering the inquiry I'd written him in London. He would be pleased to have me as his assistant, he wrote, to begin in June or September 1967. He would pay my room, board, and pocket money, and I should arrange my own plane travel and advise him as to my arrival date. I wrote back to accept, still mourning Marty but gratified that at least my postcollege future was assured.

On April 15, 1967, I participated in my first antiwar action by going to the mass march in New York called by the National Mobilization to End the War in Vietnam. My then-boyfriend, Seymour, who kept me from feeling deserted on Saturday nights more than he inspired my passion, had argued against my going. "People opposed to the war are opposed to it because their friends are, and the people who are for it are just the same," he liked to say. "That's why everyone gets so angry over it—because it threatens their emotional loyalties." I considered this psychological analysis a poor excuse to stay home from the march. Since the summer of 1966 the United States had been bombing civilian targets in Vietnam, with no pretense that the strikes were accidental. Entire towns were condemned on the grounds that they were Vietcong strongholds. Nearly a half million American servicemen were now stationed in South Vietnam, propping up a dictatorship that grew steadily more corrupt. If Johnson could be moved to change his policies by the spectacle of hundreds of thousands of people in the street, then I had a moral obligation to go.

It was a peaceful, mostly white and middle-class crowd of 100,000 that assembled in the Sheep Meadow that spring day, bearing no visible resemblance to the militant demonstration in Chester in 1963. Grass had come to the eastern campuses that year, and clouds of it hung over groups of college-aged marchers. The anarchist utopians known as the San Francisco Diggers in bright capes and hats and feathers and beads and the Hare Krishna singers in saffron gowns made the march resemble a be-in as much as a political protest. The serious edge was provided by more than 100 draft-age young men who burned their selective service cards in a ceremony in the park, a show of courage that moved me as the early freedom riders had. I wondered whether, faced with a similar dilemma, I would be able to act as fearlessly.

Four days after that march I had my chance to find out. The constitutional government of Greece was toppled by a right-wing military coup.

Alexandros, a Greek student in my honors seminars, played the devil tempter by urging me not to give up my plans to work for Broneer. Greece was an extremely poor country, he explained to me patiently, and violent political swings were to be expected. Papadopoulos, the new dictator, was an ass, but the leftist opposition he had jailed was not much better. Didn't I remember that when I was in Greece, a mail strike had stopped all letters coming in and going out of the country? This sort of disruption happened all the time, and only a firm hand could put a stop to it. Nor should I worry that, working in Isthmia, I would be affected by the repressive atmosphere. The right wing in Greece, Alexo assured me, loved Americans.

Fond as I was of Alexo, I decided that he was wrong. The Greek junta did not seem to me to differ from the South Vietnamese dictatorship against which I had demonstrated less than a week ago. Both starved and tortured the opposition. Both operated in defiance of the people's will. Both imposed censorship on newspapers. Both were rigid hierarchies, headed by ruthless, ambitious men, who were also puppets of the United States. Greece was no less dependent on the American military than was the Saigon regime of Nguyen Cao Ky. If the United States did not cut off military aid to Papadopoulos and I contributed my tourist money and labor to that country, then I was supporting in action the very policies I marched against in theory. Unless the junta fell that summer, I could not, in good conscience, take the job with Oscar Broneer.

It is possible that if the Greek government had not fallen to the junta, I would have found another reason to decline the job. The coup might merely have given me an excuse to conceal my fear of going so far from home for an indeterminate length of time—a fear I would not have admitted to my family, my friends, or myself. For as the time grew nearer for me to commit myself to a profession and begin making my own way in the world, I was increasingly worried that the responsibility was more than I could manage. In the end, I hedged: I wrote to Oscar Broneer not to protest the politics of the junta and his alleged support of the military regime, but simply to say that for financial reasons, I was postponing my departure until September. I then made plans to spend the summer living in Forest Hills and working, putting off the next step until the end of August.

I completed my senior exams with high honors and came back to Forest Hills a week before graduation to look for a job. My mother was delighted to have me home again. Both she and my father were proud of my two successful years at Swarthmore, during which I had carefully kept from them the abortion, my anguish over Marty, and other upsets that might have incurred their disapproval or caused them worry. They were not at all concerned over my sudden uncertainty about the job in Greece. In my mother's view, my classics major had always seemed impractical and my fantasies about becoming an archaeologist had the ring of escapism. For her, the test of my new adulthood was not in academia, but in finding and holding a job in the business world of New York. I gave into her pressure to cut my hair in a short, sleek, businesslike style, to buy dresses suitable for a midtown office job, and to think not only of the summer but of the long-term future when I answered the ads under "college graduate" in the *Times*.

Partly from curiosity, I made stops at the three companies in New York that published books in classics: Oxford, Cambridge, and St. Martin's Press. Quite by chance I arrived in the offices of Cambridge University Press on the day the company was interviewing applicants for a job as editorial secretary. Until my serendipitous appearance, the only applicants for the position had been young women from commercial high schools and Katharine Gibbs, none of them right for a job in scholarly book publishing. A harried administrative assistant glanced at my brief résumé and ushered me in at once for an interview with Jack Schulman, assistant manager of the firm.

Schulman was a plump, balding man of fifty or so whose geniality and canny flattery reminded me of my father. He asked a few questions about my background and then looked me in the eye. "I want to warn you," he said, "that not everyone finds our chief editor easy to work with. You've heard of difficult authors, I'm sure. Editors can be temperamental, too. But you seem to be the sort of girl who can handle tough situations."

He spoke as though I had already agreed to take the job. Awed at my luck, I remembered in time to ask him about the salary. He glanced down at my application where I had written $95 a week, $15 more than I'd made at my last summer job, as a minimum demand.

"We can meet your request," he said.

I was so dazzled then that although I would have to return to Swarthmore in a week for the commencement exercise, I offered to start work the next day.

V

In the Real World

BY MIDSUMMER THE OPPORTUNITIES at Cambridge University Press seemed limited only by my ambition. The home office in England was pressuring the New York branch to publish more American manuscripts. The New York editors were inexperienced, feuding with each other and with management. My boss, Bob Adamson, the editor in chief, was a former book salesman with no editorial experience at the time Ronald Mansbridge, the branch manager, had put him in charge of the department. Miriam Firestone, the other senior editor, was an able worker but made no attempt to hide her resentment of Adamson's nominal superiority. The department also had a part-time editorial assistant, Adam Horvath, who was completing his doctorate in English at Columbia. He was the rising star on whom I modeled myself. After I had been at the job a month, I went to Mansbridge and asked him to promote me to a position comparable to Adam's.

Mansbridge, English-born and Oxford-educated, had founded the New York branch twenty years ago. He put me in mind of a colonial administrator over evidently inferior natives. Few low-level employees came uninvited to his office. I had not been in business long enough to respect unwritten rules; my ignorance kept me from feeling intimidated. Mansbridge listened to my request. "First do a good job as an editorial secretary," he said. "That isn't easy, you know. In six months I'll consider your promotion." Encouraged that he had not thrown me out of the office, I asked if I could take off two hours a week to attend Greek and Latin classes at Columbia. I was willing to make up the lost hours by working through lunch. The eyebrows lifted above the half-rim tortoiseshell glasses. "You're a classicist, are you?" he asked in his Churchillian accent.

"Yes, sir."

"You may have the time off. And see that you get a proper lunch."

I wrote to Broneer again, finally declining the job at Isthmia.

My parents were delighted with my new success in what my father liked to call "the real world." They made me a present of the tuition money at Columbia and agreed that I should look for a Manhattan apartment before school started. I called my friend Barbara Stubbs, who was going to start studies at Columbia Journalism School in the fall. She already had plans to live with her former roommate, Jean, but said I was welcome to join them. I was disappointed but said yes. Barbara had been one of my favorite people at Swarthmore. She was gutsy and imaginative and won my admiration when she edited the newspaper through one especially lively semester, marked by student/administration controversy over the dorm rules. She had the same cynical humor I cultivated in myself, a tantalizing contrast with her snub-nosed freckle-faced good looks. I was less friendly with Jean, whom I had known at Swarthmore as Barbara's faithful sidekick, and I wasn't sure how a threesome would work out. My parents drove Jean and me around to look at apartments while Barbara was with her family in Ohio. They signed my part of the lease on a small two-bedroom apartment on West Eighty-third Street since I was a minor and my signature wasn't legal.

Barbara, Jean, and I moved in on Labor Day weekend. Barbara and I began school at once. Jean was job hunting and had more time on her hands to decorate the apartment. On weekends she went to her parents' Staten Island home, where she sewed slipcovers and curtains for the living room. The matching set in shocking pinks and oranges didn't look as dashing as we had hoped. A few days later Jean came home with a thirty-six-by-sixty-inch personality poster of Allen Ginsberg, bearded and barefoot, wearing a sandwich board that declared "Free Pot." I was nonplussed. "You're not going to put that in the living room," I said. Jean looked crestfallen, and Barbara shot me a warning look. To me, the poster suggested an embarrassing anxiety, on the part of three rather conventional young career women, to appear hip, but Jean didn't seem to see it that way. Ginsberg reigned incongruously over our living room for the duration of our stay on Eighty-third Street.

* * *

When notices first appeared on the Columbia campus urging us to "confront the warmakers" at the Pentagon on October 21–22, 1967, I assumed that my roommates and I would go together. We had all marched against the war in New York last April. Since then the bombings and troop commitments had escalated. The resistance movement had grown until we each knew a couple of men who had burned or turned in their draft cards or were planning to refuse induction or go to Canada. It surprised me when Barbara said she hadn't made up her mind. She had heard rumors at the journalism school, she said, that some of the demonstrators were planning to storm the Pentagon, hoping to incite the military police to violence. They were talking of loot-ins at Washington department stores, urinating on the White House lawn, fucking on the steps of the Pentagon. The San Francisco Diggers, who now had adherents in New York, had declared the Pentagon to be possessed of evil spirits. They were going to conduct an exorcism by levitating the building five feet in the air. "The movement has changed," Barbara said. "People are talking revolution now. It sounds crazy, I know, but it's scary, too."

Jean was by then working as David Halberstam's secretary at *Harper's*. She was beginning to be influenced by the opinions of the former Vietnam correspondent and by the electric atmosphere of the *Harper's* office, where it seemed everyone was against the war and a staggering sum had been offered to Norman Mailer to report on the demonstration. The day before the march, Jean finally decided to go with me. I was nervous myself by that time. Barbara's rumors had been repeated in the papers, and earlier in the week hundreds of demonstrators had been tear-gassed and beaten at the Oakland Induction Center. I made reservations anyway for both Jean and me on the Mobilization-chartered bus.

The trip to Washington that Saturday morning was the first time I had been alone with Jean. She was good company. The anticipation of the march made her lively, and perhaps Barbarba's absence encouraged her, too. She told me stories about working at the *Times* and on the press corps in Saigon, secondhand from Halberstam, but intriguing. We reached the Washington Monument early in the afternoon. Even after the huge April march in New York, we were amazed at the size of the crowd, already picnicking on the grass or clambering off buses parked for miles along the Mall.

If the threat of violence had discouraged more people than our roommate, Barbara, it was not evident by the numbers here. They had come from Massachusetts, Maryland, Arkansas, New Mexico, Oregon, Canada, and England. They had ridden buses and trains and planes, driven VW vans and station wagons, hitchhiked, camped out in sleeping bags they used now as seat rugs and tablecloths. There were nuns and accountants and housewives and babies in strollers and nine-year-olds in football jerseys wearing buttons that said "War Is Not Healthy for Children and Other Living Things." Couples lay wrapped in embraces as though they were at Jones Beach in July, and religious devotees danced and jingled bells. Hippies passed joints and chanted "LBJ Sucks." Scattered through the sea of people were the red, blue, and yellow flags of the National Liberation Front of South Vietnam. I assumed these were a kind of joke, like the hippies' Uncle Sam hats and Revolutionary War greatcoats.

We were too far away from the podium to see the speakers, but the sounds floated to us over the public-address system. An organizer led the crowd in choruses of "HELL NO, WE WON'T GO." The words meant something more to me than refusing military service: a refusal to cooperate with any aspect of authority. By yelling the phrases at the top of my lungs, I was saying no not only to the draft, not only to the war, but to all the values of the military and of corporate enterprise—to the religious and patriotic ideas my parents had tried to compel me to respect from the time I was a small child.

The crowd rose and surged forward. We were headed for the Pentagon—past the Lincoln Memorial and the reflecting pool, through a few blocks of the capital, and onto the Arlington Memorial Bridge. Once we reached the bridge, Jean and I were jammed together, unable to move forward or back. Army helicopters buzzed overhead. Someone said they were taking pictures of us for the CIA. Someone else said that demonstrators with NLF flags had just invaded the Pentagon. Another chant began. "HEY HEY, LBJ, HOW MANY KIDS DID YOU KILL TODAY?" I raised my voice with the others, hoping we were close enough to the White House so that the President would hear.

Halfway across the bridge, we saw the Pentagon. It looked like the capital of a space empire, coldly geometrical, with an endless lawn in front. The bridge dipped down and the building was no longer visible. It took us nearly another hour to reach the other side. Free of the bridge bottleneck, we found ourselves on a bare lot, surrounded by people running in all directions. A marshal with a bullhorn shouted from the top of a wall: "The soldiers are armed! The soldiers are armed!"

I looked at Jean. "What soldiers?"

We walked hesitantly in the direction of the Pentagon. I smelled something noxious. "Tear gas," someone said. "It's real thick farther up." Jean grabbed my arm. A few feet away a column of soldiers in rubber gas masks, armed invaders from the extraterrestrial Pentagon, were clearing a path through the crowd.

"Let's go back," said Jean. I agreed at once. The bridge was nearly clear by then. We headed back to Washington, where we caught the next train to New York.

We watched the rest of the demonstration on television Sunday and Monday. Had we been frightened away for nothing? The only demonstrators arrested that first day were those who had deliberately crossed the police line and entered the Pentagon itself. The others—thousands of them—had stayed outside, facing down the military guards. They shouted "JOIN US, JOIN US" at the barrels of the soldiers' guns. Some burned draft cards. Others draped flowers over the MPs' rifles. At night they slept on the Pentagon lawn. On Sunday they resumed the demonstration. They walked up and down the lines of soldiers, pleading with them to leave the service. A correspondent said that one soldier did. The demonstration lasted until Sunday at midnight, when the few hundred remaining were arrested. All were released on Monday.

I could hear my parents' voices in my head. Editorial secretaries who wanted to be editorial assistants didn't run around with hippies carrying NLF flags, chanting slogans, defying the police. That wasn't living in the real world. I argued back. Something had to be done to stop the war. Demonstrations had been useless. Johnson had announced over and again that he was unaffected by them. Besides, the Pentagon demonstration had been peaceful. No demonstrator had thrown a punch or kicked a cop. No guns had been fired. And headlines had been made around the world. From Chile to Thailand to South Africa, everyone now knew that the youth of America was against the war. It had been an epoch, more real than any desk full of paper work at 9:00 A.M. How had it happened, then, that after shouting "HELL, NO, WE WON'T GO!" I had turned around at the first sign of confrontation? This symptom of hypocrisy continued to trouble me as news of the movement went on dominating the headlines.

On January 29, 1968, my friend Michael Ferber was indicted by the federal government—together with Benjamin Spock, William Sloane Coffin, Marcus Raskin, and Mitchell Goodman—for conspiring to undermine the Selective Service System.

I had been slightly in awe of Michael since we were Greek majors together at Swarthmore. In my sophomore year he had played Pentheus in the Greek department's production of *The Bacchae*. His fluency in Greek and the charm he brought to the role had helped me make up my mind to major in classics. After that we had several seminars together. His weekly seminar papers were always carefully thought out and often original. He was active in the Unitarian youth movement and in SPAC. Political insight and a strong concern with ethical questions colored his interests in literature and philosophy. In my senior year he went to Harvard as a graduate student in English. He roomed with Patch, who was starting at Harvard Medical School. Lissa, then engaged to Patch, spent several days each month at their apartment in Boston. During the April 1967 Moratorium, while I was marching in New York, Lissa told me that Mike spoke from a pulpit in the Arlington Street Church. His speech, called "A Time to Say No," argued on moral grounds against cooperating with the military. Later I read it in Dave Dellinger's magazine, *Liberation*. It had the same logical strengths of Mike's best seminar papers, and perhaps because I could imagine him delivering it, it left a lump in my throat.

I had last seen Michael at Patch and Lissa's wedding in Boston. He had just begun living with a Radcliffe student who never left his side. I wanted to talk to him, but his girl friend and his new celebrity in the draft resistance movement made me shy. Through the summer and fall I thought I would call him, but never did. As I grew more absorbed in my job, I had all but forgotten him.

After the indictment I did call. He was very cordial, but I couldn't tell if he was pleased to hear from me. He said he had a fine lawyer—three or four of them, in fact. He referred to the Spocks as Ben and Jane, the Coffins as Bill and Eva. The indictment was a shock, he said, but he wasn't sorry for it. He had done what he had to. Perhaps the trial would be a rallying point for the movement. Oh, yes, he was taking a leave of absence from Harvard for a semester.

My fear for Michael changed to pity for myself. He was in danger of going to jail, but he seemed so happy! While his life had taken on such purpose, what had been happening to me? I was working ten hours a day at a job I had fallen into by accident. I hardly read the leftist press, though I kept feeling that I should. When I had a chance, at the Pentagon, to contribute to the movement, I had scurried back to the safety of New York. Michael's exemplary courage made me feel, in contrast, that my own life was slipping away from me.

After the Vietcong's Tet offensive the war looked unwinnable. As Johnson continued to invent fables of "crushing defeats" we had inflicted on the enemy, Eugene McCarthy campaigned for the Democratic nomination. I tried to feel enthusiasm for him, as Barbara and Jean did, but his speeches left me cold. Besides, I thought that he didn't have a chance. On March 12 he came in an amazing second in the New Hampshire primary. Barbara said that he did so well because New Hampshire voters thought he was related to Joe McCarthy. The next day Bobby Kennedy was in the race. I remembered Bobby from the days of the freedom riders, when he had intervened on behalf of the protesters. He had his brother's energy and physical beauty, and when he quoted Tacitus—"Will they say of us, as of the Romans, that we have made a desert and called it peace?"—I nearly cried. Perhaps he was a crass opportunist, as the McCarthyists claimed, but I couldn't help my emotional response to him. Jean brought home daily reports on the campaign from the knowledgeable *Harper's* staff. Barbara's new boyfriend, Dick Cohen, a journalism student who wanted to be a political reporter, talked constantly of Kennedy, McCarthy, Johnson. I listened avidly to their insiders' gossip and yearned for a Kennedy victory.

On March 31 the four of us settled in front of the television to watch Johnson give an address on the war. At the first sound of the hated drawl I mentally switched him off. Halfway through the speech Dick was cracking jokes. "Shh," said Barbara. He stopped. Johnson was announcing another bombing halt. This was supposed to persuade the North Vietnamese to negotiate. Dick snorted. "Why should they negotiate when they're winning?" "Shh," said Barbara again.

The face on the screen was somber, the eyes—were they actually moist?

"I shall not seek and I will not accept the nomination of my party for another term as your President."

Silence. None of us thought we had heard right. Across the air shaft, a man's voice yelled, "Did you hear that?!" Johnson's face was replaced by a commentator's. He repeated the President's words. "He's not going to run," said Barbara. "He said it: he's not going to run."

It contradicted everything we had thought about him for five years. We had accused him of necrophilia with Kennedy's corpse. We had thought that he drank the blood of Vietnamese children for breakfast, that he was a genocidal maniac, a reincarnation of Hitler. How could he not run? "I can't figure it out," Dick groaned. "I'll have to read Max Frankel in the morning before I know what to think." "Max Frankel!" yelled Barbara. Dick immediately insisted he had been joking. In a moment they were arguing over which Washington columnists were mouthpieces for the power structure, and I had tuned them out. I wished I could feel that my solidarity with the antiwar movement had contributed to Johnson's withdrawal, but the truth was that I felt insignificant.

On April 4, four days after Johnson's precedent-shattering speech, Martin Luther King was murdered.

He had been the source of my first insight into what was wrong with America. In 1963 I had begged my parents to let me go to the march he led on Washington. I was too young, they said. Now that nothing else was left, I wanted to go to his funeral.

"What do you want to do that for?" Barbara shrugged. "If I were going to take time off—which I'm not—I would go to Memphis to support the strike."

She was right. The sanitation workers' strike King was leading in Memphis needed bodies. If I meant to help, there was a place for me. That night I made plane reservations to Memphis. Then I called back and made reservations to Atlanta, too. Perhaps I could go to both.

In the end, I went to neither. The funeral in Atlanta seemed, as Barbara had warned, a celebrity bash. Presidential hopefuls, princes, journalists gathered in such numbers that it was hard to remember they were honoring a man who believed in civil disobedience and had been a prisoner in a dozen American jails. But the strike in Memphis was more confusing. Not only was it unconnected with the war, but it wasn't emotionally compelling, like the bus and school integration movements that had first drawn me to King. I believed that the sober men in overalls, wearing signs that pleaded for their manhood, were underpaid and denied their dignity. Yet I couldn't feel that I would be welcomed among them or that my solitary appearance would seem anything but eccentric.

I changed my reservations three times. I could have afforded a hotel, but wouldn't it be strange to join a demonstration after a hotel breakfast? The demonstrators would feel suspicious of me, perhaps rightly. No one else I knew had the money or interest to join me. I fretted for days, until events at work crowded the dilemma out of my mind.

Ronald Mansbridge summoned me to his office. He was dictating into a portable tape machine as I entered. I seated myself in a leather chair and swiveled respectfully away from his desk, gazing down at the shops on Fifty-seventh Street as he finished his letter. He clicked off the Dictaphone and allowed a smile to glimmer under his salt-and-pepper mustache.

"I have some news which I trust will please you," he said. "I have taken the opportunity to discuss your work with my colleagues in Cambridge and London. They have now agreed with my plan to make you an editorial assistant. I take it you have no objection?"

"No, sir."

"You will remain under Mr. Adamson's—Bob's—supervision for the time being. I know that is sometimes difficult for you, but it will be several months before we can effect all the changes we plan. I will ask you to bear with us."

"Of course, sir." It was an effort to sit still when I felt so excited.

"Your salary will be increased by"—he glanced at a note, prolonging the suspense—"twenty dollars weekly."

He nodded, dismissed me, and I concentrated on putting one foot in front of another as I left his office. Then I dashed to the bathroom to stop myself from yelling out the news. I was going to be an editor; I would have a profession, a direction. I had not felt so happy or hopeful since the day I was hired. My misgivings about my job, my worries that I was timidly holding back from what I really had to do receded from consciousness. The illusion of liberation persisted a few more weeks.

Two weeks later, on April 23, I walked through the Columbia campus in a daze. What I saw looked like a dress rehearsal for a war. At one end of the campus a group of self-declared jocks were preparing to storm Low Library and drive out the protesters occupying the building. Neighborhood residents and faculty brought baskets of food, which they passed through the windows of Low. Student committees distributed armbands in four colors: red for those who sympathized with the radical Students for a Democratic Society (SDS), blue for pro-amnesty moderates, green for neutrals, white for faculty. Yesterday's leaflets lay on the ground, spent ammunition. Out of the windows of the grand neoclassical buildings hung anarchist flags and a huge sheet painted with the words "JOIN US"—the same words the protesters had shouted at the Pentagon as Jean and I made our way back to New York. The battle of the Pentagon had come home, to the very school where I was a part-time graduate student. Although the issues inspiring the occupation were relatively obscure, the underlying causes for anger were not: the education of a privileged, largely white elite to step into traditional roles in the military and industry was no longer considered by these rebels to be an admirable goal for an institution. I knew few of the details of the protest; my very ignorance was a source of regret to me, as I would have liked to give knowledgeable support to the strike.

My class in Hesiod and the Homeric Hymns was canceled. I went for a beer with a fellow student, Gary, whom I had known since my year at Barnard. Gary, though no radical, listened to Bob Dylan and smoked grass, unusual in the Greek and Latin department. I was hoping he would know more about the student protest than I did.

"Mark Rudd's an asshole," Gary announced as we slid into our usual booth at the Gold Rail. "He must have dreamed up this occupation because he couldn't pass his courses. I don't mean that all his ideas are cockeyed. And some of the SDSers actually have brains. But plenty of them are jerks, too."

"It seems to me that most of what they say is right."

"Oh, yeah. The university's a factory. I agree with that. And the administration here is unbelievably tight-assed. Did you ever hear the profs talk about them? They hate this administration more than Rudd does."

"I was thinking about the issues. The university investments in defense. And building the gym in the black community."

"Christ. Do you think there's a major university that isn't working with the Defense Department? Harvard? Berkeley?"

"No, but . . ."

"And the gym. You know why those radical assholes are picking on the gym? Because they're so stoned all the time they couldn't pass phys ed if their lives depended on it. The guys who want the gym built are jocks who hate SDS on principle. The idea that it's a rip-off of the black community is bullshit. The administration is ready to agree that Harlem residents should have access to it. But Rudd doesn't want them to agree. You know what SDS says: 'The issue is not the issue.' "

I laughed. Gary ordered refills. It was easy for him, I thought, bent on his academic career, to avoid facing the problems raised by Columbia SDS. The university was, as the radicals claimed, preparing its students for roles in a society that encouraged racism, enriched corporate executives at the expense of the poor and minorities, and dropped bombs on a tiny country six thousand miles away. Changing that demanded a commitment to more than personal goals. If Michael Ferber thought like Gary, he would be enrolled at Harvard. If black people had nothing to complain about, they would never have followed Martin Luther King. I liked Gary, but he had disappointed me.

Our Hesiod class met later that week in the professor's apartment. I enjoyed the change; the new informality reminded me of Swarthmore seminars. Instead of translating, we argued over the occupation. I discovered that the other students were even more conservative than Gary. Their only serious complaint about the administration was that there weren't enough fellowships for graduate students. Hoping to spark discussion, I suggested that we should have less structured classes, some control over faculty hiring and admissions, an active graduate student government. This prompted the rest of the class—who had never heard me talk before—to attack me as a radical. As their voices rose, condemning the "fascist" tactics of SDS, Gary winked at me across the room, as if to say he had warned me.

After eight days of occupation the police stormed the campus. Two hundred students were injured, seven hundred arrested. One classics graduate student, who had never been in an occupied building, had his skull fractured and was in the hospital a month. The ensuing student strike lasted the rest of the school year.

Once I nearly crossed a picket line to go to a class in papyrology. It was my favorite course, held on the top floor of venerable Butler Library in a room lined with Greek, Latin, and Arabic papyri. The teacher was a young Jewish scholar, Daniel Gershenson, who knew six ancient languages and could bring the early Roman Empire as vividly to life as today's struggles over Vietnam. I also loved the papyri, incredible treasures that helped make Columbia the great university it was. For me, that room was a kind of sanctuary. Following Gershenson into the library, I almost missed seeing the picketers. "Please honor the strike," a boy with lank blond hair appealed to us.

Gershenson frowned. "Don't let those people intimidate you," he said.

The student politely stepped out of his way. He went through the door. If the picketers had tried to block my way, I might have pushed past them and gone to class. I was touched by their courtesy, in such contrast with their reputation. And it might be my last chance to do anything for the strike. I turned around and went home. The relief that coursed through me as I walked down Broadway was a surprise.

As the school year ended, Barbara planned to move to Washington with Dick. They both had found jobs on newspapers and were planning to marry when Dick's divorce was final. "Stubbs of the *Star* and Cohen of the *Post*," Barbara sang as she packed her books and clothes. I envied her degree and her life with Dick. I was no longer seeing Seymour, my last Swarthmore boyfriend, and couldn't think where I would meet the next man. Jean was equally lonely. She suggested that we go on sharing the Eighty-third Street apartment, but I thought I would be happier in my own place. My Columbia friend Gary gave me the telephone number of his landlady, who said she had a studio available on Riverside Drive, ten blocks from the university. It was in an old brownstone, had built-in bookshelves and high ceilings with cake-decoration moldings. I moved at the end of May.

I hadn't anticipated feeling so lonely. I found myself working late almost every night, to avoid the empty apartment as long as possible. When I came home, I would put Judy Collins or Richie Havens on the record player to drown the silence. I never cooked supper for myself. I took sandwiches at my desk or ate cheddar cheese and Triscuits lying on the daybed. Sometimes I ate a box of Triscuits and a half pound of cheese before I could stop myself.

My social life now revolved around the office, where all the women were single or divorced and the men were married or gay. Over Planters' Punches at the Drake Hotel across the street, I learned what the women's lives were like. One had carried on an affair for four years with a married man she saw only on lunch hours. Another had been involved for seven years with a man she wanted to marry but who kept making excuses. Others seemed not to have had dates in years. They spent their weekends with each other, which I thought was better than being alone. I was never invited to their parties. Billie Banks, secretary to Miriam and Adam, told me that was because they saw me as Mansbridge's pet and were jealous. I thought it was because I had ignored them, except for Billie, at the beginning, and they would not let me atone for that now.

On June 5 Robert Kennedy was shot. I listened to the radio until dawn, drifting in and out of sleep on the day bed. When Frank Mankiewicz announced his death, I cried. I missed my roommates and couldn't think of anyone I could call for comfort at 5:00 A.M.

I pulled on jeans and a shirt and went for a walk next to the river. I hadn't believed that Kennedy would save us, but I was sure that no one else could. McCarthy had no chance to win. It would be Humphrey against Nixon. Johnson's puppet against the old anticommunist, whom even my parents detested for his primitive red baiting, his sleaziness and con games.

The movement, as Barbara had predicted last October, had changed. Radicals now used LSD, mescaline, hash, and speed as well as grass. They listened to music by Frank Zappa and the Fugs, which hurt my ears. They bragged about orgies. They wore T-shirts in psychedelic colors, and the men had hair below their shoulders. The Diggers, hippies, Yippies, and underground press editors treated electoral politics as a bad joke. They didn't want McCarthy for President. Their candidate was a fat pink pig. Their platform was "Fuck the System." Their irreverence made me laugh. In my straight job, straight clothes, straight apartment, I felt far away from them.

I sat down on a bench next to the river. The sun was high above the Hudson. People were walking their dogs. Bobby Kennedy was dead. I was going to be late for work if I didn't hurry. Why did that seem so important to me? Whose idea of fulfillment had I bought, and at how great a price?

At the end of June, Mansbridge carried out his long-promised overhaul of the editorial department. He transferred Bob Adamson out of editorial into library promotion. Miriam Firestone announced she would resign in the fall to take an administrative job with the City University. A new humanities editor, Elisabeth Case, was hired from the University of Michigan Press. Adam Horvath became a full editor. So did I. And we had a new editor in chief, James Anzaga, formerly the sociology editor at another press. The offices were to be remodeled to accommodate the new staff. Meanwhile, Anzaga was given Adamson's old office, and I kept my desk just outside it—though as a full editor I would soon have my own office, with a door.

Anzaga, who had been hired because of his reputation as a go-getter, immediately set out to prove the image. In his first two weeks at the job he fired off letters to all his authors, suggesting that they transfer their book contracts to Cambridge. When Mansbridge learned this, he was appalled. "We are not in the habit of abducting authors from other publishers," he told Anzaga stiffly. James repeated this to me. "The old man thinks that publishing is like running a convent," he complained. "I don't know how he's stayed in business so long." I wondered if he was right. Had I been trying to learn editorial skills from the wrong teacher? I tried to ingratiate myself with Anzaga.

I found that behind his aggressive surface, he was insecure and susceptible to flattery. I took to complimenting him on his business acumen, then on his ties and choice of cologne. He praised me as one of the few employees at Cambridge who knew what I was doing. His words rang hollow. I had heard his negative remarks about Miriam and Adam, both of them more experienced editors than I was. I worked harder to prove my ability.

In August, Jack Schulman asked me to accompany Anzaga to a marine biologists' convention in Woods Hole, Massachusetts. I could help the new chief editor set up the Cambridge bookstall and he would introduce me to the scholar/authors he knew. I accepted the assignment as a compliment. Later I learned that both Miriam and Adam had turned it down because of their strong dislike for Anzaga.

At Woods Hole, we were together constantly. Our bookstall was set up in a remote part of the conference hotel. Our rooms were even farther away, in a guest lodge ten miles from the site of the conference. Since I didn't have a driver's license, I was dependent on James's rented car for transportation. I didn't worry about the suggestiveness of this. Childishly I trusted him and allowed him to set the tone.

I knew he was recently divorced. Yet it had never occurred to me to think of him sexually. He was not an attractive man. His skin was sallow and he had a potbelly. He sweated heavily, frequently wiping his forehead with a handkerchief. When he was excited, as he was often, he talked very fast, with a strong Spanish accent, and I couldn't understand him.

He asked me to go sailing with him at the end of the second day of the conference. He loved to sail, he said, and was sure I would find it relaxing. I thought he was being kind. A mile out on the bay, he ran his hand down the front of my bathing suit and kissed me on the mouth. I wanted to pull away, but I felt my body respond. The ripple of water and the sunlight were mesmerizing. He murmured that I was a sweet girl. I imagined sleeping with him. I hadn't been with a man for a long time; perhaps it would be comforting.

Dressing for dinner that night, the last we were to spend in Woods Hole, I turned on the television news. The Soviet Union had invaded Czechoslovakia.

The news snapped a wire inside me. The connections were unavoidable: the Czech rebels were to the Soviet Union what the antiwar movement was to the U.S. government. If the Czech rebels could not withstand Moscow, which was supposed to be a revolutionary government, how would the radicals in America survive? They would be crushed, and in a matter of months. Would I still be sitting on my fence when that happened? Playing tacky games for the sake of my career? The image of Anzaga's hairless, sweat-soaked skin next to mine appalled me. That I had allowed him to kiss me on the sailboat suggested how far I had lost my dignity. He would not touch me again.

I was determined to treat him correctly but coolly. Through dinner I was polite, answering his questions, shaking my head when he wanted me to share his dessert. I noticed he was drinking a good deal. He didn't seem to observe my changed manner.

On the way upstairs he draped an arm around my shoulders. I

shrugged him off. "I'm very upset about Czechoslovakia," I said.

"Czechoslovakia?" He looked puzzled. "Oh, yes. The invasion. You don't have family there, I hope?"

I must have been mad to think he would understand. "No. I'm just upset," I said. "That Moscow could invade them. It's so brutal."

To me, the message was unmistakable: I'm upset, I want to be alone. How many times had men expected me to sympathize with similar statements? James did not see. He put his arm around me again. "You're a very sensitive girl," he said. "But you shouldn't be upset. These things happen all the time."

I tried again. "Listen, I just want to be alone."

"I'm not going to leave you alone when you're feeling like this."

As I tried to close the bedroom door against him, he pushed his way in. I thought of screaming, but it seemed useless. Hadn't the desk clerk seen us register together, ride in the same car, go out on the sailboat and to meals? Besides, I had encouraged him. I had returned his embrace on the boat, had held his hand, been gracious at dinner. No wonder when I said no, he heard yes. Now he was tugging at my clothes. "Please don't," I said.

He thrust his hand between my legs. "Just relax," he murmured.

I hated him and I hated myself for being too weak to force him out. I can't bear this, I thought, as he took off his clothes. But it seemed to me that my only choice was to suffer; I held on to my integrity by yielding no signs of pleasure. Anzaga hardly knew the difference.

We took the train back to New York the next morning. Anzaga insisted on filling out my expense account. He added charges for breakfasts I hadn't eaten, laundry I hadn't done. "Don't worry. They'll never know the difference," he said. He sickened me. I thought of reporting him to Mansbridge and Schulman. But after what had happened—what, in my confusion and uncertainty, I had allowed to happen—I would be able to say nothing.

I escaped by taxi to my studio, where I collapsed on the bed. The phone rang. I ignored it, thinking it would be my mother. In the refrigerator was half of a Sara Lee cake. I was picking my way through it when the phone rang again. "How was Woods Hole?" said the voice at the other end. It was Adam.

"I didn't have such a good time," I said.

He must have heard the misery in my voice. "What's the matter?" he asked.

I began crying into the receiver, and before I had thought how to phrase the story, I said, "Anzaga raped me." There was a long silence while I tried to decide if this was a lie. Adam suggested I come to dinner with him and his wife, Joyce.

The next day, Sunday, the three of us drove to Jack Schulman's Westchester house, where I repeated my story. Anzaga had pushed his way into my room, I said, and I couldn't make him leave. That much was true. On the other hand, I left out the part about the sailboat. No one questioned my version. Jack Schulman kept shaking his head. "We made a terrible mistake," he said.

On Monday Mansbridge telephoned to apologize to me. "Don't come to work until noon," he said. "It will be taken care of then." When I reached the office, Anzaga was gone. He had been given an hour to pack his personal papers. My name, Mansbridge promised, had not been mentioned.

Anzaga called me at work in the afternoon. "When can I see you again?"

He thought we were lovers. The realization left me speechless. He seemed pathetic, not vicious: aging, unemployed, divorced. "I can't talk to you," I mumbled, and hung up. I rang the switchboard to leave a message that I was unavailable.

Guilt knotted my stomach. I went home in the middle of the afternoon. On Tuesday I called in sick.

That week Humphrey was nominated for President as Chicago police bashed the heads of Yippies and McCarthy supporters alike.

A week later I marched up to the SDS booth at the Columbia University gates and announced that I wanted to join.

TWO

Revolution

It would have been easy for him to smile at her impression that she was "in it," and to conclude that even the cleverest women fail to know when they are futile, had not the vibration remained which had been imparted to his nerves two years before . . . —the sense, vividly kindled and never quenched, that the forces secretly arrayed against the present social order were pervasive and universal, in the air one breathed, in the ground one trod, in the hand of an acquaintance that one might touch or the eye of a stranger that might rest a moment on one's own. They were above, below, within, without, in every contact and combination of life; and it was no disproof of them to say it was too odd they should lurk in a particular, improbable form. To lurk in improbable forms was precisely their strength.

—HENRY JAMES

if you do not know where the insanity factory is located, you should hereby take two steps to the right, paint your teeth, & go to sleep.

—BOB DYLAN

VI
Sam Melville

I MET SAM MELVILLE FOR THE FIRST time at the CAC demonstration at the St. Marks Arms. Tall and broad-shouldered, carelessly dressed in jeans and a work shirt with the top two buttons open, he caught my attention with his energetic stride when he was still halfway down the street. Taking a seat next to me on the stoop, he introduced himself and said he worked for the *Guardian: A Radical Weekly*. Under his arm he carried a hundred copies of the latest edition, which had a cover story by Wilfred Burchette, the Australian Marxist, on Vietnam. I had seen this paper on literally dozens of New York newsstands since I was a high school student and had never had the remotest interest in reading it. Casually I paid for a copy as though I had been intending to buy one all along.

We talked about communes. He was hoping to buy land in upstate New York with some money he was expecting from an insurance company. He said (although he had learned my name only five minutes ago) that I was welcome to visit him there. I volunteered to buy us take-out coffee at a shop down the block. He accepted the paper container without offering to repay me. (As communists, I could hear him thinking, we don't haggle over quarters—we share with our comrades.) When I left to go to work, I gave him a check for a year's subscription to the newspaper, writing my telephone number on the check before tearing it off. At work, I couldn't help telling Billie Banks, the editorial secretary, that I had met the first man who excited me since I was in college. But after eight days I had given up hope of hearing from him.

On a Wednesday night, minutes after I returned to my apartment from a Greek class, he called. "I'm Sam Melville from the *Guardian*," he said, as though he feared I might have forgotten his name. "I'm in your neighborhood. Can I come over?"

"Yes," I said, attempting to sound more indifferent than I could possibly feel.

Five minutes later the doorbell rang.

We looked at each other across the threshold. He had the larger-than-life quality I remembered from the demonstration and wore the same movement uniform of work shirt, jeans, and work boots. He had steel-rimmed glasses and a thick mustache that drooped below the corners of his mouth. His hair was thinning but hung down to his shoulders. I was still wearing the lime wool dress I'd put on in the morning, but now I wished I'd changed into something more casual. I must have forgotten to step out of his way because he said, very politely, "May I come in?" Thinking he was making fun of me, I moved aside.

His boots made the tweed carpet my mother had given me look pretentious, and when he sat in the black vinyl armchair I offered him, the chair looked inappropriate, like the office furniture it was. His back was erect; his arms and hands were powerful, his fingers curled halfway into fists. But in his face was something vulnerable. It reminded me of someone I knew well, but I couldn't think who. I riffled through the records on the windowsill and slid a Mose Allison album on the portable stereo. Before I turned around, I realized who he reminded me of: my brother, Skip. I couldn't think why. I sat down opposite him.

"You weren't at the meeting last night," he said.

"The CAC meeting? I didn't know there was one." I felt put on the spot, and wondered suddenly if he had been sent by Greg Rosen to find out the reason for my absence.

"We meet every Tuesday."

"I'll go next week," I promised. "Please tell me what happened."

The meeting, he said, had been a good one, full of energy after the impressive turn-out at the St. Marks Arms. People brought lots of ideas for more "actions" that fall, and for ways in which the group could get greater mileage out of its numbers. I found myself listening to his voice instead of his words. It was rich and melodious with an extraordinary range of tones. I kept wishing that the record would end so that I could hear him without interference. I asked questions, drawing him out.

He told me he had gone to the first meetings of CAC in the spring, and had been arrested at the sit-in at West 114th Street. He had also become involved in the Columbia strike and was on campus during the second police assault at the end of May. His trespassing case from the apartment house sit-in was still pending. Shortly after his arrest, through friends he had made at CAC and in Columbia SDS, he had gotten a job in the circulation department of the *Guardian*.

"Working for the *Guardian* is all right," he said, answering my next question. "I do a little bit of everything, which suits me fine. Handy work in the office, delivering papers, trying to build circulation. There's no hierarchy at the *Guardian*—we're all equals at the weekly staff meetings and we all get paid the same, fifty dollars a week."

He was trying to be personal, but he had no particular gift at it. His clumsiness touched me. As he went on about CAC and his job, I understood that he had not been sent by anyone else, yet I saw, too, why I had formed that impression. He constantly spoke as though he were the emissary of some higher power, even though his mission this evening seemed no larger than to get to know me. Another man would have called to suggest dinner or a movie on Saturday night, but his way was to appear at my door five minutes after calling, sit on the edge of a chair, and talk politics. I found him intensely interesting.

He asked about my job and my studies at Columbia. I tried to match his straightforwardness, stating my dissatisfactions and explaining the temptations to stay put as honestly as I could. I admitted that I liked being an editor, but more because of the prestige and security it brought than because of the work. I had less responsibility at my job than my title suggested since all final editorial decisions were made at the home office in Cambridge, England. Columbia also seemed to be a dead end. I didn't have enough time to study, wasn't absorbed by my courses, and doubted I would finish the graduate program. I gave a self-deprecating laugh so that he wouldn't think, from the sound of my high-powered job and my graduate work, that I was some narrow-minded success addict.

"How old are you?" he asked.

The record clicked off. I had looked forward to the silence, but now it made me self-conscious.

"Twenty-one," I said. "And you?"

"Thirty-two." As close to my parents' age as to mine. "Actually, I'll be thirty-three in a couple of weeks. I have trouble remembering that. I never thought I would live until my thirtieth birthday. I still don't expect to live until my thirty-fifth."

"Why not?"

"This country's about to go through a revolution. I expect it to happen before the decade is over. And I intend to be part of it." He gave a chuckle that was like a wave lapping at a beach, then vanishing. "The truth is that none of us can help being a part of it."

I didn't know what to say to that. I was about to say, "I've never met a revolutionary before," but stopped myself in time.

"Would you like to get high?" he asked.

He produced a stemless pipe and a small plastic bag from his pocket. I watched him sift through the stems, rubbing a bit of leaf off one, disposing of a few seeds from another. His fingers were long and moved capably, and his expression was one of sensual pleasure. I had never smoked grass in a pipe before and hoped the attempt to inhale wouldn't make me look inexperienced. Sam's commanding presence already had me off-balance enough. He lit the contents of the filled pipe and passed it to me, watching me intently. After one drag I began to cough. I passed the pipe back to him. He shook his head. "You finish it," he said. "There's not much left, and I got high before I came here."

Where had he smoked? On the street? Or at the pedestal of the equestrian statue at the foot of 106th Street, trying to get up the nerve to call me? The fleeting glimpse of a man who was as anxious about my response to him as I was about his to me made me smile to myself and relax slightly. He began talking politics again.

On May 21, when the police stormed the Columbia campus for the second time, he had climbed to the roof of Low Library, hauling fifty-gallon garbage cans with him. He intended to throw them down on the heads of the cops. Two policemen—he called them "pigs" in a matter-of-fact tone—grabbed him from behind, dragged him to an office downstairs, and tied him to a chair with a telephone cord. They beat him with clubs until an alarm rang down the hall, then dashed from the office, leaving him in the chair. Eventually he worked himself free.

When I expressed skepticism, he said that many protesters at Columbia had similar experiences, but the establishment press didn't report them. Didn't I know that the owners of the *Times* sat on Columbia's board of trustees? It was the same last month, at the Democratic National Convention. Only the underground press—*Rat*, the Berkeley *Tribe*, the Chicago *Seed*—whose staffs were movement activists, had the trust of other movement people and were courageous enough to report the truth. The division he made between the movement and everyone else left me uneasy. Did he think of me, too, as one of the enemy?

Wanting his acceptance, I described my feelings during the Columbia strike. I told him how angry I had been at the other graduate students and how I had decided to honor the picket line at Butler Library. I said that I wasn't very much involved with campus life at Columbia or I would have been more active in the strike. He let me talk for a while, saying nothing.

The record clicked off again. I realized, as silence settled over us, that my speech about my movement sympathies had affirmed what I had hoped to disprove. I was not part of Sam Melville's world at all.

"Is it time to go to bed?" he asked.

Startled, I looked at the clock. It was eleven-fifteen. Did he mean to leave already? Had I offended him?

"I never go to bed until one," I lied. In fact, for the past few weeks I had been almost narcoleptic, falling asleep at nine-thirty and lying dreamlessly in bed until the alarm rang in the morning.

"I noticed you right away at that demonstration," he went on. His soft voice carried easily across the room, almost as though he were speaking inside my head. "I couldn't take my eyes off you. When you went for coffee, I stood on tiptoes so I could see your ass move down the street. You were wearing a yellow dress with a sash tight around your waist. I thought about you in that dress all week."

My stomach was turning over like pizza dough. Any other man would have found an excuse to sidle next to me. Instead, Sam sat in that absurd vinyl armchair, not even leaning forward as he looked at me. What did he expect me to say? If only he would take me in his arms!

"I'm sorry if I've imposed on you," he said gravely. "I didn't mean to disrupt your evening."

Nothing he said could have won me over faster. Disrupted my

evening! His unexpected visit had been an adventure, his sexual overture an irresistible challenge. He could make matters much easier by touching me, but if the choice was going to be simply yes or no, I knew what I wanted. I would take the risk.

"I want you to stay," I said.

An amazed smile spread slowly across his face.

"Do you mean it?"

I nodded.

He stood up as though he were about to approach me. I waited for his kiss. Instead, he sat down on the bed. I understood suddenly why he reminded me of Skip. His right eye, which was a clear blue and full of intelligence, was focused on my face. The left, a paler sort of hazel color, stared sightlessly in another direction, with the blankness that my brother's had at a distance of more than two feet. Sam Melville was blind in one eye. I watched him as, still smiling, he began to remove his clothes.

He wore no undershirt, underpants, or socks.

"I gave up underpants a couple of years ago," he said. "I realized just a month or so ago that I didn't need socks either. But I've still got a bourgeois hang-up that my feet might smell."

How serious he was! His revolution encompassed everything from the universities to the wearing of socks. His face was sculpted and strong-looking with a prominent nose and chin and a wide, sensitive mouth underneath his mustache. His eyebrows were thick and straight, a darker brown than the hair that curled on his head, his chest, and (as I could tell from a quick, covert glance) his thighs and genitals. Under his cheekbones were slight shadowy hollows. I wanted to touch his face there but was too shy to make the first move. His chest was as large and muscular as it had looked under his work shirt, but his legs were fragile, his thighs thinner than mine. The smell of his sweat mingled with the odor of grass in the room was intoxicating.

I took off my clothes with no help from him. I wanted nothing so much as to surrender completely to his power: to lie inert beneath him as he stroked and kissed me into a frenzy. Not until I was completely undressed, my clothes neatly folded on the chair, did he at last put his arms around me.

"Let's have sixty-nine," he whispered in my ear.

I hesitated a moment. I had heard the expression in jokes, but that was all.

"I don't know what that means," I admitted.

"I'll show you," he said. He coaxed my hips with his hands until I understood that he wanted me to turn around. When my crotch was directly over his mouth, he drew my hips toward his head and I felt the tip of his tongue on me. Involuntarily I jerked away.

"You've never done this before?" he asked, with just a touch of condescension.

He taught me that night how to suck him, how to hold still while his tongue circled my genitals, how to kneel on all fours to allow him entry from behind. He touched my body with a familiarity no stranger had ever shown before, and he alternated teasing comments about my inexperience with compliments.

"It's really hard for me to believe you ever fucked a man before," he said. "You're ignorant as a virgin. But you have a beautiful body. Your ass is big and soft, and your tits are beautiful. You have nice fat thighs. Your cunt smells a million times better than that Madison Avenue scent you're wearing."

Radical politics, an air of masculine authority, and a deliciously illicit sense about sex—Sam mesmerized me that night. We never went to sleep. I kept thinking how miserable I would feel at work, but I didn't care very much. It was impossible to imagine falling asleep. My bed was so narrow that our bodies couldn't help touching, and nearness to him couldn't help but excite me. When the window lightened from black to pinkish gray, we agreed to close our eyes. We ended up talking instead, and we were both awake when my alarm went off. The room was full of yellow light. I went to the kitchen to start the coffee and washed hurriedly. When I came back to the studio room, his eyes were closed, his face relaxed. Quietly, so that I wouldn't disturb him, I put on my stockings and a dress. I was about to slip into my heels when Sam opened his eyes.

"You're a slut," he murmured.

"A what?"

"A slut."

He rolled his tongue over the sibilant-liquid sound. I giggled.

"What do you mean?"

"I thought you were probably a slut when I saw you on that stoop. But I couldn't know for sure. I thought so again when I watched you walk down the street by the St. Marks Arms. Now I'm positive. You're a slut."

He turned the insult into a compliment. His voice suggested

helpless lust, as though his accusation of wanton sexuality were also an admission of my power over him. On impulse, I took my spare apartment keys from the top dresser drawer.

"The round one opens the street door, the square one the apartment door," I explained. "You can come here whenever you want."

Did the warmth fade from his face as he accepted the gift? Did my overeager pursuit make him want to flee? His face was impassive, his voice gruff as he pocketed the keys and thanked me.

"I'll come when I can," he said. "It may not be tonight."

I was twenty minutes late for work; but Mansbridge hadn't come in yet, and no one else would care. The editorial department was a shambles these days, as it had been ever since Anzaga was fired. Mansbridge and Schulman had decided not to hire a replacement but instead to add the responsibility for the editorial department to the duties of David Winsor, a British-born vice-manager in charge of operations. This was safer than trying out another newcomer, but it had disadvantages. Winsor was capable but had no editorial experience, and his hands-off style seemed to me to border on laziness. When he visited the editorial offices, he preferred to discuss Plato, agnosticism, and the British monarchy rather than to hear work-related problems.

I was too inexperienced to work well without supervision, and my days at work became increasingly aimless. Manuscripts arrived, there were memos from England to be answered, and I still had my own typing and filing to do (I had been promised a secretary, though as yet no one had been hired) but I couldn't concentrate and wasn't sure what I should concentrate on. I didn't even know where to sit. I had a choice of my old, familiar desk, in the hall outside what had been Bob Adamson's office, or Adamson's office itself. Neither one felt right. The secretary's desk felt menial, the furniture of the girl who had walked starry-eyed into the office fifteen months ago, and the chief editor's office like a usurped throne, haunted by the ghosts of both Bob Adamson and James Anzaga.

But any office would have been unbearable after my night with Sam. I was too tired to keep my eyes open, the phones jangled at me, and even the typewriter stared at me in reproach. Inside the chief editor's office, I closed the door, sat at the big desk, and laid my head on the blotter. I thought of Sam calling me a slut, his tongue sidling over the word. I pictured him kneeling between my legs, felt his lips. Recalling every detail of our night kept me occupied until five o'clock.

When I reached the second floor of my building, where my apartment was, the sound of a steel-string guitar and a rich male tenor filled the hall. I thought a neighbor was playing a new record. Opening the door, I found the music was coming from my apartment. Sam was sitting in the middle of the studio room, his back to the door, singing and accompanying himself on the guitar.

I dropped to the bed to listen to him, not taking off my coat. The song, about a gambler named Diamond Joe, was a traditional cowboy tune, but Sam's arrangement was contemporary and, I guessed, original. The guitar was an expensive-looking Martin on which his left hand stretched an effortless four frets while his right hand plucked an intricate strum I had never heard before. But the magnetism was in Sam's voice. It was glorious, ranging from low to high, from piano to forte, with such accuracy and color that the walls seemed to radiate the notes.

I think it must have been in that hour that I fell in love with him. I had studied piano, violin, and guitar, hoping each one would become my instrument, but it was obvious by the time I was twelve that my only gifts were as a listener. I could play nothing unless every note was written in front of me, and even then my playing sounded uninspired. I was incapable of singing harmony and from childhood had envied anyone who could carry a tune in a round. Now, hearing Sam's voice, I was awed.

He finished the song and smiled at me.

"You're wonderful," I said.

"I used to be pretty good," he corrected me. "When I was a kid, I wanted to sing grand opera. But those days are gone."

He sang for an hour. "The Weight," "Yesterday," "Just Like a Woman," "Blackbird" from the Beatles' White Album, and a few songs I had never heard, one or two of which he'd written himself. His last song was "It Ain't Me Babe." The message of rejection in the chorus might have upset me, but he didn't seem to be singing to me. He threw his head back, closed his eyes, and appeared transported by the music.

When he put his guitar away, I praised him extravagantly. He looked bemused. "Let's go to bed," he said. "I've been thinking about you so much I haven't gotten anything done all day."

The next morning, when my alarm rang after we'd slept a couple of hours, Sam rolled over and suggested that he would pick me up at work at five. He was borrowing a car from a friend in CAC to make deliveries for the *Guardian*. He didn't have to return the car until Saturday. If I wanted, we could have dinner at a Szechuanese restaurant he knew. I had never eaten Szechuanese food, and I had a long-standing date with my Swarthmore friend Neil Perlmutter that night, but I told him I would try to break the date.

I got Neil on the telephone at noon, and made a feeble excuse that obviously hurt his feelings. I waited impatiently for the next three hours until Sam called. Then, scrunching in my chair so that no one could hear me, I sang into the mouthpiece, "I'm free! I'm free!"

Silence. Had he forgotten I was trying to break a date? Had he changed his mind about wanting to see me three nights in a row?

"I wish we were all free," he said solemnly.

I laughed, but there was no answering chuckle.

He was not going to let me forget that he was a revolutionary—that he had a grand commitment that made our own affair, however exciting, seem puny. Every so often, as now on the telephone, he was going to remind me of that. But if the trials were no worse than this, I intended to stick with him as long as he would have me.

Over the next few weeks Sam moved his few belongings—his guitar, a dictionary, some volumes of poetry and novels, a change or two of clothes—into my apartment. We spent every night together and almost every hour of the weekends. Gradually we exchanged life histories. Mine was brief and dull compared to his long romantic tales.

He had been born in the Bronx in 1935, the child of William and Dorothy Grossman. His mother already had a daughter by another man. His parents separated soon after he was born, and Sam moved with his mother and half sister to North Tonawanda, a middle-sized town between Buffalo and Niagara Falls. He had no memory of his father when he was growing up. His mother worked at odd jobs to support the three of them and, later, a second daughter, who was born when Sam was about six. Sam liked to say that his mother was the town whore—an opinion that may have had more to do with his own attitudes toward women than with his mother's moral standards. His description of her suggested a tall, robust woman, a bit slatternly, hardworking, and with the shrewdness of those who fend for themselves from adolescence. Toward her children she was fatalistic and resentful. "She wasn't a fussy mother," as Sam put it. "I got a cinder in my eye when I was a kid—oh, four or five years old, I think—and by the time she saw it was serious it was too late to save the eye. But she was okay. Until I was a teenager, I was crazy about her."

At sixteen, after several years of increasing family discord, Sam had a fight with his mother's current lover and left home the same day. He got a room in the Buffalo Y and a job stacking pins in a bowling alley. At about the same time his father had remarried and begun to look for his son. Sam had been on his own for a year when the two of them met. "I was coming out of some building in Buffalo—it might have been a courthouse—when I saw my father at the bottom of a long flight of stairs. I don't know how I realized it was him. I had never seen a picture. But I recognized him as if it was a dream. I think I must have flown to the bottom of those steps."

Meeting William Grossman and his new wife, Helene, changed Sam's life. First they persuaded Sam to return to high school in Buffalo. When he graduated, they promised, he could come to New York and live with them. Sam had been an undersized, awkward child, rejected by his classmates, but when he returned after a year's absence, he made a better impression. He had shot up to his full height, turned into a capable athlete, and his musical gifts were obvious. He joined the glee club and orchestra, discovered he was good at math, and had a facility for memorizing and reciting poetry. He liked Walt Whitman, Hart Crane, and Gerard Manley Hopkins best. When I met him, he could still recite almost all of "The Windhover," with admirable control over the Anglo-Saxon vocabulary and sprung rhythm. His main difficulty at school was foreign languages. He was incapable of passing either French or Latin, requirements for graduation, but a few teachers who liked him took pity, he said, and allowed him to graduate anyway. He was nineteen when he left Buffalo and went to the Bronx to live with his father, stepmother, and new half brother.

William Grossman had been a member of the Communist Party since the thirties. When Sam came to live with him in 1954, he was still working for the party, trying to organize a taxicab drivers' union and teetering on the edge of disillusionment. He tried to teach Sam his socialist ideals but with apparently faltering enthusiasm. "My father used to take me through Harlem and lecture me on how capitalism oppressed the Negro," Sam told me. "He was terribly serious about it, but I couldn't see it as he did. To me, those kids playing stickball and running through the streets were having a terrific time. I never wanted to have a lot of money and live in a stuffy duplex on Park Avenue. I couldn't believe that anyone else did either."

Through his father, Sam met Paul Robeson, whom he idolized for his voice and his courage in the face of persecution, and the socialist essayist Irving Horowitz, who was, Sam said, the only genius he ever knew. They and others of Bill Grossman's friends encouraged Sam to develop his musical talent. A voice teacher was found for him, and Sam began to dream of singing opera. Instead of going to college, he took a job as a short-order cook to pay for his singing lessons. Then he met Ruth Birnbaum, the daughter of a middle-class Jewish family, who had just graduated from a city college and was teaching elementary school. Sam described Ruth as "pear-shaped, with a delectable ass." In about 1957 or '58 (Sam was always vague on dates) they married. He quit his job and his voice lessons and went to work in an engineering firm.

The more Sam lived an upwardly mobile married life—big apartment on West End Avenue, $14,000-a-year job (or so he said), vacations in the Catskills with Ruth—the more he insisted that he was a communist at heart. When his father finally quit the party and moved from the proletarian Bronx to a placid suburb in Long Island, Sam, disgusted with what he called his father's sellout, refused to have any more to do with him or Helene. He even went to court to change his name legally from Grossman to Melville. Sam wanted me to believe that Melville was his mother's maiden name and that he had used it while he was growing up. Later I came to suspect that Sam had taken the name only because *Moby Dick* was his favorite book and he wanted to replace his real-life, flawed father with a more heroic ancestry.

Sam's marriage was awry from the beginning. Because of Ruth, he claimed, he was continually changing jobs, trying to increase his salary so that she could buy the furniture and clothes she wanted. He may have blamed her unfairly, but the Sam I knew was so totally uninterested in possessions that I couldn't imagine he had ever wanted much money for himself. He pretended to have a college degree in order to get jobs, first as a draftsman, then as a designer of plumbing systems. To make extra money, he taught plumbing design at a trade school for a few years. (When I appeared impressed at that, he said, "The only thing you need to teach a plumber is 'Payday comes on Friday and shit don't go uphill.' ") He hated the companies he worked for, walking out on one job after he was asked to design part of a project for the Union of South Africa. Ruth responded by calling him a communist.

They separated after five or six years of marriage, then came back together when they learned that Ruth was pregnant. Their son, Jocko, was born in 1962. Three years later they separated again, this time permanently. For a while Sam saw Jocko once a week, but he and Ruth kept fighting over the child support she thought he ought to pay (even though he was no longer working), and one afternoon, after an especially violent fight, he hit her. He had not seen her and Jocko since.

For the past three years Sam had lived with whatever woman would give him a place to stay, supporting himself at first with savings, then with occasional .construction jobs, and now on his small *Guardian* salary and the insurance money he had spoken of at the demonstration—the damages from an automobile accident he'd sustained in the last year of his marriage. His father had died six months before we met, ending Sam's last connection to family. He still saw two or three friends from his days in the Bronx, but his chief ties now were to the radical movement, which had given him friends, a vision of the future, and the language in which to express his simmering discontent with establishment America.

In April 1968, a month after his father died, he had met Diane, the friend who had loaned him her car for *Guardian* deliveries. She had stopped in Riverside Park to watch a basketball game involving Sam and five black men and had invited all six of them to her apartment after the game. A few days later Sam had moved in. They had been lovers only for a few weeks. After that Sam made his bed on the living-room couch. But Diane remained his closest friend. She brought him to his first political meeting at the CAC office, involved him in the Columbia strike, and encouraged him to take the job at the *Guardian*.

"There's something you've got to understand about Diane," Sam said, seeming anxious to head off any jealousy I might feel. "Whatever Diane has belongs to anyone who needs it. There's never less than four people crashing at her house: heads, runaways, movement freaks, you name it. Her food, her dope, her money are for the world. So many people use her Volkswagen that it's been battered into the ground. She's a little crazy, I guess, but I love her. So does everyone else."

He was so careful to explain himself and made it so obvious that he was not especially attracted to Diane that I could hardly object to their close friendship. Yet the box of clothes he still kept at her apartment and his frequent visits there for a sandwich or conversation were a barrier between us I wanted to break down. My secret hope was that in a month or two, when he was sure of me, he would bring the rest of his possessions from Diane's to my studio, establishing permanent residence with me. I understood that his revolutionary principles would not allow him to marry me or even to formalize his divorce from Ruth. I didn't care about that—as long as he never left me.

As Sam and I became closer to each other, I became drawn into the world of radical politics which I had admired from the outside for so many years and to which I'd never quite managed to gain entry on my own. I read the *Guardian* and the counterculture papers *Rat* and *East Village Other*, went to CAC meetings every week, and abandoned any lingering interest in electoral politics, learning to focus instead on grass-roots protests—riots on the Lower East Side, campus take-overs in Ithaca, New York, and Lawrence, Kansas, barricades in Paris, guerrilla war in Latin America. As an outsider to the movement I was troubled by such signs of turmoil. As I adopted the radicals' viewpoint for myself, I came to see all antiestablishment uprisings as aspects of a world revolution, which, in a slightly different form, had been predicted by Marx a century ago. Instead of feeling anxiety that the world order I'd grown up with was breaking down, I came to welcome the prospect, identifying my own discontent with that of rebels around the globe and cheering for our eventual victory.

As much as my insecurity made me ripe for dependency on a man like Sam, my background and the state of the nation made me (and thousands of others my age) receptive to the ideas of the New Left. From the antisegregation protests of 1956 to the antiwar marches of 1968, from the time my family was transplanted to Uniontown, Pennsylvania, until the first year I was on my own, political protest had formed the background of my growing up. My adolescent rebellion against my parents was sharpened both by events occurring within my family and by the growth of the New Left, which was challenging public opinion on sexual mores, drug use, race relations, and the war. The more I had tried to conform to my parents' expectations, the more I had looked over my shoulder at others my age less repressed than I, who were acting out their beliefs by hanging flags from the buildings at Columbia, passing out flowers in the streets of Prague and San Francisco, or, like my friend Michael Ferber, risking jail by resisting the draft. They seemed to me joyous and free as well as principled. I wanted nothing more than to emulate them, and I chose Sam not only because he was devastatingly sexy but because he gave me the courage to do so.

It wasn't only Sam I admired. I loved nearly all the people I met in CAC, most of them closer to Sam's age than mine and many of them lifelong radicals. Diane, a hefty, olive-skinned woman with a halo of kinky hair, taught a course at the City University she jokingly called Revolution 101 and gave her apartment for Columbia SDS to use as its headquarters, an act of generosity and courage that I marveled at. Robert Carpenter, the son of a shipping magnate, had rejected his privileged background to live in a walk-up on the Lower East Side, supporting himself as an inventor. He had a speech impediment characteristic of those partially deaf from birth, and I found it hard to listen to him; but I appreciated his sharp, original mind. Most impressive to me was Greg Rosen, who had been trained in philosophy and was solidly intellectual. The founder of CAC, he was an effective chairman to whom everyone, including Sam, looked for direction. Beneath their different surfaces—Sam's volatile and energetic, Greg's introspective—the two men had strikingly similar attitudes and had been close friends since they met.

Marxism, as interpreted by Marcuse, Reich, and Paul Goodman (whom I didn't read so much as absorb from the conversation of Sam and my new friends) fitted me like a new pair of glasses through which I seemed to see truth for the first time. I learned to take politics personally, applying movement ideas to every aspect of my life. If I was unhappy at my job, it was because it was "alienated labor": reading and passing judgment on academic manuscripts which had no relevance to anyone outside the ivy walls. If my love affairs had not worked out, it was because I expected them to conform to a "bourgeois model," leading to marriage and child rearing within a nuclear family—even though I had known all along that the ideal was a failure. The tiniest of my worries—excess pounds, for example, or the stubborn limpness of my hair—were also the fault of capitalism, which had spent billions to convince women that we ought to look thin, rich, and glamorous. By contrast, the movement held up the Chinese model: 600 million smiling men, women, and children, all dressed in identical blue, equal participants in the tasks of revolution. Like so many of my peers, fed up with the war and the injustice that grew from American affluence, I looked to China and to Cuba as utopian alternatives. I came to believe, as the governments of China and Cuba then charged, that the U.S. government, as a front for corporate capitalism, was responsible for most of the world's horrors and that the most moral thing I could do was to help dismantle it.

My beliefs were naïve and rooted as much in rage as in idealistic hope. But I needed them. I could not have fallen so overwhelmingly in love with Sam if he had not given me such an ideology. Nor could I have accepted the ideology so wholeheartedly if I hadn't been so powerfully attracted to Sam. No man had ever made me feel as sexy as he did. He insulted me in yearning tones and would beg me to walk ahead of him on the street so that he could watch me move. While other men had seemed intimidated by my articulateness, Sam bragged about me; in the middle of a discussion about, say, the Tupamaros' attack on Uruguay's democratic government, Sam would interrupt me to ask his friends, "Would you believe she's only twenty-one?" If he had been the most conventional, straitlaced businessman, I would have found his affection hard to resist. The combination of sexual love and radical ideology was more than irresistible. It consumed me.

After a few weeks with Sam, it was obvious to me that I was going to quit graduate school. I had not studied since the first night he came to my apartment. It was now too late to consider that I might make up the missed work before exams. My evenings with Sam and at CAC meetings took up the time I had once given to classes and homework and movement periodicals took the place of my Homer and Latin prose composition texts. Besides, I now understood what was wrong—"counterrevolutionary"—about attending Columbia. The university's trustees interlocked with the boards of a score of corporations. The men who ran Columbia bore ultimate responsibility for poverty in the United States and the war in Vietnam. Talking about possible reform of the university revealed only naïveté. If I couldn't dismantle Columbia single-handedly, at least I could write a stirring letter of resignation.

When I told Sam what I planned to do, he looked at me suspiciously.

"Why write a letter? Why not just quit going?"

"Because I think it's important to make a statement," I said. "The more people who speak up, the more they'll be challenged to make changes. Or at least to recognize what they're doing."

"Hell, you're talking about the Columbia faculty," Sam snorted. He was sitting at the edge of the bed as he spoke, tuning his guitar. "I saw them in action—or rather *not* in action—during the strike. You think you're going to change their minds with a letter when the New York City police force didn't make a dent?"

He was obviously right. The idea of the letter came from my liberalism, not from my new revolutionary outlook. But I couldn't not write it. I adored Howard Porter, a Homeric scholar with a whispery voice who knew all his students' names on the first day of class and was this semester's department chairman. Once he had stopped me on the way out of class to praise my facility for reading Homeric verse, a compliment I treasured. I wanted him, at least, to know that my leaving Columbia was in a noble cause. And perhaps, too, I was hedging my bets so that if Sam did leave me, I would have something to return to.

The letter came out very differently from the radical document I planned. When I tried to excoriate the university for its defense contracts, its ties to international corporations, and its aggressions against the black community, it sounded as though I were writing a speech for Sam or for Greg Rosen. I believed what I was saying, but the language wasn't mine. I threw out my drafts and instead wrote a note to Professor Porter thanking him for his concern and blaming "a complex of personal frustrations" for my decision to leave. I signed it quickly and, ashamed of my weakness, stuffed it in an envelope before Sam could see it on my desk. I mailed it in the morning, severing my last ties to graduate school.

One rainy November afternoon, after Sam and I had made love

and were drifting off to sleep, he startled me awake with a question.

"Do you have orgasms?"

The rain beat on the window for a long moment.

"I think so," I said. Actually I'd hardly considered it. I'd never had an experience that matched the description of female orgasm in books, but I had assumed the problem was with the books, not me.

"I'm not sure you do," Sam went on. "I'm not sure you've ever come with me. Maybe you've never come with anyone. I've had some bad experiences with nonorgasmic women. They tend to be very dependent. I've never thought you were like that, but now I'm beginning to wonder."

He may not have meant to hurt me as much as he did, but his accusatory tone was a shock. The charge of dependency especially alarmed me. Coming from Sam, who had always told me that he couldn't be tied down to one woman, it sounded like a threat to leave. I answered him with as much truth as I dared, hoping that honesty would persuade him.

"I guess it's possible that I don't have orgasms," I admitted. "I've never really known for sure. I do feel pleasure and a kind of wavelike sensation that I figured was probably orgasm. But it doesn't have a definite beginning and an end. I've never really worried about it."

"If you came, you'd know it," Sam said, in a tone that ended the discussion.

I started to cry. I hated myself for sniveling, but I couldn't help the tears. My crying infuriated Sam. He demanded to know what was wrong with me, and when I couldn't explain—because I was so afraid that any further sign of attachment would make him leave —he got up and left. He put on his clothes, shoved his loose change and keys in his pocket, and let the door close behind him with a louder than necessary bang. I told myself that his guitar was still under my bed and that he wouldn't move out without coming back for it. Then all my insides turned to water. I threw myself on the pillows and sobbed.

He came back about ten that night and dropped into the armchair opposite the bed. His head was damp from the rain, and his left eye was jumping as it did when he was tired; but he was grinning.

"Diane and I rented an apartment this afternoon," he said. "A communal apartment. It's enormous—six, maybe seven rooms. We were too stoned to count them. You should have seen Diane, riding her bicycle down Fifth Avenue, stoned out of her brain, hair flying in the rain. I had to pedal like a maniac to keep up."

He laughed. I wondered how this new venture connected to our argument. His friendliness gave me no clue.

"Where's the apartment?"

"Eleventh, between B and C. It's sort of a bad block, but it's convenient for me and for Elise and Alan from the *Guardian*. They told Diane they were interested in moving in, too. Incredibly cheap —sixty-five dollars a month. But I had to give the current tenants eight hundred dollars as key money. I guess we'll get it back if we ever move out." He paused a moment. "Hey—I hope you're going to move in, too."

I didn't want to live on Eleventh Street, one of the most violent blocks on the Lower East Side. I didn't know Elise and Alan, and I felt a little uncomfortable with Diane. But I did want to live with Sam, and this arrangement sounded better than the present one, which allowed him to split his time between Diane's apartment and mine.

"I almost forgot," Sam said. "There's a guy who lives in the apartment below ours who says he's a friend of yours."

"What's his name?"

"Neil something. He drives a cab, but he's a playwright. Nice guy. He's involved with some guerrilla theater troupes. He went to school with you, I think."

"Neil Perlmutter?"

"Yeah, that sounds right."

Sam was not especially interested to learn that this was the very friend I had broken a date with on our first weekend together or in the story of my motorcycle trip to Sounion with Neil, when I had decided to become an archaeologist. But as Sam kept going over the features of the new apartment, images of my shared history with Neil were flashing through my mind. The cigarettes I bummed from him when we first got to know each other during freshman year. His knee jittering at the SPAC meetings we both attended during the Chester crisis, before dropping out in mutual confusion. The Park Avenue apartment building where Neil's stockbroker father and psychologist mother lived, its lobby gleaming with marble, its doormen immaculately gloved, Neil trying not to look embarrassed by all that wealth when his friends came to visit on vacation. The joke that when Neil's parents met Neil's black roommate at Swarthmore, they tried to tip him for carrying Neil's bags. The off-campus house where Neil lived with three roommates during his last two years at Swarthmore. We called it the Stone House because of its architecture, but the name took on new meaning in 1966 when grass came to the college and off-campus apartments were the most secluded places to turn on. Many nights I had dropped off to sleep in front of the Stone House fireplace, drowsy from red wine and grass, as Beatles music played soothingly from one of the best stereo systems on or off campus.

"It's been months—no, almost a year—since I've seen Neil," I said. "I'll go down with you to Eleventh Street tomorrow, at least to say hello to him."

Sam was very gentle with me that night, as if trying to apologize for the hurt he'd inflicted in the afternoon. I admitted to myself that he'd been right: although sex was pleasurable to me, I did not experience orgasm. Yet if any man were capable of bringing me to climax, I was sure that Sam could do it. I had never been with anyone so expert or loved anyone so much. I was not going to let him slip away from me. Moving out of my apartment and into a commune with strangers seemed a small price to pay to hold on.

VII
East Eleventh Street

THE APARTMENT SAM AND DIANE HAD rented was two smallish railroad flats clumsily converted into one by a broken wall. The apartment's four fireplaces were its only sources of heat. The neighborhood was mostly broken-down tenements, and a good proportion of the population appeared to live on stoops and street corners. At night the Puerto Rican kids entertained themselves by burning cars—Cadillacs if they could find them. Sam used to watch them from our bedroom window, pointing out which of the kids were the instigators, which sneaky enough to disappear just as the fuel tanks caught the blaze. I tried to share his fascination, but the tough ten-year-olds kept me as jumpy as the grown men lounging outside the corner *bodega,* fogged by wine and heroin but not too dazed to forget to grab at my crotch when I had to pass them. Like the dedicated leftist intellectuals of an earlier era who went to work in factories for the sake of their politics, I regarded life on the Lower East Side as an exercise to toughen me for the revolution.

A few blocks to the west of us the counterculture flourished: the Fillmore East with its free community rock concerts and light shows; the Bread and Puppet, Sixth Street, and Pageant Players guerrilla theater groups; the Alternate U, offering courses in Marxism, "Spanish for politicos," women's liberation; the *Free Youth Press, East Village Other, Rat Subterranean News;* the Renaissance Switchboard, where runaways could pick up mail or recuperate from bad acid trips; the ongoing street show of St. Marks Place, where middle-class dropouts peddled roach clips, tie-dyed kerchiefs, peace symbols, hallucinogencies, jewelry, posters, vests studded with tiny mirrors, handmade leather belts—and themselves. According to long-time residents of the area, the dream had died in the summer of 1968, and what remained when Sam and I moved downtown in the autumn was just the ragtag leftovers of a movement. The authentic hippies had returned to Ohio, New Jersey, or Texas or had moved to the mountains of Nepal or the beaches of Hawaii. I didn't believe it. St. Marks Place in the fall of 1968 excited me as much as MacDougal street had in 1962. Weaving my way through the panhandlers and peddlers, buying the underground papers at Gem Spa, I felt my pulse sing with the confidence of living at the very heart of events, one of the places where the approaching revolution would be felt first. St. Marks Place and Second Avenue were more central locations; but our apartment was close enough, and when the bongo drummer across the street let loose on his instruments, it seemed as though the uprising had already started.

Elise and Alan McGrath, Sam's friends from the *Guardian,* changed their minds about sharing the Eleventh Street place when they saw it. They said it was too small for five adults, and though they were obviously right, Sam and Diane scorned them for making middle-class demands for privacy. My apprehension that Diane would want to take turns in bed with Sam vanished when she conveniently fell in love with Leon, a black handyman she met on her way to buy milk. Leon offered to fix our leaking sink for $50, took two days to finish the job, and wound up moving in with Diane. Much to my relief, the four of us divided the apartment in two, and we shared the large kitchen (the apartment's only good feature) and an adjoining room where the bathtub was. The daybed from my studio became the couch in Sam's and my living room, the inner of our two rooms. The front room was our bedroom. We used Coleman lamps for light because they gave the room the look of a mountain cabin and because Sam was ideologically opposed to enriching Con Edison. Sam built a full-sized platform bed for us, partly with lumber he found on the street, and I bought (and carried home) a thick piece of foam rubber for a mattress. We hung the walls with pictures of the two of us, taken by friends of mine upstate we had visited earlier in the fall. The photo we both liked best showed Sam playing the guitar, absorbed in his music, while I nuzzled his neck. It was my favorite because it captured the intensity of Sam's face, but it was his because of the way his right elbow surreptitiously nudged my left breast as he played.

Neil Perlmutter, who lived in the apartment below ours, completed the East Eleventh Street family. Since Swarthmore, he had grown his hair to shoulder length and sprouted a straggly black mustache. His clothes were baggier either because he had lost weight or because the cloth had stretched with age; they were certainly the same expensive slacks and jackets he had worn new five years ago, to which he now added strings of beads and occasional patches. To my surprise, Neil and Sam got along splendidly. Neil, I guessed, was attracted to the same qualities in Sam that appealed to me: his imposing physical presence, his musical gifts, his confident, hero-of-the-working-class manner. Neil's permanently sleepy look and the pauses he took between sentences had made him the subject of sometimes nasty teasing at college. They were well suited to the slow tempo of the Lower East Side, where what had been lethargy on campus was now called "mellow."

My parents were convinced that my move was evidence of self-destructiveness. When I told them that I had at last found a man I could love for the rest of my life, they responded with skeptical silence, followed by a barrage of questions about Sam's age, employment background, and marital status. Then they invited us to Forest Hills for dinner. I accepted because I wanted them to like him, but I should have known that the evening would be a disaster. The blunt outspokenness that I found so appealing in Sam was merely offensive to my parents. When my mother introduced herself as Mrs. Alpert, he looked at her coolly and asked, "Don't you have a first name?" I think he was more nervous than intent on insulting her, but the effect was the same. She looked shocked, then very prim, and said, "Yes, I do, but Jane's friends call me *Mrs. Alpert.*" My temperature rose five degrees, and I couldn't look at either of them. At dinner Sam answered their questions in monosyllables. Of course, he despised their bourgeois style and was refusing on principle to accommodate himself to it; still, I wished that he would bend a little or that they would stop acting as though he had come to sell them something.

After dinner I suggested that Sam and my father play chess. Since they were both better than average players, I thought the game would help them face each other as equals. Instead, it transferred the antipathy onto other grounds. I drank tea with my mother while Sam and my father played. My mother's eyes kept drifting from Sam's open-at-the-collar work shirt to the lugged soles of his boots, then back to me, their blankness showing she had heard nothing of what I said. My father and Sam did not exchange a word through the game. My father lost a knight early, a second in the middle of the game, and then resigned. At ten o'clock they showed us to the door. My parents never met Sam again. If they called and Sam answered the phone, they asked for me without greeting him. They would not visit the apartment, although my mother admitted (with a shudder) that they had driven by it once. I continued to have dinner with my parents in Forest Hills every month or so. If I brought up Sam on those occasions, they would talk about the weather or Skip's progress at Brandeis, where he was then a freshman. For once the two of them were in perfect accord, facing me with a wall of disapproval in which I could find no crack.

Sam and I had wonderful times together that fall. Early Saturday mornings we would ride Diane's bicycles to the Williamsburg Bridge to watch the sun rise, then pedal home, eating fresh rolls from our favorite Italian bakery. At night we would stroll along the East River, listening to the strange electrical hum of the city at night, smoking a joint, then stopping for double-dip ice cream cones at a candy store on Avenue B where they cost only fifteen cents. We had midnight dinners in Chinatown, often with Greg Rosen or Robert Carpenter, and Robert's girl friend, a graduate student in biology. One night, after a couple of joints, Robert, Sam, and I tested the almond cookies at every restaurant on Mott Street, finally buying a pound of those that won our contest and eating them until we were sick. On Thanksgiving weekend I went with Sam to Montreal, where the *Guardian* was paying him to sell papers at a Hemispheric Conference Against Imperialism. I had never been to a movement conference before, and in spite of the squabbling, I was excited at being surrounded by hundreds of people who were serious about revolution.

As I felt Sam's love for me grow, my sexual contentment with him increased. We made love almost every night on our platform bed by the light of the bedroom fireplace. I experienced my first orgasm one night when he kissed my labia. Soon after that I came for the first time during intercourse. I didn't have to tell Sam what happened; he understood my body well enough to know. "You're coming, you slut," he would whisper in my ear after that.

Whether I was or was merely on the verge, the sound of his voice would send me into ecstasy. I understood why he had been suspicious of me before I had learned to come. Orgasm was nothing like what I had pretended to feel; it was more powerful and much more self-sufficient than I had been able to guess. I was grateful to Sam for the very insistence that had hurt my feelings before. My liberation, as I saw it, was entirely due to his patience and unerring insight.

While we were still living on Riverside Drive, Sam had urged me to read *The Story of O*. This tale of the castle Roissy, where all men are sexual masters, all women their slaves, had, he said, aroused him but also left him ill at ease. The descriptions of whipping, bondage, and mutilation revolted me, but in spite of them, I found the novel powerfully erotic. O's helpless love for René and René's indifferent ownership of her, climaxing in his presentation of her as a gift to his friend Sir Stephen, expressed the very dynamic that was at the core of most of my own fantasies. I told Sam that in reality such a place as Roissy would be terrifying, but that as a setting in a novel, it articulated my own dreamworld. He was half-frightened, half-enchanted to hear this.

"In my fantasies I'm surrounded by sluts who all call me Master," he confessed. "It would turn me on incredibly if you would do that. Would you? Or does it sound crazy to you?" I was glad to do whatever gave Sam pleasure. When I found that murmuring "Yes, Master" and "No, Master" made him immediately erect and sometimes brought him to orgasm, I invented more elaborate dialogue. I would ask permission before I touched him, precede my requests to be touched with "I beg of you, Master," and thank him humbly for my orgasms. Sam swore that no woman had ever shown such intuitive understanding of his sexual needs, while I believed that any game that excited him—no matter how potentially humiliating—had to be in my interest.

Elise McGrath met every week with a group of women for "consciousness raising." Diane, who had gone to one of their meetings, said it was foolishness. "All they talked about was their orgasms. It was completely apolitical, but they think it's the most important thing that ever happened to them. I can't waste my time on that."

I asked Elise if it was true that her group had devoted a whole night to discussing their orgasms. My skeptical tone wounded her. "Orgasms," she declared, her voice an octave higher than usual, "are the most political subject there is." I went to my first meeting in mid-November.

The group met in the office of the Southern Christian Educational Fund in Grace Church. At the time I joined, its numbers had swelled to over a hundred, too many to hold personal discussions in a single room. They had just decided to divide the large group into ten or so small ones, each of which would stay in touch with the others through a leaderless network. Because certain political differences (emphasis on theory or action; the importance of Marxist analysis) had already surfaced in the large group, and because a number of the women were reluctant to leave a circle of friends for a new group of unknowns, the subdividing was a lengthy, sometimes tortuous process. It went on well into January.

A few of the women in the original large group made strong impressions on me. Elise pointed out Robin Morgan to me at the first meeting. Robin, the former child star of the *I Remember Mama* TV series, was a few months pregnant and just beginning to show. She made the rounds of her friends as if she were at a cocktail party, smiling and bubbling as other women affectionately patted her stomach. I remember that at one point after the meeting started, she quoted Chairman Mao to the group. Citing Mao was an ordinary thing to do at any movement gathering, but Robin distinguished herself by first *apologizing* for the quote. "I beg your pardon for citing a *man*," she said, italicizing the word heavily, "but at least he has a groovy wife." She had a low-pitched, commanding voice, especially striking since she was physically tiny, hardly more than 100 pounds. I thought of her often, although she did not come to future meetings.

Ellen Willis, intense and pedantic as a talmudic scholar, also prodded my thinking. Sharing a taxi with her and several others after a meeting, I heard her say that the women's movement had to separate itself from men and form wholly autonomous organizations. In future years, when men understood sexism better, we might rejoin them in a united front. If we worked with them now, when they still regarded women's liberation as trivial, we would never win our demands. I wanted to ask her what those demands were, but as I opened my mouth, the cab stopped at her building. I had time only to find out her name.

Nearly every time I came home from a SCEF office meeting, Sam would ask me what we had talked about. "Oh, a lot about how to subdivide the group," I said. "Once in a while someone makes a remark about male prejudice against women. A lot of the women agree with you that women are too dependent on men. Some think the answer to that is to break away from men completely—not just for a night or a week, but for all political organizing. I think that's stupid myself."

At such reports, Sam became morose. He told me that Henry Miller had nearly killed himself when his wife left him for another woman. I couldn't fathom the connection between this story and the SCEF office meetings. He said he knew I was concealing details of the meetings from him, but he supposed that was my right. I kept wondering what he dreaded so: that I would tell strangers how he liked me to call him Master? That I would confess to other women that he was too old for me—his secret fear? I tried to assure him that I wasn't nearly as intimate with the SCEF office women as he feared, but the more I tried to persuade him, the less he believed me.

I came home one snowy December afternoon to find a stranger at our kitchen table. She was in the middle of an animated conversation with Sam and Neil, and none of them noticed me until I had dropped my coat on one of the empty chairs. The stranger then smiled at me so radiantly that I was rooted to the floor. Neil said hello and returned his gaze to her face. I pulled off my boots and sat down opposite her. Finally Sam, sounding a bit sheepish, introduced her. "This is Pat Swinton. She's a neighbor."

She had the sort of beauty I used to envy when I haunted the MacDougal Street coffeehouses. She wore no jewelry or makeup, but her hair was the kind I had always wanted to grow, soft and thick and cascading below her shoulders. Her eyes were exactly the same shade of yellow-brown, maternally wise, set in a youthful face. She moved her hands eloquently as she talked. Involuntarily I followed the line of her moving arms up to her armpits, which were fully exposed by the sleeveless pink mohair sweater she wore. From each underarm grew a luxurious bush of crinkly golden brown hair. The sweater clung to her small breasts, at the tips of which her nipples were clearly visible. Many women on the Lower East Side cultivated that careless, sexy look, but few managed it with such ease.

The leftovers of last night's pasta and beans were pushed to one side of the tabletop. In the center of the table was an enormous chart printed on oaktag. Sam turned it in my direction like a Scrabble board. It looked vaguely familiar; perhaps it had been printed before in the *Guardian* or *Rat*. The title in inch-high bold caps read "Who Rules Columbia?" Down the left-hand side were the names of the twenty-two trustees of Columbia University. Across the top were the names of international corporations, CIA-funded agencies, and real estate holdings. Each trustee's affiliation with an institution or business was indicated, together with the corporations' roles in the defense industry and third world governments.

"Wow," I said. "Where did you get that?"

"I do a little work for NACLA," Pat said. "You know, the North American Congress . . ."

I nodded. The North American Congress on Latin America was a radical research organization with close ties to the *Guardian*.

"Is that where you two met?" I asked. "At the NACLA office?"

Neil stirred himself to assert finder's rights.

"*I* met Pat," he said, "at the Cooper Square Post Office. The lines were so fucking long today. Christmas mails, I guess. We got in a conversation about Thomas Pynchon while we were waiting."

Pat laughed. "I felt so dumb. Here was this guy in a motorcycle jacket carrying a copy of this paperback called *V*. I must have heard of the book before, but I just didn't put it together with what Neil looked like. I figured it must be some Mickey Spillane-type schlock. So we start talking, and it turns out that Pynchon is this fancy writer and the guy in the motorcycle jacket went to Swarthmore."

But she seemed to like talking political economics with Sam more than current literature with Neil.

"Can you stay for dinner?" I asked.

"My God, is it dinnertime? I'm supposed to pick up my daughter at the day care center at five."

"You're just a couple of minutes late," said Neil, pushing himself out of his chair with unaccustomed speed. "I'll walk you there."

I wondered if they had fucked before coming upstairs. Unlikely, I decided. Neil would have wanted to invite her to his place but would have feared lunging for her at the wrong moment, ruining his chances. He had brought her upstairs to be safe. Poor Neil; he always figured women out exactly backwards.

"Come back soon," said Sam as Pat shrugged into her pea coat. His voice had the deep, helpless tone characteristic of his sexual arousal.

As soon as the door closed, he grinned at me. "Did you see her ass when she got up? She's a slut."

I managed a nervous smile.

Pat lived seven blocks from us in a one-bedroom apartment on East Fourth Street with her three-year-old daughter, Jenny. At first I leaped to the conclusion that like Anita, she had chosen to bear a child without marrying, but I was mistaken. Pat's parents, government employees, were Marxists who, in the paradoxical fashion of the American old left, had brought her up both to fight for socialism and to cherish the traditional ideals of family life and financial security. She had attended a state college and majored in education. After graduating, in 1962, she spent a summer in Italy with her college roommate. In the fall she flew to Tanzania, then newly socialist, and found a job teaching in the American school. She married Spencer Swinton, an American math professor. Three years later she divorced him, returning to the United States with a new baby.

During her first months in New York with Jenny, Pat met Nate Yarrow, the son of a Baptist minister who had just quit school and come to New York from the South. Nate was then only nineteen, but his ideas were strongly formed. He had spent much of his childhood in Sweden, where he found his Swedish friends regarded American adults with contempt. As soon as his family came back to the United States, Nate understood the Swedish attitude: Americans struck him as insulated bigots, and the Vietnam War bore witness to the image. Within a month after arriving in New York, Nate had joined the Committee to Aid the NLF. He thought the Yippies were self-indulgent, but he shared their sense of the absurd. The night before an antiwar march sponsored by Youth Against War and Fascism, he had climbed to the top of the Washington Square Arch and unfurled a huge red, yellow, and blue NLF flag, visible from ten blocks' distance in the dawn light.

Nate moved into the tiny West Village apartment where Pat was living with Jenny. A year later they moved to the place on East Fourth Street where Pat still lived when I met her. During the first year they were together, Pat taught at the SEEK program at Queens College. She soon came to think of the program as hypocritical, a way to indoctrinate minority students with the capitalist ethic of the white middle class. She quit and went on welfare. Nate took a job as a layout artist for the *Guardian*. (He and Sam had a nodding acquaintance at work.) A few months before I met Pat, Nate had decided he wanted his own place and moved to an apartment on Avenue C, a block from Pat's. They had keys to each other's apartments, and although both of them slept with others, Pat still considered Nate her lover and closest friend.

Whenever I saw Pat that December and January, she was on her way to or from a night in Neil's apartment. I understood that she was not in love with Neil while he was increasingly infatuated with her. What I didn't understand was how she could be in love with Nate when she was making love with someone else two or three times a week. She answered by saying that monogamy was a kind of possessiveness and that our urge for it came from our bourgeois upbringing. Her politics had taught her that she didn't have to own a man's body to love him; she and Nate felt spiritually linked to each other even when she was in someone else's bed. Since Sam, too, had often told me he was capable of sexual relations with several women at once, I came to feel that my preference for monogamy, like my initial difficulties with orgasm, were aspects of my repression. In my attempts to become a better revolutionary, I took Pat as a role model.

Once we were washing the dinner dishes in Sam's and my apartment when she turned to me and asked casually, "Have you ever made love to a woman?"

My shock prompted me to tell the truth. "No. Have you?"

"Yes. With one woman."

"Do I know her?"

"It's Vanessa. The woman I brought here for dinner last time."

Vanessa, an exquisite Japanese woman, had sat at our dinner table in perfect quiet for nearly three hours, eating daintily with her own silver-tipped chopsticks and speaking only when she left, to thank me for the meal.

"She was Nathan's lover before she was mine," Pat went on. "He was crazy about her, and I couldn't stand it. He had slept with other women, but Vanessa was the first I was jealous of. She was so beautiful and flawless. I knew I could never be anything like her, and Nathan suggested that it might help me with my jealousy if I went to bed with him and Vanessa."

"So you did?"

"Yeah. First the three of us slept together. Then Vanessa and I became lovers on our own. At the beginning I needed Nathan there for the security but it turned out to be a lot nicer without him."

"What was it like?"

She put down her dish towel and sat down.

"Strange, in the beginning. The parts you expect will be there—

because you associate sex with a male body—aren't. Tits instead of hard chest. Tiny waist. Everything soft and round and wet. But after a while, when you get hot, it's just exactly the same. You can't wait to come, and when you do . . . well, I was actually in love with Vanessa for a couple of weeks, and it was just like being in love with a man. We haven't slept together in a while now. Still, when we're together, it's like being with a lover instead of a friend. There's always a sexual tension."

I searched my mind for some experience I could match with hers, found none. As a child I had been aroused by the centerfolds in my father's copies of *Playboy*. Later I decided that since I always identified myself with the large-breasted, slim-hipped women in the pictures, wishing I could be as attractive to men as they were, my fantasies hadn't been really homosexual. I sometimes placed women I knew as characters in my sexual fantasies, but they were almost always off to the side, stroking my breasts or holding my legs apart while a man made love to me. Pat's description made more sense than anything I had imagined about making love with a woman.

"I like your description," I told Pat. "You make me realize that it's probably just a matter of overcoming resistance."

"Would you like to try it sometime?"

I retrieved the platter I was drying before it fell on the floor.

"I guess I'd have to think about it," I said. As soon as the words were out, I felt like a fool. Someone I cared for had just asked me to make love and I'd said I'd *think* about it. It would have been more respectful simply to say no.

"I didn't mean to pressure you," said Pat. "It's just that . . . well, I've come to love you. I didn't when I first met you. You looked so straight in your office clothes: that funny coat with the fur collar. I couldn't imagine what Sam saw in you. But now I understand. You have this wonderful openness about you. You're a *big* person, not petty or mean. And as Sam always says, you've got great tits."

Her imitation of Sam broke the tension. We burst out laughing. Sam, hearing us, came into the kitchen and wanted to know what the joke was. We had to tease him onto a different subject.

Later it occurred to me it was the first secret I had kept from him.

People who knew more about the movement than I did—who had yipped in at Grand Central Station, occupied buildings at Columbia, confronted the police in Chicago—said in the winter of 1968–69 that we were facing a period of fascist repression. The Black Panther Party, the most visible sign of black militancy, was under heavy government attack, with Huey Newton in jail, Bobby Seale under indictment, and Eldridge Cleaver a fugitive. Dave Dellinger, whom I'd come to know through Patch and Lissa, was under indictment, too, together with Seale and six others, on charges of having incited a riot at the Democratic convention in Chicago. In Oakland seven radical leaders were about to go to trial for their part in the 1967 Stop the Draft Week protests. Nixon had been elected to the presidency; the Paris peace talks had been stalemated for months. In December Sam and I went to a twentieth anniversary benefit for the *Guardian* where some of the most important figures in the radical left were featured speakers: Herbert Marcuse, Rap Brown, Wilfred Burchette, Carl Oglesby, and the newly elected interorganizational secretary of SDS, Bernardine Dohrn. The evening was a fiasco. Rap Brown, former chairman of SNCC, now under indictment for riot charges, attacked the *Guardian* for having pictured Eldridge Cleaver on its cover, then attacked the audience for having supposedly voted for Humphrey. The audience—radical leftists who hadn't voted at all—hissed, and Brown walked off the stage, followed by Dohrn, who hadn't yet given her speech, and Oglesby. The most vivid impression of the evening was made by Dohrn, who cut an astonishingly glamorous figure in a velvet minidress and whose walk-off in support of Rap Brown was dramatic, unexpected, and a harbinger of splits to come.

Like much of the activist white left, CAC was falling apart. The St. Marks Arms demonstration had provided a lift that vanished when the tenants were evicted, a week or two after our protest. Greg Rosen suggested that instead of planning new actions, we research real estate holdings on the Upper West Side and hold seminars for tenants on our findings. I was willing to try his idea, but Sam complained that he hadn't joined CAC so that he could spend time in a library. We went to our last meeting in December. In January, Greg broke up with the woman he had lived with for six years and moved from the Upper West Side to an apartment on East Third Street, not far from us. With Robert, Sam, Diane, and Greg all living in a different neighborhood from the one they had set out to radicalize, CAC finally collapsed.

That winter the talk around our kitchen table turned increasingly to guerrilla action. The argument went like this: if the movement was dying, it was because the movement had never really learned how to fight. We had to stop acting like coddled children, scared off by a few arrests, a couple of canisters of tear gas. Instead of regarding ourselves as a hopelessly tiny minority, we had to realize we were more numerous than the Cuban guerrillas in 1960 or the Bolsheviks in 1917. And wasn't the overwhelming majority in the United States opposed to the Vietnam War? The radical pacifists who broke into draft boards to pour blood on draft files were unquestionably courageous. But by allowing themselves to be arrested (in accord with their nonviolent principles), they dissuaded others from imitating them. What if they had destroyed the draft files and gotten away with it? What if a hundred, a thousand, small groups, inspired by their victory, did the same? Suppose, instead of throwing money at the Stock Exchange as the Diggers had, we short-circuited the power line to the Big Board? Or poisoned the water coolers in Standard Oil's offices—just enough to keep the employees out of work for a week? Robert Carpenter was magical during these conversations. A born inventor, he knew how to hot-wire a car or build a black box to make free long-distance phone calls. Inspired by him, our fantasies grew more elaborate. We imagined the Army resigning, Washington in chaos, America's major corporations turned over to the janitors and typists, Huey Newton released from prison to form a new government.

For me, this talk was like playing Make-Believe with heroes out of Greek myths and comic books fighting a hierarchy of villains who did as they were told. And part of the game was that, if challenged, you always pretended to be absolutely serious.

On a Sunday morning in January, Pat presented Sam and me with our first LSD: two shiny purple capsules which she said were filled with a white powder that was nearly pure acid. Neil, who had come upstairs with her for the presentation, didn't entirely approve of it.

"I took acid once when I was in California last summer," he said. "I completely freaked out, nearly jumped out a window. It seems funny now, but it was terrifying when it happened. You ought to be real careful. Be sure there's someone around you who's not stoned and who knows what to do if you freak."

I wasn't afraid of jumping out of a window. My worry was a business trip I was scheduled to make Monday morning to interview prospective authors at Harvard and MIT. Although I disparaged my job to my movement friends, I was anxious for the trip to be a success. And what if I was still stoned when I had to make the nine o'clock shuttle at La Guardia? Unexpectedly Sam was sympathetic. "I've been waiting to do this for months," he said. (I knew that was true. In October he had tried to persuade Greg Rosen to sell him some acid and had been infuriated when Greg refused.) "Another week isn't going to make a difference."

Immediately after dinner he changed his mind. We had polished off Diane's stewed chicken and said good night to Diane and Leon, who had retired to their bedroom, when Sam announced that he had swallowed his capsule with his coffee. "You can take yours next week," he said. "There's no reason we have to do it together." Upset at being excluded, I put aside my scruples about tomorrow's trip and downed the second capsule.

About a half hour later Sam declared himself stoned. I still felt nothing, but my contact lenses were beginning to irritate my eyes. I decided to remove them.

My contact lens case was on a bookshelf in the room Sam and I used as a living room. I sat on the daybed, the case in my lap, and tugged at the outside corner of my eyelid to remove the lens. That gesture, the same one I had performed several times a day for the past six years of lens wearing, suddenly seemed wrong. I stared at my palm. It was enormous, pulsing with red and blue lights, crossed with lines that looked like railroad tracks. If I could manage to detach the lens from my eye, it would look like a transparent football. I would never be able to insert it in that small plastic case.

Minutes passed, or maybe hours. Voices approached me, growing louder. Hostile voices; mean, threatening laughter. In the doorway, two beams of lurid green light wavered, bent toward me. Sam's and Neil's voices came from the light beams. "What's the matter with *her*?" The green light that was Sam hovered a few inches from my face. I could see Sam's eyes, nose, and mouth, distorted as in a Coney Island mirror. Behind him was a vast glass aquarium in which Neil swam toward, then away from me, his face as expressionless as a squid's. I hugged my knees and cowered against the wall. "Jane, are you all right?" said Neil's voice. I closed my eyes. The rims of my contact lenses bit into the soft inner lids. Something trickled down my face—blood?

Sam's voice. Impatient. How long had he been talking to me? "What's wrong with you anyway?" he demanded. I couldn't answer.

A rancid smell assaulted me. We had forgotten to wash the dinner dishes. How long ago had we eaten? The nearest clock was in the bedroom, too far to walk. Sam was right to complain about Diane's cooking. She used wines and spices that didn't blend, a nauseating combination with the kitchen's usual smell of leaking gas. I should get up and wash the dishes. Impossible to move. Why didn't Sam wash the dishes?

The green lights had moved into the bedroom. Sam didn't love me anymore. He knew how weak and dependent I was, and he despised me for it. He was right. I was like a helpless child, three years old, wanting to cuddle in my father's lap, to bounce up and down on his knees.

Slowly, placing each foot carefully in front of me, I made my way into the bedroom. Neil was gone. Sam was alone, lying on the bed. I sat down next to him. He slipped his hand under my shirt. "I want to fuck you, slut," he said. His hand was a cold, slithery fish.

I wriggled away. "I can't," I said. "I'm too stoned."

"All right," he answered, and turned on his back. Mad at me again. But I couldn't help it. A few minutes later he rose from the bed and left the room. I heard the apartment door open and close.

All night I watched movies flicker on the ceiling and walls: grotesque shapes of every description, often menacing. I was frozen with terror. Occasionally someone would come in the room and ask if I was all right. Finally dawn came and the hallucinations scattered. Sam was next to me in our bed, asleep. I packed my business papers in a tooled case that had been a gift from my parents and put on my clothes. I left without leaving a note.

The raw winter morning stung my face. In the back seat of the cab, I finally managed to remove my contact lenses. The cabdriver veered aggressively through city traffic. I hoped he wouldn't turn around. The sight of another human face, close up, might bring back the hallucinations. Without my contact lenses, I retreated thankfully into the world of the unsighted.

At the Eastern Airlines shuttle I wrote a check for my ticket and boarded the Boston-bound plane. After taking a window seat, I fastened my seat belt. The plane taxied to the end of the runway, took off. The stewardess demonstrated equipment. We were halfway to Boston when the pilot's voice came on the air. "Ladies and gentlemen, if you look behind you, you will see an extensive fire." I opened my eyes and turned around. I saw the wing of the plane in flames. Before my eyes, the metal shriveled to dust. In a moment what was left of it would sizzle from the body of the plane. We would plummet to earth, blaze to our deaths.

How gruesome, to die in a plane crash! Rescue teams would pick through the rubble for days, finding more bodies. I would be one of the first to die since I was so near the wing. Why was everyone around me calm? Perhaps no one had understood. I closed my eyes again, preparing myself for the end.

We were on the ground. The pilot announced the temperature, thanked us for flying. Stewardesses walked briskly through the plane, fetching luggage. Passengers lined up to disembark. Dazed, I took my place in line. "Have a nice day," said a stewardess as I stumbled past her. Inside Logan Airport I sat down on the first bench.

So I had only imagined that the plane was on fire. Yet the pilot had made an announcement. About some other fire, as everyone else had realized at the time. Messages happened inside my head as though someone else were sending them. The one I heard now said, "Go wash your face, you'll feel better." I saw a ladies' room directly opposite. Pushing the door open, I stopped short in front of a huge mirror. Before me was a very pale, very young woman, hair pushed behind her ears like a schoolgirl's. Her fur-trimmed coat had a large stain and was missing two buttons. A run had started in her left stocking. Her eyes, half-closed with fatigue, were surrounded by dark circles.

I left the bathroom, proceeded to the terminal lobby, and bought a ticket on the next flight back to New York. Then I telephoned all the professors I was scheduled to meet and canceled each appointment, pretending I was still in New York and had awakened with a fever. I called my office and made the same excuse to my friend Billie Banks, who answered the editorial department phone.

I arrived in New York at two. The sky had cleared, and the air felt fresh as the breeze at Jones Beach. I knew I could no longer charge the day's expenses to Cambridge, but I took a cab home anyway. Sam was tinkering at his worktable when I walked in the door.

"Am I glad to see you!" he cried, wrapping me in his arms. "I've been worried about you ever since I woke up and found you gone. Are you okay?"

"I'm fine," I said, snuggling happily against his chest. The familiar smell of his sweat was all I ever wanted to call home.

* * *

A week after the acid trip Sam quit the *Guardian.*

"Why?" I kept asking him. "Did something happen at the office? Did you have a fight with someone?"

He lay on the couch, across the room from me, glaring at the ceiling. "It's done," he said. "What do you want to talk about it for?"

A few days later Jack Smith, head of the *Guardian* circulation department, called and asked for Sam. Sam came to the phone, spoke to his former supervisor for a few minutes, then hung up.

"Well?" I said.

"Well, we talked. I told him I wasn't coming back and he said okay. What did you think was going to happen?"

I didn't know. I had always thought of Sam not as irrational but as someone who lived by principles others didn't understand. Whenever I thought I had figured out what the principles were, he changed them. I remembered his description, in our first weeks together, of his walking out of his job with an engineering firm rather than agreeing to work on a project for the Union of South Africa. I had admired him for that and sympathized with him against his ex-wife's accusation of irresponsibleness. I recalled his disgust with me when I wanted to write a letter to the chairman of Columbia's Greek and Latin department. "Why don't you just leave?" he had said. "What are you trying to hang onto?" Now I wondered whether he had come to see the *Guardian* as another version of the oppressor, deserving no more courtesy than a profit-making corporation. And I began to suspect that some of Sam's hostility to "the system" was an inability to deal with himself.

I tried to quell my suspicions, but like rubber ducks in the bathtub, they kept bouncing to the surface. Could this revolutionary I loved actually be a mere drifter, incapable of commitment—to a job, a person, or even to his precious revolution?

Curiously my suspicions of Sam worked only to intensify my commitment to the cause.

On January 18 radicals called for a counterinaugural in Washington. According to Mobilization to End the War in Vietnam (MOBE), 250,000 were supposed to protest the inauguration of Richard Nixon. Probably no more than 10,000 appeared. We were jammed into a green-and-white-striped movement tent on Sunday morning, the nineteenth, where—dissension and rudeness having become epidemic in the movement—many hissed the speech of anti-war Vietnam veteran Jimmy Johnson, booed emcee Dave Dellinger when he asked for silence, and jeered, "Take it off!" at Marilyn Webb, the women's liberation speaker. Sam and I sat next to each other on Sunday school-style folding chairs. Sam was annoyed with me because I had suggested spending Saturday night at the home of a Swarthmore friend, who had turned out to be friendly with someone attending the real (not the counter) inauguration. "What kind of people do you know anyway?" he had snapped. I was still upset with him for the way he had walked out of the *Guardian* a few days earlier. In the middle of the speeches we agreed to go back to New York.

Outside the tent we nearly bumped into a handsome, lanky young man in an army surplus parka. He stared at Sam a moment, then smiled. "Nate Yarrow," he said, sticking out his right hand. "I know you from the *Guardian*." He looked at me. "You're Jane. I'm Pat Swinton's friend. You know—Jenny's mother." He held his hand waist-high to indicate Jenny. I laughed. His face was incandescent with secret mirth—at the clumsiness of his self-description? The hopelessness of the movement proceedings inside the tent? Or some still larger absurdity which he graciously assumed we knew?

"We're on our way back to New York," I said, hoping he would come with us.

"I guess I'm going to stick around till tomorrow."

We made fists at each other, a salute which had become so automatic I no longer thought about it.

On the train ride home, instead of thinking about the failure of the movement protest, I kept picturing Nate Yarrow making love with Pat. He was charming and quite beautiful, and it seemed he loved her. Why was she risking him by sleeping with Neil?

I didn't like the way Sam used his time after he quit his job. He became obsessed with body building, going through two-hour morning workouts with his friend Jim, a tattooed machinist who lived on our block, then joining the all-men's Sheridan Square gym, where he lifted weights for another two hours in the afternoon. A clerk in a health food store convinced him to give up meat. He took to preparing concoctions of banana, brewer's yeast, and protein powders in Diane's blender and drinking them instead of eating meals. He clumped around the apartment with five-pound iron weights strapped to his ankles—to strengthen the joints, he said, but he didn't explain for what. When he wasn't absorbed by his health regimen, he was talking to the leaders and groupies he met in movement storefronts. A conversation with Abbie Hoffman preoccupied him for days. "The guy's really crazy," he would say, and meant it as high praise.

Our sex life changed, too. He persuaded me to let him penetrate me anally, which at first I was glad to do, since it gave him obvious pleasure and he praised me lavishly for accommodating him. As he came to prefer anal intercourse to any other form of sexual contact, I grew resentful. The master/slut games, initially playful, made me uncomfortable when he demanded them, insisting on an elaborate verbal formula before he would condescend to touch me. At the same time I sensed that underneath his dominating behavior was a fragile core. He wasn't ready to talk about what troubled him; if I pressed, he withdrew and was silent and hostile for days. Because I was going to be away for a month and didn't want to upset him before I left, I resigned myself to endure the difficulties until my departure.

When I was first promoted to an editorship, I had agreed—had in fact been enthralled at the suggestion—to make a trip to England to meet with the editors at the home office. During the time the editorial department was reorganized, and while Sam and I were settling in together, the trip remained unscheduled. Around the time Sam quit the *Guardian*, Mansbridge summoned me to his office to let me know that the dates had been set: February 18 to March 15. I asked for a postponement. Impossible, he told me: the tickets had been purchased, the hotels booked in Cambridge and London. If I wished, I could take a few weeks' vacation after March 15, to travel in Europe perhaps.

Sam, I knew, would not be interested in London, Paris, Rome. He had been musing over a trip to Mexico, but that was different—Mexico was the third world, we could live there in about the same style as on East Eleventh Street. He would hate England; no use even suggesting that he meet me there. And what fun would it be to travel without him? None at all, when I would not only miss him but worry every day that in my absence he was deteriorating or, worse, changing his mind about our relationship.

To add to my concerns, Pat was finally showing her restlessness with Neil. In December and early January the two of them had usually eaten Sunday breakfast with us after sleeping together Saturday night. By the end of January Pat was more likely to show up at Neil's on Sunday afternoon, Jenny in tow, and insist on coming immediately upstairs to our place. Sometimes she didn't stop at Neil's at all. I always liked talking to her—she was honest and funny, and her conversation traveled more easily between the political and the personal than anyone else's—but I was apprehensive about what her visits would be like when I was in England and Sam was left to entertain her alone.

On February 15, the Saturday before my trip, she and I went together to a women's liberation-sponsored demonstration protesting a commercial bridal fair in Madison Square Garden. The mostly female crowd and the theme of the protest stirred an exchange of confidences between Pat and me. On the way home she said to me, "The one thing I don't understand about you and Sam is why you're so sexually exclusive. You're really hip people, but you're as monogamous as I was when I was married."

"I suppose it's more my choice than Sam's," I said truthfully. "I'd like to be freer, but I haven't had much experience at it."

She laughed.

"Maybe I can help you," she said. "You know I love both you and Sam. And I wouldn't do anything that would threaten your commitment to each other."

We dropped the subject, but I thought of it again when I saw her on the night before my flight. Sam and I had stopped at her apartment so I could say good-bye. As I left, she hugged first me, then Sam.

"Don't worry about anything while you're away," she said to me, leaning over Sam's shoulder. "I'll take good care of him for you."

Why did I laugh again when she said that? It was what I was most afraid of.

VIII
Visitors

I KEPT HOPING FOR A RAMBLING, newsy letter from Sam that would narrow the ocean between us and reassure me during my three and a half weeks away. Nothing about my stay in England gave me any comfort. In Cambridge the English editors appeared to disapprove of my clothes, my casual manners, and my American speech. I thought them repressed and stuffy. At a tea held at the home of an important official, I was seized with an urge to overturn the hand-painted cups and saucers, throw the cucumber sandwiches at the brocaded walls, and yell obscenities, Yippie style. I stopped short of violence and instead picked an argument about apartheid with the foppish fifteen-year-old son of my host. The hostess came to the rescue of her son, changing the subject so artfully I didn't realize until later that she had outmaneuvered me.

The New York editor Elisabeth Case, who shared the trip with me, saved me from feeling I had parted company with the human race. At home, I had considered Elisabeth prim, but in comparison with our English hosts, she was direct, lively, and the only person with whom I could relax at all. Back in our overheated rooms at the Blue Boar Inn, we mocked our hosts' pomposities until we could laugh in mutual relief and counted the days until we could leave. But while Elisabeth was looking forward to a week's vacation in Paris after the trip, I longed only to return home to East Eleventh Street, my friends, and Sam.

My first mail arrived in the second week of our stay. Instead of the fat envelope I had fantasized, the desk clerk handed me a flimsy blue aerogram. Sam's angular handwriting on the outside made my stomach pound. I raced upstairs with my prize and flung myself on the bed to read.

Sam had marked off the space inside the aerogram in six rectangles. Each of these boxes held a crude stick drawing. At the top was the title "The Adventures of Jane Darring." I read my way slowly through the dialogue balloons in each frame. The characters were a band of guerrilla revolutionaries under the direction of Jane Darring (sometimes spelled "Daring"). Their mission was to destroy Central Controls, the computer that governed the world. In the last frame, Jane agrees to lead the band to the computer through a labyrinth studded with land mines and poisoned cesspools and guarded by the well-armed imperial police. Sam had written at the bottom, "Tune in for next installment."

My head swam with Sam's presence, as powerful after reading the aerogram as if he had suddenly sauntered into the room, pinched my ass, and now stood laughing at the surprise on my face. For Sam, this aerogram amounted to intimate communication. He identified with the guerrillas in his cartoon. By making "Jane Daring" the leader of the group, he was paying me a teasing compliment. But—tucked away at the Blue Boar—I didn't think of myself either as daring or as a revolutionary. And I knew no more about Sam's daily activities at the end of the aerogram than at the beginning. Yet I was glad to hear from him in any form. The very sight of my name in his handwriting boosted my spirits.

A few nights later the second installment of Sam's aerogram series was waiting for me. There was a letter from Pat too. I read about the efforts of Jane Daring's band to penetrate the imperial labyrinth, then turned to Pat's longer letter. Two pages of cheerful gossip concluded with the news that she and Sam had gone to bed together. Sam hadn't wanted her to tell me, but she "knew that I would understand." Whatever happened, she assured me, she would continue to see my relationship with Sam as "primary."

I looked at the date. Sunday. Five days after I left New York. They hadn't wasted much time.

I threw myself on the bed in a fit of despair. After nearly two weeks of isolation, surrounded by superiors who I was sure despised me, and disillusioned with the work in which I had once invested so much ambition, I now felt that I was facing the loss of Sam. For in spite of Pat's blandishments, I couldn't imagine that Sam would continue to love me when someone so much more attractive and aware had made herself available. I told myself that I would definitely quit my job when I returned to New York and treat myself to a long vacation. If we had enough time together, it was possible that I could win Sam back, but if I continued to leave him alone all day while I went off to work, I would surely lose him to Pat.

By the end of my stay I was living for Sam's aerograms. They came almost every day. The apelike imperial guards caught Jane Daring in the labyrinth, strung her from the ceiling, raped her anally and vaginally, forced her to suck them—sort of *The Story of O in the Sierra Maestra.* Jane Daring, I noted, remained passive through these indignities but succeeded in the end in blowing up the computer that governed the world. As the computer exploded, she exclaimed, her hands over her ears but her legs straight up in the air, "That sound always makes me come." The sexual politics of Sam's comic strip were clear: through masochism, victory.

On March 12, two nights before my long-awaited return to New York, an overseas telephone message was waiting for me at the Blue Boar. "Call home as soon as possible," it said. The East Eleventh Street phone number was at the bottom.

I had to wait until 2:00 A.M. before I could get an appointment to place the call. I tried to nap but was too nervous to close my eyes for long. My throat was so dry I wondered if I would be able to speak. By the time the telephone rang I was convinced that Sam was about to tell me he was moving in with Pat. "Your party," said the operator. Sam's wonderful voice flooded over the telephone wire, more reassuring than anything I'd heard in weeks.

"Sam," I murmured, clutching the phone like a lifeline.

"Hi, babe," he said. "I hope I didn't worry you. I just wanted you to know that something far-out has happened. I can't go into it on the phone. You'll hear all about it when you come home."

"Does it have to do with Pat?" I couldn't help asking.

He was silent a moment.

"I know she wrote you. I asked her not to, but she insisted. No, it doesn't have to do with Pat. It has mostly to do with people you've never met. But I really can't talk on the phone. Suppose I meet your plane?"

His voice was loving, gentle, full of affection. I was so relieved I could hardly answer.

"Oh, Sam, I love you," I said. "I've missed you so much."

"I've missed you too, babe. You've been gone a long time."

He was waiting for me after I came through customs. He looked subtly different—or was my memory playing tricks? A new, tight pair of jeans made him look slimmer, his mustache was a bit shaggier, his hair thinner and longer. And there was something else changed—the shadows of his jawline, the play of light in his eyes. I breathed him in as we embraced.

"You've lost weight," I said, wondering if that was the answer.

"Maybe. I haven't had much time to eat."

"So what's the mystery?"

"Not now. I'll tell you when we get home."

We picked up my luggage and hailed a taxi outside the terminal. The bus was cheaper and not inconvenient, but I wanted to be alone with Sam. Cambridge could foot the bill. The landscape familiar to me from my high school years in Queens sped past the window: the signs on the Long Island Expressway, the giant globe from the 1964 World's Fair, the garish blue and orange exterior of Shea Stadium.

"How's Neil?" I asked.

"He's okay. Getting ready for his draft board physical. He's spending a lot of time high by himself, not eating, so he'll look freaked-out. He'll probably make it."

"And Nate?"

"All right. He got a little upset this weekend over a letter Pat wrote him."

"A letter about what?" My nerves were beginning to jangle again.

"About her and me," Sam said. "I don't know why she wrote it actually."

I didn't trust myself to answer, so I said nothing.

"Something about how she'd learned to love two people equally," Sam went on. "Which she thinks is a big breakthrough for her. Apparently Nate didn't take it too well."

"I thought this thing between you and Pat wasn't important," I said finally.

"I didn't think so either. I mean, I don't *think* it is. At least I didn't until a couple of nights ago."

We were in the Midtown Tunnel by this time. Even if I could

have talked around the lump in my throat, I could not have made myself heard over the vroom of the traffic.

"Look," he said. "You've been gone a long time and a lot has happened. Right now I don't know how I feel. Let's just relax, okay, and see what happens?"

I turned my face to the window to hide the tears.

Inside our bedroom I unpacked my bags as Sam filled his stemless pipe with marijuana, lit it, and handed it to me. I breathed in the smoke, hoping to put the pain at a distance.

"It's cool to talk here for now," Sam said. "We try to be careful about where we have certain discussions these days. For example, we never talk in Pat's apartment. Because of her NACLA work, the place might be bugged. But no one in this place is heavy enough to be watched."

I nodded, waiting for him to explain.

"Have you ever heard of the FLQ?" he asked.

"Sure. The Front de Libération du Québec, I think it stands for. People were talking about them at that conference in Montreal, remember? They're French-speaking people in Quebec who want to make a Marxist revolution against the English-speaking government. The founder is named Pierre Vallières. He wrote a book called *The White Niggers of America.* It's supposed to be good, but I never read it."

"You're incredible," Sam said. "I didn't know that until a week or two ago. Anyway, do you also know that the FLQ has carried out about forty—dig, *forty*—political bombings in the last year?"

"Yeah, I think I read about that."

Sam put the pipe in the conch shell we used for an ashtray.

"Two of the guys who did those bombings are here in New York. Until a couple of days ago they were here in this apartment."

He could see the shock in my face, I suppose, and it delighted him.

"It was pretty hairy for a while," he went on. "The FLQ, it turns out, was only three men. Jean and Jacques, the ones who are here, and a third guy, Pierre-Paul, who's now under arrest. Funny names, huh? They don't even speak English. Well, Jacques doesn't at all. Jean speaks a little."

The reality of what Sam was telling me dawned slowly. Two Canadian fugitives responsible for forty bombings. In this apartment. Eating in our kitchen, sleeping . . . where? In our bed? Or had Sam been there with Pat?

"Where are they now?"

"Luckily Pat had keys to an apartment of some friends of hers. A nice quiet place over in the West Village. Her friends are away until June, so we've got time to figure things out."

"Figure what out?"

"They can't go back to Canada. They'd be picked up as soon as they reached the border. And they can't stay here. Like I said, they don't speak English. This is a foreign country to them."

"So what do they plan to do?"

"They hope to get asylum in Cuba. They already know a little Spanish. And they're big admirers of Fidel. They think they could live happily in Cuba until Quebec wins independence. The problem is that to get out of the U.S., they need IDs. So far they haven't been able to get any."

"IDs aren't hard to get, are they? I thought you just pick a name out of the birth announcements in an old newspaper, write for a birth certificate, and use that to get a passport and stuff. People do that just so they can rip off welfare."

"Yeah. *American* people. But Jean and Jacques can't pass for U.S. citizens. They've got to get Canadian IDs. Either that or French."

I began to understand how the problem captivated him. His Jane Daring cartoons had come to life in the form of two live guerrillas seeking asylum. Dynamite, narrow escape, the threat of imprisonment, perhaps death—Sam's imagination could not resist such intoxicants. And where did Pat fit into this? Did her fantasies also turn to foreign revolutionaries? Or was she simply weaseling into Sam's life in my absence?

"I was hoping," Sam went on, "that you could call your friend Dave Dellinger and see if he could help. He must know all about that stuff."

I could have answered that Dave Dellinger was a lifelong pacifist who might not be pleased to help two terrorists. I could have said that I didn't want to get involved. Instead, I said, "I'll call him at the *Liberation* office on Monday."

Sam devoted his waking hours to caring for the two Québecois. He went to the post office every day to see if mail from their comrades in Montreal had arrived. At three o'clock each afternoon he bought the Montreal newspapers at the foreign newsstand on Times Square for prompt delivery to Jean and Jacques's apartment. He supplied them with money and clothes, and for the first few days, when they were afraid to go outside, he did their grocery shopping. Later, when they wanted to walk around, he drew maps of the parts of town where they were least likely to attract attention. As our attempts to arrange their safe entry to Cuba ended in one failure after another, Sam kept their spirits up, assuring them and himself, over and over, that something would turn up.

I was touched, myself, by the two fugitives. Jean, twenty-six, was slender and dapper, with mild eyes and a chivalry toward women that I realized I had missed in the radical left. Jacques, twenty-two, was somewhat huskier, olive-skinned, with a stubborn, coarse face. Jean explained that Jacques came from a large, very poor family in the slums of Montreal, had little education, and had worked in factories for subsistence wages since he was thirteen. Jean's family was better off. He had been to college and had worked for the past year as a clerk at the offices of the Canadian Broadcasting Company. He spoke halting but clear English. On certain subjects, he was eloquent: discrimination against the French in the English-run universities and businesses of Quebec; hunger, crime, and inadequate housing in Montreal's French quarter; the inevitability of independence for Quebec, perhaps in less than five years. But independence, Jean said, was a reformist, not a revolutionary, goal.

"If we win independence before we make a Marxist revolution, then Quebec becomes—how do you say it?—a colony of the United States. We do not want to trade government by Toronto for government by Washington. We want to make a communist state independent of both." I liked Jean's logical mind, his patience with my ignorance, and the spark in his eyes when he talked of revolution in his country. I never discussed the bombings with him. Perhaps it seemed too personal a subject at a time when his freedom was in danger. In any case, the rationale behind the FLQ bombings was too obvious to require explanation. They wanted to topple the power structure as quickly and effectively as possible and ultimately install a revolutionary regime.

Sam, after a few days, dispensed with theorizing and got down to what interested him: hideouts, disguises, dynamite, plastique, secret communiqués. He got Jean to describe how he, Jacques, and their arrested comrade, Pierre-Paul, had used false IDs to buy dynamite at an agricultural supply store and how they had later happened upon a quantity of high-explosive plastique, left unguarded at a construction site. Jean drew him diagrams of timing devices wired to blasting caps wired to bundles of explosive material. He explained how to stuff the bombs into briefcases that could be deposited inconspicuously in restaurants, government buildings, corporate offices. They talked of the necessity of renting a safe hiding place for explosives and, if necessary, guns; of the importance of cool storage to prevent dynamite from spontaneously exploding; of wearing appropriate disguises when planting a bomb and covering the telephone mouthpiece when making a warning call. Sam sometimes stayed up till midnight with Jean and Jacques, going over diagrams, asking questions, making suggestions. While Jean and Jacques themselves were unsure whether the U.S. movement ought to adopt their methods, Sam had no such qualms. He would come home bursting with excitement, unable to sleep until he had put in another three or four hours at his worktable, tinkering with fuses and wires.

I might have taken this new interest of Sam's more seriously if I hadn't been so preoccupied over his affair with Pat. He spoke of Pat often, though he never specifically told me when he had seen her or what they had done. But Neil, forlorn since Pat had dumped him, said she and Sam had been together constantly in the week before I returned. They had acted, Neil said, "very exclusive—always giving each other secret looks and making me feel like shit." Every morning, when I went off to work, I assumed that Sam went to Fourth Street to roll around in Pat's bed. Every night I expected him to tell me that he was tired of living with me and was going to move in with her.

For my own self-protection, I cultivated my friendship with Pat. She kept disarming me by always answering my questions. According to her, she didn't see Sam often and had slept with him only once since my return from England. But it was clear that she was powerfully attracted to him and would have liked to divide her time equally between him and Nate. Whether Sam returned her feeling for him, neither of us could figure out.

It was my suggestion that Sam, Pat, and I go to bed together. This was for several reasons. First, I thought that if I could actually see Sam make love with Pat, I might lose my fear of their intimacy. Secondly, I had felt curious about making love with a woman ever since Pat had raised the subject in the East Eleventh Street kitchen. Sam's presence would add safety to that experiment—as long as a man was there, it wouldn't be "real" lesbianism. Finally, Sam's continual repetitions of fantasies had persuaded me that group sex might actually be arousing and at least that it couldn't hurt to try. I told him that if he still wanted to sleep with two women at once, as he had often claimed he did, I was willing to try it. He looked amazed, then, as he realized I was serious, ecstatic. He got Pat to agree. We set a Saturday when Jenny was going to Philadelphia with her father as the date.

I remember the early hours of that Saturday evening as the first time since my return that Sam, Pat, and I had felt comfortable in the same room with each other. Pat was wearing the sleeveless pink sweater she had on the day we met. Sam teased that I should grow my underarm hair, like Pat's, and give up wearing bras. His voice was good-humored, not offensive, and I laughed. We joked about Pat's straight husband, who had come that morning for Jenny. I liked the feeling that Pat, Sam, and I were an enclave of hipness that was horrifying to the straight world.

We smoked a couple of joints. Pat dimmed the red-shaded lamp over the mattress she used as both couch and bed. We took off our shoes and lay on the mattress, rolling over to brush each other's bodies lightly. Sam slipped one hand around to the fastening of my bra, the other inside Pat's sweater. Pat pulled her sweater over her head, smiling radiantly at both of us. Sam undid his work shirt. I took off my clothes, unable to remove my eyes from either of them.

Sam looked beautiful to me, strong and well muscled, a bohemian Gregory Peck. Pat had long legs and high, small breasts. Her body reminded me of the tall East African women pictured in *National Geographic* except that her skin was fair. I put a hand on her shoulder and tried to let it slip gracefully to her breast. Pat, smiling, was very still.

"You feel so different from me," I breathed, "doesn't she, Sam?"

He laid one hand on each of us. "Yeah, you have very different muscle tone," he announced. The first round of physical contact became a game, reducing the tension for all of us.

Filled with tenderness, I kissed Pat on the mouth. Her lips opened at my touch. My tongue moved inside her mouth, tasting the crevices of her palate. If I could have thrust my tongue into a conch shell, like the one in the East Eleventh Street bedroom but with a creature still living inside it, warm and pulsing with life, it would feel like Pat's mouth. I felt her arms go around my back, the surprising pressure of her breasts against my own.

Sam interrupted us. Had the sight of our kiss aroused him or did he merely need to reassert control? He touched first me, then Pat, and finally drew her attention exclusively to himself. I watched their intimacy grow, trying to suppress my alarm. At last Sam, ignoring me completely, wrapped Pat in his arms, turned her around on her back, and mounted her. I had to scramble out of the way.

I thought they were disgusting: like stray dogs that fucked on street corners oblivious to hooting bystanders. I got up from the bed. Their bodies shifted, occupying the space I left. I went to the kitchen, thinking of food.

I started to saw a thick slice from a loaf of rye bread. My hand was trembling so that I had to stop. It wasn't bread the knife was cutting but the necks of my lover and best friend, fucking in the next room. I saw their shocked faces, their blood pooling on Pat's dingy sheets. I saw myself weeping, begging their forgiveness. My ears strained for any recognizable noise, but I heard only the refrigerator hum. I returned to the living room, willing myself to appear calm.

I discovered them still locked together, in the middle of what appeared to be orgasm. In a plastic ashtray I found the remains of a joint. I lit it and breathed in. Sam rolled over and lay next to Pat. I offered him the roach. He took it, passed it to Pat.

"Come here and lie down, Jane," Pat said. "You look so far away over there."

I lay down next to her. She stroked my hair and forehead. Sam's arm reached around her so that his fingers brushed my shoulder. For a long time no one spoke.

I had wanted a peephole into the intimacy between Sam and Pat, and I had gotten more than I bargained for. Now, into the silence, Sam said, "I want to fuck Pat more."

I could feel Pat's heart beating rapidly next to my arm. Her expression was confused, but her voice, when she answered Sam, was calm and hopeful.

"I thought you weren't interested in me anymore," she said. "In the last couple of weeks I've hardly seen you. I figured you had changed your mind."

"I haven't changed my mind," said Sam. "It's just a difficult situation." I supposed he meant me.

"If you want to sleep with Pat, no one's stopping you," I said belligerently. "You're free to leave whenever you want."

"Christ, you're insecure," Sam exploded. He sat up. "I didn't *say* you were stopping me. Can't you just relax?"

I had never in my life been able to get terribly upset without bursting into tears. The more furious I got, the more uncontrollably I cried. I was now so choked with tears that I didn't dare try to answer Sam's accusation. I concentrated on swallowing back the sobs and holding my eyes wide open so the tears wouldn't flow.

"I think we should talk about this later," said Pat. Suspecting what she felt for Sam, I marveled that she had settled for the role of peacemaker. "It's four A.M. Why don't we turn out the light and try to sleep?"

No one answered. Pat clicked off the light. Before settling back down on the mattress, she deftly rearranged herself so that Sam was between her and me. Sam did not touch me. I turned on my stomach, buried my head on the pillow, and released my tears. If either Pat or Sam heard me, they gave no sign.

A couple of days later Sam called me at work. Our dope dealer, Sunshine, had picked up a shipment of pure LSD, direct from San Francisco, and was willing to sell 100 capsules for $75—a bargain price. I had grown fonder of acid since my calamitous trip to Boston, and Sam took it two or three times a week. What we didn't use ourselves, we could sell to Pat or Nate or other friends. I agreed to take the cash from our account and meet Sam at Sunshine's apartment after work.

Sunshine lived in a small Bleecker Street studio that glowed purple, even in the middle of the afternoon, and made me lightheaded from the combined fumes of marijuana, hash, and opium (he did not permit tobacco, which he considered unorganic). When I came in, Sam was sitting on a low-slung couch. His body was peculiarly rigid, and he barely acknowledged my entrance.

"What's the matter?" I asked at once, sitting next to him and peering anxiously at his eyes. The right was extremely dilated while the left jumped nervously in its socket.

"I—I don't know," he said, not looking at me.

Sunshine, skinny and spaced-out, turned to me. "There's nothing wrong, lady."

He put a tiny chunk of hash in a carved pipe and passed it to Sam. "Try some of this Lebanese shit, man. That will calm you down."

We smoked for about half an hour. I kept asking Sam how he felt. He shook his head and murmured, "Heavy stuff. Heavy stuff." Suddenly he gripped my wrist and stared me full in the face. The look in his eyes was undisguised panic. "Please take me home," he groaned.

"You gonna pay for this acid or what, man?" Sunshine demanded.

I withdrew the $75 from my wallet and counted it out for the dealer. The bottle of iridescent blue capsules went into my purse. Sunshine unlocked the door. Sam staggered to his feet and took my arm as I led him outside, one step at a time, to the corner of Bleecker and Seventh. He blinked at the light and started at the sounds of traffic. I told him that instead of waiting for the cross-town bus, I intended to hail a cab. He didn't answer. I stuck my arm out for the next taxi. The driver screeched past us, stopped. I half dragged Sam to the door.

Because of an accident on Houston Street, it took us almost half an hour to cross town. Sam stared ahead for the whole ride, saying nothing. I thought I might have to get Neil and Diane to help me bring Sam upstairs, but when we finally reached our building, Sam opened the taxi door himself, got out, and looked around him. "We're home," I said. He held my arm tightly as we mounted the four flights of stairs to our apartment.

Once inside, Sam went directly to the bedroom, lay down on the bed, and stared at the ceiling. I asked him if he wanted me to leave. He clutched my arm again. "No," he said distinctly. "Stay with me." I sat next to the bed in a chair, waiting for him to explain. He neither looked at me nor said another word. When I rose and tiptoed from the room, although his eyes were open, he appeared not to notice.

Diane suggested I get some Thorazine and make Sam take it.

She had none herself. Neither did Neil, Greg Rosen, or anyone else I called. I tried Pat. "I don't have any Thorazine, but I'd be glad to come over if you'd like company," she said. I didn't feel a pinprick of jealousy; I was scared for Sam and thought only of helping him. I urged her to come.

Neil, Diane, Pat, Jenny, and I gathered in the bedroom that evening, some five hours into Sam's death trip. I sat next to Sam on our bed, underneath his favorite photo of the two of us. Jenny sucked her pacifier. Pat, who had a longer history with acid than the rest of us, said Sam would probably be all right, but it might take a few more hours for him to come down. I touched Sam's hand. Like an infant presented with a rattle, he grabbed it and held on. "What's the matter, Sam?" I asked. I leaned close to him to hear the answer.

"Guilt and shame," he muttered hoarsely. "The demons of guilt and shame."

A few minutes later he sat up. He looked at us with a confused expression, got out of bed, walked to the bathroom. The toilet flushed. Sam came back to the bedroom and spoke his first coherent sentences since leaving Sunshine's apartment. "That acid is death," he said. "I'm not going to let any of you take it. Give it to me. I'm going to flush it down the toilet."

Pat looked petulant.

"Don't be ridiculous, Sam. You're not going to destroy seventy-five bucks' worth of acid because of one bad trip."

"That acid is death," Sam said. "No one I love is going to take it."

I glanced at Pat, warning her to keep quiet. She took Jenny's hand, still annoyed.

"I've got to go," she said. "Jen and I are getting up early tomorrow."

I walked her to the door.

"You're right about the acid," I said. "I'm pretty sure there's nothing wrong with it. But why don't we let Sam think that we've gotten rid of it—at least until he comes to his senses? Meanwhile, you take them home."

It didn't seem particularly odd to me that on Saturday night I had wanted to kill her for going to bed with Sam, while today we were collaborating to deceive him. Our cooperation was as natural as our rivalry and sprang from an affection as deep as our mistrust.

I put the bottle of blue capsules in Pat's hand. She looked at it. Then she smiled. She was still angry, and the smile had only a quarter the power of her high-beam radiant look; but the message was clear: whatever had happened, we were still friends.

On April 1 Pierre-Paul Geoffroy was sentenced to 124 concurrent life sentences. Jean and Jacques, who had now spent over a month in hiding in the apartment of Pat's friend, learned the news from the Montreal paper bought for them the next day. The reporters described how Pierre-Paul, defiantly proclaiming his belief in revolution, raised his clenched fist to a courtroom full of supporters as he was led back to prison. Jean and Jacques were morose. They grieved for their ally, chafed at their own idleness, and said that they now knew, without any doubt, that they could not return to Quebec. I hadn't realized that they had harbored such a hope until I saw their devastation at losing it.

In the past month all our attempts to get IDs for them had failed. Sam now decided to go to Montreal to meet with one of their friends, an FLQ sympathizer who was supposed to have underground connections. I convinced Sam to let me go with him. We went on the first weekend in April and stayed in the same hotel where the Hemispheric Conference Against Imperialism had been held in November. Sam met Jean and Jacques's friend in a café. He returned with no promises, but the hope that IDs would be available for the two fugitives in a week's time. The next morning as we were about to leave, a visitor came to our hotel room. "Royal Canadian Mounted Police," explained the man in khaki, showing his badge. "Just a routine check. May I have your name and home addresses? Some identification, please?" I produced my passport, Sam his driver's license. The RCMP copied the information. On the way back to New York we convinced ourselves that the inquiry was a coincidence.

A week later when no word had come from Montreal, Sam made another trip to the border, this time alone. At the checkpoint he was forbidden to cross. Instead of returning or thinking up a good alibi to explain why he needed to reach Montreal, he hitchhiked fifty miles to the next checkpoint and attempted to cross again. He was taken into custody and held for twelve hours. When he was released—he had committed no known illegal act and could not be held further—he was warned that he could not enter Canada again unless he obtained written clearance from Ottawa.

The story frightened me. And a persistent doubt lingered that Sam had somehow fucked up and that as a result, we were no longer quite safe.

Of course, I had to quit my job. I had made up my mind to do that when I was in England. The complications raised by Jean and Jacques and by Sam's on-again, off-again involvement with Pat confirmed my decision. As the moment of my resignation approached, sadness overrode any anger I had about Cambridge. I kept thinking of the personal interest Mansbridge and Schulman had taken in me, the way they had fired Anzaga on the strength of what I told them, their praise and encouragement since. I knew what Sam would say: he would tell me I was a fool to think my employers had done me favors, that they had gotten their money's worth and more from my work, that they would pay anyone else more to do what I did. None of my other friends would understand my regret. They had never heard me speak well of my job or of my pride in my close relations with several authors and in the first manuscript I had acquired for the press (a study of the early Romans). These achievements had no place in my life on East Eleventh Street; they belonged to a world of which I was no longer a part. I decided to resign as of April 30, giving my employers two weeks' notice first.

At nine-thirty on Wednesday morning, April 16, I caught Mansbridge's eye through the open door to his office, and he nodded at me to enter. I sat down and recited my carefully rehearsed speech. I was leaving, effective in two weeks if that was suitable—longer if he needed time to replace me. I was sorry to resign so soon after my trip to England, but that visit had confirmed what I had suspected beforehand: that my main interests lay outside publishing and that I could no longer give my editorial duties the attention they required.

He gazed at me over the rim of his bifocals. He did not look nearly as surprised as I thought he would. Perhaps he had guessed something already. He could not have missed noticing my sudden reluctance, starting last fall, to travel or put in overtime—after I'd lobbied through my first year to be given more responsibility. He was astute enough to have observed my new indifference to my hair and clothes.

"Do you mind telling me what you'll be doing?" Mansbridge asked, not unkindly. "It's none of my business, of course, but I would like to know."

The question took me by surprise. I hadn't thought of what I would be doing.

"I plan to get more involved in political work," I said, hoping that sounded responsive but also vague enough to discourage further questions. "I've been doing some things in the movement for the last six or eight months—since I quit Columbia—and I hope to do more."

He tapped a pencil on his desk.

"You're not in trouble, are you?"

I had a wild temptation to stutter the truth to him. Suppose I said: Yes, Mr. Mansbridge, I am. When I was in England, my lover got involved with two foreign revolutionaries, wanted on bombing charges. He also started sleeping with my best friend. We were questioned last week when we went to Canada. A couple of days ago he was forbidden to cross the border. I think he's about to do something terribly dangerous—and that if I try to stop him, he'll take up with my best friend again.

Then I realized what Mansbridge meant by "trouble." He was wondering if I was pregnant.

"No, sir," I said. "Not in any way I can't take care of."

"If I can help you, Jane, let me know." He nodded his head, concluding the interview.

Later that afternoon a report I had sent to Mansbridge on Cambridge's participation in an Asian Scholars' conference came back to my desk. I thought it was returned accidentally, then saw the note at the bottom in Mansbridge's graceful script. It read:

> This is an excellent report. You express yourself clearly, you say what we are doing wrong and what we are doing right, and you make compelling recommendations for the future. I don't know what you are going to do with the rest of your life, but I hope that you will one day return to publishing. I believe you are a born editor.

I closed the door to my office, laid my head on my desk, and cried.

Sam was pacing the apartment when I came home, bursting to talk with me.

"I had a long talk with Jean and Jacques this afternoon," he told me. They've done a lot of hard thinking. And they've come up with a plan."

I assumed this meant they had resigned themselves to staying in the United States at least for a year or two, which I didn't think was a dreadful alternative.

"They want to hijack a plane to Cuba," he said.

"You're not serious."

"Babe, it's not me. It's them. They've been talking about this for weeks. And now they've decided it's their only option."

"What about staying here? We could get them U.S. IDs; they could learn English, get jobs, maybe eventually go back. If they hijack a plane to Cuba, they'll never get out of Cuba."

"Forget about them staying here. They both say they'd rather be dead."

"But, Sam, a hijacking! Think how dangerous it would be! It's totally crazy."

Sam shook his head.

"That was my reaction, too, in the beginning. It's not the way those two look at it. Jean says he thinks it would be safer than a bombing. Their plan is that all they'd have to do is *threaten* the pilot to get him to change course to Cuba. They'd accomplish their mission without firing a shot. No one gets hurt. At worst, they get arrested and go to prison. They face that anyway, so what's the difference?"

I couldn't think of an answer.

"They're going to need a gun, preferably two," Sam went on, watching my face for a reaction. "I thought of these friends of Nate's and Pat's who might help. A guy named Ben Warren, about forty years old, used to be a professional stock car racer. He and his old lady, Dana Powell, are active in the Yippies. They're supposed to be very cool and have a lot of connections. I'm going to see them tonight."

The threat of being left out was enough to make up my mind.

"I'll help you," I said. "In any way I can."

* * *

I went to the Donnell Library to read up on hijackings. I remembered studying in the same green and salmon plastic-furnished room in that library on an autumn night in 1962. As I left, it had started to rain, just hard enough to make me intensely, joyously aware of the physical world. The tabloid headlines blazed from the subway newsstand: KENNEDY THREATENS NUCLEAR WAR OVER CUBAN MISSILE BUILDUP. I had felt like a young soldier that night, believing in my country, ready to die if necessary, but achingly in love with the lights of the city, the mist, the wet pedestrians huddled at bus stops. I had written a poem, probably my last, which I thought of now, poring over the *Times* index so that I could advise Jean and Jacques on hijacking a plane to Cuba. I believed in what I was doing: I thought that the two Québecois were heroes whose courage would be applauded in revolutionary Cuba. In helping them escape, I was becoming the young soldier of my imagination—though my allegiance was to a utopian ideal, not to my country.

The research excited me. Since January 1, 1969, an astounding twenty-one planes had been successfully hijacked to Cuba —an epidemic, admitted airlines officials. Only two hijacking attempts had failed. Neither of the unsuccessful hijackers had carried guns: one had a spray can wrapped in brown paper that he tried to make the pilot believe was a bomb; the other had attempted to intimidate a stewardess verbally, but she had stood up to him and eventually talked him out of going to Cuba. This last attempt was hardly worth the label "hijacking," but was a page-one story. Successful hijackings, on the other hand, received back-page coverage.

I found the explanation for this peculiar editorial judgment in a story dated March 25, 1969. Airline officials admitted that their attempts to detect would-be hijackers before boarding, to deter them with criminal prosecutions, and, most important, to persuade Havana to return them had all failed. Their only effective tool was public relations. Accordingly, they had papered the air terminals with posters announcing "AIRCRAFT HIJACKING IS A FEDERAL CRIME PUNISHABLE BY DEATH," offered a $25,000 reward to anyone providing information that would lead to a hijacking conviction, and convinced news editors to report prominently on foiled hijackings, while downplaying successful ventures. And the bluff appeared to be working: hijackings had declined slightly in March and were down further in April.

Ironically a determined hijacker now had a better chance of succeeding than ever before. Aircraft crews were under strict orders to obey immediately the commands of any armed person. Defiance of a would-be hijacker, the airlines officials feared, might lead to scuffles in aisles, hurt passengers, and expensive lawsuits by innocent injured parties. They considered it wiser to accept the detour to Cuba, with a near guarantee that the passengers would return unharmed the next day. On the basis of these reports, I concluded that Jean and Jacques could certainly get to Cuba with a gun.

Sam's affair with Pat was waning. Pat told me they had gone to bed with each other only once after the night the three of us had spent together. (Typically, Sam had never mentioned it.) Sam, she said, had been remote. "I think he's turned off by me, and I don't know why. If he'd just tell me what he doesn't like about me, I'd feel better, even if he never spoke to me afterward. But that goddamned coldness of his makes me feel like shit."

I couldn't see, actually, why she was complaining at the loss of Sam. She and Nate, now that they were past the tension created by his moving out of her apartment, were again sleeping together regularly. Besides Nate, Pat already had a new lover—Greg Rosen, Sam's closest friend. From what I could judge, Greg was crazy about her.

On Thursday, May 1, the day after I left my job for good, Sam came home from Ben Warren's with the gun.

"Where is it?" I asked. I looked about our bedroom, half-fascinated, half-fearful.

"Don't you see it?"

I shook my head.

Triumphantly Sam lifted his right pants leg, revealing a leather holster.

"I looked all over the city for a leg holster. I figured that would be safer for them than a shoulder job." He withdrew a small black object from the leather straps and placed it in my hand.

The gun was hardly larger than my palm and only a bit heavier than a toy.

"Does it work?" I asked.

In answer, Sam took it from me, pushed a button on the side, and withdrew the clip. I looked inside. Slim, pointed metal pellets were stacked neatly from top to bottom.

"You release the safety," Sam said, showing me. "That automatically cocks the gun. The clip's fully loaded. The six bullets can be fired in a couple of seconds."

I thought of the shots that had killed Martin Luther King and Robert Kennedy. I thought of a movie I had seen in which a man's brains had exploded across the screen. I thought about my pacifist friends Dave Dellinger and Mike Ferber and about the so-called Panther 21, arrested on April 2 for an alleged conspiracy to blow up department stores and the Bronx Botanical Gardens. The Panthers had campaigned for several years for their right to bear arms. They liked to quote Mao Tse-tung: "Power grows out of the barrel of a gun." Another of their slogans was: "The only good pig is a dead pig." I had chanted those slogans myself at rallies. But this was no slogan; it was real.

"I really don't see why it needs to be loaded," I said, my voice unnaturally high. "I mean, they're not going to fire it."

"Of course not. But it doesn't make sense to carry an unloaded gun."

"Where are you going to keep it?" I asked.

Sam patted his leg.

"Right here. I kind of like the way it feels."

I knew from his tone that it was useless to argue.

Theoretically Jean and Jacques could board a flight going anywhere, but a Miami-bound flight was the most practical, requiring the least rerouting and extra fuel. Three airlines went to Miami. Of those, I eliminated Eastern, which was experimenting with metal-detection devices at its passenger gates. Then I eliminated weekend flights, which were likely to be crowded. Our chief worry was a patriotic marine type among the passengers who might play hero, jumping Jean and Jacques and attempting to take away their gun. The fewer the passengers, the better the chances of avoiding the marine. But I decided against first-class seats, which might subject them to scrutiny. I narrowed the list of regular flights to Miami to three. Sam went to the airports to observe the boarding calls at each of them. He came back with the report that Atlantic Airlines' flights from La Guardia were the least crowded, the clerks the most casual about checking identification and baggage. We chose Flight 301, leaving La Guardia on Monday, May 4. I made two reservations over the telephone in the name of Peter Dufay—neutral enough to stretch over a number of different ethnic origins—and withdrew enough cash from my savings account so Jean and Jacques could pay for the tickets.

The Québecois came to our apartment on Friday night. Neil—who had been told they were leaving, but not how—came up to say good-bye. Pat and Nate came over, too, with Jenny. The seven of us told jokes, reminisced about the hair-raising incidents of the past two months, and refrained, out of respect for the straitlaced Québecois, from lighting a joint. I wondered, as I had before, if Jean and Jacques found us Americans scatterbrained and naïve—the counterpart to Pat's finding them superstraight, repressed, and narrowly ideological. But when I put the $300 for tickets and other expenses in Jean's hands, he looked as though he might cry. "How can we thank you?" he said.

"We all are fighting for the same cause," I answered earnestly.

After Neil, Pat, Nate, and Jenny had left, and the glow of self-congratulations had subsided, we held a rehearsal for Monday's performance. We arranged chairs as if they were airplane seats on either side of an aisle. Jean strapped the gun to his leg. Jacques tucked inside his pants a seven-inch hunting knife Sam had bought for him. The two men sat down, on either side of the aisle. I walked between them while Sam, in front of us, pretended to be in the cockpit. As I passed their seats, Jean practiced grabbing me from behind and sticking the (unloaded) gun in my back. He was very shy and would not use any force on me, in spite of my insisting that he practice in earnest. Jacques rose on the other side, shielding the scene from imaginary passengers. Sam and I told Jean what to say. We kept the sentences simple and rehearsed him until he was word-perfect.

We wanted to go to the airport with them on Monday, but Jean wouldn't have it. "If anything happens and they know you are with us, they arrest you, too," he said. "Forget it." We agreed that Sam and I could go in a separate cab and watch them from a safe distance.

We were at the Atlantic Airlines passenger gate on Monday as Jean and Jacques, trimly dressed in new American suits and carrying light canvas bags, presented their tickets to the clerk. Our hearts stopped a moment when the clerk looked at a seating chart. We had forgotten to warn them about picking their seats before they boarded. Would they understand? Jean pointed at the chart. The clerk nodded, marked their tickets, gave them back. Our eyes followed our two friends as they walked—nervously, we thought—across the boarding area and sat down in two laminated chairs. Jacques was pretending to read an English-language paper. Jean said a few words to him and looked around the terminal. Our eyes met. I smiled. Jean's eyes barely glimmered before he looked away. Sam's elbow was in my ribs. "Did you see that? He knows we're here."

The boarding area was only half-full, but one man, a grizzly fifty-year-old in a jovial Hawaiian shirt, worried us. Jean and Jacques eyed him too. "They'll be okay," whispered Sam. It was more a prayer than a prediction.

Our friends looked like two young sales executives on their way to do business in Miami. "Swimming pool contractors," I said to Sam. He chuckled.

At last the plane was boarding. Jean and Jacques took their place in line, a little too hurriedly. Sam and I could not manage a word as they disappeared inside the waiting jet. We stayed at the airport a long time after they were gone from view, watching until the plane had lifted off the runway.

We listened to the news that night on WBAI-FM, hoping that the listener-sponsored station wouldn't censor news of a successful hijacking. The first report was read from the AP wire.

"Atlantic Airlines Flight Number Thee-oh-one from New York to Miami has been diverted to Cuba, where it has now landed. The plane carried seventy-five passengers. It changed course about forty miles from Miami, with no word to ground controls. This is the twenty-fourth hijacking since January 1, 1969."

Sam and I hugged each other, whooped, jumped up and down, and ran to call Pat. We were so excited we told Neil, too, although we had agreed not to, and our screaming woke up Diane and Leon. "Those little bastards," Sam kept saying. "They did it. They did it."

At four o'clock that morning we lay in our bed, unable to sleep. Sam was listening to Bob Fass's all-night radio program. My attention kept wandering. Sam got up, opened the window, stared out it a few minutes, came back to bed.

"You know," he said, wrapping his arms around me, "I'm going to miss those two little fellows. I'm going to miss them like hell."

IX
Another Move

IN THE WEEKS AFTER THE QUÉBECOIS left, the weather turned warm. East Eleventh Street teemed with pushers, knife fights, acid rock blasting from transistor radios, card sharks, tactical police maneuvers, sirens, outbursts of arson, gunfire. We kept our front windows open to cool our apartment. Cries of "Up against the wall, motherfucker!"—and the Spanish equivalent—rose from the street into our bedroom. Leaking gas, released by the underground pipes Con Edison never repaired, perfumed the kitchen. Violence erupted on St. Marks Place. Formerly the refuge of flower children, it was now the battleground of speed freaks and junkies, fighting the local merchants who catered to customers from Queens, New Jersey, Brooklyn, and Westchester, lured to the East Village by the hippie myth. Several times a week the police raided the street people, arresting them for drug possession or petty theft or suspected solicitation, and the freaks (as the street people called themselves) resisted with rocks, bottles, feet, and fists. Similar scenes took place, we heard, in Cleveland, Boston, Los Angeles, Berkeley, Austin—wherever the counterculture had planted seeds.

High school students published papers celebrating pot, sexual freedom, the Tupamaro guerrillas in Uruguay, and the expropriation of American oil interests in Peru and calling for student strikes to protest "prisonlike" high school conditions. At City College, black and Puerto Rican students demanded more programs on third world interests and more control over admissions and faculty hiring, a protest that shut down the college for weeks. Black students at Cornell occupied a building, brandishing bayonets and guns before national television cameras. Fifty-six Dartmouth students went to prison for holding an anti-ROTC sit-in. Queens College closed its library after receiving three bomb threats in a single day. The faculty of Pratt went on strike against an administration plan to expel students involved in disruptions.

Even more than in the winter, the word in the spring of 1969 was "repression." The Panthers were in jail or in exile; the Chicago 8—representing a cross section of the male half of the movement—were about to go on trial. In San Francisco the Presidio 27 were court-martialed for a protest at an army base, where they had sat down together and sung "America the Beautiful." J. Edgar Hoover assigned 2,000 agents exclusively to investigate New Left groups, assembling dossiers on individuals and preparing material for possible future indictments. Assistant Attorney General Richard Kleindienst announced that when "people demonstrate in a manner to interfere with others, they should be rounded up and put in a detention camp." SDS issued a "Bust Book," explaining what to do if called before a grand jury, questioned by the FBI, or arrested at a demonstration. The authors couldn't explain how to respond when the police opened fire, as they did in May in a "People's Park" in Berkeley. A hundred were injured, one was blinded, and James Rector, nineteen, was killed—the first white youth, though not the first student, to die that year at the hands of the police.

Only the Vietnamese seemed to be winning. Their victories had forced one American President to decline to run for a second term and compelled his successor to negotiate from a position of weakness. On May 14, 1969, Nixon proposed the first phased withdrawals of troops from Vietnam, to be followed by internationally supervised elections. Three days later the North Vietnamese rejected the proposal. They would settle for no less than complete withdrawal of all U.S. troops from their country. We in the American left were awed by their courage: Look how long they've been fighting imperialism, we told each other; look how they've been decimated by artillery, land mines, napalm, crop defoliation, the destruction of their railroads, highways, harbors, the torture of their soldiers. Not only have they refused to surrender, but they're on the brink of victory. They've proved that the United States government is a paper tiger. We categorized our friends as "political" or "apolitical" depending on how seriously they took the Vietnamese as a model for their own actions.

Neil was one of the apolitical ones. He had suffered through a bad winter—first the trauma of his rejection by Pat, then near acceptance by the Army. With the help of a letter from a well-connected psychiatrist and a week alone in his apartment, tripping on acid and contemplating suicide, he managed to win a 4-F on psychological grounds. After that he announced he was moving to Berkeley, together with some musician and street-theater friends. He painted an idyllic picture of California life—organic food coops, bread baking, year-round sunshine, a hammock under every tree and a marijuana garden in every backyard. Diane, too, was leaving New York. She had resigned her teaching position at City College and convinced Leon to go to East Africa with her. She claimed that by bringing Leon to Africa, she was actually serving the revolution since the experience would politicize him and he would return to New York as a militant black. I wasn't sorry to see Diane go. We hadn't been close since the pressing needs of Jean and Jacques and Sam's affair with Pat had absorbed my attention. I looked forward to living with Sam without the tension caused by Diane and Leon's presence in the house.

When I said "we," I meant the movement. In particular I meant Sam, Pat, and Nate Yarrow. As I came to know Nathan, I often wondered at how astoundingly free he seemed—much more than Sam, Pat, or I—of middle-class values: of fear of established authority, of sexual possessiveness, of any lingering taste for luxury or even domestic stability. Pat had said as much when she talked about him, and all my observations bore out her view. Perhaps it was because Nathan's parents were so outlandishly reactionary that he had accomplished his rebellion against them at an early age and no longer felt the pull toward their world that I felt toward my parents'. He had quit college at nineteen, made his way to New York on his own, immediately found a job to support himself and joined the farthest left group on the scene. His sexual jealousy, judging from his long-term, open relationship with Pat, was minimal. Was that the result of his radicalism, or did it have more to do with the confidence that came from his physical beauty? I loved his accent, a unique combination of Tennessee drawl and the Swedish he had learned as a child. I loved the way his smiles—in response to a piece of my sarcasm or to a private joke—lit up his fine-boned, solemn face. He had large, sensual hands. Watching him take Jenny's hand to cross the street or pick her up in his arms was an erotic delight.

While Pat's affair with Sam continued, Nate and I had eyed each other with politely disguised curiosity. Pat, who couldn't help noticing our mutual interest and who must have felt some guilt at the escalation of her involvement with Sam, suggested that all four of us sleep together. I stalled for a while before saying yes. I didn't want to watch Sam and Pat make love again, not even with Nathan as a buffer. Eventually my attraction to Nate and my determination to overcome my own jealousy, which I saw as a deep character flaw, led me to say yes. One Saturday afternoon, toward the end of Jean and Jacques's stay in New York, the four of us gathered in Sam's and my bedroom. We shared two tabs of acid among us and took off our clothes. As Sam and Pat moved toward each other, Nathan smiled at me. He was very gentle with me; as we made love, I felt he was saying, "I know what you're going through. It will come out all right." Later Pat and I watched, breathless, as Sam rested his fingers on Nate's shoulders. Nate was very still. Would the two men kiss? I could not believe what I was seeing. At the next instant Sam had withdrawn his hands. But they had looked at each other with a frank, sexual affection I had never seen Sam display toward another man.

We didn't think of ourselves as libertines seeking new thrills. We were much too serious for that. For my part, I came to think of the four of us as a family. At times we seemed a single consciousness, divided randomly into four bodies, four biographies, but sharing a vision to which we had implicitly sworn loyalty. We believed that the world could be cleansed of all domination and submission, that perception itself could be purified of the division into subject and object, that power playing between nations, sexes, races, ages, between animals and humans, individuals and groups, could be brought to an end. Our revolution would create a universe in which all consciousness was cosmic, in which everyone would share the bliss we knew from acid, but untainted by fear, possessiveness, sickness, hunger, or the need for a drug to bring happiness. The left had taught us that what we learned in school, in newspapers, on television, and from political leaders was suspect. Acid had given us the idea that by merging into the cosmos, we would transcend our own deaths. We found it difficult to put our ideas into words for the benefit of those who did not start by sharing them. With each other, we needed no words. Once, I formulated my idea of revolution like this: I said I wanted to smash a hole in the wall of imperialism, through which the liberated armies of the world would march.

Thrillingly cut off from the world I had grown up in—my parents, my college friends, and now my job at Cambridge—I had never felt less alone. Since my first yearnings toward the civil rights movement, I had wanted to sacrifice myself to a cause that was larger than my own identity. Sam had stirred me into giving up some of my attachment to things, to the privileges of my white skin and middle-class background, to the idea of sexual monogamy. Now that I was not one, not two, but four people, I took it for granted that we would make some extraordinary difference to the movement. Through Nate's work at the Committee to Aid the NLF and the *Guardian*, Pat's background in NACLA, and Sam's and my involvement in the Columbia strike and in CAC, we were connected to virtually every left activist in New York. Beyond the core group of the four of us, we had dozens of friends whose thoughts were similar to ours: Greg Rosen, who was about to take over chairmanship of the Alternate U on Fourteenth Street; Robert Carpenter, whose fearlessness and mechanical inventiveness appeared endless; Ben Warren and Dana Powell, who had given Sam the gun for the hijacking, who had been active in the movement for almost a decade, and who between them knew everyone we didn't—the women's liberationists, the Yippies, the National MOBE organizers, the Cubans at the U.N., the SDS national officers. By helping Jean and Jacques escape to Cuba, we had proved what we were capable of. Now when we talked of blowing up army induction centers or the Chase Manhattan Bank, I had no doubt that we could do it and that thousands would support us, cheer us, imitate us.

Pat bought Bob Dylan's new record, *Nashville Skyline*. I listened to it entranced, at first barely able to recognize the famous voice. Instead of surreal laments about heel-clicking sword swallowers and women on Rue Morgue Avenue, Dylan now crooned, "Love is all there is/It makes the world go round," and "Throw my troubles out the door/I don't need them anymore." The sneer, the petulance, the obscurity—the traits that had drawn me to Dylan's music in high school and had become his trademark—were gone.

Sam, the most musically knowledgeable of the four of us, pronounced the record a disappointment. He knew one or two songs from every previous album of Dylan's by heart, but after two hearings he'd had enough of *Nashville Skyline*. Nathan liked the record but reported that the women at the *Guardian* considered the lyrics sexist. Pat scoffed at this; she said (and I agreed) that "Lay, Lady, Lay" was the most seductive song Dylan had ever recorded. I spent hours in Pat's apartment, playing the record over and over. I heard a message in Dylan's voice that I couldn't explain until Nathan told me about an interview Dylan had given a rock critic. The critic had asked Dylan to explain the drastic change in his voice and his music. Dylan answered something like "You don't understand. All I ever wanted to do was sing." I thought I knew what he meant. In the beginning of his career he had struggled so hard to be himself that his voice had always been strained, his lyrics contorted and difficult. Success had come to him at the same time as hardships: a motorcycle crash in which he almost died; the end of a love affair; the escalation of the war in Vietnam. Now, at twenty-eight, he was a survivor, had fallen in love again, had discovered that life could be startlingly, lyrically easy. *Nashville Skyline* distilled the spring of 1969 for me, when I had prepared myself, after returning from England, to lose Sam and found myself instead initiated into a higher love, a more intense happiness than I had thought possible.

About a week after the hijacking I paid a visit to the seedy loft on East Fourteenth Street in which *Rat Subterranean News* had its office. I thought I might interest the editors in a piece on how to hijack a plane. Slim, bearded Jeff Shero, founder and chief editor of the paper, told me to write up the piece and let him read it. "I should warn you," he added, "that we don't pay for articles. We'd like to, but we've got no money."

I explained that I lived with Sam Melville, who once worked for the *Guardian*, so that I knew about finances on radical papers. I added that since I had just quit a high-paying "straight" publishing job, I had enough money to live on. My interest was in contributing to the movement, not getting rich. Shero, who I later learned had worked for years as an SDS campus organizer, looked at me with increased interest.

"That's pretty impressive," he said. "Too many folks seem to be going in the other direction. Listen, if you really want to help out around here, we need a secretary. The chick who's had the job hardly ever comes in anymore, and she's been saying that she wants to quit. We could pay you twenty-five dollars a week—not much, but it's the same as everyone else gets."

It was obvious that the paper needed a housekeeper. Bundles of old papers were strewn about the two dusty rooms, stacks of correspondence waited to be filed, the windows hadn't been cleaned in months, and not a square inch of desk space was free of the clutter of mail, paper clips, torn Prestype, canceled stamps, pencil stubs, cigarette butts. The Swarthmore *Phoenix* had looked considerably more professional.

"I'd like to help," I said. "But I just quit my job a week ago, and I need some time to think things over. I'll write up the article and bring it around, though."

Shero pressed the point. "Come for layout night, why don't you? Every other Tuesday. I know a lot of people here would like to meet you. And you'll get a feel for how the paper works."

He was a good organizer. I left feeling flattered, looking forward to layout night and with the tiniest bit of regret that I hadn't accepted the job he had offered me. On second thought, I decided Shero's offer had been sexist: he wouldn't have asked a male in my position to be his secretary.

The longer I lived with Sam, the more clearly I saw how erratic he was. At the time I didn't seriously consider that he might be mentally ill, though in retrospect the signs were unmistakable. He alternated, as if unable to help himself, between tenderness and abrupt withdrawal. For example: his fluctuating love and hate for the *Guardian*, ending in his sudden resignation for no apparent reason. Other examples: his moody treatment of Diane and eventually Pat. Glad as I was to be the woman in his life, I was always afraid of his hostility—not so much of physical violence, although he was capable of it, as of his doing something bizarre and unpredictably dangerous, either to me or to others. Several incidents that spring heightened my apprehension.

The first was relatively minor. While I was bringing my hijacking notes up-to-date in the library, I also looked up birth announcements in newspapers published near the dates of Sam's birth and mine. I thought it was a good idea for us to have false ID; even if we never used them, having them would save us from a predicament like Jean and Jacques's. So I copied down the names of a female born within a couple of weeks of my birthday and a male born within a few weeks of Sam's, together with their parents' names and the hospitals where they were born—enough information to write to the department of records for birth certificates. I asked my friend Billie

Banks, from Cambridge, if she would receive a piece of mail for me at her address, and she agreed. I told Sam that he should find some similarly straight friend to receive "his" birth certificate. Obviously, I added, it shouldn't go to Pat's address or Nathan's any more than to our own, since as movement activists they were as likely to be under surveillance as we were. Sam nodded and thanked me. A week or two later he mentioned, rather casually, that he was looking for the birth certificate to arrive at Pat's. I stared at him in amazement. At first I thought he was joking. When I realized he wasn't, I started to yell. His face went expressionless as a stone. As on other occasions, I had an intuition that he hadn't been able to stop himself from doing what he knew he shouldn't. Dismayed as I was, in the interests of peace I let the subject drop.

The second incident occurred one hot afternoon when I was alone in the apartment. I was cooling off in the bathtub, located in Sam's workroom, when the front door opened. I looked up, expecting to see Sam. Instead, a clean-shaven stranger in a white shirt, striped tie, dark business suit, and a fedora stood staring at me. A nightmare roused itself in my brain: I felt a gun at my head, cold as if it were actually there, heard a harsh command, saw the water splash from the tub as the burglar lunged for me. The stranger took a step toward me. "Hello, babe," he said in Sam's voice.

My heart wouldn't quiet down even after I realized that the stranger was Sam, minus his mustache and the beard he'd recently grown, and wearing a businessman's disguise. What was he rehearsing for? I knew he had talked with Jean about the importance of wearing unobtrusive clothes to plant a bomb and of going to and leaving the site unrecognized. But why shave and put on business clothes in order to walk around his own neighborhood?

"We can't afford to look like hippies anymore," he told me, deadly serious. "They're not playing games out there. We've got to stop kidding ourselves. The revolution ain't tomorrow. It's now. You dig?"

I didn't, but I shrank from contradicting him. Still, my astonishment appeared to have an effect. He went into the bedroom and changed into his usual work shirt and jeans.

The third incident happened a couple of nights later. After working until midnight on my *Rat* article, I found Sam lying in bed, listening to WBAI. Bob Fass was taking calls about the turmoil at City College. The caller on the air was condemning the strike leaders as "bourgeois racist revisionists" who were into "capitalist get-aheadism" and had to be "smashed" along with other "enemies of the working-class revolution." I recognized the language as the rhetoric of the Progressive Labor Party, the more-Maoist-than-thou group currently battling the leaders of SDS for control over the radical organization.

"How long has this jerk been on the air?" I asked Sam as I crawled into bed next to him.

He made no answer. To my surprise, he was wearing his clothes under the sheet. Then he said in the darkness, "I'm going to blow up WBAI."

I stared at his face, partially visible in the moonlight. His left eye was jumping.

"Are you stoned?"

"No," he said. I didn't believe him.

"Tell me why you want to blow up WBAI."

"Because they're liberal assholes. It's time they learned that things are serious."

"But, Sam, they're the only station in New York that gives the movement any airtime at all."

"That's exactly why we need to shake them up."

"You're crazy," I said.

The words came out of me before I thought of censoring them.

"Don't you talk to me that way," Sam said, sitting up.

I cannot remember what I said then, but it must have been another mistake. Sam leaped from the bed, gripped the edges of the six-foot mirror mounted on our bedroom wall, and tore it from its brackets. For one terrifying moment, he held it over me while I covered my head with my hands. Then, coming to his senses, he relaxed and laid it gently against the wall.

Trembling, I got up and let myself out the door.

Avenue B was unusually quiet that night. I walked rapidly, not thinking of where I was going. I knew that what I had said was true: that Sam was crazy and that I was not going to be able to change him. Jean and Jacques had seen bombings as the means to a particular political end. For Sam, politics was an excuse. He was as likely to turn his violence toward me or toward Nathan or Pat or WBAI or the *Guardian* as toward the people we agreed were the enemy. He clung to the movement not because he believed its ideas, but because he needed its rationale for his insanity.

I reached the corner of Fourth Street and Avenue B, where Pat lived. I hesitated to ring the bell at 1:30 A.M. but decided to risk waking her. She buzzed me in and welcomed me at the door. While we squatted on pillows, leaning against the wall, I told her what happened. I said I had decided to leave Sam although I wanted to remain on friendly terms with him and to stay in the neighborhood, which after six months I had come to think of as home.

"Sam is sort of crazy," Pat said, "although probably not much crazier than the rest of us. You just see it more clearly in him because you live with him. Here's an idea: Danny, who lives in this building, just broke up with his wife. She's living with another guy and Danny has been going nuts. Now he's decided to take off six months and split for Europe. He's been saying he wants to sublet his place—it's a terrific apartment and only sixty-five a month—and I could put you in touch with him."

It sounded perfect. I could get away from Sam, but still remain in the neighborhood close to him and all our friends, in the same building as Pat, and walking distance from *Rat*.

"Fantastic," I said. "Give me his number. I'll call him in the morning. And tell him not to give the apartment to anyone else."

My announcement that I was going to move produced an immediate change in Sam. Suddenly he was tender and considerate, showing an interest in my ideas and my writing, even accompanying me to the grocery store and helping in the kitchen. Once while he was making the bed in the morning, he looked at me and said, "I just don't want to live apart from you." The show of vulnerability touched me, but I thought it best not to give in.

"We'll see a lot of each other when I'm living on Fourth Street," I said.

A few days before my birthday, May 20, Sam proposed that we go to the country for a week. I was taken aback. Although we had plenty of money, it was inconceivable that we would spend money on a hotel, and except for a few friends of mine near Ithaca Sam didn't much like, we knew no one who could put us up.

Sam answered that his friend Irv Schwartz, a social worker he had known since he lived in the Bronx, owned a house in New Jersey, near Port Jervis. Irv and his wife used the place only on weekends, and they had invited Sam to go there during the week.

"It's really nice," Sam went on. "Dairy country, lots of cows and meadows and very green. There's not much to do, especially without a car. But I would like it if we could just be together."

How could I say no?

Our five days in New Jersey were still and hot as summer. I felt as though I'd been let out of prison and got drunk on fresh air. I had forgotten how sunshine felt on skin when the air wasn't full of soot and smog and how food tasted cooked in a country kitchen. The smell of honeysuckle and new-mown grass wafted through the open windows. We went to sleep to the sounds of crickets and cicadas and woke up to the crowing of a rooster.

Pat had given me a bit of mescaline as a birthday present. I had enough for two, but Sam decided not to take any. "I don't seem to react well to drugs anymore," he admitted. "I don't know if it's the mood I've been in or my age or what. But I think I should lay off for a while." For Sam, this was a rare display of self-restraint.

I was pleased. "It would be more fun if you wanted to trip, too," I said. "I have a feeling that no one could have a bad time in such a beautiful place. But I'll be glad just to have you around."

The afternoon after I took the mescaline, I lay naked in a meadow, listening to the hum of insects. I imagined I was a giant crocus stirring in the breeze. Sam fanned me with a maple branch. My ears hummed. The sun warmed my legs and belly and face. I stretched in the heat, unfolding myself like petals. At one point Sam said, "Babe, there are about a million flies around you." I opened my eyes and saw an immense horde of winged creatures buzzing around my eyes, nose, mouth, feasting on my sweat. There's enough room for all of us, I thought, and closed my eyes again. I thought of trillions of insects birthing, copulating, feeding, dying, birthing. An unearthly bliss filled me; so this is the famous Om, I thought, all the insects in the world buzzing at once. The peaceful country around us was a land of fairy tales, of old women who lived in shoes and cows who jumped over the moon. I felt ageless. I felt deeply bound to Sam, joined to him by forces greater than our separate powers to choose.

It rained as we ate dinner. After we finished our chicken and rice, we sat on the porch and listened to the water beat on the roof. "Let's take off our clothes and walk outside," Sam said. We peeled off everything and stepped off the porch. I shivered in the damp cold. Once the light of the house was behind us, it was as if we were buried in black velvet. "The well is only about fifty feet away," Sam whispered. "Let's run." I held his hand and we made a dash for it. Huddling in the shelter of the well, we watched the rain fall, a curtain closing around the stage we played on. Sam's naked body was wet but miraculously warm. I hugged him hard, my skin drinking in the radiance from his.

Later in the week we talked to each other as we had not talked since our first weeks together. I told Sam how hurt I had been when he seemed to be in love with Pat. I said that he never seemed to appreciate the changes I made in my life, though he was the cause of most of them. I said that I was afraid of his irrationality and thought of moving out as a way to protect myself. He listened quietly, seeming to take in everything I said. "I think you're wonderful," he said. "I love you and admire you the more I know you. When I met you, I thought you were a cute, naïve kid. You're much more than that: I learned that in the last few months. And that article you're writing—it's great. I never even realized how much talent you had."

If he paid me those compliments simply to flatter me, I think I would have seen through them. But he meant what he said. The fear of losing me had brought him to risk telling me how he felt, and his words nourished me more than food, mescaline, or sunshine. I needed the reflection of myself Sam gave me. As long as he kept holding up that particular mirror, I could not leave him. And for all I had seen of his madness, I still thought of him as brave and strong and knowing. I felt secure with him.

By the time we left New Jersey we had agreed to take the apartment on Fourth Street together.

Our new apartment on the fifth floor of 235 East Fourth Street was sunny and relatively spacious, with an exposed brick wall that divided the living room from the eat-in kitchen and a snug bedroom in which Sam built a loft bed and a combination desk/worktable area underneath for us to share. We put up a few shelves in the living room for my portable stereo, records—Dylan, the Incredible String Band, and a modern composer, Harry Partch, Sam liked—and the few books we had acquired since moving to the Lower East Side. (I had sold my college collection of books shortly after we moved to East Eleventh Street. Hesiod and Plato no longer had much to do with my life, and Sam kept complaining about how the boxes cluttered the apartment.) We found that the heat in the bedroom rose to the height of the loft bed and practically suffocated us as we tried to sleep, so we called up an electric appliance store and ordered an air conditioner. The air conditioner was Sam's idea. It pleased me out of all proportion to its actual contribution because such indulgences weren't usual in our life together and because it seemed symbolic of our new domesticity. A few days later Sam mentioned that he had referred to me as his "wife" to a local storekeeper. I wanted nothing more than for our tranquillity together to continue.

Shortly after we moved, we acquired two puppies, the offspring of Dana and Ben's two grown dogs. Sam called the black and tan male John Keats, a name inspired by the puppy's sad, soulful eyes. I named the frisky tan female Bernadette after Bernadette Devlin, who had just delivered her maiden speech in the House of Commons, defending Northern Ireland's insurgency. I would have preferred to start with one puppy, but Sam insisted that a single animal would feel lonely with only humans for company. Bernadette learned to climb the stairs to the loft bed while John Keats would stare up at us mournfully, wagging his tail and whimpering until we carried him up to join us.

The Tuesday before *Rat* was to publish my piece, I went to help with layout. The cover story of that issue was about John Lennon and Yoko Ono, who had just been labeled dangerous aliens and refused admission to the United States but who had allowed U.S. reporters to interview them in their Montreal hotel suite. Page 2 featured letters to the editor, a price list for grass and hash sold on St. Marks Place that week, a recipe for a homemade bomb said to "yield at least one pig car in flames," and a ballad for James Rector, People's Park victim. On page 3 was a long review of Black Mountain poet Gary Snyder's *Earth House Hold*, and on page 4, my article. I was thrilled to see my first piece of writing in print, although a little annoyed when my by-line was misspelled "Albert." Actually, I had intended to tell Shero to leave my name off the piece, but in the excitement before publication I had forgotten.

Shero again offered me the secretarial job. I said that the title of "secretary" had sexist implications that I resented but that I was willing to help out in the office on an informal basis two or three days a week. Shero looked embarrassed. "We haven't been as good on women's lib stuff as we ought to be," he admitted. "If things work out, maybe you'd like to take on a couple of reporting assignments." I promised to think it over. Meanwhile, he gave me my own office key. I soon fell into the habit of going to the office at about ten or eleven each morning. Because I was the first staffer to arrive—and the only woman who showed up regularly—I ended up as the de facto secretary in spite of my initial protests. I opened the day's mail, put the subscription files in order, answered long-neglected correspondence. My sole lingering protest against sexism was my refusal to clean the office. The male staffers teased me by inventing new titles for me on the paper's masthead: Important Female, Princess. I enjoyed their attention and the relaxed, playful atmosphere of the office. Our easy rapport typified the best of the movement. I often contrasted the atmosphere at *Rat* with the tense competitiveness at Cambridge and felt glad about the change in my life.

Pat and I went to a citywide women's liberation conference at the New School. I had not been to a feminist event since the bridal fair protest before my trip to England. I was impressed by the growth of the women's movement since then and by the angry, independent spirit of the conference. Kathie Amatniek (later Sarachild), a pixieish blonde with a long background in the civil rights movement, interrupted a dispute to shout "Women unite! Women unite!" Pat fell into a conversation with Robin Morgan in which Robin told her essentially what Ellen Willis had said to me six months ago: that the left was hopelessly male-dominated, would never accept women as equal to men or pay more than lip service to women's oppression. Robin went one step farther than Ellen Willis had. Instead of asserting that women should form independent organizations, Robin thought that we should take over the left. The idea that women might kick all men out of leadership roles at *Rat*, the *Guardian*, Youth Against War and Fascism, the Communist Party, Progressive Labor, and the two new divisions of SDS—Weatherman and Revolutionary Youth Movement-2—electrified me. Rationally, I held that such a step was an extreme overreaction, even if it was possible to pull it off. Emotionally, I couldn't resist the appeal of so daring a proposal.

Among the mimeographed papers we took home from the conference was one by Ti-Grace Atkinson called "The Institution of Sexual Intercourse." Although Atkinson wrote in the pretentious language of a sociology graduate student, her thesis attracted me strongly. She claimed that sexual intercourse was not in women's interests and did not contribute to our pleasure. Instead, she argued, it was merely the most efficient means of propagating the species. With the development of extrauterine conception and incubation, sexual intercourse could no longer be said to be necessary. If it continued as an accepted practice, the only reason was that men liked it and managed to convince women that they should too. The part of Atkinson's paper that most affected me was the conclusion, in which she argued that what women liked was not vaginal penetration but being touched. This thesis closely matched my personal experience. Although I had managed with Sam to have orgasms for the first time, it was still difficult for me to reach climax through sexual intercourse; I much preferred oral or manual contact. If that was the case, then why did I need a man as a lover at all? Why was I still resistant to the idea that Pat and I could give each other sexual pleasure more intense than we each experienced with men?

As a direct result of the conference and of reading Atkinson's paper, I wanted to try making love with Pat again. Up until this time we had made love tentatively in the presence of Sam and of Sam and Nathan. I now wondered whether the men had inhibited us and if in front of them Pat and I had repressed the deep feeling we had for each other. I persuaded Pat, who appeared to share my mixture of curiosity and reluctance, that we should sleep together on the next night possible.

I told Sam what I was about to do, and though it evidently made him unhappy, he could hardly object. I went downstairs to Pat's apartment on the appointed night while she was putting Jenny to sleep. Jen sat up at the sound of my footsteps. Soon she had commanded both Pat's attention and mine. We read her stories and sang to her and allowed her out of bed twice. I think Pat and I were glad for the diversion. Jenny prolonged her last drink of water as long as she could.

In the living room Pat and I shared a bit of hash and talked and joked nervously, waiting until Jenny's breathing became regular. Once or twice Pat checked on her. We talked long past midnight, going back and forth to the refrigerator for orange juice as our throats became dry from apprehension and from our compulsive conversation.

At last, when, in spite of our efforts, silence had descended, we took off our clothes and went to bed. We made love to each other for a long time, but neither of us was able to come. It felt as though some will or drive essential to the act were missing in both of us. We were performing, not feeling.

"Let's stop, Pat," I said finally. "It's not important that we have orgasms, is it? It's what we feel for each other that counts. I love you. I love to be with you. It doesn't matter to me whether we can make each other come."

"I think we're too tired," Pat said hopefully. "It's late, and we smoked a lot of that hash."

I agreed.

Pat turned out the light. We fell asleep with our arms around each other. I felt closer than ever to her and not sorry for our experiment, but it was Sam I wanted for my lover, not Pat.

I went directly to the *Rat* office from Pat's apartment. That night was layout night again. I called Sam at about 10:00 P.M. to tell him I would be coming home in another hour. Would he pick me up at the office? I hated to walk alone in our neighborhood late at night. He sounded gruff but agreed.

I knew as soon as I saw him that he was in a blind rage. He would not stay to be introduced to Shero and the other staffers. Instead, he waited on the landing outside the office while I got ready to leave. I took his arm when we reached Fourteenth Street. He shook me off.

"What's the matter, Sam? Are you upset about my spending the night with Pat?"

"No."

"Because if you are, I can reassure you. We didn't have great sex. I doubt we'll ever do it again."

"I'm not upset. I just don't feel like talking."

We walked the next twelve blocks without speaking or touching. Once in the apartment, Sam climbed up to the loft bed, wearing all his clothes, turned his head to the wall, and went defiantly to sleep. I wept on my pillow for almost an hour, but he refused to acknowledge me.

The next day I came home from the office to find him cheerfully at work at his desk.

"What are you doing?" I asked.

He looked like a man with a delicious secret.

"I called Ben Warren this morning," he said. "I convinced him to drive me to this blasting site in midtown. There's this little green truck that carries the explosives to and from the site every day. This morning we followed the truck up as far as the Major Deegan Expressway. Look, here's the route."

He handed me a yellow pad on which he had drawn a crude street map marked with X's and arrows.

"What are you going to do with this?"

"In another day or two we'll be able to follow the truck to its destination. When we do that, we'll know the location of the supplier for the biggest blasting site in midtown Manhattan."

I knew the reason for Sam's suddenly renewed interest in bombings. Since we had moved to the Fourth Street apartment, I had grown increasingly independent of him, first by working at *Rat*, then by going to the women's conference at the New School, and finally, two nights ago, by sleeping with Pat. His impulse to follow the dynamite trucks was an attempt to reassert his authority—as at an earlier point in our living together he might have gone off to play basketball when I was expecting him home for dinner. He could no longer score points against me, as he had at first, through his knowledge of radical politics or the breadth of his sexual experience. In his frustration he had concocted this silly scheme with Ben to win my attention and boost his self-esteem. For several days I ignored his hunt for the dynamite warehouse. At last, fed up with his cloak-and-dagger clumsiness, I suggested that he look up "Explosives" in the Yellow Pages. To his amazement, he discovered three listings, one of them in the Bronx. The next day he and Ben drove up to the Bronx address of Explo, Inc., and that night Sam told me that he, Ben, and a third man, Scott Trowbridge, were going to rob the warehouse at gunpoint.

We had talked about bombings that spring at such length that Sam's intentions were not completely surprising. I did not feel shock or dismay so much as anger at being left out—especially after the contribution I had made to the hijacking and all the other ways I had proved myself. Why, after Sam, Pat, Nate, and I had been so close—had become a kind of family—was Sam insisting on taking such a risk with two relative strangers?

Sam said there was no place for women in his scheme.

"First, we've got to climb a concrete wall to get into the warehouse. Ben and I barely got over it when we cased the place last night. You wouldn't be able to make it, and neither would Pat. Second, we've got to carry a couple of hundred pounds of the stuff. Third, we've got to be fast. You're not in bad shape, but you're small and slow, and you've got no experience in this kind of thing."

"And you do?"

"I'm a man," he said, as though that answered all questions. "I've played sports all my life, and I'm not afraid to throw a punch. So has Ben. Scott I'm not so sure about, but he's providing the gun, so we've got to let him come. He seems to be really into it."

"And why don't you ask Nate?"

Sam had no good answer for that, but I figured out the reason later. The very intimacy among the four of us that had helped me to feel invincible inspired fear and resentment in Sam. Part of the excitement the new dynamite plot held for him was that it involved strangers, allowing freer reign to his fantasies. When I realized that, it seemed as useless to argue against the scheme as it did to tell him not to sleep with other women. I gave up, temporarily, resigning myself to being an observer of Sam's adventure.

The three men fixed Sunday, July 6, as the night they would rob the dynamite warehouse. For three days Sam practiced push-ups and weight lifting, clumped around in ankle weights, and took no nourishment except high-calorie health drinks of tiger's milk and brewer's yeast. He copied all the phone numbers of his friends and acquaintances into a new notebook, writing them in alphabetically reverse order and omitting last names. His phony birth certificate, made out to David McCurdy, had arrived at Pat's. He told Pat and Greg Rosen—but not me—that from now on he was to be addressed as David. But he appeared to forget his instruction the day after he had given it.

Ben and Scott were supposed to meet at our apartment at nine o'clock that Sunday. At seven, just as Sam and I came back from walking the dogs, Dana arrived with Ben. Apparently they had been quarreling for most of the day. They had come on Dana's insistence; she glared at Ben frequently to make sure he said what she wanted. The problem, according to Dana, was that the men hadn't bothered to disguise their faces and they hadn't decided what to do if the elderly night watchman woke up—except to shoot him, an idea Dana pronounced macho and absurd.

Dana was exactly Sam's age. She had married at twenty, while still a college student at a midwestern university. In 1961 she and her husband, a political science Ph.D. named Dick Powell, visited Cuba, a point from which Dana dated her revolutionary consciousness. Together she and Dick became prominent figures in the New Left, contributing articles to the theoretical journals, becoming friends with Tom Hayden, Rennie Davis, Carl Oglesby, and other leaders, appearing at all the important SDS conferences. Their child, Max (named after Max Weber), was weaned on demonstrations and radical meetings. In 1967 Dana drifted into the countercultural wing of the movement while Dick took a more traditional leftist line. They split up at the time of the Columbia strike, Dick going abroad, while Dana began an affair with Ben, a former math teacher/construction worker/stock car racer a few years older than she. Max, then nine, spent an unhappy year with his mother and her new lover before he moved in with Dick's parents, who lived in a sumptuous East Side apartment and enrolled Max in an expensive private school.

As Dana and Dick Powell had been known for their theoretical contributions to the left, Dana Powell and Ben Warren were notorious for the bizarre Yippie-style protests at which they were frequently arrested. "Women always tell me," Dana bragged to me once, "that I'm their example of a liberated woman. If you totally understand what the movement's about, you don't need women's liberation." I had already seen enough of her troubled relationship with Ben, his sadistic streak and her dependence on him, to doubt her claim. But she was forceful, smart, and articulate. At thirty-two she hadn't settled for an easy life; a courageous intelligence could be seen in her hazel eyes and the determined line of her mouth. I felt comforted by the interest she was taking in the proposed robbery; she seemed to possess more common sense and maturity than either Sam or Ben.

I supported Dana's argument to postpone the robbery another forty-eight hours, giving the men time to improve their disguises and to rehearse a plan for handling the night watchman. Eventually they decided to bring a length of stout rope with them and to tie the watchman loosely to his chair. Sam was convinced that the guard would not resist if he knew his life was threatened. I agreed that sounded reasonable. By this time I was hoping for no more than that the men wouldn't get caught.

On Tuesday the three men and Dana assembled at our apartment. Dana was more subdued than she had been on Sunday. I guessed that she and Ben had been fighting again. Ben had something of the punch-drunk boxer about him, his short, muscular frame tensed as if for a fight, an uneasy belligerence in his boyish face. Scott was the least likely-looking member of the group. The youngest of the three by some ten years, he had been trained as a pacifist, still worked as a draft counselor (an activity many radicals now regarded as reformist and slightly contemptible), and was studying kundalini yoga with an Indian guru. He said almost nothing, while Sam went about checking the gun, rope, and ski masks that were serving as disguises, and Ben told sexist jokes. Dana asked if she could stay with me until the men returned. I gratefully accepted the suggestion.

They left at eleven. Dana chain-smoked Kools. "I've been arrested three times," she said, "but I'm still a coward. I'm glad they didn't want us to come along—even if it was for sexist reasons. Guns terrify me. Ben thinks he knows all about them because he was in the Army in Korea. He doesn't know shit. Oh, more than I do, but not enough to mess around like this. I just hope they'll all come back alive. You're lucky to be as young as you are—you're probably not half as scared as I am."

I liked being assigned the role of the young, fearless radical; it helped me from feeling intimidated by Dana's age and sophistication. We talked of other subjects: her visit to Cuba, the SDS split, Pat and Nate Yarrow, whom Dana had known for nearly five years. Midnight came, then one o'clock. Dana got up every five minutes to look for Ben's car.

They burst into the house at one-twenty. I didn't know how frightened I was until the first sound at the door, when Dana and I instinctively grabbed each other's hands. Sam, then Ben, then Scott entered the kitchen in triumph. I tried to look calm, to smile. Without looking at Dana, I knew she was doing the same. Sam deposited two large boxes on the kitchen floor. Ben and Scott put down one each.

"Jesus, did you have to bring that stuff here?" Dana demanded. My heart went out to her. Her voice was pure challenge, but I knew her heart knocked against her rib cage as fiercely as mine.

Ben put his arms around her.

"Where else should we have taken it, silly?" he asked. "I don't suppose you wanted it at our house."

"No, but it's not fair to Sam and Jane to have to live with it."

Scott sank into a chair. His face was white, and his knees were shaking so hard I thought he might knock the chair over.

"We're going to have a meeting on Saturday and decide where to put the stuff," Sam said. "In the meantime, I guess it can stay here."

Dana stared at me.

"Is that okay with you, Jane? This is your apartment, too."

I hadn't thought ahead to this moment. It hadn't been real until now, when four boxes of explosives lay on the kitchen floor.

I didn't like being so close to it, but what else was to be done? Scott was obviously not going to take it, Dana didn't want it, and we couldn't ask anyone else—certainly not Pat or Nathan, whom Sam had excluded from all his plans.

"I guess it can stay here till Saturday," I said.

"I've got to get home," Scott said. His teeth were actually chattering, though in the July heat Bernadette and John Keats were lying next to the window panting for air.

"We've got to go," said Ben, playfully lifting Dana out of her chair.

After the three of them had left, Sam turned to me with a radiant smile. "We did it, babe," he said. "We've got a hundred fifty sticks of dynamite and fifty blasting caps. It went just like we planned; once the night watchman saw our gun, there wasn't a peep of protest out of him."

"You didn't hurt him?"

Sam snorted. "We tied him up so loose he's probably out of the ropes by now."

My breath came out in a long, quavering sigh. I told Sam I was proud of him. Then my glance fell again on the four boxes, each of them marked in large black letters "DANGER—EXPLOSIVES." "Where are we going to hide this stuff?"

"In the refrigerator," Sam answered promptly. "It's the only safe place in this heat."

He opened the refrigerator, tossed a container of cottage cheese, some leftover salad, and a quart of yogurt into the garbage and slid the four boxes inside.

"Can I look inside the boxes?" I asked.

"Sure."

Gingerly I lifted the cover of the top box. Inside, like layers of candy in a Whitman's sampler, lay paper-wrapped sticks of dynamite. On each stick was printed "NITRO-GLYCERINE—HIGHLY INFLAMMABLE" and, in finer type, the name of the manufacturer and technical specifications. How much damage could this dynamite do? Was it enough to blow up our building? Would it level the whole block? Two blocks? Half the city? I thought about the bombs dropped on Vietnam and, in the past month, on Cambodia. I thought about Jean and Jacques and the seventeen Black Panthers who had or had not planned to blow up the Bronx Botanical Gardens. I thought about WBAI and the instructions for a Molotov cocktail in *Rat*: "Yields at least one pig car in flames."

"Let's go to bed," said Sam. He was jollier than he had been in weeks.

We smoked half a joint and made love. Was it our first sex since I slept with Pat? Certainly it was the most tender and passionate in a long time. Sam had been invigorated by his success. He kissed me good-night and dropped off to sleep. I closed my eyes, but too many thoughts were speeding through my brain. As dawn came through the window, I saw the outlines of buildings along the East River beginning to come clear beyond the gutted tenements and smokestacks. Our refrigerator was full of dynamite, neat as the tubular chimes of an orchestra, waiting to be struck. How had I gotten here? What was the point after which I couldn't turn back? I would have given a great deal to know.

X
To the Quicksand

THE MORNING AFTER THE ROBBERY I woke up ill. My eyes burned with fever. Lifting my head was an effort. I was so dizzy I almost fell climbing down from the loft bed. In the kitchen I automatically put on water for coffee, then turned it off. I was too nauseated to eat breakfast, and besides, the idea of opening the refrigerator terrified me. What if a sudden rush of warm air caused the dynamite to explode, the way a soufflé could fall if you opened the oven too soon? I abandoned the kitchen for the safety of the living room, where I lay down on the daybed. The India print spread was covered with dog hair and made me sneeze, but I pulled it over my head anyway. The center of my body pulsed heat like a giant furnace, but my skin sprouted goose bumps from cold.

Sam woke up after me. He followed me into the living room, leaned down, and peered at me under the spread. "What's wrong with you?" he demanded. I didn't know then that the dynamite was making me ill. In the same way I had convinced myself that sexual possessiveness was reactionary, I was now trying to overcome my scruples against bombings, which I was convinced were a residue of the same bourgeois upbringing. I was afraid to seem cowardly: I didn't want Sam or anyone else to accuse me of timidity or conservatism, and I didn't want to be excluded from Sam's plans for the future. The anxiety I couldn't express turned itself on my body. I had come down with the flu as a result, and without speculating about the reasons, I simply told Sam I was sick.

I needed, at the very least, to be able to talk frankly to someone about what I felt, and part of what troubled me as I lay ill on the couch was the necessity of keeping the robbery a secret. For before Scott, Ben, and Dana had left our apartment, we had agreed that no one except the five of us should know we had the dynamite, at least until we had a meeting to discuss what we would do with it. Scott had wanted to amend the agreement so that he could tell Frank Weiner, a close friend who had provided Scott with the gun the men had used for the robbery. This request sounded reasonable, and everyone had approved it. I was aching, myself, to tell Pat, my best friend, but since I had no good reason for involving her—besides my emotional needs, which didn't count—I accepted the burden of silence. To my shock, on Friday afternoon, Sam told me that he had not only let Pat in on the secret but had given her permission to repeat it to Nate.

"But how could you do that after your promise?" I asked. I was so stunned and hurt that I nearly forgot I was sick, sitting bolt upright until the throbbing in my head persuaded me to lie down again.

Sam shrugged. The secrecy I had accepted as a necessary part of group discipline meant nothing to him. A few days later I found out he had also bragged about his exploits to Greg Rosen and Robert Carpenter. He seemed unable to understand that each time he enlarged the circle he increased the likelihood that we all would be informed on, regardless of how trustworthy each individual he told might be. Within a week of the robbery three men had carried out, eleven people had, in one way or another, been invited into a conspiracy. The lack of self-control and disregard of collective principle that Sam exhibited that week ought to have served as a warning to the rest of us, but no one yet took his mistakes seriously.

As soon as Pat learned that we had the "stuff"—as we almost always called the dynamite, in spite of efforts to come up with a more imaginative name—she wanted to come to Saturday's meeting. I would have liked her to come, too, but Dana and Ben rejected the proposal. The problem was that Scott had already invited Frank Weiner and Frank's fiancée, Heidi Marks, neither of whom knew Pat and Nate. I chafed at joining forces with two strangers while my closest friends were left out. Weiner, an economics professor who was also an official in a prominent antiwar organization, and Heidi Marks, an administrative assistant with no movement credentials except her engagement to Frank, were, as far as I could tell, upwardly mobile liberals who wanted to keep their middle-class respectability along with their pretensions to revolution. I considered their intention to marry reason enough to exclude them. No one else took my side, and I was forced to give in to the majority. And so, through Scott, Sam had entangled our lives with two people, Frank and Heidi, who felt no commitment yet either to us or to our ideas, while Pat and Nate, with whom we had forged the most intimate of bonds last spring, were to be shut out.

I recovered from my flu—or whatever it was that ailed me—by Saturday night's meeting, which took place in our apartment. There I met Frank and Heidi for the first time and formed an immediately unfavorable impression. Weiner was verbose in the style of a man who loved, above all else, to hear himself talk, and in Heidi he had a devoted, uncritical listener. I quickly—perhaps too quickly—raised the subject of expanding the group to include Pat and Nate. Weiner was opposed to enlarging the group any further, and Dana and Ben supported him. Sam, who had created the problem first by excluding our friends from the robbery and then by telling them it had taken place, paid no attention to the group discussion. He leaned against the living-room wall, which was as far as he could remove himself from the cluster of people around the couch. Scott was his mirror image, sitting against the opposite wall, concentrating on flexing and unflexing his knees and ankles. The other five of us were soon mired in a fruitless debate, as abstract as if four boxes of dynamite and blasting caps were not sitting in our refrigerator, inches away from Scott's head.

In the heat of an intimacy that was ideological as well as emotional and sexual, Nate, Pat, Sam, and I had often discussed the morality, the effectiveness, and the precedents for terrorism, with the idea that someday soon the four of us would become a functioning political cell. We had spoken of physical destruction aimed at the enemy as the only course left for revolutionaries. We had speculated whether or not others in the movement would follow the example of a few and how we could communicate our ideas and intentions to political sympathizers. We had discussed targets: army induction centers, major corporations in the interest of which the war in Vietnam was fought, the Pentagon. I had become convinced then that bombings, aimed at property rather than people and accompanied by clearly written communiqués that we would send to the press, were the necessary next step in the evolution of our movement. And I had no doubt that the love the four of us felt for one another was enough to sustain us through whatever dangers we would face—which we fully believed might include capture and life imprisonment.

After all that emotional preparation, it was frustrating in the extreme to be compelled to start all over again with strangers. In this group, paradoxically, the combination of our unfamiliarity with one another and the presence of the dynamite itself made candor impossible. No one wanted to admit that with explosives already in our possession, we were having second thoughts about using them. No one wanted to be the first in the group to look like a coward. We seven ordinary movement people, indistinguishable in our ideas, behavior, and ability from thousands of others across the country, were suddenly, by virtue of a harebrained robbery, a vanguard. Not one of us was capable of handling this new power; not one of us was brave enough to back away from it.

Except perhaps Ben, who proved to be a most ingenious and aggressive procrastinator. On the night of the robbery Sam had told me that Ben had a case of cold feet just as the three men approached the night watchman's station. He had argued so persuasively for turning back that Scott was on the verge of agreeing. Only after Sam showed that he was ready to go ahead without the others did Ben give up his objections and follow. Now, before my eyes, Ben gave a demonstration of exactly what Sam had complained of. When his turn came to talk, he said he had been thinking all week about the robbery, and though he himself could hardly wait to go ahead with an "action," he believed it would be objectively racist (a favorite movement expression) for us to carry out a bombing without first consulting the leadership of the Black Panther Party. While everyone else thought this was, on principle, an idiotic proposal, Dana offered a suggestion no one could refuse. Next week she and Ben were going to attend the Panthers' United Front Against Fascism conference in Oakland, where they would stay with friends who were close to the Panthers' California leadership. If they believed that our group should go ahead with plans to use the dynamite, we could take that as an okay from the Panthers themselves.

It took us the entire evening to decide whether or not we were going to consult with the Panthers in some fashion, and since we still had made no plans, it wasn't even clear what we were going to consult with the Panthers about. Not only had we failed to discuss methods of operation, security, or goals, but we hadn't even settled an urgent practical matter: what to do with the four boxes of dynamite, which now had been in our refrigerator nearly a week. Finally, as the meeting broke up, Scott agreed to help Sam look for a cheap apartment in the neighborhood where the explosives could be stored safely. I was uneasy about settling a crucial question so offhandedly, but it was better than leaving the dynamite in the kitchen indefinitely. And willing as I was to be part of a bombing, I wasn't entirely sorry that we were postponing a definite action for at least a few weeks.

On Monday morning Sam and Scott found a tenement apartment on East Second Street available for less than $60 a month in rent. Since the only false ID they had was the David McCurdy birth certificate Sam had ordered sent to Pat's address, they used that name on the apartment lease. I wasn't pleased at this news, but I was delighted that the boxes of nitroglycerine and blasting caps would no longer be in our kitchen. From the day they were moved, Sam regarded daily trips to the storehouse apartment as his primary responsibility. He claimed that if he didn't spend at least a few hours each day at "McCurdy's place," the landlord would grow suspicious. Since Scott, Frank, and Ben all lived in other parts of town and had jobs, they couldn't share the routine checks with Sam. Nate, however, had just quit the *Guardian* and lived only a block from the McCurdy place. Within a week after renting the apartment, Sam gave Nate a spare set of keys. They agreed to visit the apartment on alternate days, checking to ensure that the explosives were intact—and that the building hadn't come under police surveillance. And so Nate, excluded from the robbery, was quickly elevated by Sam into an active conspirator, although he was never to attend a meeting with the others.

Meanwhile, I made plans to attend the Panthers' Oakland conference with Dana and Ben, their friends, and a few other *Rat* staffers. I was flattered at Dana's eagerness to have me along and excited about seeing California for the first time and attending my first movement conference without Sam. But after the flight over the Rockies and the thrill of visiting Tom Hayden's house with Dana (a highlight of which was a personal letter from Robert Kennedy that Hayden had framed on his wall), the conference was a letdown. We dutifully sat through endless panel discussions on "fascism"—by which the Panthers meant the very real repression of the Black

Panther Party—choruses of "Power to the people" and "Off the pig," and a screening of a badly damaged print of *Z*. I stayed with a few of Dana and Ben's friends in a tiny apartment on Polk Street in San Francisco, where I passed most of one evening in conversation with George Demmerle, a thirty-eight-year-old founder of the group known as the Crazies. Demmerle, who liked to call himself Prince Crazy, used to show up at demonstrations in a purple cape and plumed helmet. I had always considered him fatuous, but in San Francisco I saw his serious side. He earnestly tried to convince me to help him drop chemicals in manholes in New York's financial district in order to blow out the supply of electricity to major Wall Street corporations. Under his silly helmet, his face looked like worn-out rubber. I sympathized with his destructive urges, but I thought his plan was ludicrous.

When Mary Jo Kopechne drowned at Chappaquiddick on the second day of the conference, most of the people around me, if they cared at all, felt she got what she deserved for having worked with the establishment. That was also the weekend American astronauts prepared to walk on the moon, an accomplishment greeted at the conference with choruses of boos. In the auditorium, members of the Revolutionary Youth Movement (later Weatherman) faction of SDS picked out members of a rival faction for the Panthers to drag into the street and beat up. Onstage, black revolutionaries called for community control of the police, a program white radicals were unwilling to advocate in white neighborhoods. Action, almost any action that would give the appearance of bringing down the state, was what we longed for. At moments I caught Dana's eye or Ben's and felt that we shared a magical secret: the dynamite. What white radical at this conference would not have envied us if they knew? It was inconceivable that either the Panthers or Dana and Ben's friends would deny their blessing to our plans, and of course, they didn't.

Saturday, July 26, was the sixteenth anniversary of Fidel Castro's raid on the Moncada barracks—a risky adventure that ended in failure but helped inspire a revolution. We thought of a ragged band of guerrillas hiding out in the Sierra Maestra, ready to die if necessary to save their country from imperialism. We wanted to play the same role in the United States: to be the vanguard of a movement that would topple the government, even if we ourselves did not live to see it happen. Sam and I were eating breakfast in the kitchen on Fourth Street when he asked me how I was planning to observe the day.

"What do you have in mind?" I asked.

"I was thinking of leaving a bomb at the United Fruit warehouse."

Every movement activist knew what United Fruit was: a major investor in Batista's Cuba, now forced out but still heavily involved in the Latin American economy. Pat's kitchen walls were studded with decals from United Fruit's Chiquita bananas, revealing the range of United Fruit's holdings: Panama, Nicaragua, Guatemala, the Dominican Republic, an empire extending a thousand miles south of the U.S. border. Sam's proposal made perfect theoretical sense, but I wondered if we were ready, after only one meeting of the group, to carry out a bombing.

"The warehouse is on a pier on the Hudson, near the bottom of Manhattan," Sam went on. "I've passed it lots of times; it says 'United Fruit' in mile-high letters across the top. The last couple of days I've been checking it out. It's completely deserted after six o'clock at night. We could stroll over there after dinner, leave the stuff on the pier, and be home before we ran into anyone."

"What about the group? Shouldn't we talk to them?"

Sam shrugged. "Let's just ask Pat to come along."

That was what I had wanted from the beginning. If Pat came, I didn't care whether our official group approved the action or not In fact, I would have been happy if the group had dissolved and left Nate and Pat and Sam and me to deal with the dynamite ourselves.

The three of us met in Pat's apartment about eight o'clock that night. Sam had assembled two bombs from dynamite, blasting caps, and wind-up alarm clocks an hour earlier at Second Street and put them in capacious vinyl pocketbooks. Pat and I took turns carrying one. Sam took the other. As Sam had promised, the area around the warehouse was deserted and our target itself was plain since the owners, in what we thought of as proud ignorance, had blazed their corporate name across the top. At the street end of the dock we stopped and listened: no sound but the river lapping against pilings, no sign of human presence.

Sam took Pat's pocketbook and crept along the pier next to the warehouse. Pat and I kept our eyes on the street. A car exited from the West Side Highway a few blocks up and came toward us. Pat and I held our breaths, but the car passed without stopping. We heard a sudden noise in back of the warehouse. I grabbed Pat's arm. Then Sam's face appeared on the other side of the building. Empty-handed, he hurried toward us.

"I heard something inside the warehouse at the last minute," he muttered. "So I had to leave the stuff outside, on the dock. Give me the other one."

I resisted. "That's enough, Sam, let's leave while we can."

"No, no, it's cool. I just panicked for a minute, I don't know why. Give me the bag."

I handed it to Sam, and he hurried away. In seconds he was back. "Let's go," he said. His voice was tense. After five or six more blocks, when it was clear that no one had followed us, we relaxed and began to recount our separate versions of the event. It had been astonishingly easy. We could hardly wait for the news reports.

We listened to the radio until late that night but heard no accounts of the bombing. In the morning I combed the *Times* and the *News* for an announcement. Nothing. Perhaps the bomb hadn't gone off. Sam suspected that the water might have absorbed all the impact of the blast. I thought that the police might have deliberately covered up the news. On Sunday afternoon we decided to call WBAI-FM and offer our item as a news tip.

We were afraid to use our home phone in case the FBI had tapped the WBAI telephone and could trace the origins of an incoming call. Sam dialed from a pay phone, and spoke through a handkerchief into the receiver. "The United Fruit Company warehouse," he said, "was blasted by a bomb at midnight, in celebration of Cuban Independence Day. If you have any doubts, you can verify this information with the police."

Later Sunday evening we heard the announcement on WBAI's news program. The announcer reported our "anonymous tip" about the bombing and went on to explain that the pier, though owned by United Fruit, was leased to a tugboat company. The bomb had blown a large hole in the pier and wrecked the door to the warehouse, but inside, thirty tons of peat moss had absorbed the explosion.

"We ought to have checked who was using the warehouse," I said, embarrassed at our carelessness. "And we should have realized that an action on July twenty-sixth wasn't going to be reported until July twenty-seventh. Besides, I think we got the name wrong: the Cubans don't call it Independence Day."

Sam wasn't as bothered by verbal inaccuracies as he was by the fact that the bomb did minimal damage.

"I used up forty sticks of dynamite on that job," he mourned. "That's one-quarter of what we've got. It was stupid to leave the stuff outside the warehouse door."

Still, it was a beginning. I looked forward to congratulations at the next group meeting.

Frank, Heidi, Scott, Ben, and Dana were furious with us. Scott was disturbed that he had learned the news first by hearing the announcement on WBAI. Dana was irritated that we had used the phrase "Cuban Independence Day." "It sounds right-wing," she complained and, using the *Fidelista* word for the exiles, added, "People will think *gusanos* did it." I suspected she was right. Frank announced that revealing the existence of the dynamite to strangers had been Sam's first transgression, carrying out the action at United Fruit his second, and if there was a third, he was leaving the group.

At least everyone agreed that a brief notice of the United Fruit bombing could appear in the next issue of *Rat*. I volunteered to write this up, pretending (for the benefit of the *Rat* staff) that I knew of the action only because of the WBAI report. Then Dana and Ben, true to form, asked if we could postpone any important decisions for at least two weeks. This time their excuse was the Woodstock Festival scheduled for August 15–17. Their group, the Crazies, expected to run a booth at the festival and Dana and Ben were up to their ears in plans. Until Woodstock was over, they would be too busy to think of anything else.

At *Rat* I was beginning to get regular writing assignments. I covered a protest at the Electric Circus, wrote about two junior high school girls who had been suspended for refusing to salute the flag, and did a long piece on contraception and abortion for which I interviewed a number of feminists, including Robin Morgan and leaders of the abortion law repeal movement. The more deeply my work drew me into the movement, the more resentful Sam seemed to become.

I had not been surprised when, shortly after ending his affair with

Pat, he began sleeping with my friend from Cambridge, Billie Banks. I realized Billie had a crush on Sam one evening when the three of us had dinner at the Eleventh Street apartment and Billie had become so tongue-tied that she couldn't answer a simple question. Sam took her home, and when he came back home later, I assumed they had slept together. A week or so afterward he tried to coax her into sleeping with both of us, but she refused. I figured then the affair was over until one afternoon early in August, when I came home to find Sam and Billie in bed.

I tried to act casual, but I'm sure I bristled with hostility. I knew Sam had bullied my friend into sleeping with him in our apartment. He sat next to her, his hand on her head in what I took as a pretense of tenderness. "Hello, babe," he said to me. "Billie was just getting ready to go." I refused to leave the room, so Billie had to dress in front of me. She put on her clothes and left without a word.

The next morning Sam looked up from his breakfast coffee, stared me in the face, and said, "I want to break up." A chasm opened in my stomach.

"Why, Sam?" I asked.

"It's just over, that's all," he said. His voice was icy. I bit my lips to keep myself from reacting, knowing that a tearful scene was what he wanted.

"If you want to go, then go," I said. "I'm not holding you here." I was afraid he was going to argue over his right to the apartment, but he said nothing. He packed his clothes and a few books in a duffel bag, which he dragged into the living room.

"Mind if I leave these here for a couple of days?" he asked. "It'll take me awhile to find a place of my own." I shrugged.

For the next three days I alternated between rage, grief, and an eerie calm in which I felt nothing at all. Pat tried to convince me that I needed to go to bed with someone else. I let her give my phone number to a friend of hers named Steve, but when Steve called, I pleaded an excuse. Preparations for Woodstock were keeping me busy, I told him. Would he get back to me after the festival? I knew it would be weeks before I could face a strange man and talk of any subject but Sam.

On the third morning after Sam left me, he called. "It's Sam," he said, as if nothing had happened. I heard a woman burble in the background.

"Where are you?" I asked.

"I'm at Billie's. She says to tell you hello." He paused. I said nothing. "I thought I'd come home for breakfast—that is, if you're going to be there."

"I'm on my way to *Rat*," I answered. I was surprised, after the turmoil of the past seventy-two hours, at how sane I sounded. "I can wait a few minutes. But you'd better hurry."

Billie's West Village apartment was a twenty-minute walk from East Fourth Street. Sam was at the door in ten minutes. I fixed coffee and waited to hear what he had to say. He studied his coffee cup. "Your friend Billie's nice," he said after a while. "But she can get pretty boring." It was as much of an apology as I was going to get. That afternoon Sam unpacked his bags. We went on almost as if the three days hadn't happened. I wonder now, looking back, if Sam's sudden departure was an early sign of the madness that seized him periodically. What happened over the next few days confirmed that something was seriously wrong.

The night before I was leaving for Woodstock with Dana and Ben, Nate and Pat, and Jenny, Sam said he wanted to come too. He had shown no interest in the festival until then, and I thought he had been looking forward to a weekend alone. I accepted his about-face as an effort at reconciliation.

Dana and Ben picked us up in the morning in Ben's ancient station wagon. We were six adults, one child, and two dogs, plus sleeping bags and cooking gear, but after a pipeful of hash and a few cold beers none of us minded the crowd. We didn't mind, that is, until we were within ten miles of the festival grounds, stalled in traffic for over three hours, unable to sing Jenny to sleep—and it started to rain.

All around us, people were abandoning their cars and walking to the festival grounds. Sam and I decided to try our luck. I had a map of the grounds that showed where the movement booths and sleeping areas were located. We told our friends we would meet them at "movement city" and took off on foot, using extra copies of *Rat* to protect our heads from the drizzle.

It was nearly midnight before we found movement city. Under a large circus tent, every square foot of space was occupied by bodies, most sleeping, some talking, some shushing others who were trying to talk. Along a hundred-yard stretch of meadow next to the public tent, people had set up private tents, many large enough to hold entire families. Sam and I walked up and down the meadow, looking for a group that had room for us. Cold and soaking wet, I squeezed back into the public tent and curled up on a corner of a stranger's air mattress. By dawn I had managed about an hour of sleep. Sam, who suffered from claustrophobia, wandered in the rain all night.

We found out in daylight that movement city was more than a half mile away and on the other side of a hill from the concert stage. While the fans were packed in stoned delight in front of the mammoth Woodstock stage, straining their necks for a glimpse of the rock stars, cheering lustily at music so distorted by the public address system that the cheapest home stereo sounded better, over at movement city the Crazies were talking to the Yippies, the Meher Babaists were talking to the yogis, and a few curious onlookers were trampling unread leaflets in the mud. I roamed back and forth, wishing I had brought a book, while Sam fell into conversation with George Demmerle, who was manning the Crazies' booth.

When I found someone at the concert who was driving back to New York that evening and had room in his car, I ran to tell Sam. Still deep in conversation with George, he asked me if the driver had room for all three of us. George said at once that he didn't want to leave. "But, man, you're exhausted," Sam protested. "Let someone else take care of this booth."

George shook his head. "I don't mind, really I don't," he said. "Have a good trip."

"That George." Sam chuckled as we trudged to the parking lot to meet our benefactor. "He really is crazy. I offered to spell him at the booth, but he wouldn't let me. He said only bona fide Crazies ought to work the official booth. All he's doing is selling buttons, but he really takes it seriously."

"That's because he's old," I said. "He wants to be a twenty-year-old freak, but he's still got all these straight ideas in his head. If he'd stop trying so hard, he'd have a lot more fun."

Sam said nothing. Too late, I realized I had offended him. I had forgotten that he was closer to George's age than to mine.

Pat's friend Steve called to remind me that I had promised him a date after Woodstock. My impulse was to turn him down. My second thought was to accept. Sam and I were getting along well again, but I hadn't gotten over my anger at him for the three days with Billie. Pat's advice was probably sound: it would do me good to go out with someone else. And Sam had been telling me for months that I ought to be more independent of him; perhaps he'd be pleased if I made a date with someone else. Steve and I settled on Wednesday night, the twentieth. He agreed to call me at the *Rat* office before meeting me there at eight o'clock.

Alone at *Rat* that evening, I began to regret my decision. I pictured Steve as someone who would try to wrestle me into bed and would see every no as an invitation to further pursuit. Whatever problems Sam and I had with each other, I could not imagine feeling a strong sexual attraction to anyone but him. When Steve called, I told him I had changed my mind. I worked in the office for another forty-five minutes; I didn't want to seem to be rushing back to Sam as if expecting a reward for my fidelity.

I came home to find Sam in the loft bed, listening to the radio. He started when he saw me.

"I thought you had a date," he said as I climbed up to join him.

"I changed my mind."

"Why?" he asked.

"Because I'd rather be with you," I said, and lay down next to him.

He did not respond. I sat up and looked at him.

"What's wrong, Sam?"

"I planted a bomb this afternoon."

"You what?"

"I planted a bomb."

His voice was not tearful or anxious or threatening. He avoided our usual euphemisms; not a word about "action" or "stuff." He appeared calm.

"Where did you plant the bomb?"

"At the Marine Midland Bank."

I had never heard of Marine Midland. We had not discussed it as a possible target at a meeting, nor was it part of the litany of leftist enemies, the way Chase Manhattan and Dow Chemical were. I didn't understand what Sam was telling me.

"Why Marine Midland?"

"No particular reason. I just walked around Wall Street until I found a likely-looking place. It's one of those big new skyscrapers, millions of dollars of glass and steel, some fucking phony sculpture in the front. You just look at the building and the people going in and out of it, and you know."

"What time did you set the bomb for?"

At last, he showed reluctance before answering.

"Eleven o'clock," he said.

I knew that Sam was impulsive, at times uncontrollable. I had often suspected he was crazy. But I wasn't prepared to hear that a bomb he had placed in a randomly selected office building was going to explode in the next two hours.

"Sam, you never even cased that building. Do you know what the Wall Street area is like at eleven o'clock on a weeknight? People work there until after midnight. Cleaning women, file clerks, key-punch operators. Did you make a warning call or anything?"

He shifted away from me.

"Sam, we've got a little over an hour. Please, let's call the building and warn them."

"It won't do any good," he muttered. But he reached for his shirt.

As we walked up the street to the pay phone, I insisted that Sam allow me to make the call. He stood next to me as I dialed the building number for Marine Midland, 140 Broadway.

I took the wrong tone with the night guard who answered the phone. Instead of threatening him, as he would have expected a bomber to do, I pleaded. He answered me as if I had begged him to fix my washing machine first thing in the morning. "I'd like to help you, lady, really I would," he said. "But I don't leave this post until midnight when I make rounds."

"But the bomb's going to go off at eleven," I said. "You can leave your post for an emergency, can't you?"

"I see your point," he agreed, under duress. "I'll do what I can."

We heard the news at a little after eleven.

"An explosion has ripped through the eighth floor of the Marine Midland Bank building in lower Manhattan, blowing out windows, wrecking furniture, and littering the corner of Broadway and Nassau Streets with flying glass, concrete, and plaster. About a hundred fifty employees were working in the building at the time of the blast. At the present time we have no word on the number or extent of the injuries."

I couldn't look Sam in the eye. We stayed riveted to the radio most of the night and soon knew the worst of the news: twenty employees, mostly female clerks, were taken for emergency treatment to Beekman-Downtown Hospital. All were released within a few hours, more frightened than physically injured.

To Sam, I vented my rage at the night watchman, calling him a sexist bastard for not responding to a warning call from a woman. But I knew the fault was Sam's, not the night watchman's. The uncontrollable temper that had led me nearly to leave him in May had erupted again. His behavior had nothing to do with the ideology we supposedly shared. He had given no thought to what Marine Midland meant to the left or to the general public, nor had he thought of how he might explain his action to our group, to the press, or if necessary in the courts. Because I had threatened to abandon him, even for one night, by sleeping with another man, he had taken revenge on a skyscraperful of people.

In retrospect I have to ask myself why, after seeing so many demonstrations of Sam's imbalance, culminating in the Marine Midland bombing, I didn't decide to leave him—or at the very least why I didn't adamantly refuse to have anything more to do with his bombings. One answer is that I still believed that bombings could serve a useful political purpose, and having put so much effort into making them work, I wasn't going to back down because of someone else's mistakes. It must also be true—although I don't completely understand how—that Sam was a kind of lightning rod for my own craziness: I was attracted to bombings out of a deep irrational rage, not unlike Sam's own; but I was too inhibited to carry out my fantasies, and I let Sam act them out for me. A third reason is pure competitiveness. Seeing Sam fail inspired me to take over and do it better. Most of the tasks associated with the bombings were extremely simple and required less coordination than preparing a dinner party. Rather than leave the stolen dynamite in Sam's less-than-competent care, from then on I placed myself at the head of the conspiracy and prodded everyone else into action under my direction.

Besides these personal motivations, the continuing involvement of the United States in the Vietnam War remained the essential condition for all our bombings. Nixon, since taking office in January 1969, had reneged on virtually every promise he made in the campaign. He had produced no "secret plan" for peace; he had widened rather than called a halt to the air war; and instead of withdrawing troops, he had instituted the paper-shuffling tactic of lowering troop ceilings. Photographs of children on fire from American napalm and adults shot down in cold blood by American soldiers had become part of the steady diet of news programs and part of our political assumptions as well. While public opinion polls showed that a majority of Americans opposed the war, reports of atrocities multiplied—all of them officially denied by the administration. We in the radical left believed we were facing a situation similar to that which had prevailed in Nazi Germany. If we could only manage to interfere materially with the work of the U.S. Army, we believed we would have widespread support, and the destruction we caused would be its own justification.

To Dana, Ben, Frank, and Heidi I argued on the day after the bombing that if they abandoned Sam now, they would be violating the principle of collective responsibility no less than Sam himself had. As revolutionaries we were pledged to take care of one another. That was what we meant when we called each other "brothers and sisters" or framed on our walls the famous quote from Che Guevara: "The true revolutionary is guided by great feelings of love." For the six of us (seven, including Scott), our first meeting after the robbery had sealed our commitment. To desert Sam when he was obviously in emotional trouble would be, in my eyes, pure, selfish cowardice. "Look at the conduct of the whole group first, before you lay all the blame on Sam," I told them.

And I was amazed to see the effect of my argument on the others. Dana's sympathy surprised me least. She was loving and generous, and as I had seen the night of the robbery, her difficulties with Ben were similar to mine with Sam. Ben followed her lead. "I've got to admit that the rest of us have been fuck-ups," he said. "We got so involved in Woodstock we forgot about calling another meeting. To tell you the truth, Sam's got a right to be fed up with us."

Heidi, showing compassion I hadn't suspected, simply asked me how I thought Sam could be helped. I answered that if everyone in the group now shouldered the responsibility we had agreed to take on in July and if we actually carried out an action as a collective, I believed that he would calm down.

Heidi said that made sense to her and turned to Frank for approval. Frank had news of his own. Since our last meeting he had seen Rap Brown. He lowered his voice as he said the name, a sign of deference perhaps related to speculation that the former SNCC leader was not going to show up for his scheduled trial on riot-conspiracy charges in Baltimore. Rap Brown had one of the toughest images in the black movement. He wasn't an esoteric intellectual like Stokely Carmichael or a life prisoner like Huey Newton, and he spoke so dismissively of "whitey" that I was surprised to learn he was on friendly terms with any white radicals—especially a poseur like Frank. Yet he had told Frank of his plans to assemble a secret militia which would attend a two-week "training session" on a midwestern farm in September. Rap was interested in recruiting white men with special skills for the group, and Frank had recommended Sam. I knew Sam would be flattered at the invitation, and I had some hope that Rap's political astuteness would act as a brake on Sam's impetuosity.

Pat was less concerned about Marine Midland than were the other four I spoke to on the day after the bombing. Since she learned about the bank in the same casual way that she had been told about the robbery and invited to join the United Fruit bombing, she didn't see how it was different. She was sure that NACLA maintained a file on Marine Midland. A few hours after I spoke to her she was able to tell me that the office building Sam had bombed was a bank controlled by W. R. Grace, a major corporation that owned land, railroads, sugar plantations, and shipping companies throughout Latin America. I was cheered by her news, but not by her explanation of how she learned it. Instead of going to the NACLA office herself, she had called a friend and asked her to look up the file on Marine Midland. The friend not only was a regular NACLA worker but also contributed to *Rat* and was sure to have figured out the reason for Pat's request—one more movement person who knew more about the bombings than should have.

I tried to find Scott, but he was never home. A new girl friend was apparently taking up most of his time. I guessed from his obvious discomfort at the last few meetings that he was on the verge of leaving the group anyway. When the seven of us finally met at Sam's and my apartment, Scott confirmed my impression. "I just can't handle this group anymore," he said. I suggested that we might be able to make changes in the group that would meet his objections. Dana murmured that I should leave him alone. Scott got up and left, and for a few minutes the rest of us stared unhappily at the bit of floor that had been his accustomed seat. I had come to like Scott, and I took his departure as a personal failure. I wished he had explained his feelings. Perhaps none of us could handle what was happening, and Scott alone was independent enough to admit it.

A burst of activity followed his departure. The six of us worked until late at night on a letter explaining the Marine Midland bombing, to be sent to the *Guardian, Rat,* and Liberation News Service, the wire service for the underground press. The letter began, "The explosive device set off at the Marine Midland Grace Trust Company on the night of August 20th was an act of political sabotage," and went on to state that we made a warning call that had been ignored. I volunteered to type three copies of the finished letter on a public typewriter, to slide one copy under the door of the *Rat* office and to mail the other two to the *Guardian* and the LNS. Before the meeting broke up, I insisted that we not allow another month to elapse before we met again. No more excuses: if we were going to carry out a collective action, we needed to plan and execute it while our determination was fresh. Our final deadline should be the week Sam left for Rap's training session. If we couldn't do anything in the month remaining, we should admit our failure and decide instead how we wanted to dispose of the dynamite.

While the establishment press denounced in huge headlines the accidental injuries at Marine Midland and called for the immediate apprehension of the bombers, I had the impression that the left approved of our action and that our communiqué explaining the warning call went a long way toward allaying objections. I was especially gratified by the reaction of *Rat* editor Jeff Shero when he slit open the envelope containing our typed communiqué. "Far fucking out!" he yelled after his eyes had passed over the first half of the page. "Hey, folks, listen to this." He read out loud the words I had helped to type the night before, his evident excitement reassuring me that we had support. I made a point of hanging around every staffer who read the letter that day. If anyone showed disinterest or disapproval, I questioned him closely to find out why.

The leftists from whom I expected the most sympathy were the Weathermen, the hundred or so SDS activists, including Bernardine Dohrn and Mark Rudd, who had split from the rest of the organization in June and were now trying to organize a militant demonstration in Chicago, October 8–11. Unlike most national groups, the Weathermen did not see themselves as a mass organization. Instead, they hoped to appeal to a small but significant number of white working-class youth and inspire them with a revolutionary ideology. To this end they ran across beaches carrying NLF flags and beating up anyone who got in their way; they broke into schools, barricaded classrooms, and lectured students on imperialism; they provoked scuffles with police at hamburger joints, shopping centers, and other places where working-class teenagers would notice. They attracted few followers but a great deal of publicity and some grudging admiration from the rest of the movement. By the end of the summer most of them had been arrested, some on felony charges carrrying high bail. I thought they were masochistic and mostly wrong, but far from dumb. In mid-September two of them, Jeff Jones and Phoebe Hirsch, came to the *Rat* office to persuade their old friend Jeff Shero to run a pro-Weatherman piece in *Rat*.

When I joined the conversation, Jones and Hirsch had been trying for some time to explain the reasons behind the Weathermen's anti-monogamy line. It was obvious that their position annoyed Shero, although his soft southern drawl never rose above conversational level. "I just wouldn't expect this kind of attitude from the two of you," he told Jones and Hirsch. "You've been together for years, and that's a good thing. What do you stand to gain from breaking up your relationship?"

The two Weathermen defended their view in terms I recognized easily from my long talks with Sam, Nate, and Pat. They said that the desire to have exclusive rights to another person's body came from the same source as wanting to own property. It wasn't easy to give up the longing, but it was a necessary part of becoming a revolutionary. I couldn't help breaking into the conversation to hint at my own experiences as a militant, and a sexual radical, so apparently similar to theirs. Soon Shero withdrew from the dialogue, leaning back in his swivel chair and watching us in that quiet way of his that absorbed more than he let on. Later he wrote a piece critical of the Weathermen, and I realized that I had probably talked too carelessly and eagerly to people I didn't know.

On September 18, at three o'clock, as Nixon was delivering a speech at the United Nations meant to explain how his B-52 raids on Vietnam, Laos, and Cambodia were contributing to peace, Heidi, Frank, Ben, Dana, Sam, and I met at the Fourth Street apartment. In the presence of all of us Sam assembled a bomb from a Westclox wind-up alarm clock, a blasting cap, and fifteen sticks of dynamite he'd brought over earlier from the McCurdy apartment. (He was still the only member of the group who could assemble a bomb with any degree of skill and confidence.) He placed the device in a large purse I had stolen from a midtown department store. Carefully

I slid the strap over my right shoulder. The other five wished me luck. I felt very solemn, acutely conscious that I might never come back home. I saluted them and left.

I stopped at Pat's second-floor apartment. Because Frank continued to insist that he would not meet anyone else Sam and I knew, she couldn't join the group upstairs. "I'm on my way," I said as she opened the door.

Her eyes widened. "Do you want me to go with you?"

"No," I said. "It's all been worked out, and this is safest. I'll see you when I get back." I kissed her, holding the purse away from us.

I boarded a bus headed downtown. I was wearing a white A-line dress, kid gloves (to avoid leaving fingerprints), and a touch of makeup. I looked as if I were going to a business lunch or a matinee. I felt as I imagined I would on my wedding day, if I ever married. A kind of agitation coursed through my body, heightening all my faculties. I cushioned my purse on my lap, protecting it from the bus's sudden jolts. I noticed the large, calloused hands of a Puerto Rican woman opposite me, the dirty toenails of a sandaled teenager next to me. I was absolutely happy and, in spite of my racing pulse, felt very calm, as when the first rush of an acid trip subsides.

I got off at Foley Square and walked to 26 Federal Plaza. The Federal Building, some sixty stories of tinted glass and steel, dominated the landscape at the foot of Foley Square. Sam and I had sat outside the building every night for the past week, watching until the last light went out on the thirty-ninth and fortieth floors. Near quitting time on this Thursday afternoon, the lobby bustled with civil servants, secretaries, messengers, clerks, maintenance men and women. Tonight at 2:00 A.M., when the bomb exploded, the halls would be dark and deserted, the people who worked here safe in their beds—or so we hoped. I found the right bank of elevators and rode up to the fortieth floor, occupied entirely by the Department of the Army.

The fortieth floor, as I had determined from a previous trip, had two possible locations for placing the bomb. One was a broom closet; the other, a somewhat larger room holding electrical equipment. I walked purposefully toward the broom closet. As I was about to open the door, a woman came out of an office around the corner. I answered her gaze with a sheepish smile and turned back toward the elevator. The woman kept going and disappeared into the next office.

I could not now return to the broom closet. If the woman saw me loitering there again, she might call a guard. I thought the electrical room a poorer choice because there were fewer objects to hide the purse behind, but it would have to do. I made sure no one was around before I opened the door. I found a space for the purse behind a bulky piece of machinery, pushed the straps out of sight, and closed the door behind me as I left. I rode the elevator down to the lobby alone and emerged again into the swirling crowd. A guard stared at me as I went out the glass doors. Had he noticed that I came in with a pocketbook and left without one? I turned my head to avoid giving him a good look at my face.

This was to be the group's first wholly collective action. Once I had volunteered to place the bomb, Ben had promised to write the communiqué, Heidi to type it, and Dana to mail copies to the major newspapers and radio and television stations. At 1:00 A.M. on September 19 we reassembled on the roof of the building where Frank and Heidi lived. Frank had a small telescope which he focused on 26 Federal Plaza. It was easy to spot; although the lights on most floors were extinguished, the central building lights stayed on. At the top of the skyscraper, far above the surrounding buildings, an airplane beacon winked.

At a few minutes before two, all the lights in the building went out.

"Holy shit," Ben whispered.

"Did you see that?" asked someone else. I was too awed to speak.

In a moment everyone was talking at once. I don't know what the other five were feeling, but at that moment my joy was undiluted. I had shown Sam that he didn't have to act alone; I had caused real injury to the work of the U.S. Army; and I had, perhaps, brought revolution an inch or two closer. An hour later the radio news confirmed our success. The explosion had been massive but had injured no one. For a few hours that night I wanted no more happiness.

The next morning when I was walking the dogs and buying the newspapers, Sam took a telephone call from the new tenants at the Eleventh Street apartment. Two FBI agents had just come to their door, asking for Sam and me. When the young couple said they didn't know where we were, the agents replied, "If you happen to run into them, ask them to get in touch with us." They gave the couple their calling cards and left.

Sam panicked. He wanted to call the FBI immediately and insist that the agents explain their business with us. I said that was too dangerous to consider: the fear that would inevitably betray itself in our voices would arouse more suspicion; one question would lead to another; any lies would be held against us. Surely the call had nothing to do with our current activities, or why would the agents have gone to a six-month-old address? They must be following a tip from Canada. The Mountie in the Montreal hotel who had taken our names and addresses when we were still living on Eleventh Street must have forwarded his report to the FBI. Eventually the FBI would track down our current address (they only had to ask telephone information for my number), and when they did, we could ask a movement lawyer to represent us. Until then we had nothing to worry about.

Sam couldn't understand my reasoning. In his view, either the FBI was after us and would soon have us, or they weren't after us and we were safe. The notion that they might have only a few pieces of the puzzle, and that it was within our power to figure out what those pieces were, was beyond him. But because he was afraid of the agents, he really didn't want to talk to them, and he was glad to have an excuse not to return their call.

On Wednesday the following week the New York police descended on the *Rat* office, armed with search warrants. I knew they were at *Rat* when I was still a block away: their patrol cars, with lights flashing, were parked two deep outside the office, blocking traffic all the way to both corners. Dope raids and pornography busts were frequent occurrences at other underground papers, so I didn't leap to conclusions. I called the office from a pay phone on the corner. George Tama, an assistant editor, answered.

"I see you have a few visitors," I said.

He sounded nervous.

"They're looking for that letter about Marine Midland. I told them that we always throw out the copy after the issues are printed, but they don't want to believe me."

I felt sorry for George. Shero had left New York on Monday for an extended leave of absence during which he hoped to finish a book about poor whites in the South. He had persuaded two friends of his from the Chicago *Seed,* Abe Peck and Paul Simon, and Gary Thiher of the Austin *Rag* to help run *Rat* in his absence, but George, as the senior permanent member of the *Rat* staff, was to be nominally in charge. A dreamy-eyed composer of anguished prose, he wasn't up to coping with much pressure, and to be hit with a police raid two days after Shero's departure must have sent him reeling.

I walked to Gramercy Park and stopped in a doughnut shop for a second cup of breakfast coffee before finally circling back to *Rat*. The police cars were gone, but I called the office to make certain. Gary Thiher answered and assured me that I had missed all the morning's excitement.

Gary, Paul, and Abe had all arrived ahead of me. George, more relaxed now than he had sounded on the phone, was eager to tell me about the exploits the other three had already heard. "They searched the office up and down for the Marine Midland letter," he boasted. "But all the time I had the latest letter—the one about the Federal Building bombing—right here in my pocket. I was sure they were going to body-search me, but they never did."

"Did they find anything at all?" I asked.

"They got the copy for that announcement we ran about United Fruit. Was it you who typed that?"

"I don't remember. Did you tell them that?"

"No. I told them I didn't know who typed it. Then they asked me who opened the mail the day the Marine Midland letter came."

The scene flashed in front of my eyes: Shero opening the Marine Midland letter, shouting "Far fucking out!," handing it to George.

"What did you tell them?"

"I said I didn't know."

"You didn't give them any names at all?" I pressed.

"Well, yeah. They asked me who usually opened the mail in the morning. I said you did."

If I told him he was an idiot, he would know how scared I was. I let my face say it for me.

"I guess I shouldn't have done that," he said, shuffling papers on Shero's desk.

"Hey, George, you did all right," said Gary. "It's just too bad you had to handle them by yourself."

I supposed Gary was right; George had been in a jam, and he didn't think he was giving away important information. After all, my name was on the masthead. Still, I was worried about the trail of clues: Sam's aborted trip to Canada; the David McCurdy birth certificate sent to Pat's address, then used to rent the Second Street apartment; Pat's slip with the NACLA worker; the loose way in which many of us in the group talked about bombings with others; the United Fruit copy, which I had typed myself, left around the *Rat* office, now in the hands of the police. They would have us soon if we didn't change course.

Fortunately Sam was leaving that very night for a two-week training session on a North Dakota farm with Rap Brown. When he came home, he would have to make plans to leave New York.

After Sam's departure I went to see Hank DiSuvero, a movement lawyer who had represented Dana and Ben on a half dozen minor cases. Hank was young, thin, nervous, and very gentle. After he gave me a little encouragement, I poured out the whole story of Jean and Jacques, including the trips to Montreal, the failed attempts to get false IDs, the gun, and the hijacking. With a bit of prodding, I probably would have confessed the bombings to him, too, but his raised eyebrows at the hijacking told me he'd heard enough.

"It's possible that they've got information about your Canadian friends," Hank said. "But it's just as likely that they're investigating you for the counterinaugural last January. Your friends Dana and Ben are likely to be indicted for that, and you and Sam are close enough to them to arouse suspicion."

I told Hank that sounded too good to be true. He laughed.

"Why don't you let me call these agents on your behalf?" he said. "I'll just tell them that I'm representing you and try to find out what they're after. If it's something like the counterinaugural, you may want to talk to them to get them off your tail. Otherwise, I'll let you know."

A couple of days later Hank called me at home.

"The agents want to question you and Sam about a matter involving a foreign government," he said. "They don't believe you're directly involved. They think you have information about some foreigners who are. I told them you don't wish to talk with them. Is that all right?"

I said that was fine.

"I don't think they'll bother you again, now that they have a record of your attorney," he went on. "But if you find them at your door, just refer them to me."

Immediately after hanging up, I memorized Hank's phone number. When Sam came back from North Dakota, I would see that he did the same.

On October 8, while Sam was still away, Nate Yarrow planned and carried out, virtually unaided, the bombing of the Whitehall Induction Center.

Whitehall was the place where every draft-eligible male in the borough of Manhattan reported for his army physical and where, if he was drafted, he was inducted into the Army. The target of demonstrations since the beginning of the antiwar movement, it had enormous symbolic importance for all of us who were opposed to the Vietnam War. Whitehall was also of material importance to the Army: the selective service records of thousands of draft-eligible men were filed in its vaults. If those were destroyed, selective service would fall far behind schedule and might never fill its quota of inductees.

But our group realized early that sneaking a bomb into Whitehall was not like what we had done at United Fruit, Marine Midland, and the Federal Building. At Whitehall, two guards stood twenty-four-hour watch at the main doors, checking the briefcases and parcels of everyone who entered. Other security personnel were posted in the hallways. The building crawled with military officers, presumably experts at detecting hidden weapons or explosives. We agreed it would be splendid to blow the place up, but who would take the risk of going inside with a bomb?

Early in October Nate told me he had devised a way. "I guess you should tell your group what I'm planning to do," he said, "so that you don't have the sort of hassle you got into after the United Fruit action." He told Ben and Dana his idea. I said to Frank and Heidi that a close friend, a member of what we sometimes called "the other group" and someone who had shared responsibility for the McCurdy place from the beginning, was planning to use several sticks of dynamite for an action I wouldn't specify. Not surprisingly, Frank and Heidi approved. I'm sure they were pleased at the idea that the "stuff" was disappearing quickly without their having to take responsibility for it.

I had come to know Nate as a curiously dual personality. For weeks on end he would be remote, distracted, almost impossible to engage in conversation. Without warning the solemnity would vanish and the funny, playful Nate would emerge. During the weeks he thought out and executed the Whitehall maneuver, only his serious side was evident. The night of October 8, when his task was accomplished, he appeared at our door in a different mood. He wore his most radiant smile, and instead of a greeting, he giggled. In the kitchen he pulled a crumpled note out of the pocket of his fatigue jacket. It said:

"Tonight we bombed the Whitehall Induction Center. This action was in support of the NLF, legalized marijuana, love, Cuba, legalized abortion, and all the American revolutionaries and GIs who are winning the war against the Pentagon. Nixon, surrender now!"

It wasn't the sort of note I would have written. It made no attempt to persuade the uncommitted or even to explain to the committed. It was simply Nate's declaration of beliefs—brief, direct, unapologetic.

"Do you want me to type this for you?" I asked.

He shook his head.

"I already did that. And mailed it out."

"You brought it just to show me?"

He nodded and laughed again. I laughed with him. Still smiling, but as abruptly as he had entered, he turned around and left.

That night the Whitehall Induction Center was virtually leveled. There were no injuries, and the joy of the movement was palpable everywhere we went.

Sam came home late the following night. He was pale, anxious, and disheveled. Roberto, a young Puerto Rican Harry Belafonte look-alike, was with him and even more agitated. They dropped on the couch and looked around furtively, as though FBI agents were hiding behind the bookshelves. I asked Roberto if he wanted to spend the night on the couch.

"I can't, man. My wife is expecting me. She must be a nervous wreck, we're hours and hours late."

"Where have you been?"

The two men looked at each other.

"Everywhere," said Sam. "Three different cities in one day. Minneapolis, Chicago, and . . . where was the last place?"

"Milwaukee, I think," said Roberto.

Sam dropped his voice to a whisper.

"We were planting bombs," he said.

I kept my mouth shut. Roberto glanced at me and decided to leave at once.

"I got to get uptown," he said. "Brother, man, I'll be seeing you."

They clasped each other around the back and hit a few hard slaps on each other's shoulders. I could imagine the tension that had made them feel so close to each other after only a brief acquaintance. Sam rarely showed such affection to anyone who knew him well. Roberto turned to shake my hand. I hugged him and silently hoped he would never come back.

The next morning I got up before Sam and walked the dogs. Sam awoke while I was out and decided to buy bread and cream cheese for breakfast. On his way upstairs, when he reached the fifth-floor landing, he ran into two FBI agents at our door. He quickly replaced his keys in his pocket.

The agents, seeing he was about to ring our doorbell, produced their calling cards.

"We're looking for Sam Melville," said one of them. "Does he live here?"

Sam pretended to be puzzled. "Sam Melville? I think he used to live with a woman in this apartment. But he moved out some time ago."

"Can you tell us where he lives now?"

"No. I don't know. I was just going to visit the woman who lives here."

"That's Jane Alpert, right?"

Sam nodded.

"And your name is . . . ?"

"David McCurdy," said Sam.

I told Frank and Heidi and Dana and Ben that Sam had to leave town again at once. The agents had certainly realized that he was lying, and that was sufficient grounds to arrest him whenever they pleased. The rest of us had a few more weeks, perhaps, but Sam had to go.

Dana proposed a temporary solution. An old friend of hers, a Puerto Rican radical named Bobo Lopez whom she had known since her 1961 trip to Cuba, was in New York. In a couple of days he was leaving to visit friends in New Mexico, Colorado, and California. She trusted Bobo like a brother and saw no danger in telling him the whole story. If he agreed to take Sam west with him, that would solve the immediate problem. Meanwhile, we could think about a long-range remedy.

Sam agreed. Bobo agreed. Sam said the long-range problem was already solved. Rap Brown's militia was holding another session on the North Dakota farm in mid-November. Before that took place, Sam would ask the people who lived on the farm if he and I could spend the winter with them. It might be a bit bleak, but we'd be safe from pursuit and we'd have a few months just to be quiet, to walk in the woods, and to think.

"Sure," I said. I was living from moment to moment like a visitor in a hospital waiting room. As long as Sam left town at once, I was willing to say yes to anything.

When Bobo understood the extent of the danger, he speeded up his departure plans. The two of them flew to Albuquerque together on October 13.

The movement churned with preparations for another mass demonstration, this one in Washington, called by National Mobilization Against the War for November 15.

Pat, Nate, and I, exhilarated by our recent successes at the Federal Building and the Whitehall Induction Center, decided to do our part. We picked out the headquarters of three corporations with close links to the war effort, Chase Manhattan, Standard Oil, and General Motors, and set Monday, November 10, as the target date to plant bombs at all three.

Frank was apoplectic. "Don't you understand that this demonstration is the most important effort anyone is making to end the war?" he bellowed at a meeting—at which, naturally, Pat and Nate were not present since Frank still refused to meet them. "And you're going to ruin it with this foolishness?"

I wanted to know why, if bombings were foolishness, Frank had joined the group in the first place.

"In July, okay. In August, okay. But not the week of what might be the biggest antiwar demonstration in history!"

I was on the verge of reminding him that he'd also opted out of acitvity in July and August. To my surprise, Ben took his side.

"I admit I was wrong last July when I wanted to check things out with the Panthers," he said beguilingly. "That was probably a cover for my own cowardliness. But this time I think Frank is right. We shouldn't do anything that's going to interfere with MOBE's plans. Why don't we wait until December?"

Heidi sided with Frank. Dana equivocated. I shrugged. I had never liked this group of six anyway. I was perfectly content to ignore them and work with Pat and Nate. We set another meeting for a week away, but I had no expectation we would come to an agreement.

Sam called. Bobo had left him about three or four days into their trip. For a while he had stayed at a commune in New Mexico, but that hadn't worked out. He'd hitchhiked to another commune where he was given shelter for a night. Since then he'd been sleeping in the desert. He was cold and had run out of money. Would I wire him some money to buy some warm clothes? We had $500 left of our savings, which I'd been planning to use for our trip to North Dakota. I sent him $100, hoping that would keep him warm and safe until he could go to North Dakota.

If I'd had a moment to reflect that fall, I might have realized how thoroughly angry and upset I was with Sam. When I had first learned from him of the Marine Midland bombing, I had acted to protect him and to hold the group together. At the end of another two months it was not clear why I had bothered. The most successful and effective bombing, at the Whitehall Induction Center, Sam had nothing to do with. His bombings in the Midwest with Roberto were hastily executed failures. The bomb in the Chicago Civic Center had been discovered by police before it exploded, presumably yielding clues to the identities of the bombers. He had exposed the name under which our dynamite storehouse apartment was rented. Now he had shown himself an incompetent even at hiding out. Inevitably he would soon be back in New York, continuing to endanger the rest of us.

Perhaps I should have locked him out of the apartment. Or perhaps I should have let him in, since by rights the place was half his, and moved out myself. When I think back on that time, it seems to me that I must have still loved him, in spite of his failures. His mistakes may have made him even more appealing to me than he was earlier in our relationship, when I saw him as all-knowing and powerful. And beyond my attachment to him, the very danger we were in exerted its own hypnotic effect. It appeared to me that the bombings had made us the toast of the movement and the talk of all New York. Our identities were the subject of speculation wherever radicals gathered. Weighed in the balance against the fear of arrest was the anticipated thrill that we would soon be openly celebrated as heroes. If I raged at Sam for inviting our capture, I also—subconsciously—may have needed him to ensure that it would happen. For all those reasons, when he called for a second time and announced he was coming home, I didn't object.

On the very day after he returned, Sam talked to George Demmerle. As Sam reluctantly admitted to me, he gave Demmerle a full, detailed account of all the bombings. He told him where and how he obtained the dynamite, which buildings in New York, Chicago, and Milwaukee he had placed bombs in, how many sticks of dynamite he had used in each bombing, even the fact that he was involved in several different groups simultaneously. He had concealed nothing except the names of the other people in the groups. He was proud of having kept this information secret since George had pumped him for it.

"He asked me if you were involved, and I said no," Sam told me. "He asked about Dana and Ben, and I said they weren't either."

"Who else?" I asked.

"I can't remember. Oh, yeah. He asked about Pat."

"And you said no?"

The answer came after a brief pause.

"I said she was just a courier."

I couldn't react. Since Sam's encounter on the stairs with the FBI, I had been numb to reports of his lapses. Pat was bewildered, but not nearly as angry as she had a right to be. Nate was enraged. None of us liked or respected Demmerle, but Nate believed he was actually an undercover agent. When Sam asked his opinion of George, Nate had said so. Still, Pat, Nate, and I decided we would go ahead with our simultaneous bombings. I can't think why, unless my two friends were motivated by the same subconscious wish for capture that seems to have affected me.

Monday afternoon, November 10. Pat, Nate, and I met in the McCurdy apartment. It was my first time in the place, which looked like an arsenal. In plain view were a rifle, two submachine guns, an automatic pistol, boxes of batteries and wires and ammunition, stacks of military instruction manuals, dismantled alarm clocks and watches. Nearly all the gear was Sam's, collected piece by piece since early summer. I felt I was looking at the inside of my lover's brain. What had all the afternoons he'd spent here done to his mind, surrounded by a virtual munitions plant?

Nate, who had become something of an explosives expert himself in the weeks he guarded the apartment alone, assembled the bombs, while Pat and I watched. I felt grateful for his expertise. Although I believed in what we were doing, I was still afraid to attempt to wire dynamite to a blasting cap connected to an alarm clock. I had practiced the simple technique several times, but never with live explosives. I couldn't help picturing the stuff blowing up in my face as soon as I touched a wire to it.

We changed into clothes we'd stored in the apartment a few days earlier. I left first, then Pat, then Nate. We left our bombs as agreed, set to go off at 2:00 A.M. I went home and wrote a press release:

> During this week of antiwar protests, we set off explosives in the offices of Chase Manhattan, Standard Oil, and General Motors.
>
> The Vietnam War is only the most obvious evidence of the way this country's power destroys people. The giant corporations of America have now spread themselves all over the world, forcing entire foreign economies into total dependence on American money and goods.
>
> Spiro Agnew may be a household word, but it is the rarely seen men, like David Rockefeller of Chase Manhattan, James Roche of General Motors and Michael Haider of Standard Oil, who run the system behind the scenes.
>
> The empire is breaking down as peoples all over the globe are rising up to challenge its power. From the inside, black people have been fighting a revolution for years. And finally, from the heart of the empire, white Americans too are striking blows for liberation.

Wearing gloves, I typed the letter on a machine at the McBurney Y, and mailed eight copies—to the three daily papers, UPI, AP, LNS, the *Guardian,* and *Rat*—at the boxes on Thirty-fourth Street, outside the Central Post Office.

Later we were to learn that undercover agents, dressed as derelicts, were lounging on the steps of the McCurdy apartment and had the three of us under surveillance as we went in and out. Why they didn't arrest us on the spot, I cannot imagine.

Monday night, November 10. Sam said the bomb squad was watching us. I asked how he could tell. He said a white Mercury sedan had been parked outside our building all day. Two agent types were sitting inside. They took turns spelling each other, going out for coffee, stretching their legs. But the car didn't move.

I looked out the window. I saw the car and the man at the wheel. He might have been from the bomb squad. Or he could have been a salesman waiting for a customer, a mobster waiting for his partner, or a narc setting up a drug bust.

"I'll close out the savings account tomorrow," I said. "How soon can you leave for North Dakota?"

"Thursday, I guess. On Wednesday night, I'm supposed to do an action with Demmerle."

"Maybe you should skip that."

"No, it's cool. I'll leave on Thursday."

Tuesday, November 11. The bombings of Chase Manhattan, General Motors, and Standard Oil overwhelmed almost all other city news. As we had planned, the bombs exploded on vacant floors. At Chase Manhattan, a clerk had paid attention to our warning call and evacuated the building. Warning calls to GM and Standard Oil were ignored, but the only suffering was endured by some fifty middle-aged couples dancing in the Rainbow Room forty-five stories above the Standard Oil offices; they were unhurt, but they did have to walk from the roof of the RCA Building to the street level after the explosion knocked out elevator service. Property damage was calculated in the millions. All over the city, switchboards lit up with warning calls—most of them, police insisted, made by practical jokers who wanted a day off from work, although we were convinced that many callers were politically motivated.

At night Ben and Dana came over. Ben had had another of his changes of heart. He was so excited by the news reports of the bombings that he finally realized I was right and Frank was wrong. He'd been a sellout, a shmuck, a coward—but now he was ready to atone. Would Sam help him carry out a bombing?

The white sedan was still outside the apartment. Sam was meeting Demmerle tomorrow night to bomb a couple of army trucks. Thursday morning he was leaving the city for good. But he said yes. At eight in the morning he would meet Ben at the McCurdy apartment. Together they would leave bombs in the Criminal Courts Building, where the Panther 21 trial was proceeding. Ben said he had figured out the whole plan; Sam only had to be there.

Wednesday, November 12. Sam left to meet Ben at the Second Street storehouse. I stopped at Pat's on my way to the *Rat* office. She didn't answer the doorbell, so I let myself in with the key. Pat was awake but still in bed. Her eyes were clouded with depression, and she did not stir as I came into the room. She was usually busy getting Jenny's breakfast at this hour, but Jenny was in Chicago spending a week with her father.

"You look like you want to be alone," I said.

"No, I want to talk to you. But you have to promise not to be too angry with me."

"What happened?"

"I had a terrible fight with Nathan. The worst ever. And I did something awful."

The fight arose because Pat had made a date with Bobo—the Puerto Rican radical who was now back in town—for this evening. Nate didn't want her to keep it. Pat thought this was simply jealousy. Nate insisted it wasn't. The quarrel had grown to monstrous proportions, ending with Pat's demand that Nate return her keys.

"He said we were no longer comrades and he couldn't be part of the group," Pat said miserably. "Now I feel like I've fucked over everyone."

I told her not to be silly.

"You don't think I've ruined everything?" she pleaded. "You think it's okay that I took the keys? And that I'm going to see Bobo tonight?"

I said I thought it was fine. Nate still had keys to Sam's and my apartment, as he had for months. We wouldn't stop being friendly with him because he and Pat had fought. She could handle her relationship with him as she pleased.

On my way to the *Rat* office, all my thoughts were trained on Sam's meeting with Ben and their planned bombing of the Criminal

Courthouse. If that went well, we would be safely out of New York and on the farm in North Dakota by the end of the week.

Wednesday night, November 12. I forgot to look for the white sedan on the way home from *Rat*. When I came into the apartment, Sam was standing in the dark, peering out from under a half-drawn shade. He turned to me and put a finger to his lips.

"They're back," he said.

His face, a few feet away from me, was a mass of shadows. I could see his pale left eye jumping with fear. The dogs whimpered.

"You're sure?" I asked.

"Same white car. Same guys. On the other side of the street this time."

"Sam, if you know it's the bomb squad, then don't go out. Stay here until they leave."

He put his arms around me and held me for a few moments without speaking.

"I can't stay," he said. "I promised George I'd meet him."

I watched helplessly as he shrugged into an army jacket with colonel's stripes and slung his knapsack over his shoulder. He kissed me once more, then left.

The next time I saw him, we were on opposite ends of a hallway in FBI headquarters, both of us in custody.

XI
Exit

AT THE WOMEN'S HOUSE OF DETENTION they took my watch away along with my sailor pants and boots and a shirt of Sam's I had shrunk almost to my size. They made me shower and wash my hair with a delousing shampoo. I had to spread my buttocks for the matron, then lie on a table while a doctor examined my vagina. "Do you use drugs?" he asked me. "Any health problems?" I wondered whether I should admit to wearing contact lenses so that he would let me keep my plastic case and wetting solution. I decided not to risk it; if he responded by confiscating the lenses, I would not be able to see. The matron handed me back my clothes and a pair of broken, mismatched shower clogs and told me to dress. The clothes stuck to my scrubbed flesh. As the matron led me out to the elevator, I glimpsed a clock: 4:10 A.M. Six hours ago thirty FBI agents and New York State police had banged on my door, yelling, "Open up! We've got your friend!" and heaved against the hinges until the plaster cracked and I unlocked the all-but-useless bolt. I felt desperately tired.

The matron took me upstairs to a solitary cell, six feet wide and perhaps eight feet long. A thin ray of moonlight illuminated a narrow mattress on a frame suspended from the wall. "You're quarantined for three days," the matron said. "Then you'll get a roommate like the other girls."

"But they told me I was going to court in the morning."

"I don't know about that, sweetheart," she answered, and clanged the iron door shut.

The cell smelled of decay, my hair of disinfectant. Under the scratchy blanket I closed my eyes, expecting to fall asleep at once. Instead, I found myself thinking of the last friendly voice I had heard, the lawyer Hank DiSuvero's. I had called him a few hours ago from the FBI office, using my one permitted phone call for the purpose. Awakened from a sound sleep at 2:00 A.M., Hank agreed to telephone my parents and to meet me at the courthouse in the morning. "Was anyone else picked up?" he asked me.

"I can't tell you now," I said, looking at the agent sitting three feet away from me.

"Okay, I guess I'll hear about it on the radio," Hank said as if he understood my reticence. My gratitude to him swelled now into a fervent belief that he would get me and my friends out of jail first thing in the morning.

I reviewed the government's transgressions, convincing myself that they were sufficient to get the case dismissed. Nate and I had been talking quietly in the bedroom, waiting for Sam to come back as we listened to the news on the radio. Neither of us had been involved either in the morning's bombing of the Criminal Courthouse or in Sam's venture with Demmerle tonight. Yet—on the basis of no evidence, as far as I could see—the police had burst into the place as though they were putting out a fire. They slammed me against the wall and snapped handcuffs on Nate's wrists as he emerged from the bedroom. "Yarrow, it's Yarrow," they announced to each other excitedly. Without stopping to produce a search warrant they had dumped the contents of shelves and drawers on the floor, chortling at discoveries which ranged from electrical wire in a closet to water-chestnut flour in a paper bag. While a couple of dozen cops stayed in the apartment, the others led Nate and me downstairs into separate unmarked cars. One of them kicked John Keats and Bernadette back into the apartment when they tried to follow.

The spectators who filtered onto the street must have thought we'd shot a cop, so long was the procession of police cars that headed north to the FBI office on Sixty-ninth Street. Once inside the office, the agents took me into a small room and began to ply me with innocent-sounding questions. "Where did you go to school, Jane? Do you have any brothers or sisters? How long have you lived on Fourth Street?" I had heard dire stories of what happened to people who let the FBI get chummy. I refused to admit that my name was Jane Alpert, answering every question with "I want to talk to my lawyer."

Before they took me to the women's house of detention, I was led to another room to be photographed and fingerprinted. As we waited outside, Sam, escorted by agents, appeared at the door. He stared at me in dismay. "Call Hank," I mouthed to him. He shook his head, uncomprehending. Could he have forgotten the lawyer's name after all my warnings?

My parents. How would they react to the lawyer's call? I hadn't talked to them about anything that mattered since the night almost a year ago when I brought Sam home for dinner. On our occasional dinners together in restaurants or in the Forest Hills apartment, Sam's name never came up. We didn't discuss the war or Nixon or the Black Panthers or my job at *Rat*. I felt almost glad that they would now be compelled to look at my real life. They would be horrified, of course, but at least they would know now what I believed and how far I was willing to go.

My eyes were shutting at last, but my contact lenses, which I had not dared take out, scratched and burned me. I looked around in the moonlight for a place to put them. The cell was bare except for the cot, a toilet, a sink with an open drain, and a roll of toilet paper. I tore off a length of toilet paper and wiped the sink dry. Then I tore a second length, folded it several times, and laid it over the drain. Removing my lenses, I placed them on the folded tissue. If no one entered the cell while I was asleep and if I remembered not to run tap water over them, they would survive.

My last thought was of the dogs. Would the police lock them in the apartment when they left, take them to the pound, or let them run wild? If Pat were free, she would care for them. But if she had come back to Fourth Street last night after her date with Bobo, she had surely been arrested. The door to her second-floor apartment, I remembered, had been standing wide open as the police took me downstairs. Too confused and tired to think what this meant, I went to sleep.

A blaze of electric light woke me up. I couldn't have been asleep more than an hour. Peering through the slit in my cell door, I saw my fellow inmates shuffling down the corridor. At the metal gate at the corridor's end they shifted about, yelling at someone on the other side to "bust the gates." A voice called, "Breakfast, ladies," and I heard the gate open. Then silence.

A few minutes later my own breakfast was pushed through a slot in my cell. A matron yelled through the opening: I was to clean my cell and get dressed before she returned for the empty tray. I had to be quick about it since I was going to court in an hour. I looked at the food: gluey oatmeal and a liquid that I supposed was meant to be coffee. I scraped the food into the toilet. Then, after rinsing my lenses under the tap, I inserted them. The cell leaped into focus, fouler than I had imagined. By squeezing myself in a corner, I could see the shops of Greenwich Avenue through the barred window. In the corner of the cell someone had left a pencil stub. I picked it up and inscribed on the wall one of the Panthers' slogans: "Put the pigs in the pokey and the people on the streets." It reassured me to see the militant phrase there, reminding me who I was.

The marble hall of the federal courthouse was packed with spectators, most of them reporters. Gradually I picked out my friends. The *Rat* staff had come, and I smiled and clenched my fist in their direction, trying to look brave. My ex-roommate Jean and other college acquaintances were there, too, sober and concerned. The biggest shock hit me when I spotted my father. He was wearing oversized dark sunglasses and a hat that covered a large part of his forehead. In the set of his mouth I recognized, with a start, my own unconfessed fear and shame at what had happened last night. To dispel this sudden dread, I put on a glad-to-see-you smile and waved vigorously. My father acknowledged me with a slight nod. His lips did not move. Feeling my face flush, I looked away. To my relief, I then spied Hank DiSuvero making his way through the crowd.

The marshals cleared a space next to the window so that we could talk. Hank allowed me to scan the front pages of the newspapers he'd brought. FOUR ARRESTED IN BOMB PLOT, read the *Times*' front-page story. The *News*' cover had it as FBI NABS 4, DYNAMITE. Sam and George Demmerle had been arrested, bombs in hand, at the site of the army trucks they had planned to blow up. Nate was described as my boyfriend, living with me at the Fourth Street apartment. Pat Swinton was named as a fugitive.

"Listen," said Hank, "they're not going to give us much time now. Do you know what's about to happen here?"

I shook my head.

"It's an arraignment. A formality before a magistrate so that bail can be set. It's going to be very high because of all the publicity—

maybe fifty thousand dollars, maybe more. That doesn't matter. It can be lowered later. For now we've got to get you settled with a lawyer."

"You're my lawyer," I said.

"Your father showed up with someone else. Guy named Todel. I think he'd like it if you went along."

I was annoyed.

"Why did my father go ahead and hire someone when I already have you?"

"Your father doesn't seem to like me much. In his mind, I'm associated with the people who got you into this mess."

"Why won't he talk to me?"

"He's afraid of being recognized by the reporters. He says your mother works for the public school system and her job would be in jeopardy if she got in the papers."

I still wanted Hank, whom I liked and trusted, but he argued forcefully against that. "Go along with your father," he urged. "He's a nice man. He loves you, and he's willing to stand for your bail. Judges like that. Later, when you're out, if you still want me as your lawyer, we can talk about it."

Since he seemed to have made up his mind, I reluctantly agreed to accept Todel.

A moment later my new lawyer, an executive type in a silk tie and $400-suit, and I were standing before a railing opposite a black-robed magistrate. Sam and George Demmerle were represented by a very young lawyer from the radical left Law Commune, Bill Crain. Another member of the Law Commune, beefy, curly-headed Fred Cohn, represented Nate.

The U.S. attorney, Robert Morgenthau, read the charges against us. We were said to have conspired together with Patricia Swinton, fugitive, to place bombs in eight buildings, on the United Fruit pier, and in four army trucks. Dynamite and arms had been seized at Sam Melville's East Second Street apartment (the McCurdy place). Information against us came from "an unimpeachable source" and had been corroborated by a full confession made by one of the defendants to the FBI. Full confession! At this news my brain started to spin.

Then the magistrate pronounced bail: $500,000 for each of us!

A marshal took my elbow to propel me out of the room. My friends jammed into the hall to wave. Standing a little apart from the others was Dana. Joy at her freedom broke through my stupor. I flashed a smile and raised my fist in triumph. She looked at me exactly as my father had, with stunned terror. My smile froze on my lips. If Dana felt things were so bad, we were in much worse trouble than I had allowed myself to think.

When the cell door clanged shut on me again, the reality of $500,000 bail struck at last. No one had that much money. Not even a tenth that much. The government was going to keep us in jail forever. This cell was going to be my home. Unable to hold back the fear I had restrained for the last twelve hours, I threw myself on the cot and burst into racking sobs.

Prison, court, and prison succeeded each other in a kaleidoscopic whirl so that I lost track of the days. One morning Nate, Sam, George, and I were in court for a new determination of bail before Judge Marvin Frankel. Todel told me that we were lucky since Frankel generally gave low bail. Nate sat next to me and hissed, "We can't go out on bail until the Panther Twenty-one are freed."

My heart sank. I didn't want to stay in the house of detention, not for the sake of the Panthers or the white radical movement or any other cause.

Nate saw my resistance. His eyes clouded with irritation.

"Look, Sam and I have already talked this over. We're in complete agreement. If we get our bail lowered now, it's only because we're white and middle-class. To accept that while the Panthers have already been in since April—without ever having bombed a building—well, that's just white-skin privilege."

When he put it that way, it was hard to say no. And I could even see a personal advantage to staying in jail. I might get to know the two women in the Panther 21 case, Afeni Shakur and Joan Bird, connections no one else in the white movement had. We wouldn't have to stay in forever. A couple of weeks would be enough to make our point. Nate hadn't said that, but I figured he would be open to renegotiation at a later date.

"All right," I said.

Nate inclined his head, pleased that he had won me to the side of honor.

My father came to visit me in the house of detention, bringing dresses, a contact lens case, and money for the commissary. We spoke to each other through a thick pane of glass over an internal telephone, a line of inmates on one side, a line of visitors on the other. I told my father that I wasn't going to leave jail until the Panther 21 were freed.

"The who?" my father yelled.

I explained. Months later my father said that this conversation was a turning point for him. I had appeared so unshaken by the grotesqueness of my surroundings and so sure of my beliefs that he decided on the spot that I should choose my own lawyer and conduct my case as I saw fit.

Todel came to tell me that my bail had been lowered to $20,000 and that I would be free in a day or two. He said he had spoken with Nate's lawyer and with Sam's and that it was all right with everyone.

Afeni Shakur sent me a message confirming what Todel said. "Revolutionaries belong in the streets, not in the jails," she wrote. From the Panthers' point of view, if we were free, we could publicize their case, a more productive use of our celebrity than staying in jail.

On Thursday, November 20, eight days after my arrest, I was released on $20,000 bail under severe restrictions, including the requirement that I report daily to the U.S. attorney's office. Nate was released on $25,000 bail provided by a lien on his parents' house. (Though he was not in close contact with his parents, they proved as concerned as mine in the crisis.) His restrictions were the same as mine.

Sam's bail was $50,000, twice as high as ours because he had been caught red-handed and—unwilling as I was to believe it—had made a full confession to the FBI. He later claimed to have done this in the spirit of Pierre-Paul Geoffroy, who had bought time for Jean and Jacques through his confession. This made no sense to me since Sam's confession came *after* he had seen me in the FBI office. It also repeated in every detail what Morgenthau's "unimpeachable source" had reported.

The unimpeachable source was George Demmerle. Having successfully posed for the last three years as the craziest of the Crazies, living on the Lower East Side, dating movement women, and urging his friends to help him blow up bridges or power lines, he turned out to have been an undercover agent all along. From the moment of Sam's first conversations with him about our bombings, every word Sam said had gone directly to the FBI.

Released from jail on his own recognizance, Demmerle, fearing retribution from the movement where he had posed as a friend, went immediately into hiding. Six months later he collected his reward: $25,000 offered by the Marine Midland Bank for information leading to the conviction of the bomber.

I emerged from the isolation of jail into a furor of publicity. My parents, to get away from the reporters camped outside their door, had checked into a motel for a week, changed their telephone to an unlisted number, and, when they returned home, substituted an alias for the name on the mailbox and lobby intercom. Journalists had sought out my high school teachers and principals, publishing colleagues, and even elementary school classmates. An ambitious *Times* reporter made her way to the Fourth Street apartment on the first Sunday morning after my release. I refused to give her an interview, but she got a sufficient glimpse of the living room to describe it in her front-page story entitled "Girl Next Door Turns Radical." Poring over hers and other stories, I wondered if these Sweetheart of Sigma Chi portraits of me were true or whether the reporters, for all their assiduous research, had simply been trapped by their own clichés.

If to the straight world I appeared a nice young girl drawn tragically into crime, to the movement I was a fearless Amazon. On my first day back at the *Rat* office my fellow staffers greeted me with cheers as though I had been elected to office, not released on bail. Shero had flown back from Mississippi and plunged into arranging a benefit for *Rat* and the so-called Alpert-Yarrow-Melville Defense Fund. Rock bands were going to perform songs written for us; actor Rip Torn had promised to appear; leftist academic John Gerassi was helping to raise money. Now that Nate and I were free, we would be the featured speakers. What would I say?

"It doesn't matter," Shero assured me. "People just want to know what you look like."

Although much about my sudden fame left me uneasy, my new status at *Rat* was a delight. In the week of my release Shero ran my article "Inside the House of D" on the cover—my first lead piece. The next week, when he returned to Mississippi, the acting editors again ran a piece of mine, this one on the Panther 21, on the cover.

I soon discovered I could do no wrong. I no longer had to sweep or file or type. I didn't even have to come to the office. The telephone rang for me twenty times a day—reporters, old friends, movement stars from other cities hoping to meet me—and the *Rat* staff dutifully took all the messages and never once complained.

Over tuna fish sandwiches Sam's lawyer, Bill Crain, and I discussed my choice of attorney.

"Do you have any idea how much your parents are paying Todel?" Crain asked me.

"I know they paid him a five-hundred-dollar retainer."

"If he takes your case, he's likely to charge around twenty-five thousand dollars."

He paused, letting the staggering figure sink in.

"If you went with a movement attorney instead, the fees your parents paid could be split among all three of us. That's the only way Fred Cohn and I are going to see any money from this."

I didn't think of this suggestion as unscrupulous. Aligning myself with the movement's interests against my parents', I thought Crain's proposal was fair enough: why shouldn't our lawyers receive equal compensation?

"Okay," I said. "Who do you suggest?"

We finally settled on Sanford Katz, a leftist lawyer with fifteen years' experience, a close friend and an associate of Leonard Boudin (who had represented Spock and Coffin and was the father of Weatherwoman Kathy Boudin), and the senior attorney on the Panther 21 case. I checked Sandy's reputation with Dana, who approved, and then made an appointment with the lawyer myself. I found him charming and very bright and told my parents I had made my choice.

My parents liked Katz well enough but were shocked at the fee he named. "I want you to have the lawyer of your choice," my father assured me, "but twenty-five thousand dollars—frankly, it's more than we have." I felt chagrined, suspecting—although I couldn't know for sure—that Crain was behind the request for such a high figure. Eventually Sandy and my parents agreed on a lower but still very substantial sum.

Our case was transferred to Milton Pollack, a judge who our attorneys warned us was known for taking the prosecutors' side.

Crain warned that we should try to get Sam out on bail as soon as possible. If we lost our pretrial motions, the prosecutor could ask for an increase, and even if we won them, the state of New York was readying its own charges against Sam, on which he could be held on no bail. Through the winter Dana, Greg Rosen, who was devoted to Sam, Robert Carpenter, our friend from CAC, a few others, and I devoted all our energy to raising the collateral required for a $50,000 bond.

Our case had a certain avant-garde chic among well-placed liberals, and we were treated kindly. Chris Cerf, the publishing heir, gave us several thousand dollars. Gloria Steinem provided the list of contributors to Norman Mailer's mayoralty campaign, which yielded us several hundred dollars and more names. Frank Weiner, in his one token effort to help his co-conspirators, introduced me to Susan Sontag, who expressed some interest in taping a conversation with me. (This project never materialized.) Honor Moore, the friend of a college friend, showed up at *Rat* and offered her inheritance, a considerable sum. Gradually we approached our goal and with it Sam's freedom.

With Sam himself, communication was all but impossible. Nate and I could see him only in the presence of lawyers at meetings which took place in the basement lockups of the federal courthouse. This mildewed dungeon, resounding with the slamming of iron, was the preserve of the U.S. marshals, who had a special loathing for political radicals. They frequently transported Sam from his cell to the lockups on no more than whim, kept him there all day on the pretense that he was going to see his lawyer, and then transported him back to prison without explanation. When we did manage to meet, the marshals would lock all six of us, lawyers and defendants, in a windowless concrete room with a small spyhole in the door through which they kept an eye on us.

For me, these encounters with Sam were replays of bad acid trips. The stiffness of his body communicated his suffering, but he would not talk to me. I would hold his hand and kiss him, trying to give him comfort. Sometimes he wouldn't respond at all, while at other times he would thrust his hand up my dress or pull me onto his lap, as though a display of sexual dominance might restore his self-esteem. Inevitably the marshals would burst into the room and order us to break it up. To divert Sam, I brought photos of the dogs, cared for by a neighbor while I was in jail and noticeably grown since Sam's absence, and copies of underground papers I thought would interest him. He seemed incapable of absorbing any but the simplest information—although Dana, Robert, and Greg, who visited him in jail, assured me that with them he was quite articulate.

In early December I learned that Sam's affair with Billie Banks had continued up until the week we were arrested. I heard this not from Sam himself but through an alarming coincidence. In midsummer Billie had gone to work for a book editor, Kurt Nelson, who published a number of radical left authors and was a friend of Sandy Katz's. It seems that Sam had told Billie that he was the one responsible for the bombings and that his involvement was the reason he was frequently out of town. For whatever reason, to protect me from suspicion or to persuade Billie that she had no rivals, he also said that he and I had separated in August and that we never saw each other. When Sam and I were arrested—or perhaps before—Billie poured out the story of her affair with Sam to Nelson, begging him for help. I finally heard the tale at a party at Kurt Nelson's house, to which Sandy had invited me. I had nowhere to go with my rage that night: Sam was in jail, and I had to return alone to an apartment that was still half his, wishing he were there only so that I could beat his brains in.

During one of my early meetings with Sandy in his office—which, with a paranoia I respected, he always treated as if it were bugged—he held up a scrawled note: "Do you know where Pat is?"

I shook my head. "Do *you*?" I asked him.

He scrawled again, "In USA."

Sandy didn't explain how he knew this, and I didn't ask. Instead, he agreed to introduce me to a woman named Maude Tolliver who was in contact with Pat. Sandy arranged my encounter with Maude through more notes and guarded messages, in the course of which it became clear that Maude wished me to know as little as possible about her in advance of our meeting.

Our rendezvous took place in a smoky pub with a loud jukebox in the West Village. Sandy had described Maude only as tall and blond, which turned out to be an understatement. The striking woman who waved to me from a rear seat was nearly six feet, extremely slender, with light fine hair down to her waist and a face that looked deprived of flesh. She wore thick gold-rimmed glasses and smoked a cigarette in a plastic holder. If the pub had not been so dark, she would have been a center of attention.

Apparently she had the same misgivings about me. "You ought to buy yourself a new hat," she said, nodding at the blue mohair scarf wrapped around my head. "I'm sure I'm not the only person who recognizes that babushka from the picture in the *Times*."

While prudent activists treated all movement homes as potentially bugged, Maude took this precaution a step further and would not discuss sensitive subjects even in a restaurant. While she finished her whiskey and soda and I drank a Coke, we chatted awkwardly, passing the time. She told me she was trained as an x-ray technician, had an interest in the movement for socialized medicine and was writing a book on the subject. She had come to New York in the last year from Texas after her marriage to an antiwar Vietnam veteran had broken up.

Maude was a person in whom the habits of secrecy were ingrained. She would have behaved with the same reserve she displayed in the pub even if she were not involved in hiding fugitives from the law. Unlike Dana and Frank Weiner, she never dropped names; unlike Sandy Katz, she didn't hold up scraps of paper or talk out of the side of her mouth. She relied on silence and on her instincts, which generally flashed yellow lights. I liked her enormously.

As we walked down Hudson Street later that night, she told me exactly the amount of information she felt I could be trusted with. On the night of our arrest Pat and Bobo had been in the home of someone she knew. When the news came over the radio, the friend had telephoned Maude, who had arranged for both Pat and Bobo to fly to the West Coast under aliases and to stay with friends of hers until more was known about the charges. (Jenny, fortunately, was with her father.) After a week or ten days Bobo, much to Maude's annoyance, had deserted Pat, going off on his own with the ID Maude had provided. Concerned that Bobo might be picked up for questioning and lead authorities to Pat, Maude arranged for Pat to move again. She was now somewhere in the South, where she had hopes of staying permanently, but Maude suspected that a third move might be necessary.

If I liked, Maude said cautiously, Nate and I could write to Pat and she would forward the letters. But we had to be careful to include absolutely nothing in the letters that would reveal the identities of senders or recipient.

The more I saw of Maude's discretion, the more surprised I was that she was willing to risk involvement in a group that had behaved as foolishly as ours. I think now that Maude was one of many movement sympathizers who lived outwardly conventional lives but carried out bombings in fantasy and dreamed that someday the United States would produce a genuine revolutionary movement. Many such friends were to help me over the next years, but few were blessed with Maude's prudence or with her amazing range of connections.

Among the celebrities whose paths crossed mine that winter was Mark Rudd, leader of the 1968 Columbia uprising and a founder of the Weathermen. I saw him for the first time in December at a demonstration for the Panther 21 where he appeared in a full beard and cowboy hat.

"Rudd's in disguise," someone had muttered to me then. "You know the Weathermen are planning to go underground rather than face trial for the Chicago action."

Why would someone about to go underground broadcast his intention by appearing in so transparent a disguise in full view of the police? It didn't make sense. When a few weeks later his lawyer, also a member of the Law Commune, suggested that Rudd wanted to meet me, I was sufficiently intrigued by what I'd heard and seen to agree to a rendezvous.

We met in a coffee shop near the courts. Rudd said he had no money. I volunteered to pay for his breakfast—I was surviving then on my *Rat* salary and spare cash from the bail fund for which I was working more than full time. Rudd ordered coffee and eggs, and while we were waiting for our food he began to boast about his last plane trip when he and a few other Weathermen had roamed the aisles of the plane demanding cash handouts from their fellow passengers.

"You've gotta overcome a lot of bourgeois hang-ups to do that, but, man, it feels great," he assured me. "Didja ever do that?"

How could he brag of panhandling to someone who was about to go on trial for eight bombings? I tried to get him to talk about the Weathermen's plans to commit sabotage and go underground, but he clammed up. Irritated, I decided I would put him out of my thoughts. Yet something about him—his hulking walk? the insolent look he gave me whenever our eyes met?—stayed in my mind in spite of myself.

On December 29, 1969, Sam's friends and I appeared in federal court before Judge Pollack with the $50,000 bond drawn up by a bondsman. Pollack would not consider accepting it until he had interviewed on the witness stand all the people who donated to the fund, questioning them about their motives. At the end of this unprecedented hearing he ruled that none of the witnesses was an individual toward whom Sam would feel any sense of personal responsibility and that therefore bail was denied. However, if we could produce one responsible person who would agree to take Sam into custody and who would also put up the entire bail unassisted, he would reconsider. He then doubled the required amount to $100,000.

In mid-January Bill Crain worked a small miracle by persuading a wealthy young woman to fill the role the judge had defined. She appeared before Pollack in chambers and, according to Crain, succeeded in making a favorable impression on the crusty old man. But we were too late. That same day the state of New York also indicted Sam for the bombings. While Dana, Greg, and I were waiting in federal courthouse for the good news from Judge Pollack, state police were already transporting Sam to the Criminal Courts Building four blocks away. There, at the site of his last successful bombing, a state judge ruled that Sam was to be held without bail until his trial.

I came home from this last bail hearing with just twenty-four hours to leave the Fourth Street apartment, which Sam and I had on a sublet for only six months. I went immediately to one of the Lower East Side's rip-off rental agencies and took the first place offered me, a small, dark apartment at the corner of Third Street and Avenue A.

The landlord, recognizing my name, didn't want to let me sign the lease. He had nothing against me personally, he assured me; he just didn't want any trouble. I called Sandy, hoping he would sign the lease for me. He wasn't home. Fearing that I would be put out on the street if I couldn't move into this apartment, I called my father. He drove into the city at once, signed the lease, paid the rent plus deposit, and gave me extra money so I could fix the place up. Then he took me out for dinner before driving back home to Queens—one more demonstration of love and concern to pull at my heartstrings as my life continued to move away from his.

As I came into contact for the first time with movement activists from all over the country, my sense of the prospects for revolution began to shift. I started to see that we radicals had nothing that could be called an army, no national unity or organization. Exhausted from demonstrations, trials, police brutality, and jailings, many leftists had already abandoned the cause for yoga, meditation, communes in Vermont and California, religious groups, or simply a hobo existence from city to city and job to job. Ironically I came to see the unlikelihood of revolution at precisely the moment when I could no longer abandon my commitment to it. Already under arrest and facing some seventy years in prison and in the spotlight of movement attention besides, I would have had to explain any change of heart to those whose eyes were fixed on me in the months before the trial. And any show of disillusionment might have hinted that I was getting ready to inform against Sam, Nate, Pat, and others—and that, of course, was anathema.

Bound as I was to the movement, I couldn't help feeling disappointed in it. Having been convinced only a few months ago that thousands of white youth were prepared to give their lives for social change, I now believed that even such enthusiasts as the Crazies and the *Rat* staffers had been less than serious all along. *Rat* itself, I noticed from the corner of my eye, was deteriorating from a lively radical journal into a sophomoric joke sheet. My worst suspicions were confirmed on a night in January when the Elgin Theater was hosting a benefit for the defense fund.

Paul Simon, *Rat*'s art director and a loyal supporter of our cause, was hawking the newest issue outside the theater when Dana and I arrived. "We had a great idea after you left layout last night," Paul confided to me. "We decided to turn the issue into a sex-and-porn special."

"Oh?" I said. I accepted my copy and walked into the theater with a sense of foreboding. In the not-yet-darkened theater, my eyes fell first on a page 3 story about Sam's last court hearing. Written in impressionistic half sentences that made it impossible to figure out what had happened at the hearing, the story was illustrated with the photo of Sam and me in which Sam was surreptitiously rubbing my breast with his elbow while pretending to concentrate on his guitar. An article on pornography was illustrated with cartoons of disembodied male hands resting on female thighs, models in bizarre sexual costumes, and a pile of feces. Another story, discussing female masturbation, was headlined CLIT FLIT BIG HIT. And so on.

"Dana, is this disgusting or not?" I asked.

"It looks like *Screw*," she agreed.

The movie began. "I'm going to resign from the paper," I whispered.

"That's bourgeois individualism," she hissed back. "You're not the only person insulted by this issue."

"But I'm the only woman on the regular staff."

"Shh," exploded a woman behind us.

We were quiet for a few minutes. Then Dana whispered, "Tomorrow we'll go talk to Gary and Paul. We'll tell them to give the paper over to women's control for one week. It's about time they did that anyway."

As soon as Dana and I persuaded the male editors to agree to an all-women's issue, I called Robin Morgan to invite her to help us. Robin sounded thrilled. The next day she brought over thirty women to join Dana, me, and a few others at the first all-female meeting held at the *Rat* office. Inexperienced as we were, I was afraid we wouldn't manage to pull it off—but the women's issue of *Rat* rolled off the press exactly on schedule.

Looking back on that issue, I see something less than an epoch in journalism. My long front-page interview with Afeni Shakur of the Panther 21 is bloated with rhetoric and largely obliterated by a drawing of a fist we had superimposed on the page. A piece called "Winter Doldrums" on page 3 attempts to encourage readers to "guerrilla actions" but in a tone so despondent that no one could be inspired. The writing is pedestrian, the artwork amateurish, the overall impression not only humorless but unironic. The one exception to the mediocrity is Robin Morgan's piece "Goodbye to All That," which was to become a feminist classic.

Robin opened by calling for a permanent take-over of *Rat* by women. The essay continued as a scathing indictment against nearly every well-known man in the left, mingled with expressions of disappointment toward the women who allowed those men to retain power. In a paragraph that sent shivers through me, Robin wrote: "There is something every woman wears around her neck on a thin chain of fear—an amulet of madness. For each of us there exists somewhere a moment of insult so intense that she will reach up and rip the amulet off, even if the chain tears at the flesh of her neck."

The article concludes with a call for a revolution led by women and aiming at the creation of a totally genderless society. Although Robin's version of feminism puzzled me, I couldn't doubt her seriousness, either in person or on the page. Her intellectual energy was immense, and unlike most of the people I saw around me, she could put it to highly effective use. Inspired by Robin's militance, most of the other women and I decided we wanted to keep the paper permanently.

At a meeting called soon after we had published the issue, the men resisted our demands, then caved in. The truth was that with Shero away in Mississippi, the paper would probably have died of natural causes in a few more months. In women's hands, it stuck out another two years, undergoing three more take-overs by splinter groups before it ceased publication forever.

If "Goodbye to All That" was the eye-opening delight of the new women's regime, Dana's sudden aloofness was the deepest disappointment. Instead of helping me edit the women's issue as I had expected, she virtually disappeared from the office. When I learned that Ben was so hostile to the women's take-over that he was refusing to sleep with Dana until she changed her mind, I figured that was the reason she was staying away. At last she told me that her absence had nothing to do with Ben. She hadn't been around because she and Ben were spending a great deal of their time with John Jacobs, known as J.J., a leader of the Weathermen and an old friend. What J.J. and the Weathermen were doing, why they needed to have so many meetings, and why she had said nothing about this for weeks, she wouldn't hint at.

Dana's evasiveness drove me mad. Since the arrest she had been the one friend with whom I could speak with complete freedom about Sam, the bombings, the lawyers, and the upcoming trial. We had never kept secrets from each other, and I could not understand why she was starting now. What did the Weathermen have to offer that the *Rat* women didn't? And why wouldn't she tell me?

Given these anxieties, when Rudd telephoned me at the *Rat* office one day in February—the first time I had heard from him since our breakfast meeting—I was relieved. He identified himself as Tony and said he wanted to see me again. We arranged to meet near my apartment a few evenings later.

Sitting at my kitchen table, we shared a tab of acid, and it broke down inhibitions. In the darkened bedroom, the walls of which nearly touched the sides of the bed, we made love and murmured of our feelings for each other without worrying how our words would sound when the drug had worn off.

He asked me how I felt about jail. I said I figured I could handle it, short of torture. He wanted to know where my defeatist mentality came from. "Getting arrested doesn't mean it's the end, you know. The big struggle is still ahead. Why shouldn't you be part of it? If you want to be a revolutionary, you've got to fight and keep on fighting."

At first I didn't understand what he was driving at. Thinking he was merely condescending to me, I got angry, and, dismayed that the tenderness between us had ended so quickly, I walked him to the door. Hours after he left, what he had been trying to tell me struck me like lightning. *He was going underground.* And so, no doubt, was Dana. And all the rest of the Weathermen. That's what her meetings with J.J. were about and why she couldn't tell me more.

The next night my buzzer rang at midnight. "It's Tony," said the voice over the intercom. Leaving a guest stranded in my apartment, I pulled on a jacket and ran to meet Rudd, who said he had only a few minutes. We walked around the block, our arms around each other. Rudd apologized for being hard on me, and I told him I was sorry not to have caught on quicker. He said we would talk more when he could find a safe place for us to meet. He hailed a taxi and, with one hand on the door, held me and kissed me for a long time.

Two days later a Greenwich Village town house belonging to James Wilkerson, father of Cathy Wilkerson, burned to the ground after a powerful explosion. Kathy Boudin and Cathy Wilkerson escaped alive and promptly disappeared. Two or possibly three others were said to have been killed. The cause was the apparently accidental detonation of an enormous quantity of dynamite the Weathermen had stored in the basement and with which they were making bombs. It was several more days before I was able to corner Dana and find out that Rudd was definitely not among the dead.

The town house tragedy forced the Weathermen to advance their plans to go underground. By March 6, the day after the explosion, every member of the organization had vanished. Dana and I drew together in the crisis; she loosened a bit and confided to me that she and Ben were both going to join "the Beatles" within a few weeks—our code name for the Weathermen in these conversations, coined by Ben because they were young, rich, and white. Because monogamy was forbidden in the organization, she and Ben were going to different cities, she to San Francisco, he to Boston. It was possible that, through Maude, she would bring Pat with her to San Francisco.

It was easy to conclude that everyone who remained active in the movement was going to be underground within a few months. On March 10 Rap Brown failed to appear at his riot conspiracy trial at a Cambridge, Maryland, courthouse. On the following day, as if in explanation for his absence, a bomb exploded in the courthouse. On March 12 after Robin and I had finished dinner in a Chinese restaurant and while we were in my apartment discussing whether the women's movement would ever go underground—a group called Revolutionary Force 9 set off explosives in three midtown office buildings. (Robin later suspected that I had been using her to provide an alibi. In fact, I was as surprised as she was.) Left-wing sabotage was becoming epidemic: an army installation in Madison was struck by explosives dropped from a helicopter; a Bank of America building in Santa Barbara was fire-bombed. Even the Catonsville 9, Catholic pacifists arrested in 1968 for pouring homemade napalm on draft files, were rumored to be on their way underground.

Writing about these events in the March 20 issue of *Rat*, I proclaimed: "The real division is not between people who support bombings and people who don't, but between people who will *do* them and people who are too hung up on their own privileges and security to take those risks." I was addressing myself more than anyone, trying to make up my mind if I still believed in the revolution enough to become a fugitive for it.

Nate said that for his part, he wanted to go to prison rather than underground because he felt what he needed most was time to be alone and think. Maude told me the decision had to be mine, but whatever I chose, she would help me. She could provide ID in advance of my departure and arrange a safe place for me to stay. She would also become a coordinating point through which Dana and Ben and Pat and I could keep in touch. Finally Robin Morgan threw her support on the side of my going underground. She had no love for the Weathermen, whom she had roundly denounced in her *Rat* piece, but she believed that in another year or two, radical feminists would also be going underground to escape a repressive government. She promised me money and support and eventually a circle of women who would help me when I needed it.

The question of my parents' bail money remained. If I failed to show up at my trial, their $20,000 would be forfeited. I truly loved my parents, for all our misunderstandings, and I had been touched by the extent of their support for me since the arrest. The idea of costing them their life's savings (as I believed the bail money was) caused me many sleepless nights. But in the end, my wish not to hurt them gave way to the political commitment I had put before everything else.

In April Maude arranged the first telephone contact between Pat and me since the arrest—pay phone to pay phone. A fugitive's lifeline depended so much on these untraceable pay-phone connections that the Weathermen used to joke about calling their collective autobiography *Meet Me in the Phone Booth.* This call, for which I waited in a booth on the corner of Washington Square at a precisely appointed time, was to be the first of many hundreds for me. I could hardly believe that I was actually going to hear Pat's voice on the other end. Yet when the phone rang after a wait of about ten minutes, the long, exhaled "Hello" on the other end was unmistakably Pat's.

Our conversation, I'm sure, was ordinary. What I remember of it is not the words, but the quality of Pat's voice from which I tried to flesh out a picture. What did she look like now? What name did she go by? What did she do all day? I didn't dare ask her those questions. Underground: even in conversation with a beloved friend, it seemed to exist more in metaphor than reality.

* * *

On Dana's last morning in New York we sat on a bench in Abingdon Square, gazing toward the river and trying to avoid the pain of separation in each other's eyes.

"What it comes down to," Dana said, "is a few people you love and the commitment you make to each other. Everything I care about is here: Ben, you, Max, Sam. The Beatles are nothing to me, I hardly know them."

She was silent a moment, as if struggling for words.

"It's so goddamned hard to give everything up," she burst out. "I could stay in my apartment forever, planning dinner, getting ready to have the draperies cleaned, feeding the dogs, going to Crazies' meetings. But there's no point to that anymore, is there?"

Except for holding her hand and promising we would be together soon, I could say nothing to help her.

Through Clare and Arthur, two unindicted members of the Weather Underground who remained in New York, a meeting was arranged between me and Rudd. I had to travel to Philadelphia to see him, the first time I had violated my bail conditions since the arrest. As a disguise I wore a dress—unusual for me—and sunglasses and tied a silk scarf around my head.

We met in a formica coffee shop near the Market Street station. Rudd was disguised as an Italian hood in dyed black hair and mustache, wraparound glasses, and a black vinyl jacket. He hadn't changed his hulking walk or the exaggerated swinging of his arms. I was inordinately pleased to see him again and wished we had days instead of hours.

I told Rudd I was planning to leave New York before my trial and make my way to San Francisco, stopping first at a safe house to make sure I wasn't tailed. Rudd was more forthright about the organization than he had been before.

"I'm not sure that things are in great shape on the West Coast," he admitted. "But I suppose you'll be safer there than in the East. Your face is known in New York. If California doesn't work out, get in touch with me."

"How?"

He glanced around him. "Right here. This place is open every day of the year. I'll meet you here, let's say, on Thanksgiving. At noon."

It sounded ludicrous, but without fixed addresses or phone numbers, I could think of nothing better.

We went back to the apartment where Rudd was staying and made love. I felt we had moved inside a drama with certain conventions that made themselves known as we played out our roles. My eyes fell on a string of blue glass beads Rudd was wearing.

"Will you give me those beads?" I asked.

"They were given me by a friend," he answered. "But I understand what you're saying. You want to know if I love you. I do."

He slipped the beads off and handed them to me.

He didn't love me, of course, nor did I love him. We shared a physical attraction heightened by the drama of our underground encounter. But the words suited the moment and perhaps our underlying needs as well. We both were more frightened by the future than we were able to admit.

Our trial was to begin on Monday, May 4. I planned to leave the Friday before that. Since my bail conditions now required me to report only on weekdays, this would give me two days to get ahead of the FBI's expected pursuit. Maude had made all the arrangements and purchased my travel tickets. In her zealously prudent fashion she would not tell me where I was going until the night I was to leave.

On the night before I was to depart, I took Bernadette and John Keats to Maude's apartment, where they were to be picked up by friends of Maude's and moved to a farm in New England. They leaped into the back of the waiting station wagon and wagged their tails at me expectantly. I kissed their noses and tried not to cry. The motor started. Bernadette pressed her nose to the glass. John Keats shoved her out of the way. I watched them until the car disappeared, and then Maude put her arm around me and walked with me until I managed to stop the tears.

I came home to find a message from Bill Crain, Sam's lawyer, pinned to my door. He had to see me urgently. It was nearly midnight, but I walked up to his Murray Hill apartment to find out what was on his mind.

Crain was jubilant. The U.S. attorney's office had finally agreed to what he believed was a lucky break. If Nate, Sam, and I were all willing to plead guilty to lesser offenses instead of going to trial, then the state would sentence Sam to no more than eighteen years in prison. The charges to which Nate and I were to plead, conspiracy to destroy government property, carried maximum penalties of only five years each. Sam, Crain assured me, was ecstatic; this was the only opportunity he had to get out of jail before he was an old man.

Ecstatic? Over an eighteen-year sentence? Surely Crain was exaggerating.

"You should talk to Sandy first," Crain advised. "But Sam really wants you to go along. He's begged you to put off leaving until Monday so the deal won't collapse."

I had told Sam of my plans on the understanding that he would not repeat them to anyone, least of all the lawyers, and I was incensed to learn he had confided in Crain. Besides, I thought the plea was altogether a bad idea. Not only was eighteen years a staggeringly long sentence, but it would look awful for three revolutionaries to stand up in court and cop a plea.

I hoped for support from Nate, but to my surprise, he was on Sam's side. He was elated at the prospect of avoiding a court battle and of going to prison for as little as five years. With both my codefendants voting to accept the deal and considering my own plans to go underground anyway, I saw no choice but to go along.

So it happened that on May 4, instead of beginning my underground life, I was standing before Judge Pollack with my codefendants and lawyers, a packed courtroom of sympathizers behind us, admitting that I had conspired to destroy government property. We had to agree that we were pleading solely because we were guilty and not because of any expectation of a reduced sentence. In about ten minutes it was over. We were now convicted felons. Bail was continued for Nate and me until sentencing.

Even the marshals appeared touched by the solemnity. For once they kept their distance as Sam and I embraced. I hugged him tightly, unable to believe that it was going to be the last time.

"Are you going to leave today?" Sam whispered in my ear.

Still furious at his betrayal, I refused to answer.

THREE

Underground

The country beneath
the earth has a green sun
and the rivers flow backwards;

the trees and rocks are the same
as they are here, but shifted.
Those who live there are always hungry;

from them you can learn
wisdom and great power,
if you can descend and return safely.

—MARGARET ATWOOD

XII
Initiation

I STEPPED FROM THE PLANE IN THE Montgomery, Alabama, airport and was momentarily blinded by the sun. I was now as far along toward my destination as I could manage without further assistance. A friend of Maude's was supposed to pick me up here, but Maude had not told me her name or phone number or even the name of the town where she lived.

Since the week's delay necessitated by my guilty plea on Monday, the conspiracy that propelled me here had grown more elaborate. Greg Rosen had plied me with questions about the future—how would I stay in touch with Sam? did I want him to visit me?—until I grew tired of faking replies and told him the truth. In response, he had asked if he could use my department store charge cards to buy some equipment he needed. It shouldn't make any difference to me since, by the time the bills came, Jane Alpert would not exist. Together we went to Macy's and Bloomingdale's where I signed my name to hundreds of dollars of purchases: traveling clothes for me, and for Greg a stopwatch, a camera, and binoculars, all for a reason he refused to divulge.

Because Maude was going to be out of town on the night of my departure, I asked Robin Morgan to help me with my disguise. She had already given me a gift of $1,000 toward my expenses, wrapped in a Sunday *Times*, and on the night I was to leave she met me at Maude's apartment (to which I had the keys) disguised in a curly wig and glasses. She helped me bleach my hair with a shampoo-in blond coloring, made up my face with theatrical pancake, and gave me a crash course in changing my walk and voice. I filled the card holders of a new wallet with the false ID Maude had left for me: I was now going to be Frances Ethel Matthews, born in Virginia, age twenty-five. My nickname would be Maddy. Maddy Matthews: I kept repeating it to myself, trying to make it my own.

Pennsylvania Station had been packed with antiwar protesters on their way to Washington to demonstrate against Nixon's invasion of Cambodia. Their camaraderie affected me as usual with painful longing. I wanted to be part of them and drew little comfort from thinking that they would cheer me if they knew who I was. I imagined their resenting my new straight appearance—my print shirtwaist and lipstick and the tortoiseshell glasses I had substituted for my contact lenses. Once secluded in the privacy of the Pullman car Maude had reserved, I immediately removed the glasses, wiped off a layer of Robin's pancake, and brushed the spray out of my hair. Shadowy fears kept me awake in my bunk bed all the way to Baltimore.

From Baltimore I took a taxi to Dulles Airport and then boarded a plane to Montgomery. The frequent changes had been Maude's idea, as was the plan for me to spend two weeks with her friend in Alabama before going on to meet Dana and, I hoped, Pat in San Francisco. It seemed as though I were rushing headlong into a vacuum. And now that I had arrived, I felt like a fool, in a place where I knew no one and was waiting to be met by Maude's nameless friend.

A slender woman in a bright sundress waved at me cheerfully. "You must be Maddy," she said, taking my bag. "I'm Leslie."

"But how did you recognize me?"

"It was easy. You're the only woman on the plane under sixty. But I did think you were going to be blond."

My hand went to my hair, to which I'd applied two full bottles of color last night.

"What color would you call it?"

"I think it's brown," said my benefactor. "Maybe a little on the reddish side."

I trudged after her to the parking lot, wondering how safe it would be to discuss a new bleach job with her.

Leslie lived in Selma, where she worked as codirector of a project that allocated federal assistance funds to black farmers in the southwestern part of the state. Her boyfriend, B.T., a Mississippi black, was codirector and shared the quarters rented by the project in the poor black section of the town. It was a cheap frame house with an asbestos roof but more comfortable and clean than what I was used to on the Lower East Side. My bedroom on the rear porch was furnished with a bed, a rickety bureau, an armchair, and a faded rug and smelled of citronella and roses. When we arrived, Leslie showed me around and then left me alone in the room to recuperate from my trip.

I allowed an hour to pass so that I wouldn't seem overanxious. Then I went out to buy hair dye. In the black section of town residents cooled themselves on their porches or weeded scraggly gardens. In the white section I was the lone person on foot. I imagined hundreds of eyes staring at me behind the dimity-curtained windows, memorizing my features.

Once back at the house, I locked myself in the bathroom and opened the box of Clairol. This product was especially designed to turn dark hair light, unlike the gentler potion I had used at Maude's last night. It came in three parts: a stripper, a package of pink plastic curlers shaped like wishbones, and a glass bottle of murky dye. I washed my hair and applied the stripper, then waited twenty minutes for it to take effect, leafing through my copy of *Revolution in the Revolution?* as I sat on the edge of the tub.

The stripper left my hair looking like tangerine straw. I wet it again, rolled it on the thirty-six plastic wishbones, and then applied the dye to each rolled section. The tub and sink were now stained gray, and the bathroom smelled like rotted chicken meat. I waited another fifteen minutes, removed the curlers, rinsed my hair, and waited impatiently for it to dry.

At the end it hung limply about my face in a rainbow of shades, salmon and copper and egg-yolk yellow. In junior high school I had known a girl who tried to bleach her hair the color of Marilyn Monroe's. Something had gone wrong, and she'd had to cover the result with a scarf for the next six months. I thought of her when I looked in the mirror and saw a nightmare out of the fifties. I would have burst into tears if I hadn't been afraid of attracting Leslie's attention and drawing her too deeply into the plot.

Leslie and B.T. were getting ready for the arrival of the summer volunteers, college students from up north who donated several months of their time to the privately funded project. To Leslie and

B.T.'s neighbors, I passed as one of these volunteers, although I had come a bit early and would be staying only a few weeks. Leslie kept telling me how much more helpful I was than the college students. I cooked and cleaned up after myself and was always ready to help in the house as well as with office work. Of course I was grateful to my hosts and could not have acted otherwise.

B.T. was a thickset man with a southern accent so strong I couldn't understand him. Leslie told me he was a gifted organizer but superstitious: he kept a bowl of water and a fork under their bed to scare away the "haints." The "haints" were supposed to stop to drink the water and get trapped by the fork. One night he startled me by entering my room after I was in bed. "You're real nice, Maddy," he said, sitting on the edge of the bed. "You're different from the others." He tried to crawl under the sheets. I talked him into leaving.

In the morning I told Leslie what had happened. She looked amused. "Well, that's B.T. for you," she said. "You weren't scared, I hope?" I assured her I wasn't.

After that B.T. kept urging me to join him and Leslie at church meetings or visits to the rural districts. It didn't sound like a prudent move for a fugitive, but he seemed not to know what my problem was, and I wasn't sure I should tell him.

JANE ALPERT'S BAIL IN BOMB PLOT CASE DECLARED FORFEITED, announced the headline on a back page of the May 15 *Times*. I read the brief article in the periodicals section of the Selma public library. It said I had forfeited my bail when I failed to keep my appointment at the U.S. attorney's office on May 11. Sandy Katz had told the court that neither he nor my parents knew where I was and that my parents would suffer a "substantial financial loss" if the bail were revoked. Pollack had agreed to allow one month's grace time. He had sent Nate to jail at once, though, saying he did not believe he would show up for sentencing otherwise.

Substantial financial loss. The news was no surprise, but the way I felt was. And Nate in jail—I hadn't been prepared for that. I walked slowly back to the house, utterly wretched.

Leslie, B.T., and I set out on the first Sunday after my arrival for a visit with the Johnsons, a politically active black family who lived in the rural part of the state.

On the highway I saw shacks built of papery stuff that looked as though the next wind would topple them, scrubby patches of collards and turnips that, Leslie said, provided the diet of large families, and children in rags with distended bellies, staring vacantly after our car. B.T., who traveled with a shotgun in the back seat for protection from red-necks, appeared to take these sights for granted. Leslie, a northern white herself, was more attuned to my dismay. She explained that we were driving through one of the poorest parts of the country where illiteracy approached eighty percent, contraception was unknown, and deaths from malnutrition not uncommon. These were the horrors the project aimed at correcting, through organizing the rural poor to demand the federal assistance to which they were entitled by law.

I was relieved when the Johnsons turned out to be a well-nourished family living on a productive farm. Leslie, B.T., and I joined three or four Johnson adults, a couple of toddlers, and a high schooler in the living room, which was presided over by the Johnson matriarch. I followed the others' lead by refusing lunch but accepting a grape Kool-Aid. Conversation turned to mutual friends, and my mind wandered. A poster of Rap Brown holding a lighted match caught my eye. Brown was now underground, having failed to show up at his trial for rioting in a Cambridge, Maryland, courthouse. I wondered how easy it was for him to fade anonymously into homes like the Johnsons' and whether he found it possible to continue his political work.

One of the Johnsons wanted to take a group picture. Unable to think of an excuse, I put on sunglasses and trooped into the yard. As the camera clicked, B.T. put an arm around me and I made an effort to smile, in spite of my fear of exposure.

The photograph, which I was allowed to keep as a souvenir of my visit, was a memento of those early months underground. My paleness stood out in contrast with the rich brown skin of the Johnsons, and B.T. My outsized sunglasses were framed by luridly colored, stringy hair. After my week of inactivity, my Bloomingdale's shirtwaist was too tight in the bust and hips. The picture, in fact, was startlingly like the one taken with the Alperts and the Schors when I was fourteen, when, to escape my family, I had dreamed of becoming a hero in the civil rights movement.

I went to the Montgomery airport with Leslie to meet the first of the summer volunteers. I felt like an old hand at the project after ten days and was beginning to wish I could stay on through the summer. I loved the work; it combined the satisfactions of fighting a corrupt system with giving help to those who truly needed it. I couldn't imagine that what I was going to in California would feel half so productive. By the time the volunteer, a gangling redhead named Peter, stepped from the plane, my envy and rivalry were at high pitch. I took the back seat on the ride back to Selma and steamed in silence over each naïve question Peter put to Leslie, thinking how much more I knew than he did.

Leslie proposed that the three of us take the day off to go swimming at a reservoir a few miles out of town. She was in the water when Peter addressed me directly for the first time, asking where I was from. I gave him a fictitious answer in a bored tone.

"You look very familiar to me," Peter said.

I thought he was flirting and ignored the remark.

"In fact, you look like a famous person."

"Oh."

"You look like Jane Alpert."

Leslie was out by the deepwater buoys, swimming laps.

"Who is Jane Alpert?" I stalled.

"Oh, you know. She's the girl who bombed all those buildings in New York. She went underground last week. It was in the papers."

I got up, walked to the edge of the reservoir, and after plunging in, swam toward Leslie. As far as I knew, not even she had been told my real name. But she had been told enough to help.

I explained that I had been recognized and had to leave Selma at once. She said that after we got home, B.T. would drive me to the airport while she diverted Peter so that he wouldn't realize I was leaving. That seemed important to me. If he were an agent, he could alert the FBI and they could arrest me before I got out of town.

With Peter sipping a drink in the living room and Leslie fixing dinner in the kitchen, B.T. started the car in back of the house. I tossed my clothes into my suitcase and escaped by the back door. I slid in the car, and B.T. stepped on the gas and sped down the street.

B.T.'s hand slid questioningly up my thigh. I wriggled away. How had things gone so wrong when I had been so careful? Where was the mistake? Whatever it was, my arrival in San Francisco would wipe the slate clean. This would be the real beginning of my underground life.

* * *

My flight to San Francisco was outwardly uneventful, but I experienced it as full of threat. I could not copy Robin's skill at disguise, and to me every stranger in the airport and on the plane was a potential enemy, on the verge of touching my elbow and murmuring, "Don't I know you from somewhere?" I also wasn't certain that Dana would receive the message I had telephoned to an agreed-upon contact point in San Francisco. I wasn't officially expected for another three days.

No one was waiting for me when I landed in San Francisco in the morning. I boarded a bus for the city, remembering that that was what Dana and I had done when we attended the Panthers' conference a year ago. I hoped she would be waiting for me at the city terminal; if not, I would have to leave a second message and include some way she could find me that wouldn't reveal my whereabouts to strangers.

I was overjoyed to see her waiting on the ground floor of the terminal, wearing her familiar bell-bottoms and a pair of sunglasses. I rushed down the stairs, ready to fling my arms around her. She drew away. "We can talk outside," she said. I followed her into the bustle of downtown Mason Street.

"Your hair," Dana announced, "looks frightful."

I was too happy to see her to feel insulted. "You've got to admit it's different," I said cheerfully.

"You really ought to do something about it. It's awful."

We labored up a steep hill past souvenir shops, giant drugstores, and porno theaters, saying nothing. I couldn't understand why Dana wasn't happier over my arrival. She hadn't even asked me how my trip was and had said nothing at all about herself.

"Where are we going?" I asked, breaking the silence.

"The YMCA," she said tartly.

"Are you serious?"

"I'm serious. It's cheap and anonymous, and it should be safe. Right now I don't have any better ideas. Do you?"

"No. Is that where Pat is?"

"Leah," Dana corrected. "No, she's staying with friends of hers. You'll see her tomorrow. We thought that would be safer."

This promise of seeing Pat was the first news I'd heard that made me feel welcome.

The Y looked like a post office with an American flag outside and a lobby full of loiterers and harassed clerks. For one miserable moment I thought Dana was going to leave me there alone, but after I paid for a room with twin beds and signed a false name on the register, she agreed to accompany me. The room was linoleum-tiled with a small black and white television and a view of an air shaft. Dana sat down on one of the beds. "This place is heaven compared to where I'm staying," she said.

At first Dana was wary, fearing to give away Weather Underground secrets. After a few days her story came out more readily. She had picked up Pat and arrived with her in San Francisco about a month ago. She had expected that the two of them would stay together and that later I would join them, but the Weathermen said no. Pat was a stranger and a fugitive, and they would not risk exposing their people to her. Instead, the Weathermen wanted Dana to find an apartment she could move into with four or five of the younger organization members. Since Dana was not hiding out to avoid arrest, she was to use her connections to raise money for rent and food. Periodically she was to report to the Weather Underground West Coast leadership: Bernardine Dohrn and Jeff Jones who, in spite of the official dictum against monogamy, were living together as lovers in an apartment on the beach.

I slowly understood that the Weathermen had managed, more or less on a whim, to break up Dana's four-year-old relationship with Ben, remove her from her home, and finally send her to live with five kids whom she was expected to support and care for as a virtual den mother.

"The apartment is horrible," she admitted. "I keep thinking that everything in it is plastic: the dishes, the people. Even this dog that one of them picked up is like a plastic dog. They always forget to walk it, so I wind up taking it out. Little yappy thing that shits all over the house.

"I talk to Ben every day. We use phony credit cards. Sometimes we talk for the whole afternoon. I miss him so much I don't know how I can go on. I miss my apartment and the dogs . . . I want to go home. But if I go, they'll just pick me up and try to get me to talk about the Beatles."

Dana's face brightened only when she talked about Pat. Undaunted by the Weathermen's rejection, Pat had telephoned Neil Perlmutter, her ex-lover and my friend, who was now living in Berkeley.

"Wasn't that pretty dangerous?" I wondered. I had figured I would never talk on a home phone to anyone I had known in my former life since there was no telling whose receiver the FBI would tap.

"Well, of course she couldn't stay in a movement center like Berkeley. But Neil introduced her to these friends of his—Ned and Janine, their names are. They've got an apartment in San Francisco. Leah's staying there."

Ned Gorgas and Janine Foster, like Neil, were friends from Swarthmore. They had never been politically active, and I was surprised to learn that they were willing to house a fugitive.

Dana insisted it was safe. The Weathermen had also contacted some of their college friends, reasoning that the FBI had no way of tracking down all their nonpolitical associations. This made sense but contrasted with the paranoia Dana displayed on most other occasions. Once at a drugstore counter, she made me leave a half-eaten sandwich because she thought the man next to me was staring too hard. Another time, on a bench in Union Square, she suddenly jumped up.

"That man just took a picture of us," she hissed.

I turned and saw a stout middle-aged man with a camera.

"I think he was taking a picture of the cable car," I said. But Dana insisted that we leave the park. We wandered the streets for an hour before she would sit down again anywhere.

"It's easy for you," she said. "You know as long as you're free that you're also safe. But I'm not a fugitive. If they find me, they'll just keep tailing me until I've led them to someone they want. I'm never safe. I can't sleep. I keep imagining them outside my door laying a trap. I don't know how I can keep living with all this fear."

She was shaking when she said this. Dana, who had always seemed the sanest and strongest of all, was beginning to lose her reason.

I met Pat in a delicatessen on Mason Street on the second morning of my stay. She had cut her hair and dyed it red, but otherwise, she was her old self, tender and expressive and funny. Over bagels and on a long walk through North Beach (which Dana had insisted was an unsafe area for a fugitive), she told me of her life since the night of our arrest. After her impulsive flight she had lived in many different homes, sometimes staying indoors for weeks because her hosts were afraid she would be recognized on the street. In virtual isolation she had missed Jenny fearfully.

"I read books on prayer because I didn't know what else to do," she confessed. "I felt silly at first, but they really helped. You know, there's a center inside you where nothing that happens on the outside matters. If you can get to it, you feel only peace. I practiced doing that. And when Dana arrived on my doorstep . . . well, how could I have asked for more of an answer? As soon as I saw her, I thought: 'This is the messenger.' And now *you're* here. It's like a miracle to me."

I was delighted to see Pat so full of vitality, but I wasn't sure how far her new calm would take us. Dana was on the verge of a breakdown, and the Weathermen hadn't been exactly helpful. Pat said I shouldn't worry; something would work out.

I left the Y and moved into Ned and Janine's living room with Pat. Our hosts were marvels of tolerance, not only enduring the danger and inconvenience of having us but also agreeing that the Weathermen might visit us there one night while they were out with friends.

Bernardine and Jeff Jones came disguised, wearing broad smiles and bearing grass. As if granting us a privilege, they read to Dana, Pat, and me the first press release of the Weather Underground, due to reach radios and newspapers later in the week. Pat leafed through yesterday's *Chronicle* as they read. I sympathized with her boredom but tried to appear receptive. Dana glanced back and forth between us like an overanxious hostess. I was waiting for some discussion of our living arrangements, money, transportation, ID—anything to show that the official underground was prepared to help. Instead, Bernardine and Jeff raved about the movie *Woodstock,* which they had seen eight times. Pat pointed out that the three of us had been at the actual event. This did not faze the Weathermen. They left with kisses and hugs and a promise that we would meet again in a week or two. They failed to keep the next appointment.

Dana decided to return to New York. Whatever dangers awaited her at home, she preferred them to pretending to be a fugitive. Pat and I discussed our dilemma in phone calls with Maude and Greg Rosen. It was agreed that the two of us should not try to come east before September, when the hunt for us would have died down. In the meantime, Maude and Greg would send enough money to keep us alive and we should try to fend for ourselves. In September we would all gather again and discuss the next step.

Suppose Pat and I took the next three months to drive across the country? We could save money by sleeping outside, visit scenic wonders, and have an altogether splendid vacation while fulfilling our main obligation: not to get caught. Pat had camped and hiked in East Africa when she was married and could choose our equipment and provide basic skills. Ned and Janine would advise us on our itinerary, and Dana would help us pick out a used car before she went home.

Our joy over our new plans was marred only by Dana's deteriorating emotional state. To save money, she planned to share a ride with a stranger who had advertised on a Berkeley bulletin board. Then she worried that she would be asked too many questions. Instead, she reserved a driveaway car at an agency. The car was supposed to be ready a few days after Pat and I left for Yosemite, our first stop, in the 1963 Rambler Dana had helped us buy.

Pat and I departed on schedule on a brilliant June morning. We learned later from Ned and Janine that Dana had changed her mind for the third time. Deciding she wasn't safe in San Francisco for even a few more hours, she got Ned and Janine to take her to the airport and boarded the next flight for New York.

Six hours from San Francisco we caught our first glimpse of the Sierra Nevada. Those jagged peaks, the crisp, heady air, and the amber light dazzled our senses. We fell in love with the mountains, and after some early mishaps we became moderately good campers. At first we had only a couple of Dacron sleeping bags, a styrofoam ice chest, a plastic jug, and a light knapsack, but after the first week we had augmented our supplies by using our phony IDs to rent down bags, real backpacks, and a tent at a store in Fresno. Pat became expert at cooking combinations of whole-grain flours, powdered milk, nuts, and dried fruits over a campfire. I learned to stake a tent, build a fire, identify Jeffrey pines by their vanilla-scented bark—and, under Pat's direction, to drive a car, a skill I'd never acquired in New York.

When we felt lonely, we cheered ourselves with a myth about a network that stretched across the country. Maude and Greg were part of it, and so were Ned and Janine and Neil in California, standing ready to help if needed. Sylvia, the friend of Maude's who printed our false IDs and with whom Pat had stayed for a month or two, belonged. So did Leslie in Selma (even though I was no longer in touch with her) and potentially hundreds of others. We told ourselves that we didn't need the Weathermen or any other official organization; our friends and sympathizers would be enough. Whether "enough" meant simply staying alive and out of jail or whether we had some larger political purpose, I'm not sure we could have said.

After four glorious weeks in the Sierras we headed back to San Francisco to restock our food supply and enjoy the luxury of hot showers at Ned and Janine's. We spent a few days feeling seduced by the city but then pulled ourselves away again. This time we took the coastal route toward Big Sur, planning to reenter the Sierras in the southern part of the range and climb Mount Whitney.

Two hours south of the city, just before we planned to camp for the night, we picked up two hitchhikers. Lonnie was extremely tall and slender with curly hair and a dreamy baby face. His friend, slightly built with a pointed chin and ears, did most of the talking. Lonnie was from Cincinnati, Ray from Ann Arbor. They had met a few weeks ago in Berkeley, where they both were working for the *Tribe*, the more political of the community's two underground papers. Pat and I slipped into movement jargon with them, and they responded like charter members of the network. Yet when we encouraged them to camp with us for the night at a spot called Half Moon Bay, they declined. We dropped them on the road and turned in toward the ocean. We were building a fire in front of a cave when the two men approached us. Could they change their minds and share our dinner after all? Of course we said yes.

To me, Lonnie was obviously the more attractive. I was afraid that Pat would snare him. Instead, she seemed happy to give her attention to the loquacious Ray. After dinner the two of them retired to the rear of the cave while Lonnie and I gazed silently at the Pacific. When I suggested a plunge into the ocean, Lonnie smiled shyly before taking off his clothes and dashing in.

We dressed and walked along the dunes. Lonnie told me he had recently got back from Vietnam. He had enlisted from high school in the hope that imminent departure would win his girl friend back. It hadn't worked. She married someone else, and Lonnie found himself in the middle of a war. He came to love the Vietnamese and hate the American soldiers who were devastating the country, and he dreamed of deserting to the Vietcong. He spent almost a year in the stockades and was finally shipped back to the States. As soon as he won his discharge, he joined a Weatherman collective, with which he intended to go underground. But when the Wilkerson town house exploded and the Weathermen became fugitives ahead of schedule, Lonnie was in the hospital with hepatitis. He had been trying to find them ever since; that was the chief reason he had come to Berkeley.

The coincidence struck me as remarkable. When Lonnie and I made love on the warm, damp sand, the urge to tell him the truth about myself was almost irresistible. If I had been alone, I would not have hesitated, so much alike did our stories seem. But of course, I had to consult Pat first.

Lonnie and I returned to the cave at dawn. When Pat and Ray awoke, I took Pat aside and repeated Lonnie's story. She was not as impressed by the coincidence as I was, but she saw no harm in our confiding in Lonnie. Nor in Ray who, while no Weatherman, had been active in leftist organizations in Ann Arbor for many years.

We broke the news to the men together as we squatted by our morning fire outside the cave. After our weeks of anonymity, their response to our names was gratifying. Ray, amazed, kept shaking his head. Lonnie won my heart by saying softly, "I remember staring at your picture in the *Tribe*. But I wouldn't have recognized you. In the photos, your hair looks dark."

Pat and I canceled our plans to climb Mount Whitney. Instead, we headed for a commune in northern California which some of Ray's friends from Ann Arbor had founded. Lonnie had lent his new Maverick to the communards for the summer, and in return for the favor, the two of us were given the privilege of a bedroom to ourselves.

If Lonnie showed signs of being less than the perfect revolutionary in those first weeks, I was too infatuated with him to notice. No man had ever made love to me the way he did, moving his hands and tongue and hips in slow, mesmerizing motion. Lonnie wasn't articulate, but I thought our souls must be in silent communion in order to have the kind of sex we did. We hardly left the bedroom and saw Pat and Ray only at meals or when we went for a dip in the communal swimming pool. Pat assured me that she too was enjoying the conviviality of the commune and was in no hurry to leave.

Eventually we did leave, heading up the Oregon coast. Almost from the moment of our departure our troubles began. I quickly came to dislike Ray, who was on a mucus-free diet which he talked about incessantly. He was also a hypochondriac who wouldn't swim and loathed hiking. Afraid of starting a fight, I kept away from him. After breakfast Lonnie and I would wander into the woods, where he would tell me stories of the Mekong Delta and the stockade that made me feel I had been there myself. Pat began to resent us for never doing our share of the cooking and cleaning, which I hardly was aware of.

We were camped next to a stream in the shelter of a granite cliff when Pat asked to talk to me alone. She and Ray had reached a decision that the four of us should separate. She and Ray would drive the Rambler to Ann Arbor, where Ray had invited her to stay. Lonnie and I could return to the commune and pick up Lonnie's car. Then we were to make our separate ways across the country to New York for the September rendezvous with Maude and Greg—which both Lonnie and Ray wanted to be part of.

I was stunned that Pat would have reached such a conclusion without consulting me. As enamored as I was of Lonnie, my commitment was to Pat, not him. How could she make such a crucial decision without asking me first? She told me it was obvious to her that the separation was the best step. It couldn't possibly make so much difference what we did for just a few weeks. I disagreed strongly but could not budge her.

That afternoon the four of us drove to Interstate 5 near Portland and divided up our gear. Pat and Ray took the rented (or, rather, stolen) goose down bags and one backpack. Lonnie and I took the Dacron bags which we'd been using all along since they zipped together. We had about $200, which we split down the middle.

"You'll certainly have more than enough cash," Pat said, "since your car is brand-new."

"Yes, we'll be fine," I answered in a rush. The vision of the two of us arguing over money was too depressing to contemplate.

Lonnie's zippy Maverick was waiting when we arrived at the commune, but we were in no hurry to leave. I suggested that we try to stay until Labor Day, only two or three weeks away, when Maude and Greg might be ready to receive us in New York. As long as we were willing to camp on the grounds of the commune and chip in for meals, no one had any objection.

On the second afternoon of our stay, I applied myself to a stack of magazines in the communal living room. On the couch opposite, a commune leader, a blond midwesterner like most of his housemates, was holding a one-volume collection of articles from the radical press, but I realized that what he was really doing was staring at me. He would look at the page in front of him, then at my face, back at the page, and then at my face—as if he were trying to identify me from a photograph. After a few minutes he put down the book and left the room.

I got up and looked at the table of contents. Could this possibly be the volume for which an editor had asked permission to reprint one of my *Rat* pieces? Yes, the piece was listed. My heart stopped when I turned the page. Next to my piece was a full-page photograph of Nate and me at a demonstration. My profile was unmistakable: beaklike nose, straight hairline, firm chin. I dashed outside to tell Lonnie we had to leave at once. He suggested that we head for his parents' house in Cincinnati, and having nothing better to offer, I accepted.

As we packed the Maverick, I cursed my carelessness. I should have known—and so should Pat—that a commune founded by Ray's leftist friends from Ann Arbor was not a safe place for us. I had been recognized here for the same reason I was spotted by Peter, the volunteer: movement activists and sympathizers, having seen my face in the papers they read, would recognize me. And where the movement gathered, so did the FBI. I was going to have to learn to be much choosier about the places I stayed. I didn't kid myself that this would be easy, for if I couldn't stay with movement folk, then how much meaning did the network have?

Lonnie and I spent our first night on the road at Lake Tahoe, which was not the wilderness retreat I pictured. We had to squeeze our pup tent between monstrous Winnebagos and suffer the tantalizing smell of steaks cooked on middle-class families' charcoal grills. At night the temperature dropped below freezing and neither of us could sleep. Lonnie leaped into the car and started the motor. I got in next to him with our gear. We crossed the Nevada border and headed south.

Outside Reno at 3:00 A.M. we picked up a hitchhiker on his way to Denver. If we drove him all the way, could he give us a place to stay? He said he was visiting friends who might let us sleep on their floor. The sun rose on the moonscape of central Nevada. We kept driving, doing eighty on the nearly empty interstate. In midafternoon we raced through the blazing reds and yellows of the Utah canyons. At dark we approached the sheer heights of the Colorado Rockies. The car swerved sharply as we switchbacked up and down the slopes. Twenty-four hours after leaving Lake Tahoe, having stopped only for gas and candy bars, we descended into the foothills of Denver and drove through block after block of identical middle-class houses, trying to read the street signs.

"Look out!" yelled the hitchhiker.

Lonnie jerked on the steering wheel. We bumped over a pothole at about forty miles an hour. The car struck the curb and careened back into the middle of the street, then went dead.

The hitchhiker telephoned his friends from a pay phone as Lonnie worked on getting the car started. We drove slowly after that, the car rattling ferociously through the sleeping town.

We spent the night on a living-room floor where five or six others were also rolled up in sleeping bags. In the morning, after banging on the bottom of the car for a while, Lonnie announced that all was well. We were almost at Limon in the plains east of the Rockies when both front tires blew out. Getting the car towed to a Limon service station took most of the rest of our money. The mechanic said he would look at the car tomorrow. With the few dollars we had left, we rented a space in a dusty trailer park on the outskirts of town and staked our tent.

Lonnie telephoned his parents in Cincinnati—to whom he had not spoken since leaving for Berkeley—and asked them to wire $100. His father said he would send $75. He also had some bad news. It seems the FBI had been to Lonnie's parents' house, saying they believed Lonnie might know the whereabouts of a few missing Weathermen.

I let this news sink in. The FBI was looking for fugitives through Lonnie. His father now knew that Lonnie was stranded in Limon, waiting for a money order. If Lonnie's father repeated that to the FBI, my freedom would end with the arrival of the money order.

Continuing on to Cincinnati was out of the question. But whom did I know within a thousand miles of Limon, Colorado?

Dorian. My dear friend Dorian, who in 1966 had referred me to the doctor who performed my abortion. After graduating from college, she had returned to St. Louis, her hometown, where she was living with a classical musician and taking graduate courses. St. Louis wasn't all that close, but it was the best I could come up with.

A call to St. Louis information produced Dorian's number.

Amazingly she knew my voice almost at once, though we hadn't spoken in at least a year and I didn't say my name. I had to trust that she knew my story. By all means, she said, she would find me a place to stay. And Lonnie, too, if I wanted. I blessed her silently.

Lonnie and I used every precaution in picking up the money order at Western Union. We talked the mechanic who was repairing the Maverick into driving Lonnie to the Western Union office. That way the license plate of the Maverick would not be observed. Lonnie looked about him before he entered and left the office to make sure he was not noticed. In the mechanic's car, he watched the rearview mirror to determine that he was not followed. When he met me at the trailer park, he assured me that we were in the clear.

In that case why was a police car tailing us for our first twenty miles on the highway? We were driving well under the speed limit. Finally the cop signaled us to pull over. He walked over and demanded to see Lonnie's license.

"I've got to give you a warning," he said, "for driving in the passing lane when you're going under the speed limit."

I was convinced it was a ruse so that the cop could take my picture with a secret camera.

After that I was sure we were followed by unmarked government cars that kept a steady distance behind us. One of them actually followed us into a gas station, and I was convinced that while Lonnie and I had used the bathrooms, the driver had secreted a bug in our car to pick up our conversations. They would have arrested me on the spot, but they hadn't quite figured out which of the Weathermen fugitives I was.

I forbade Lonnie to talk while we were driving, fearing that all our conversations were taped. I studied a map to figure out where I could hop on a bus for St. Louis. Hays, in the middle of Kansas, seemed the only likely spot. Silently I pointed it out to Lonnie on the map. He nodded, as tense as I was. Hays was still hours away. For miles we passed nothing but cornfields rolling into the far horizon. And always the tails.

In the town of Hays, a diner doubled as the Greyhound bus terminal. As soon as I left the car, a sheriff's car pulled up next to us. I turned my face from the sheriff and entered the diner. He followed me. He sat down at a front booth from which he could have heard anything I said to the ticket seller at the counter. I continued straight to the back of the diner and walked into the ladies' room. Standing over the toilet, I shredded every bit of information I had that could lead to someone: names, phone numbers, a small photo of Sam. I hid a water pipe Ned and Janine had given me behind the toilet. When I looked in the mirror, I thought it might be the last time I saw myself outside a prison cell. I combed my hair. Then I shoved open the door and headed straight toward the sheriff, looking firmly ahead.

He didn't budge. Not daring to believe my luck, I went out the door to the parking lot. He didn't follow. I walked very fast in no particular direction, wondering whether Lonnie had left town already.

He was waiting for me two blocks away, pale and shaken. He opened the car door, and I got in. I didn't say a word. Nor did he. We hit the interstate again and headed east, driving exactly at the speed limit. The unmarked car kept following. Or so I was convinced.

We reached Kansas City in the evening rush hour. Urban pollution had never filled me with such relief. In a crowd like this, James Bond himself couldn't find me. On a piece of notepaper I wrote to Lonnie: "Let me out."

We exited at the busiest possible spot and drove into the middle of the city. Cars, trucks, motorcycles, pedestrians, bicycles. Huge crowds hurrying home. Bums. Junkies. I loved them all. Leaving everything in the car except a change of clothes I had stuffed into my shoulder bag and $40 in cash, I hopped out. I walked a half mile through the honky-tonk section, confident for the first time since morning that no one was in pursuit of me, and checked into a cheap hotel. The desk clerk leered at me, but he could have been welcoming me to heaven for all I cared. That night I bought a bus ticket to St. Louis and a bottle of hair dye. I bleached my now-dark roots in the hotel bathroom, cleaning the rancid mess from the sink as well as I could. I loved that shabby room. On that night even the foul odor of the dye smelled to me of freedom.

Dorian and I strolled through a city park, hunting for topics we still had in common. She had broken up with the musician and was now involved with Paul, a medical student, who was about to move in with her. I talked a little about Sam, more about Lonnie, and described the best parts of camping in the Sierras. Dorian wondered whether I was concerned about getting caught. I said I felt perfectly safe now, which was true. Dorian might have agreed to house me out of political sympathy as well as personal generosity, but the FBI would never know that; she had never been an activist. In fact, I was astounded and grateful that she was willing to help me. She said I was welcome to stay in the house Paul rented. His roommate was away for the summer, and Paul, since he was moving in with Dorian, would not be using the place.

After a couple of days in Paul's house—with its color television, stereo system, walls of books, and electric kitchen equipment—I missed Lonnie sorely. Although I had decided in Limon that it was unsafe to travel with him, I now convinced myself that we could work out a way. I telephoned him at his family's house in Cincinnati. He immediately agreed to take the next bus to St. Louis—leaving the Maverick, through which he might have been identified, behind. Dorian and I picked him up at the station.

In the sedate academic world in which Dorian and Paul lived I realized for the first time that Lonnie was less than completely sane. He used enormous quantities of drugs—speed, mescaline, grass, whatever he could get his hands on. He giggled to himself over jokes he couldn't explain. He helped himself to the clothes in Paul's closet, appearing not to realize that Paul might object. Once, while I slept, he painted a Day-Glo mural directly on the living-room wall.

At times I was appalled. At other times I responded exactly as I had to Sam, competing with him to prove that I was the more daring radical. Reverting to the persona I had left behind in New York, I devoted my time in St. Louis to writing an article that advocated kidnapping as a means of freeing political prisoners. Lonnie, naturally, loved it and made a drawing to accompany it, showing the young revolutionaries of the world—Vietnamese, Cubans, Chinese, black American—with linked arms and banners. Strangely, every face in the drawing resembled mine.

Through Maude, Pat and I managed to reconnect. We talked on the telephone for the first time since our separation. She had arrived in New York, where she was met by Greg and Robert Carpenter, at around the same time I reached St. Louis. The three of them were staying in a cabin Robert owned in western Massachusetts. They were trying to rent another cabin temporarily, which would have room for me and Maude and perhaps Ben and Dana, who also wanted to visit us.

"And Lonnie," I added.

"Oh, you're still together?" Pat asked. Her tone was condescending. After some coaxing she told me what had happened to her and Ray.

Within days after leaving us in Portland, the Rambler had developed engine trouble. They had spent all their money on repairs and from then on were forced to steal their food and gas. In Missoula, Montana, Pat was caught at a check-out counter with a jar of peanuts in her pocketbook. She and Ray were hauled into court and given a choice of going free on $25 bail or pleading guilty on the spot. They didn't have the money. The judge sentenced them to six days in jail—long enough for Pat's fingerprints to be checked with the FBI's central office. Before that could happen, the judge commuted their sentences to six hours and let them go.

The experience had devastated Ray. When they finally reached Ann Arbor, he told Pat he couldn't take fugitive life anymore. Pat had then left him the Rambler, which he promised to sell for us, and flown to the East Coast with money provided by Greg and Maude.

I wondered whether my friends would accept Lonnie after Pat had managed to work her way free of Ray. Pat assured me that it was fine if Lonnie came east: Greg and Robert and Maude would certainly understand and would help me find a place where he could stay, too.

After I hung up, my pride asserted itself. Damn right they would find a place for Lonnie. He was my lover and more than that—my mad self, my child. We would not be separated. If my friends cared for me, they would accept him, too. And keep their opinions to themselves.

XIII
Disintegration

THE LONG-AWAITED REUNION TOOK place in a cottage Greg had rented for the purpose on the shore of a tiny lake in the Berkshires. For one weekend eight of us gathered there: Greg and Robert, Pat, Maude, Lonnie and I, Dana and Ben. In spite of shared politics and interlocked histories, we were an uncongenial group.

Maude, who hated such large gatherings, had driven up from the city with Dana, who since her return from San Francisco had practically become Maude's personal charge. Listless and withdrawn, she talked little to Pat and less to me.

Pat and Robert Carpenter, who had met only briefly before, had found themselves strongly attracted to each other and were sleeping in Robert's private cabin not far from the lake. Pat was sleeping with Greg, too, an arrangement which appeared to suit her. I had rarely seen her so euphoric as during those first weeks back east.

Lonnie and I were awarded the private bedroom in the lakeside cottage. Lonnie frequently retreated there not to be with me but to escape the interrogations of Greg, Robert, and Maude, who remained suspicious that he might be another Demmerle.

Ben refused to meet Lonnie at all. He had come up from his Boston Weatherman collective on that condition and would not even stay overnight, for fear of bumping into the stranger. Greg warned me to watch my tongue with Ben since anything I said could go back to the Weather Underground. I couldn't see what we had to fear since the entire occasion was little more than social. Pat and I had pinned our entire summer to this event, and I now wondered just what we had expected to happen.

After Ben had returned to his collective and Maude and Dana to New York, the purpose of the gathering became clearer. Greg told me that he had been waiting all weekend to talk to me alone and suggested that we go for a drive. In the car he explained that Pat already knew what he was about to tell me but had been sworn to secrecy until the others had left. I was to repeat his confidence to no one, not even Lonnie. My curiosity aroused, I gave my word.

"Do you remember when you left New York and I charged all that equipment on your store accounts?" Greg asked.

I nodded.

"Well, that was so Robert and I could carry out this plan. Last spring, when Robert was on a hike in the woods behind his cabin, he discovered an abandoned shed. You're not going to believe this when I tell you, but it's true: that shed was packed to the roof with dynamite. We don't know for sure, but we figure it's owned by some construction company that uses it for a warehouse. Anyway, with the help of the stuff I bought with you in New York, Robert and I were able to break in three times, and now we've got access to all the explosives we could possibly use. We can hit whatever target we want."

I was supposed to express elation, but I felt only dismay. I didn't know why. Having just completed an article advocating political kidnapping, I could hardly claim to have turned against violence. Yet I did feel disappointed in Greg, who had maintained a pacifist stance ever since Sam began his bombings. When I had wondered whether we were doing the right thing, my thoughts had turned to Greg as exemplifying a different kind of activism, nonviolent but no less committed than ours. This new glint in his eye reminded me painfully of last fall and of the madness that had led to our arrest. I didn't know what to say.

"Now that the others are gone," Greg went on, "I think that you and Pat and Robert and I should get together at Robert's one night and talk about this. Do you think you can make some excuse to Lonnie?"

"I'm sure I can," I said. I was thinking that would be the easy part.

Sitting around the Franklin stove in Robert's cabin with my friends, their faces lit by the plumbers' candles Robert used instead of electricity, I kept remembering the first time Nate, Sam, Pat, and I had talked of bombings, after I had returned from England. A thrill of possibility had beckoned to me in that room on the Lower East Side as we had hunched against the walls, keeping our voices low. If Sam and Nate were here now instead of Greg and Robert, would I be experiencing the same urgency again?

Robert said one possible target was a nuclear power plant on the outskirts of New York City. In such discussions one was never to look shocked, but I wasn't sure whether Robert was serious.

"Wouldn't that kill a lot of people?" I asked.

"It's just a suggestion," Robert said. "I think it's a good idea not to limit your imagination at the planning stage."

For a moment he reminded me of Dr. Strangelove, fiddling with his hearing aid, his eyes rolling. Sam had sometimes called him a mad genius and lamented that he wasn't more political. I felt grateful now that the two of them had never gotten together for more than guitar-and-banjo jam sessions.

"We've got some other targets in mind," Greg, the reasonable one, broke in. "For example, the IBM plant in Newburgh, New York, is vital to the global computer market."

I caught Pat's eye. She beamed as if to say, "Isn't this wonderful?" No wonder. She was involved once again in a sexual triangle with two vanguard radicals competing for her attention. I wondered if what was true for Pat and me was also true of women in the Black Panther Party and the Weather Underground. Did all of us feel interested in bombing buildings only when the men we slept with were urging us on? Was it love for Sam that had allowed me to lose my head a year ago and objectivity toward Greg and Robert that was allowing me to keep it now?

"Listen," I said finally. "This all sounds great, but it's a bit much for me to handle at the moment. Pat and I still need to get ourselves settled. We need a car and a place to live. When we're straightened out, we can figure out the next step."

Amazing how a hint that the men had been unchivalrous snapped them to attention. "Of course," Robert said. "There's no rush. I thought that tomorrow morning we could look for a used car for you."

"As a matter of fact, I've got a place for you to stay just about lined up," Greg added.

Under the pressure of immediate needs, the topic of bombings was shelved. By the time it next came up it had the smell of last week's lunch, saved in the refrigerator for an occasion no one could remember.

Pat required new ID since hers had been tainted by the Montana shoplifting arrest. Lonnie, who still planned to stay with us, would also need ID, and I was sick of the name Frances Ethel Matthews. Maude's friend Sylvia went to work printing new licenses for us all, to be ready in a month or so. Robert helped us pick out a 1963 aqua Chevrolet that cost only $100 and that he assured us was in top condition. Relieving a burden that had weighed on me heavily, I wrote a note to my parents assuring them I was safe and well and gave it to Greg to pass on to Sandy Katz for them. Then Greg and Robert returned to New York while Pat, Lonnie, and I moved into an unheated summer house in Connecticut lent to us by people Greg knew. At that point the three of us began house hunting in earnest, again relying on money provided by our friends.

Since Pat's ID was unusable and Lonnie's revealed his true identity (and a possible link to the Weathermen), mine was the only set among us that would stand up to inspection. I took turns house hunting with Lonnie, pretending to be a newly married couple, and with Pat, pretending to be Montessori-style schoolteachers who had earned a year's leave to write a book. We had bad luck in conservative Connecticut, where Lonnie's bushy hair and wild-eyed look alienated homeowners, so we moved our search to western New York. I was on the verge of admitting to myself and Pat that Lonnie was more a hindrance than a help and that he perhaps ought to leave when we found a perfect farmhouse: furnished, with an apple orchard, located on a private dirt road, and only $100 a month. We promptly moved in and within a few days had equipped the kitchen with items from rummage sales, baked dozens of pies from the orchard's apples, and acquired two kittens from a neighbor.

Lonnie, Pat, and I had been in the farmhouse less than a week when, without warning, Greg's ancient Ford pulled into the driveway. He had brought dire news from the city. It seemed that Sylvia had finally completed our new IDs and mailed them to a prearranged drop—but after two weeks, they had not arrived. She and Maude had concluded that they had been intercepted by the FBI and that in order to be safe, Pat, Lonnie, and I should leave our new home at once.

Pat and I protested. Even if the IDs had fallen into government hands, how would the agents conclude that they were intended for us? And how would they know where we were? Greg said that Sylvia was already under suspicion (or believed she was) for having harbored Pat and reminded us that when we moved in, we had ordered a new telephone for the farmhouse using the surname that was to be on the IDs.

Pat had grown used to obeying the wishes of others in her early months underground, and though she was upset, she did not protest. I was furious. Pat and I had been as cautious as any two people could be under difficult circumstances. We always addressed each other by aliases, kept our friends' phone numbers in codes, and had never talked about our situation or our friends in the hearing of strangers or over home telephones. We had suffered one bout of paranoia in the past week when the owners of the farmhouse showed us around and one was a shutterbug who kept snapping our pictures. Since then I had felt positive that we were safe. No local people were going to recognize our faces. Pat's disappearance had received no publicity for a year, and mine had not been covered since May 15. With Rap Brown, the Weather Underground, Eldridge Cleaver, and most recently the disappearance of Angela Davis to keep them busy, I figured the FBI was not expending much effort on finding Jane Alpert and Patricia Swinton. And this fuss over a piece of lost mail struck me as ridiculous. Greg evaded my argument by insisting he was only a messenger and that Maude, on whom we were dependent for IDs, had given orders.

When I finally understood that logic was useless, I telephoned our landlord with an excuse to cover our sudden departure. Then Lonnie, Pat, and I packed our belongings and the two kittens in the Chevy and drove east into the Catskills. After a miserable week in the cheapest rental cottage we could find, and no luck with house hunting, we went on to New Hampshire, where Greg had suggested that rents might be lower than in New York. In the industrial town of Manchester we took a furnished room over a trucking yard where the rumble of engines woke us before dawn each day.

In mid-October Lonnie and I found a house for rent outside the town of Jaffrey in southern New Hampshire. It was a find: a white frame colonial with wood-paneled library, fireplace, five bedrooms, and only two or three other houses within a quarter mile of the property. Jubilant, Lonnie and I signed a lease in the aliases Richard and Ellen Davis Blake—the names printed on the IDs that had finally arrived from Sylvia. The only problem was that we couldn't occupy the house until November 1. In the meantime, the landlord in the Manchester rooming house discovered our kittens and evicted us.

I couldn't bear the idea of calling Maude or Greg to ask for help. Instead, Pat and I agreed to relax our usual precautions and call a movement connection of mine in Boston, Jeanette, a woman I had met at a radical left press conference. She immediately offered to meet me at a pizza parlor in a suburb of the city and to find a place the three of us could stay until November 1. The next day Lonnie, Pat, and I moved in with a young couple who worked in a day care center in Somerville, Massachusetts. The couple, friends of Jeanette's, didn't know our real names and might not have recognized them. The fact that we were radical fugitives was sufficient to win us their help. They gave up the bedroom in their two-room apartment to the three of us, a token of their personal generosity but also of something else: the extent to which even apolitical young people in the early seventies yearned for social change and were willing to believe that an underground of penniless, scared fugitives had something to do with accomplishing it.

My parents were to call me for the first time at a pay phone next to a shopping center across the street from the Somerville apartment. When the telephone rang—on the stroke of seven—I picked it up with a cheery "hello."

The answer came after a long silence. My father began to say my name, then remembered. "Is this Ellen?" he asked. The ragged edge to his speech told me everything I had hoped to avoid knowing. Sandy Katz had told Greg that my parents had refused to believe I had deliberately jumped bail, even after receiving my first note. At first they thought I had been mugged and thrown into the East River. Then they believed I had been kidnapped and drugged. Hearing my father's voice, I felt that whatever insecurity I'd experienced in the past six months was minuscule compared to their suffering. I hated myself, and for a moment I hated my father, too, for his inability to hide the cracking of his voice.

"How are you, Daddy?" I said.

They were all right. Well, they'd had a few problems. My mother, who had started having nervous spasms in her hand, had had to take a leave from teaching and was suffering from severe insomnia. Otherwise, everything was fine. How was I?

I assured him I was well and happy. In a few weeks a friend and I would be moving to a lovely house only five or six hours from New York. If they liked, they could visit us there.

"That would please your mother," my father said. He said he had to go then but would write to the new address I had sent. I promised to send a home phone number as soon as I had one. He hung up, sounding on the verge of tears.

I walked very slowly back to the house, ill at ease and dimly aware that something in my underground life was now permanently changed.

While we were still in Somerville, Pat and I decided Lonnie had to go. My fierce attachment to him had dwindled to mere fondness, and I couldn't in any case go on allowing him to drain our friends' meager resources. After a few downcast days Lonnie announced he would return to Cincinnati. He claimed he was going to get his parents to give him a lot of money which he would then hand over to Pat and me. Pat and I humored him. He left us to hitchhike back to Cincinnati a few days before Pat and I were to occupy our new house. We breathed more easily once he was gone and thought we would never see him again.

Pat and I moved into the Jaffrey house on the appointed day under cover of darkness, hoping to keep the neighbors from noticing that we were not man and wife, Richard and Ellen Blake, and also to hide from them our ragtag possessions, collected over five months of vagabond life. I barely remembered the house from the day Lonnie and I had signed the lease, and it took us awhile to find it in the dark. Once inside, it looked dowdier than I remembered—like a set for a fifties movie, Pat said. Taking in the formal dining hall, the starched curtains, and the empty credenza waiting to display our heirlooms, I had to admit that it was not quite us.

It was a hard time for revolutionaries. Fugitive Pun Plamondon was picked up in Michigan when he chucked a beer can out the window of a car. Angela Davis was arrested in New York. The bombings in Southeast Asia escalated in spite of huge demonstrations against them. A grand jury refused to indict national guardsmen for killing four students in protests at Kent State. Pat and I, worn out by months as fugitives, no longer imagined we would accomplish political goals. Nor did anyone else we knew. Maude was making plans to move to Kentucky after her boyfriend took a job there. Greg was looking for a position in Europe. Robert was cross-country skiing and working on his inventions. His affair with Pat continued sporadically. When he visited, they made love in the upstairs bedroom, as I knew from the bellowing that accompanied Robert's orgasms. The sounds reminded me unhappily of my own sexual isolation as I stared out the living-room window at the falling snow.

Sometimes I imagined that when Sam got out of prison, perhaps in ten or twelve years, we would love each other again. Of course, I knew myself better now and would not follow him in the same stupid mistakes I made a year ago. But perhaps he had changed, too. Greg, who visited him every month at Attica prison near Buffalo, said Sam was becoming an intellectual, immersing himself in Marx, Lenin, and Engels. Through Greg I sent Sam assurances that I still loved him and begged to know whether he felt the same. His answer was smuggled out by Greg on five squares of toilet paper.

"To speak of love," he wrote, "especially love between one desperate man and woman, limits our vision and ties us to the past. When I am not weeping over such obvious extremes of our blindness (or about my own loneliness in spite of knowing the blindness) i'm laughing bitterly at the absurdity of your fearing i have lost love for you. You can believe if i never smell or taste you again it's a real motherfucking loss!"

He went on to lecture me about our "desperate vision and inheritance" which his "new teachers" (Marx etc.) called capitalism. "Recriminations," he wrote, "have no part in expanded love." I was to use my guilt "to realize more meaning for the rest of humanity."

In the end, he expressed affection—characteristically, with an insult. "Yes, sweet bitch, i love you. And if they ever let me out and the wind is right i'll find you."

I became worried that Greg had told Sam about Lonnie and that as a result, Sam had written me off. Greg admitted that he had. I wanted to write a letter explaining that Lonnie had never taken his place in my heart. Greg refused to risk smuggling one of my letters into Attica and offered to memorize my words instead. I found this so inhibiting that I never finished the letter. Sam and I lost touch.

The fiercest snowfalls in a half century piled the drifts high in our yard, blocking both front and back doors. The temperature dropped to thirty below and stayed there. During the thaws, neighbors visited us, wondering if we needed anything. They were obviously curious about two young women who had so little to do. We tried to avoid inviting them indoors. Once the owners of the house, a middle-aged couple who lived in Massachusetts, came to visit. We prevailed on Jeanette, my movement connection in Boston, to come with her boyfriend, Vince, so that Vince could stand in as Richard Blake. For two excruciating hours we made small talk with the landlord and landlady, elaborating on the fiction that Vince was a children's book illustrator, Pat my recently widowed sister, and I a housewife. Although we collapsed in merriment when the owners finally left, our laughter rang hollow. The minute-to-minute dread of discovery had been an ordeal none of us cared to repeat.

Pat gradually retreated into the meditative existence she'd led in her first months underground. She instituted a strict vegetarian regime, practiced yoga and exercises to improve concentration, and kept a daily journal of her spiritual state. I devoted a month to Isaac Deutscher's three-volume biography of Trotsky, my first serious reading since graduate school. Deutscher's masterpiece added to my disillusionment with the neo-Stalinist militant left. The book convinced me that Trotsky was a genius, guilty of cruelty and of serious errors of judgment but politically radical and awesomely courageous, the real heir to Lenin's revolution—while Stalin was responsible for the revolution's crimes. I tried to convince Pat to read the Deutscher book. Instead, she picked up Emma Goldman's *Living My Life* and insisted on quoting passages critical of Trotsky which I thought simplistic. As I tried to engage her in argument, she withdrew, practicing her new spiritual discipline by holding her tongue.

Pat's parents came to visit us in New Hampshire from their home in Washington, D.C. Having belonged to the Communist Party through the witch-hunts of the fifties, they knew how to travel incognito and talk in code. Pat was eager to see them because they were in touch with her ex-husband and had visited with Jenny. I had met her father once before in New York and recognized in Pat's affectionate friction with him aspects of my own relationship with my father. Her stepmother was warmer than Pat's descriptions had led me to expect. In conversation alone with her, I learned a version of Pat's childhood different from the one Pat had told me. Pat had always claimed that her mother abandoned her when she was small and that her father had then placed her in an orphanage where she was brutally mistreated until he remarried and took her back home. Pat's stepmother told me that the institution had not been an orphanage but a home that provided temporary care for the children of couples who, for one reason or another, were unable to keep their children with them. Pat's father had visited her there every weekend for the duration of her stay. Hearing her stepmother's version, I wondered at the self-pity reflected in Pat's own account. I wondered, too, whether Pat's memory of abandonment was now reliving itself in the mind of four-year-old Jenny.

A week or so later my own parents came to Jaffrey in a station wagon my father had borrowed from a business associate—to avoid the possibility that his regular car would be tailed as he left the city. The three of us spent an emotionally charged but not especially frank two days together. We did not discuss the financial loss I had caused them or my reasons for going underground. Once my mother sat up suddenly in her chair before the fire and said she was feeling so comfortable she had nearly forgotten why she was here. In my parents' minds, they were visiting a prison. Nothing about my life in Jaffrey struck them as chosen.

Shortly after their departure I found a job through the state employment agency at a place called the Hancock Inn. My tasks were to serve breakfast to the inn's few winter guests and to help clean rooms afterward. Working less than twenty hours a week, I barely earned enough money to pay for the cost of gasoline between Jaffrey and Hancock, a half hour's drive. I was also a terrible waitress. I spilled coffee and dropped plates and never could learn to balance a tray on one hand. Still, I was glad to leave the house at least a few times a week. And the Hancock Inn was exquisite, originally built before the Revolutionary War and with some of the original wood fixtures intact.

One December night a call came from Greg and Robert. Pat and I were to go at once to a pay phone and telephone the number they had given us in code. The news they gave us then was disheartening: Ben and Dana and several others had just been arrested in an unsuccessful fire bombing. Because the FBI had decided that they were all Weathermen, their total bail came to nearly a million dollars.

Later I learned that the bombing conspiracy had been Ben's idea. Dana was not supposed to be part of it, but at the end she couldn't bear being left out—in spite of her suspicion that one of the conspirators was an undercover cop. She was right. When the group reached their target building, the police were waiting to arrest them, having been informed of the plan by their undercover man.

Eventually all the conspirators were released on bail. Not surprisingly, none of them chose to become fugitives. Dana went to jail for a year. In August 1971 Ben was sent to Attica.

The tension between Pat and me became worse. Once she called me at work to ask me to come home early. A tab of acid she had taken had plunged her into an abyss. My return to the house deepened her fear; she saw me as the enemy. I found this easy to understand. Isolated as we were, we each tended to project the reasons for our unhappiness onto the other. Once during a quarrel I threw a gallon jar of molasses at Pat. It barely missed her head, and I spent days cleaning the goo from the walls.

It occurred to me that we might be able to ease the tension between us through physical affection. One evening in January, when we were watching the sunset on a hilltop near the house, I asked Pat if she would sleep with me again. She looked surprised, then shrugged.

"I guess, if you want to," she said. I tried to experience pleasure at her agreement but felt only dulled and numb. That night in my bed Pat and I brought each other to orgasm for the first time, but the act was without joy. She went upstairs to her own room, and I fell into a fitful sleep.

The next day I didn't have to work. I was eating breakfast while Pat practiced her yoga routine when the doorbell rang.

On the porch, shaking the snow from his boots, was Lonnie.

He had returned in triumph with nearly $5,000 in cash coaxed from his parents on the pretext that he was going to school. His secondhand Volkswagen van parked in the driveway was stuffed with new possessions, including an expensive tape deck, an electric juice maker, and a camera. Pat and I exchanged glances. It wouldn't hurt, we agreed, to invite him in and find out what he was up to. Lonnie unloaded the van and brought the contents into the house. When he removed his wool cap, the curly hair was completely gone. He had shaved himself bald.

Obviously he intended to stay for as long as we would let him. Possibly to secure his status with us, he wanted to give me the entire $5,000. When I refused to accept it, he proceeded to dispose of it at an alarming rate. Within a few days of his arrival he had bought hundreds of dollars' worth of records, clothes, stereo equipment, even books, which he didn't read. Fearing that he would go through the rest of the money and that we would be stuck supporting him again, I got him to drive to Massachusetts (I didn't want his name on bank records in New Hampshire) to deposit what was left in a savings account.

At some point since Pat and I had last seen him, Lonnie had gone over the edge. We slept together for the first few days of his stay, but after that Lonnie, while he continued to share my bed, refused to have sex. He filled sketch pads with Bosch-like drawings of menacing figures, leaving the pages wherever I would be sure to see them. I once found him in the upstairs bathroom, naked, greased from head to foot with Vaseline, and masturbating for what I guessed had been most of the afternoon. He played with a broken pistol that friends from Boston had left with us for safekeeping, claiming that he knew how to fix it and had plans to use it. What remnants of his army tour or other misadventures had resurrected themselves in his dazed brain? He had turned so inward that neither Pat nor I could tell.

Crazy as he was, I still felt an inexplicable fondness for him—and I saw his car, his money, and his continued attachment to me as a way to get out of Jaffrey. Boredom and isolation had made me desperate. I conceived a plan to go to Hawaii, where I thought I could sleep under palms and live on pineapples that dropped from trees. Lonnie said he would drive me to California, where he wanted to look up an old army buddy, and I could fly to Honolulu from there. I was still weighing this idea when I was unexpectedly fired from my job at the Hancock. I came home and told Lonnie I was ready to leave whenever he was.

I said good-bye to Greg, Robert, and Maude by telephone. Neither Greg nor Maude had visited us in months—though they had continued, faithfully, to send money orders—and Robert came only to sleep with Pat. I did not doubt that they all would feel relief at my departure. I told my parents my plans, and they gave me the number and address of a safe friend through whom I would always be able to reach them.

Much as I still loved Pat, I didn't think of asking her to come. In the past months we had been thrown on each other's company more than was healthy for either of us. I felt sure that the break would do us both good and that eventually we would be together again. After I tossed my backpack and sleeping bag in Lonnie's van, I hugged her tightly and promised to write. Lonnie gave her $1,000 to pay the next few months' expenses. Pat said good-bye to him with more warmth than she'd expressed toward me. Not until months later, when she wrote me a letter accusing me of "leaving her life—both spiritually and physically," did I realize she thought I had abandoned her. Yet I believed that we both had recognized the need for separation while fearing to admit it and that I was only coincidentally the first to act.

Lonnie wanted to have his tape deck repaired before heading west, and Boston seemed the best place to do it. We stayed with the couple in Somerville who had put us up earlier. Before we left Lonnie gave them $1,000. I have no idea why. He also gave me $1,000 which this time I did not refuse.

Toward evening of the day we left Boston, we crossed the Delaware River into Pennsylvania. Lonnie was in a foul mood. He didn't like the way his tape deck sounded, and he couldn't get a buzz off his grass. I tuned out his complaints until he let drop something about a pistol.

"Lonnie," I said, "you didn't take that gun out of the house?"

"Why not?" he cackled. "You and Sasha [Pat's current alias] sure weren't going to use it."

"And you are?"

"You bet," said Lonnie. Remembering that he had been angrily muttering about his parents, I had a horrifying thought.

"Lonnie—you're not thinking of using that gun on your parents?" He didn't answer.

I began to calculate how quickly and where I could get away from him.

The van's engine was steadily losing power. On an uphill section of the interstate Lonnie could not coax the car to the minimum legal speed. We left the highway for a side road. Lonnie proclaimed the van was shot and not worth repairing. We chugged to a halt in front of a neon-pink motel called Scotty's. He proposed that we spend the night there and in the morning hire a taxi to take us to the airport. I reminded him that I couldn't go to Cincinnati because of the FBI visit to his parents' house last summer. This gave him a moment's pause. Then he suggested that we go to Columbus and stay with his married sister. Since he still had the gun, I was afraid to antagonize him openly. I said Columbus sounded fine. In the morning Lonnie paid a motel employee an exorbitant sum to drive us to an airport from which we flew to Columbus. He left the van with all his possessions in the motel parking lot.

Lonnie's sister, businesslike and alert, was suspicious of her brother's freaky appearance and behavior and seemed to be wondering how I was mixed up with him. To avoid tainting my ID, I was calling myself Foxy, a nickname originally given me by Ben. Lonnie's sister thought this strange, too, as she did my vague answers to questions and occasional contradictions to Lonnie's version of events. In my eagerness to avoid disaster, I hit on an idea that Greg or Maude would have instantly vetoed and that I would have as well if I hadn't been so desperate.

I telephoned one of the founders of the Yippies, Terry Axel, who had moved from New York and was living in Indianapolis with her boyfriend, a former SDS organizer. I didn't know Terry very well, but she was the only person I could think of in the vicinity who might help. I was immensely grateful when she agreed to meet me at the Indianapolis bus terminal. Pretending to Lonnie and his sister that I would be gone only overnight, I boarded the next bus that left Columbus. I volunteered no address or phone number where I could be reached, and I trusted Lonnie would never find me again.

In the belief that no one would any longer remember what I looked like, before leaving Jaffrey I had dyed my hair back to its original dark brown. I realized from Terry's reaction to me in the Indianapolis bus terminal that this had been a mistake. She and her boyfriend, Ed, insisted that I buy a wig before taking me to the place where I was to stay. At a department store I picked out an inexpensive honey-colored hairpiece and, to ease my hosts' alarm, replaced my contact lenses with the tortoiseshell glasses. I thought the disguise superfluous but a cheap price to pay for a place to stay.

Terry and Ed took me to the apartment of a couple of undergraduates, Clyde and Susan. I had intended to remain only until I could collect my wits and then to fly on to Hawaii, but on my first night with the students all the money Lonnie had given me was stolen from my pocketbook, presumably by a visitor. Clyde and Susan, although they had been warned by Terry that I was a hunted fugitive, begged me not to worry. I could live with them as long as I pleased. Their complete fearlessness made me feel welcomed. Instead of treating me as a burden, they seemed to look up to me. Clyde sought my advice on the campus political scene; Susan, on her relationship with Clyde. We played chess and cooked together, and I began to think of finding a job in Indianapolis and remaining indefinitely.

Even though I knew Clyde was involved in local radical politics, I didn't feel concerned about jeopardizing him or Susan by living in their apartment. I think my relaxed attitude reflected my laziness at the end of a strenuous winter and the draining separations from Pat and Lonnie. I was more exhausted than I knew, and I needed the emotional support my new friends gave me. I therefore pushed any sense of danger out of my mind, allowing myself to forget both my own predicament and the possibility that if I were discovered, anyone who sheltered me could be charged with harboring a fugitive.

Terry Axel and her boyfriend, Ed, both prominent movement organizers, were not so naïve as to overlook the threat. They had left Indianapolis the day after depositing me at Clyde and Susan's. When they returned three weeks later to discover I was still there, they were appalled. Telling me we would have to talk alone, they drove me to a park outside the city where they ordered me to leave Indianapolis immediately.

Where could I go? Huddled on the grass, I shivered as much from the force of their reprimand as from the March chill. My money, I reminded them, had been stolen as soon as I arrived in Indianapolis, and I knew no one in the vicinity except them. Terry, gazing at me with an expression that was probably pity but that I interpreted as rebuke, delivered her analysis of my behavior. She and Ed felt that my undisguised appearance at the bus terminal, the theft of my money, and my blind insistence that I was safe with Clyde and Susan were evidence that, deep down, I wanted to be picked up by the police. If that were really my wish, Terry told me, I ought to turn myself in. She could see that I was having a hard time, and no one would blame me for surrendering.

If I had felt any confidence in the importance of maintaining a radical underground, I might have risen to the occasion. While many of the people who had helped me had done so only out of personal generosity and goodness, Terry and Ed, radicals who had publicly endorsed violence against the state, were in a different category. They claimed to represent the revolutionary movement for the sake of which I had become a fugitive, and it could be argued that they bore some ethical responsibility for helping me to stay out of jail. Instead of telling them that, I mumbled some tearful excuses.

I was filled with shame over my dependence on others and, in that moment of humiliation, felt determined to relieve the world of the burden of caring for me.

And yet I was thoroughly unwilling to turn myself in. I wished neither to go to jail nor to make such a public gesture of weakness and defeat. This left me few options: I could throw myself once again on the mercy of Maude and Greg or I could ask my parents for money. Reluctantly I chose the latter course. I left a message at the number my parents had provided for me and asked them to call me back. It turned out that my father was on his way to the Midwest on business and would route his trip through Indianapolis, where he would meet me and give me some cash.

I also needed a place to stay. And hesitant as I was to call another stranger, who else was there? I thought of a woman I had met in St. Louis last summer, Lynn Gottlieb, a graduate student at the University of California in San Diego. A friend of Dorian's to whom Dorian had confided my identity before I arrived, Lynn had pressed my hand and urged me to call her if I needed anything. I took her up on her offer now, identifying myself on the phone as Foxy, which was the name I was using when we met. It was a second before she remembered me, but she responded with the abundant open-heartedness I later learned was part of her nature. I promised I would stay in San Diego a week or two at most, and she promised to be at the terminal when I arrived.

I met my father at the Indianapolis airport. We ate dinner in a revolving restaurant high above the city, taking food from each other's plates and getting a bit drunk, laughing like old lovers. He gave me several hundred dollars which he assured me he could easily afford and never brought up the many thousands I had already cost my mother and him in bail and lawyer's fees. Alone with him, I felt only his kindness, pillowing me against the hardships of the last months and the ones to come. "I wish your mother could be here," he said, spooning half his dessert into my plate.

Lynn Gottlieb had arranged for me to live in a houseful of graduate students on the beach north of San Diego. The students didn't know who I was, and they treated me and each other coldly, locking their rooms and labeling their food. Hurriedly I concocted a plan to spend the next few months on a solo hitchhiking-and-camping tour of the Southwest. I had hitchhiked in Europe in 1966 and again with Lonnie in the past year, and I wasn't particularly afraid. I believed that as long as I maintained a friendly but self-possessed manner, took rides only from drivers who looked honest, and didn't stick my thumb out after dark, I would be fine. And I expected that camping out would be pure pleasure, like last summer in the Sierras. It was already March, and I thought the Southwest would be warm and blooming. For a couple of days I shopped for supplies and determined an itinerary from studying maps.

On the night before I left, Lynn's brother Warren, who also went to graduate school in San Diego and whom I had met with Lynn in St. Louis, asked me to join him for dinner at his San Diego house with his roommates. Both Warren and his roommate Malcolm were conscientious objectors who were politically sympathetic to me. Tim, the third roommate, had more mainstream views, and at first I was uncomfortable to learn that he too had been told my identity. Yet he seemed more than sympathetic; he seemed intrigued, never taking his eyes from me at the dinner table. After dinner he advised me on the scenic spots I shouldn't miss on my trip and urged me to keep in touch with him through postcards. I liked him very much, and if he had suggested that I give up my trip and move into the spacious house with him and his housemates, I would have accepted on the spot. No such offer came.

I had a ride from a friend of Lynn's almost all the way to the Grand Canyon. My first sight of the canyon struck me with fear. Those vast strata of limestone and shale and purple quartzite dropping into the earth's heart! I had planned to hike to the bottom on one of the little-used trails. I gave up that idea and chose instead the safety of the paved Bright Angel Trail. After a few hundred steps it occurred to me that without a partner to share jokes and complaints, I lacked the motivation for so strenuous a hike. My pack, which contained everything I owned, weighed far more than I could carry comfortably. At the halfway mark, four hours down, it started to rain. I took shelter under a lean-to, where I decided to retrace my steps and spend the night on the canyon rim.

In the morning I pointed my thumb toward the east, intending to visit the Painted Desert and Petrified Forest. In the beginning my luck was good. The sites were dazzling; the rides, at least tolerable. A Basque priest drove me from Globe to his community in Show Low and pressed $10 on me. I didn't refuse since my money was dwindling more rapidly than I'd expected. A grizzled logger asked if I was a hippie and believed in free love. He was creepy but didn't try to touch me. Still, I was starting to wonder if the trip was such a good idea. The dust storms made sleeping outdoors unpleasant, and the more remote the territory, the longer I had to wait for rides. With fewer opportunities to choose my drivers, I ran into more kooks. One man pretended he was making an academic survey of breast types and wanted me to remove my jacket so he could examine mine. Another warned me of maniacs on the road in a tone that suggested he might be one of them. In southern Arizona, after a wait of nearly six hours, I caught a ride with two male speed freaks from Los Angeles who were going all the way to Albuquerque. Although I usually refused rides from men in pairs, these two were so obviously gay that I felt safe and a four-hundred mile ride to anywhere was not to be lightly dismissed. I sat on the transmission of their sports car as they zipped up the road at ninety.

One of the two men was a bowling shark. He kept making stops in Arizona gulch towns so he could take on the natives in the bowling alleys. As I waited for the games to end, my mind turned on its now-habitual path, and I began thinking of safe places to stay. What I wanted most of all was to call up Tim in San Diego and ask if I could come back, but I felt too shy to try that. Instead, I phoned a married couple who taught at a crafts institute in Santa Fe. Gene, who recognized me from my first name and a reminder of our last encounter in college, said he and Louise would be glad to have me as an overnight guest. The bowling shark agreed to drive me the extra fifty miles from Albuquerque to Santa Fe.

Gene and Louise lived in the chic Anglo section of Santa Fe in an adobe filled with hanging plants and beautifully carved oak furniture. Gene told me Louise was away for a few days but I should make myself at home. I took a luxurious bath, dressed again in my filthy sweat shirt and jeans, and stretched out in front of the fireplace. I was thinking how relieved I was to get away from the weirdos on the road when I felt a hand on my back. It was Gene's. He began caressing my shoulders.

I had come to expect such overtures from men on the road. From a married acquaintance who had never before displayed the slightest sexual interest in me and on whose hospitality I was now dependent, the gesture took me completely by surprise. I shrugged away. Gene had the grace, at least, to apologize.

My silent anger at Gene was probably disproportionate to his offense, but I had not been having a wonderful few weeks. As the tension accumulated between us, I felt I could not bear one more night on the road. Overcoming my shyness at talking to Tim again, I got Gene to drive me to a pay phone, from which I called the house in San Diego.

Tim answered. I asked if he and his roommates could possibly spare me their living-room couch while I looked for a job. He said he would check with the others and returned to the phone a minute later.

"You'd better hurry," he said. "Malcolm's dog, Rusty, is going to give birth any day, and if you're back in time, you can watch."

I hung up in a daze of happiness. The thought of going to a home that I wouldn't have to leave in a week's time—where I was wanted enough to be included in such major events as the birth of puppies —I had not allowed myself to know how much I longed for that until now. I began hitchhiking back to San Diego very early the next morning.

Thinking now only of how fast I could get to San Diego, I grew careless about the rides I took. One pair of truck drivers took me three hundred miles but insisted that I ride in a rear compartment, where one of them sat next to me, feeling me up and laughing as I tried to push him away. At a diner I was turned over to another truck driver who was going almost all the way to Los Angeles. This man left me at a deserted gas station outside the city limits at 3:00 A.M. I walked a mile along the road looking for a place to unroll my sleeping bag. I found, instead, a diner full of breakfasting patrons, where I asked a waitress whether any of her customers was headed for San Diego. She inquired around and then pointed out a stocky man in the corner, eating pancakes.

"Dean over there, he'll take you," she said.

Dean looked harmless, so when he began telling off-color stories as we barreled down the highway, I paid little attention. Then I noticed with a start that he had drawn his penis from his pants.

"Okay if I do this?" he asked. He was massaging it like a piece of clay.

"Okay if I don't look?" I answered, contemptuous.

"Oh, c'mon. How can you look at a poor, wilted pecker like mine and not try your hand on it? Don't you want to get it up?"

"No." I tried to remain calm by telling myself that flashers weren't molesters.

The humor disappeared from his voice.

"Look, this is how I see it," he said. "You're a girl that's been around. Probably you've had a lot of men. I can tell by how you look. You may be the one girl in the world who can get me hard. And you're not getting away until I've found that out."

I tried reasoning with him. I told him if I were looking to trade sex for a ride, I would have made that clear. If he couldn't behave himself, he ought to let me out of the car.

"Damn straight I'll let you out of the car. At sixty miles an hour."

He grabbed my hand and puled it toward his crotch. I got it away from him. He cursed me. He leaned across and, still driving at sixty, unlocked the button on the door next to me and opened the door. I fought back with all my strength and managed to force his hand off the door. It swung wildly.

All I could think of was my backpack on the rear seat. It contained not only my few belongings but all my precious Ellen Davis Blake ID. If I survived the fall from the car and was taken to a hospital by police, I could be identified by fingerprints and arrested.

I managed to close the door. Dean belted me across the face.

"Which'll it be?" he barked. "Hands or mouth?"

If I went down on him, I thought, at least I wouldn't have to look at him. I could pretend he was someone else.

"Mouth," I said.

He slowed down to perhaps forty. I put my mouth to him. He had told the truth about his impotence: his penis was limp as an empty sock. I couldn't make it stir. In a moment he pushed my head away.

"It's no good," he said. "Stop. It's no good."

I thought he was going to turn violent again. Instead, he became abject. He begged my forgiveness. He hadn't meant to hurt me. He wouldn't really have thrown me out of the car. It was a joke. He hadn't hit me too hard, had he? The sun was rising now, and he couldn't bear it. Each dawn made him want to kill himself. But he was too gutless. Would I mind if he put his arm around me just for a few minutes?

Too amazed to protest, I let him hold me. He wove down the highway another few miles. Then he admitted he was too tired to keep driving. He had never intended to go to San Diego anyway—he was just trying to help me.

He stopped the car on the shoulder and let me out. I put on my backpack and began walking. A polite young man stopped for me.

"If a cop finds you walking here, you'll get arrested," he told me. "Let me give you a ride to the next exit."

Believing that even another ride with a stranger was preferable to arrest by the police, I got in the car, and the young man took me to the exit without incident.

I was sitting on my backpack, wondering what to do next, when the highway patrol caught up with me. The cop looked at my New Hampshire license and copied everything down.

"Do your parents know you're all the way out here?" he asked.

"Yes, sir."

"I can't stop you from hitchhiking at an exit, but I wish like hell I could. You can't imagine what sort of gruesome things have happened to girls who hitchhike here."

I was still wondering if he was going to offer me a ride to San Diego—which I would have accepted on the spot—when he wheeled around and left me on the side of the road.

XIV
Awaking

A CONVERSATION WITH GREG A FEW days after I returned to San Diego brought the distressing news that Pat was thinking of turning herself in. He assured me that he, Maude, and Robert were doing everything possible to talk her out of it. A letter Pat sent me at the end of May suggested that they had succeeded.

"i had sort of thought that all i had to do was make the damn decision and then it would all be done, all be carried through," she wrote. "but of course that was naive of me. in any case now that i know i cant do it, now that ive stood back from the thing a bit, i can perceive the desperation more clearly in such a decision. . . . the reasons—no not 'reasons' actually but rather *feelings*—which led me to that decision in the first place you must know well enough yourself: the anxiety, the insecurity, the restrictions on my life, the uprootedness, the sham and deception, at times the fear, THE ISOLATION." But after reflection—and what sounded like intense pressure from our friends—she had decided it was her own emotional problems, not fugitive life, that were to blame and that little was to be gained by "the simple expedient of going in for a few years."

I was a bit surprised to gather from Pat's letter that she had never tried to discuss her situation with a lawyer. Now that Sam, Nate, and I had pleaded guilty, it seemed to me that the chance she would be convicted was rather slight. She had mentioned fear of prosecution for unlawful flight, but it was hard to imagine that she would receive a sentence of more than a year on such a charge. Once it was over, she could reestablish a relationship with Jenny, which she had always claimed was her fervent wish. It was possible, of course, that the government had more evidence against her than we knew or that the judge would throw the book at her for unlawful flight. Still, I wondered that she was willing to rely so completely on the advice of a few loyal but hardly disinterested friends.

Meanwhile, my contentment in San Diego made my escape from New Hampshire and the last hellish months on the road seem well worthwhile. My fantasized romance with Tim did not materialize. After we slept together a few times, I realized he did not return my strong interest in him. I suspected this was because he was resistant to becoming entangled with a fugitive, and I couldn't blame him, although the rejection hurt. Still, I loved the cheerful clutter of my new home, where I made a corner of the living room my own and adopted the runt of Rusty's litter, called Grundoon by my housemates. I cured her of an eye infection when she was a few weeks old, and she soon grew to German shepherd size and became my devoted companion.

More importantly my housemates had helped me to get a job as a medical assistant-trainee with their landlord, Dr. Ching, who ran a family practice. Ching paid me only $1.05 an hour, but he supplied my uniforms free, cosigned a bank loan so that I could buy a used Opel, and promised me that eventually I would earn a certificate qualifying me to work as a lab technician anywhere in the country. I began to envision a long professional career in the name of Ellen Davis Blake in which my past as a radical bomber would never have to intrude.

In June my housemates left San Diego for summer vacation. The rent was paid for the month (generously, my housemates had never asked me to chip in), and Ching had promised to rent me one of the smaller houses he owned when the lease expired. In the meantime, I rattled around in the six empty rooms with Grundoon and Rusty and Malcolm's pet goat, Guinivere, for company. I read Joan Didion, played British rock on my roommates' superb stereo, and marveled at how peacefully my life was working out after all.

Reading in bed late one night, feeling safe and sheltered, I received a telephone call from Robin Morgan. My first response, blurted out in alarm, was: "Where did you get my number?"

From Maude. I should have known at once. On the night I had left New York, I told Robin that if she needed to find me, Maude would always know where I was. Since then Maude told me that she and Robin—both writers, both keenly intelligent, and both with a feminist skepticism toward men that appeared innate—had become friends. Maude had praised Robin's sense of discretion, and I had said to Maude that it would be nice to see her again someday. But I hadn't expected it to come about, and after so long a separation I wasn't entirely pleased to hear a voice from the turbulent past.

Misinterpreting the anxiety in my voice, Robin hastened to explain that she was on a promotion tour for her recently published anthology, *Sisterhood Is Powerful*, and was calling from a hotel on a safe telephone. Maude had told her some time ago that I was settled in San Diego; but this was the first time she'd visited the area in months, and she was hoping to see me before she returned east.

"Where are you?" I asked.

"Denver."

Robin's sense of geography was to become a joke between us over the next years. She seemed unaware that we were still separated by 1,200 miles, and when I pointed that out, she was unconcerned. She had already booked a flight for the following night (in an alias, she assured me) and was wondering if I could meet her at the airport. Or should she take a taxi, just to be safe? She would have to fly back early the next morning, but she was very much looking forward to seeing me. Surprised and flattered, I told her that of course, I would pick her up.

I went to the airport directly from work, still wearing my white uniform, white stockings, and white shoes which I hoped Robin would consider a sufficient disguise. Robin was not disguised herself, but she had clipped her long hair up to her ears and had given up blue jeans for trousers and an overblouse of some soft, clinging material. She was wearing an exotic scent which made me think of a tropical garden and which she would not have touched in the *Rat* days.

"Good grief, it's been a goddamned year or more!" Robin exclaimed after we hugged, holding me away from her and smiling. She said it as though nothing could be more natural than our reunion—although when I thought of all the close friends with whom I'd lost contact since going underground and of how slightly I'd known Robin, the remark seemed odd.

On the way home Robin, a consummate actress had me in stitches with imitations of mutual acquaintances and what I took to be mock alarm at my driving. (Maude had warned her that I'd had a license less than eight months.) In the living room, a comical tilt of her eyebrow expressed her distaste for the hippie chaos around us. She petted the goat and kissed Grundoon, and, when I served her a supper of pork chops and burned peas, exclaimed, "God, what a relief you're not a food fascist! The vegetarian atrocities I get served at feminist communes and have to pretend to like!"

She seemed to expect that we were both going to stay up all night since we had so much news to exchange and who knew when we would next see each other? In fact, though I would have been glad for a longer visit, I had little to say to her. There was nothing to tell Robin about what was going on in the left. Nor could I describe what had happened to my political convictions since I'd last seen her. And to speak of my personal life before I arrived in San Diego would have divulged information I had no right to give away.

Robin did most of the talking, giving me a lively account of the last year. She told me how she had become disappointed in *Rat* when it failed to take more feminist direction and how publication of her anthology in the fall had finally spurred her to quit the paper. As she toured the country to promote her book, she discovered, to her surprise, that thousands of women who didn't give a damn about the leftist beliefs on which *Rat* was predicated were thrilled at what feminism had to offer. Two bits of news she thought would particularly interest me. The first came from a conference of radical feminists she had attended in Detroit, where she had delivered a paper proposing a "summer skills session" to train feminists in firearms, self-defense, emergency surgery, and the use of what she euphemistically called "tactical chemistry"—as well as more mundane skills, like plumbing, carpentry, and conversational Spanish. Dozens of women had responded enthusiastically, including two from Wisconsin, Chris and Emma, whom Robin considered so sympathetic that she predicted they might someday harbor me. The other news concerned a well-known feminist, formerly associated with the abortion rights movement and now gathering an all-women's militia which was going to train in Cuba. Robin thought me a natural prospect for this training. But she couldn't recommend the proposal because the woman had recently shifted her views from radical feminism back to Marxism—a transition about which Robin displayed her feelings by an eloquent curl of the lip.

I was a bit nonplussed by Robin's assumptions about my interests. It had been a long time since I thought of myself as a revolutionary guerrilla, and I wasn't sure quite how to explain my transformation. Finally I said that although I very much appreciated her suggestions, I was no longer much interested in firearms or explosives or in joining a militia. Personally I'd expended most of my energy in the last year on survival. Politically I wasn't sure that the women of America, for all the feminist growth Robin had described, were going to be receptive to such tactics.

Robin's surprise showed in her face. She said I was a very brave woman. I wondered if that meant she agreed with me. Then she asked if I wanted to hear some of her new poems.

It was past 3:00 A.M., and though I had earlier asked to see the poems, I now wanted to go to sleep; but Robin seemed to have her heart set on a reading. In fact, she was a marvelous reader, and the poems jolted me awake—especially one called "One Last Word to the Men" (and later titled "Monster"), more a political statement than a poem, which Robin read with great theatrical skill. At last, though, my eyes closed, and Robin allowed me to show her to a spare room and then go to sleep.

I missed her after she left. Once again her ferocious energy had impressed me deeply. She lived her life at a higher pitch than anyone I knew or had ever met, and once she was gone, the life with which I'd felt such contentment seemed drab and flat. At a bookstore in San Diego's hip community I bought a copy of Shulamith Firestone's *Dialectic of Sex* which Robin told me had helped convert her away from working at *Rat*. Much of Firestone's application of Marxist dialectic to the struggle between the sexes was familiar to me from *Rat* meetings, but several of her passages struck me with particular force. One of these I copied into a notebook on a page I headlined "The Failure of Left Politics."

"Politico women," Firestone wrote, "are unable to evolve an authentic politics because they have never truly confronted their oppression *as women* in a gut way. . . . Their inability to put their own needs first, their need for male approval—in this case anti-establishment male approval—to legitimate them politically, renders them incapable of breaking from other movements when necessary and thus consigns them to mere left-reformism, lack of originality, and, ultimately, political sterility."

Was that a description of me in the left? Nearly every risk I'd ever taken had been urged on me by a man or by my need for male approval. Even after the women's take-over at *Rat*, it was important to me that leftist men continue to respect the paper. I had been one of those who helped bury articles on day care, rape, or lesbian rights on a back page while the conviction of eight men for inciting to riot at the Democratic convention was cover material. And where had my loyalty to the male left gotten me? Knocking about in an empty house with nothing better to do than play with my dog.

In early July, shortly after moving to a new apartment rented me by Dr. Ching, I went to my first meeting at the San Diego women's center.

I had considered for a long time the dangers of walking into the women's center in the downtown Y. A feminist I'd known in New York might drift in and spot me. Or a local leftist might recognize me from an old photo. It was even possible that my picture would be on the wall in the same way that at *Rat* we had kept an "Eldridge Welcome Here" poster in honor of Cleaver's Algerian exile. And how would I describe myself? I knew how women's meetings functioned: I would be asked to introduce myself and explain what had brought me to the meeting. How much could I say without giving myself away or telling so grotesque a lie that my participation was pointless?

When I walked through the open doors of a cavernous meeting room, no flicker of recognition showed in the eyes of the two women at the desk. I asked about the open meeting and was pointed to a group of five or six women squatting in a circle.

"That's a new consciousness-raising group that's just getting under way," said one of the staffers. "You're welcome to join it." It sounded risky, but I went over and sat down anyway. All the women were white, wearing jeans or sundresses, and ranged in age from nineteen to about forty-five. They gazed at me with mild curiosity.

When my turn came to identify myself, I said I was Foxy Davis (the name I used at work) and that I came from Boston, where I had worked for the *Old Mole*, a leftist counterculture paper. I admitted to attending a few women's demonstrations in Boston but described myself as new to the movement. None of the other women had ever attended a women's meeting before, and only one or two had political experience of any kind. Slowly my fear of discovery abated. Later I learned that the group had been impressed not only by my mention of demonstrations and a radical newspaper but by the plastic bag of tobacco and papers I used to roll my own cigarettes

—an affectation that convinced them at once that I was the real thing, a radical feminist.

The group continued to meet weekly and, after growing to twelve members, divided by lot into two. In my group Meg, at thirty-four, was the oldest, recently married with a new baby. The youngest was nineteen-year-old Patty, who worked for the telephone company. Roslyn, a VISTA worker, lived in a commune, and Vera, an immaculately groomed blonde, worked as a lab technician and had a child a year older than Meg's. Maureen, at twenty-four the same age as I, had already had two husbands and three children, whom she supported with welfare checks and by occasional topless dancing in a bar. A southerner who had dropped out of high school at sixteen, a provocative dresser, and a flirt, Maureen made the more straitlaced members of the group, Meg and Vera, uncomfortable. While we were superficially unalike, I felt a special kinship with her. I understood both her vulnerability and her hostility to men and that having come through two horrendous marriages, she was determined not to repeat her mistakes. My friendship with Maureen was therapeutic for both of us, though she never knew who I was until I left.

One Sunday morning Maureen called me up in a panic. Her ex-husband had picked up her youngest child, his son, on Saturday on the pretense of taking him to Disneyland. When they had not returned at dinnertime, Maureen became convinced that he had spirited the child away to Pennsylvania, where his mother lived and where Maureen would have to go through the courts to get him back. She had no car, and she begged me to drive her to her ex-husband's home in the suburb of Chula Vista, which she had unsuccessfully been phoning since last night.

We drove down together. The Chula Vista house was locked and deserted; her ex-husband's car, gone from the garage. Maureen smashed the windows in the living room with her bare hands. Inside the bedroom she began frantically to go through papers, looking for clues to her son.

Responding to a report from a neighbor, the police arrived and took us both into custody for breaking and entering. Horrified when she realized she had gotten a friend in trouble, Maureen assured the police I had nothing to do with the incident. I was released before I was fingerprinted. Although I had once again narrowly escaped detection, I felt as much uneasiness as relief, as though I should not have gotten off so easily for a rage with which I thoroughly identified.

To avoid giving myself away to my c-r group, I talked as little as possible about my past. Yet my new friends seemed to sense my difficulties, if not the reasons for them, and gave me more positive emotional and intellectual support than I would have imagined possible from a group of strangers. I could not have stayed in San Diego as long as I did without their continuing affection.

As one result of the new self-esteem I gained in the group, I became dissatisfied with my job at Dr. Ching's. Although he had raised my salary and shown other flashes of generosity, he was a tyrannical boss and his practice was so sloppily run that I realized I would never be able to use my experience with him to get another job. I came to think that with a carefully prepared résumé, I might be able to obtain enough free-lance editing and proofreading work from Los Angeles publishing firms to support myself while still living in San Diego. One day in early September when Ching showed up three hours late at the office and yelled at me, I turned on my heel and left for good.

I telephoned the publishing firms listed in the Los Angeles directory and set up interviews for the following Monday. Then I went to work on a résumé that would reflect my work experience while providing plausible but untraceable references. By Thursday afternoon I was so pleased with the result that I gave myself a treat and drove to one of my favorite oceanside spots.

At the beach a husky, clean-cut man in white trunks struck up a conversation. He said his name was Jack and that he was a truck driver from Minneapolis with a weekend to kill in San Diego. He seemed kind and safe, the first man who had appealed to me in the many months since I'd nursed my disappointment over Tim. We left the beach together and bought ice cream cones. We were on the way to Jack's truck when I saw the headline on an evening paper: INMATES RIOT AT NEW YORK'S ATTICA PRISON. Below the headline was a picture of a fortresslike compound. Sam's prison.

I was frozen before the page so long that Jack wondered what was wrong. I explained—because I couldn't think of another excuse—that I had a friend at Attica. The secret out, I paid for the paper and read the article while standing on the street. It told me that guards had been taken hostage and that one had had his skull fractured when inmates threw him from a parapet. Inmates still controlled the prison yard.

"Don't you want to call someone?" Jack asked. First I said no. Then I changed my mind. At a phone booth, violating security precautions, I dialed Greg directly at his new home in upstate New York. When he answered, I suggested that he call me back from another phone.

"No point," he said. "I don't know any more than you do. I'll phone you at home when I have some news."

Jack became fascinated with me after learning I knew someone at Attica. I fended off his questions but went back with him to his motel, where I drowned my anxiety in the pleasure of sex.

I didn't hear from Greg on Friday, Saturday, or Sunday. During that time the crisis at Attica mounted as dozens of notables flocked to the prison, some sincerely trying to ease the tension between administration and prisoners, others bent more on publicity. I kept trying to find out whether Sam was directly involved, but very few inmates' names appeared in the San Diego press, and never Sam's. The major news over the weekend was the death of the guard whose skull had been fractured on Thursday. From then on, all the rioting prisoners became subject to potential murder charges. They vowed they would never surrender control of the yard unless they were granted amnesty. Governor Rockefeller declared that if they did not surrender peacefully by Monday morning, September 13, he would send in troops.

Over the weekend Malcolm, the owner of Rusty, came back to San Diego and temporarily moved into my living room. On Monday morning he drove with me when I went to keep my appointments with Los Angeles publishers.

In the car I fiddled with the radio dials until I found a station broadcasting the news. Troop helicopters were buzzing over the Attica prison compound. We stopped the car at an address on La Cienega Boulevard where I was almost late for an interview. Malcolm promised to listen until I returned.

When I came back, it was over. The troops had retaken the yard. At least thirty were dead, possibly more.

"Well, that's it," I said, staring ahead. "He's dead."

"Oh, c'mon," Malcolm said. "Statistically there's a better than ninety-five percent chance that he's still alive."

Malcolm waited in the car again while I called the UPI office, hoping for names of the dead. They had a few names, all of them guards. I tried Greg again. No answer. Perhaps he knew it was me.

We had dinner at the home of friends of Malcolm's, a married couple in Venice with a new baby. The husband passed around color photos he'd taken of his wife during the delivery. The blood reminded me of the prison yard and turned my stomach. I went to the bedroom and tried Greg. Still no answer. Dinner was interminable: dessert, coffee, the obligatory joint. Malcolm and I drove back to San Diego, reaching my apartment after midnight.

At 6:00 A.M. the ringing of the telephone in the living room awakened me.

"He's dead," said Greg's voice. I began to cry and couldn't stop. My sobs woke Malcolm, who looked at me as though he wished he could drop through the floor.

Greg had waited until morning to get official confirmation from the prison. He was now trying to make arrangements for the body to be shipped to New York. This would take up to a week. An autopsy would have to be performed. As a further complication, Sam's ex-wife had also claimed the body in the name of Sam's son.

Perhaps the death of a lover enforces its own rules like the need for water or sex. I knew I had to be with Sam's body. Nothing else would make his death real to me.

"I want to come east," I said to Greg.

"That probably wouldn't be smart right now. Things are going to be pretty hot for a while. But I'll get back to you, okay?"

I hung up the phone and cried some more. "He's dead," I repeated to Malcolm. I called Grundoon and drove with her to a hill overlooking the ocean.

On a manzanita slope where the trilling of larks competed with the sound of traffic below, I found the response that felt most authentic: relief. Sam was dead and I was free of him. I no longer had to worry over how much loyalty I owed him or whether I was betraying him when I said, "I love you," to another man. I didn't have to wonder whether he was angry at me and could give up my guilt at having stopped writing to him. I could even surrender the fantasy, less frequent now but still recurring, that when he got out of prison, we would be together again. I could try to feel grateful that he died in a way he would have chosen, in the middle of a battle that was as close as he would come to his dream of revolution: a thousand of the oppressed against the armed strength of the state.

And yet—and yet—I would have liked to say good-bye. I would have liked to tell him that my love for him had been as genuine as any feeling I had ever had and that some of it had lasted, in spite of the anger. I would have liked to tell him that he had taught me something about my own sexuality and about trying to live life on my own terms. The bombings may have been wrong, but our impulse to defy the American establishment, especially at the height of the Vietnam War, had been right, and without Sam I would never have acted on it. I knew his blindness and craziness, yet I honored him still. I cherished the idea that whatever changes I went through, I would always be a woman he could love and that I would never lose whatever spark of faith and courage and openness to change had drawn him to me and held him, at least for one tumultuous year.

Pat called me from the house in New Hampshire where she had been living since the summer. She had heard from Greg that I wanted to come east and she and her new lover were prepared to have me as their guest if that would help me feel better. Determined to see Sam's body if at all possible, I accepted Pat's invitation. I cleaned out my savings and flew east the next morning. Pat met me at the airport and drove me to her new home.

During the time I spent with Pat and her lover, Thorsten, in New Hampshire, Greg and Sam's ex-wife, Ruth, resolved their dispute over the corpse. It was agreed that the body would be flown to the city, where for three days it would be on display at the Washington Square Church, allowing members of the left community a chance to pay their respects. After that Ruth would receive it for cremation in a private ceremony. Greg told me not to count on anything but that maybe, with luck, while the body was at the church, I would be able to see it. Meanwhile, the ever-resourceful Maude—who was now living in Kentucky but had come to New York to help in the crisis—was arranging a safe house for me in Manhattan.

For my first trip to New York since becoming a fugitive, I boarded the plane in heavy disguise—my Indianapolis wig and much-despised glasses. Maude's boyfriend, Bob, met me at La Guardia and drove me to the home of the poet Genevieve Porch, who had learned through a friend of Maude's of my predicament and offered me the guest room in her Central Park West apartment.

A longtime liberal activist, the author of six volumes of poems and winner of many literary prizes, Genevieve was a different sort of benefactor from the people who had helped me until then. Her apartment, with its walls of books, contemporary sculptures, and imposing view of Central Park, represented to me an almost unimaginable wealth, both of money and of intellect. I thought she was wonderful—lucid, passionate, sensitive, and extraordinarily kind. Her face, unmade up, showed all her forty-two years and was beautiful. At first she was solicitous of my privacy, but when she saw me responding to her overtures, our talks went on later and later into the night. Genevieve, who was to become a leading lesbian/feminist in the mid-1970s, was then new to the women's movement. She seemed especially interested in whatever I could tell her about feminism and about Robin Morgan, whose poetry she respected.

Maude, Greg, and Robert (with a little help from Maude's boyfriend, Bob) put to work the guerrilla skills they'd honed for the last three years so that I could have my wish to see Sam's body. At two in the morning they picked me up at Genevieve's and drove me to the Washington Square Church. Bob and Greg staked out the street. Maude preceded us into the sanctuary. Robert checked the basement of the church, cleared signals with Maude and with Bob and Greg, and then took my arm and hustled me into the church, keeping a little ahead of me so that my face could not be seen. (Later I learned that we had successfully escaped the notice of some late-night volunteer workers in the church basement as well as the FBI, which claimed to reporters that it had the church under twenty-four-hour surveillance.)

From a rear corner, hidden by shadows, Maude waved. I walked quietly down the center aisle to the open casket in the front and looked down at the man I had loved. The restlessness that had possessed me since the news about Attica broke was stilled, and I felt for a few moments the peace of moonlight on stained glass and of the eternity of what lay before my eyes.

Physically Sam was as I remembered him: high forehead, jutting nose, wide sensual lips, bald spot on his head. I leaned closer, trying to pinpoint what made me think of a counterfeit bill or of wax rather than flesh. His skin had been made up with suntan-colored pancake, and I caught a whiff of formaldehyde. Greg had said Sam was killed by a bullet in the neck. I pulled at the starched collar, looking for the hole. My hand drew back: Sam's flesh was as starched as the shirt. I had not meant to cry because what I felt wasn't really grief. Yet tears were rolling down my cheeks, and if I'd tried to talk, I would have sobbed out loud. For this was not Sam, but the shell of Sam—the husk into which an irreplaceable life had once been poured and from which it was now gone. Where to? Did it hover in the church? Straining to listen, I heard a sound that resembled Sam's voice, more like music than speech. I laid my fingers on the cold forehead and then on the bald spot on his head that Sam had loved to press between my thighs. I kissed the baldness.

The tears came fast now, dropping onto the face of the corpse. I kissed the icy mouth and chin and the place on his cheekbone where his beard used to stop. I laid my head on the neck and chafed the right hand, wondering if I could warm it a degree or two. I said good-bye. Then I signaled to Maude that I was ready to leave.

On my last night in New York, Greg and Robert took me to a tiny Szechuanese restaurant, where I sat with my back to the door so as not to be observed by passersby.

"What would you think," Greg asked me, "if we signed a book contract to publish Sam's prison letters?"

Few proposals could have excited me more. I had so far read only the letters Greg received from Sam until the time I left New Hampshire and had found them fascinating. Having just quit my job, I had plenty of time to work on the project. I also had a few unrealistic notions about how much I could participate in a publishing venture while living underground. I immediately volunteered to take the letters back to San Diego with me and begin editing them.

Greg told me to slow down. There was no sense in starting to edit before a contract was signed. All he wanted to know was whether I was willing to provide an introduction of 10,000 words or so. I wouldn't be included in the contract, but dropping my name discreetly to the publisher might make the proposal more attractive. I was thrilled to be included on any terms at all, and agreed at once.

Back in San Diego I immersed myself in the introduction. I had to work around several restrictions: I could give no clues at all suggesting Pat's involvement in the bombings since she was already under indictment and any evidence would weigh heavily against her. I had to be equally careful about revealing the identities of the other conspirators who could be indicted at any time before the five-year statute of limitations ran out. These limitations handicapped me less than my own emotional bias—for immediately after his death, my memory of Sam was suffused with a romantic glow and I kept looking back on my year with him as the last time I had known pure joy. And so unwittingly I excluded material that hurt too much to think about. The carelessness of the Marine Midland bombing worked its way into my essay, but not the date I made with another man that had precipitated it. I referred obliquely to the affair with Billie Banks, but not to the fact that Sam had boasted of the bombings to her. I admitted that Sam had been advised against talking to Demmerle but then tried to rationalize his having done so. I wasn't deliberately falsifying; I was telling as much of the truth as I was able to face.

Because the essay was completely preoccupying me, I talked about my work on it to my c-r group. I assumed that none of them was interested enough in the left or in prison riots to inquire about my deceased friend's identity, but this turned out to be naïve. Nineteen-year-old Patty had started attending the meetings of an anti-imperialist coalition that was organizing against the plans of the Republican Party to hold its nominating convention in San Diego. One of her leftist friends in the coalition had prompted her to ask me the name of my friend who died at Attica.

"Why, uh, Mel," I said, seizing on the unimaginative nickname Sam had used during the bombing conspiracy.

Patty nodded. "I think I've heard of him," she said as my heart sank into my sandals. I tried several times to sound her out further but was unable to determine how much she knew without giving it all away.

Greg had generously promised to give me half the $7,500 advance for the book, out of which I could meet my expenses on another trip east. In October when I'd finished my essay, I flew to his home near Albany, hoping to spend a week or two helping him edit the letters. To my disappointment, Greg had barely started his own essay and had still not touched the letters. He allowed me to read them but insisted he would do the editing himself. Having paid little attention to the plans he laid out in the beginning, I now felt iced out of a project that had become very dear to me. I was bitter when I left him, continuing on to New York to retype and mail my essay from Genevieve's. I followed the instructions Greg had mapped out, mailing the essay to Sandy Katz with a cover note suggesting that it was his to publish as he saw fit. Of course, Sandy had prior instructions to forward the essay immediately to Greg, who would see that it became the introduction to the letters.

On the night Sam died, Robin had called me in San Diego to express condolences. She had also mentioned that she and her husband and child were about to move for three months to Sarasota, Florida, where she would be teaching feminist courses at an experimental college. She felt sure that she would not be under surveillance there—as was always a possibility in New York—and said I was welcome to visit her. With the prospect of my half of the advance, I decided to take her up on the invitation.

On the beach in Sarasota, Robin and I walked with our arms around each other while she pointed out coquina shells. She was thrilled to learn that I had joined a women's consciousness-raising group and amused when I told her that the other women thought of me as a feminist, though I didn't consider myself one.

"You were always a feminist; you just couldn't admit it before," she said. "When you were waiting to go on trial for the bombings, you were like a character in a Greek tragedy who kept turning to the audience whispering, 'Help—I don't want to be in this play.'"

I was amazed at her astuteness; no one else I knew had caught on to my act so acutely.

She hugged me. "Having you here is like being with family," she said. "I'm so surprised that you came—and so glad."

Encouraged by her warmth, I decided to show her my essay on Sam. It had already been read by Greg and Genevieve, both of whom had praised it, and I felt confident that Robin would think well of it, too. Instead, she was so appalled that she said nothing at all. She simply asked if it would be all right for her husband, Kenneth, who was a writer himself and shared her feminist politics, to read it also. Their opinions coincided, and what they told me over the next few days was to alter my life profoundly.

After dinner, when two-year-old Blake had been put to bed, Kenneth and Robin went through my essay page by page, pointing to examples of Sam's cruelty that I had glossed over with humor or self-blame. He had pressured me into moving out of an apartment I liked into a commune with strangers. He had refused to help me put up bookshelves in the new apartment, compelling me to sell off my library. He had disdained tickets to a Carnegie Hall concert that I had bought to please him. He insisted on sleeping with other women, which I had presented in my essay as an aspect of his radical politics but which Robin and Ken insisted was no more than philandering disguised as "liberation."

What upset them most was my description of the Jane Daring aerograms Sam had sent me in England. "Don't you realize what the character of Jane Daring is?" Robin demanded. "She's the masochist in *The Story of O*." I had not mentioned either in the essay or in conversation that *The Story of O* was a favorite book of Sam's and the basis for his sexual fantasy life. Robin's insight struck me as uncanny—and made me intensely uncomfortable. She was conscious of a truth not only about Sam but about me that I had tried to avoid facing for years.

Eventually Ken went to sleep. Robin and I talked until nearly dawn. She was trying to convince me that Sam had never been a leftist at all. He had pretended to believe in equality and freedom, but my revelations about his sexuality made his real proclivities clear. Far from being a communist, Robin said, Sam was a fascist. He wanted power over me for the same reason he wanted power over the world: to shore up his crumbling masculine ego.

I could not answer her attacks on Sam. They matched too well what I had sensed about him and been afraid to admit. Finally I summoned the nerve to ask her the question that most weighed on me: if Sam was so worthless, wasn't there something wrong with me for having chosen and stayed with him?

Ah, Robin said, that was different. As a woman I innately understood that I lived in a society in which I would never achieve more than second-class citizenship. Like many women, I had identified my oppression with that of others—with black men and Vietnamese and college boys who burned their draft cards—and fought for them as for myself. I couldn't have known back in 1968 that my real fight was against male supremacy, not capitalism, or that my real allies were not the men in the radical left, but other women. I had moved to the Lower East Side with Sam for the same reasons that other white middle-class women went south to fight for integration in the early sixties. My mistakes were understandable because at the time I made them I had no other options. Now that feminism was at last a powerful movement, and the left as I knew it defunct, wasn't I free to admit my error and move on to where I would always be welcome—the women's movement?

Robin's argument explained more of the mysteries of my life than any set of ideas I had ever come across. She had accounted for my lifelong attraction to radical men, my participation in the bombings, my long, irrational attachments to Sam and to Lonnie, and my drift into a women's consciousness-raising group after my brief affair with Tim failed to work out.

For months after that night in Sarasota my memory would prompt new bits of information to be examined, explained, and fitted into the feminist scheme. I came to see the lives of other women as further examples of submission to male oppression. I became infinitely more wary of involvements with men—any men. And I became deeply suspicious of anyone, male or female, who looked at the world through the spectacles of the left. The male right and the male left, I believed, were the Janus faces of patriarchy, and I needed to maintain independence from both.

It was brilliant of Robin to recognize that I had clung to Sam in order to enact a revolutionary fantasy. It was also helpful that she guided me, in Sarasota and later, away from involvements with men that jeopardized my safety as a fugitive as well as my self-respect. But her scheme had a serious flaw. She was wrong to think that only men appealed to me as spiritual directors. Female power had a primitive, awesome quality for me, and intimacy with a woman could reduce me to greater abjectness than I had displayed with any man. In time I was to play out the same psychic drama with Robin that I had with Sam.

But I didn't know that then. That night in Sarasota we forged a friendship of rare intensity which supplied each of us with what she needed most: for me, an ideology I could live by, and for Robin, more substance for the mythmaking that was central both to her politics and her poetry. In the bond we formed that night, the foundation was laid for my break with the past and for my surrender to the government two and a half years later.

Back in San Diego I did my best to make brief revisions in my memoir that would reflect my entirely changed interpretation of Sam. I had little hope of salvaging what now seemed to me an embarrassing whitewash, but I sent the alterations to Sandy Katz anyway, begging him—that is, Greg—to have them included if at all possible. Greg did not call to confirm receipt of my message, an omission which made me frantic for weeks.

In my now-frequent contact with Robin through pay telephone calls and mail drops, we discussed the possible threat to my safety in San Diego. The Republican convention was scheduled to meet in the city in June, and a flood of advance men was already arriving. I continued to worry that Patty's friends in the anti-imperialist coalition were going to figure out who "Mel's" friend was, if not now, then when the book was published in February. Publication of the book could also lead to news stories and the reappearance of old photos of me as well as to increased FBI interest in the case. Robin suggested that I move. When I mentioned that New Mexico appealed to me, she immediately offered to get in touch with Rosemarie Dryden, a painter she knew who had recently settled in a town near Albuquerque. A little after this conversation she called to say that a temporary home for me with Rosemarie and her eighteen-year-old daughter, Stephanie, had been arranged.

My c-r group had provided me my closest friendships in San Diego, and I didn't want to leave these women without some sort of farewell. I could see little harm in revealing my identity to them on the night before I was to go and in giving a forwarding address to at least one of them, through whom the others could also write me. At my last meeting I asked Roslyn, the VISTA worker in whose house we were meeting, to close all the doors and windows so no neighbors could overhear. I was not expecting any difficulty, but after Roz had complied, the prospect of exposure before these five women overwhelmed me. I stammered and shook, unable to say my real name. Roslyn held me in her arms, assuring me of the group's support, no matter what my problem was. Gradually my tremors passed.

My story, halting at first, came out more easily when I had said my name and finally unrolled wildly as yarn in a kitten's paws. The women listened in amazed silence. When I came to a halt, they hugged me, one by one. Patty was crying.

"I wish I'd known," she said. "I never would have said a word about you or your essay to anyone."

"It doesn't matter," I told her. "I probably would have had to leave anyway. Something would have happened."

Silence fell again as no one could think of what to say next.

I left San Diego soon after that, Grundoon and a few possessions stowed in the Opel. I felt that in leaving my c-r group, I was losing something I would never replace. Yet with Robin looking after me, I also felt a brand-new security. I drove toward New Mexico with regret but no deep remorse, comforted by the idea that I would now be a thousand miles closer to the person who mattered most.

XV
Fugitive Encounters

SHORTLY AFTER I ARRIVED IN NEW Mexico, a message Greg had sent to San Diego was forwarded to me at Rosemarie's house. Along with a money order for $500, which Greg claimed was what was left of the half of the advance he had promised me after deducting travel expenses, and a copy of the just-published book was a letter informing me that *Evergreen Review* had bought the rights to reprint my essay on Sam.

Isolation, frequent moves, and the other tensions of fugitive life were taking their emotional toll, and I vented my frustrations on Greg. I was already upset with him for not having shared the editing of the book with me and for the many weeks in which I'd had to wait for confirmation that my revisions were being made. Although I was relieved to see my changes incorporated into the published essay, everything else about his message infuriated me. I found it hard to believe that half of a $7,500 advance could have been reduced to merely $500 by my two trips across the country when round-trip airfare was under $200. (Later Greg explained to me that the funeral expenses for Sam had also come out of the advance, but I didn't understand this at the time.) I thought the finished book was ugly and sloppily edited, but what made me angriest —foolish though it seems to me now—was the news about *Evergreen*. Knowing my increasing commitment to radical feminism—and about my feelings on pornography as far back as the *Rat* take-over —how could Greg have promised my piece to a magazine which advertised itself as "literary erotica"?

Greg had warned me after Attica that he considered his telephone completely unsafe. I didn't dare call now when both his safety and my new hideout in New Mexico could be jeopardized by a tap on the phone. Robin, whose outrage at Greg exceeded even my own, helped me devise a plan to stop *Evergreen*'s publication of the piece. I sent a letter to Greg care of Genevieve threatening a public denunciation of him if he did not immediately withdraw my writing from *Evergreen*. To ensure that Greg received the letter, Robin told Maude to tell Greg to pick it up at Genevieve's immediately, even if that required him to make a special trip to the city. Greg eventually received the letter and was able to cancel publication plans, but only because *Evergreen*'s financial difficulties happened to delay its schedule. He never understood why I was so angry, and the harshness I displayed in my letter permanently alienated him. We never again were on friendly terms.

Meanwhile, Rosemarie Dryden's house was becoming an unsuitable hideout. Her daughter Stephanie's involvement in left-wing protests at the University of New Mexico made me fear the house might be watched, and I was getting along badly with Rosemarie's lover, Eric. Stephanie, to whom I was becoming close, arranged for me to move to Santa Fe and stay at the home of a friend who was vacationing out of state for a week.

At the Albuquerque HEW office I had applied for a new Social Security card in the name of Carla Weinstein—Weinstein because, after two years of "passing," I wanted my Jewish identity back and Carla because it suited my new surroundings. I planned to use the Social Security card to obtain a driver's license under the same alias. Until the card arrived at Rosemarie's, I was in no position to sign a lease. In case I failed to find a place to live when Stephanie's friend returned, I telephoned Pat in New Hampshire to ask if, in an emergency, she could take me in again.

Pat answered that she had less room than when I'd visited her in September and that she knew no one else who could put me up. Then, to my astonishment, she launched into a tirade at me for the letter I had written Greg. How could I dream of denouncing him publicly when he was on our side? I tried to explain the ways in which I believed he had betrayed me, but Pat wouldn't listen. Then she added that my essay had wounded her deeply. Instead of feeling relieved that I had made no mention of anyone in the bombing conspiracy who resembled her, she felt hurt that I had left her out.

This proved, she said, that I had never considered her important. We hung up in mutual anger.

I was on the verge of pleading with Stephanie's friend to allow me to stay in the house after he returned when, by a stroke of good fortune, I learned of a young white woman named Polly living in the Santa Fe *barrio* who had a two-bedroom house to share. I immediately drove to see her. A thin, shy woman with a hint of apology in her voice, Polly explained that her last roommate had left her in the lurch to go off to California with a new boyfriend. She needed someone who could move in at once and help with the month's rent of $90. The bedroom she showed me was already furnished with a bed and a desk and had a view of the Sangre de Cristo Mountains to the north. I gave her $45 from what was left of the advance for the book and moved in with Grundoon the next morning. Polly, who was employed as a maid and worked at home on her weavings, proved to be an ideal roommate, gentle, unobtrusive, considerate and kind. I came to count on her absolutely, and she remained one of the best friends I made in my years as a fugitive.

Faced with a few weeks' wait before my Social Security card arrived and with some money Robin sent to tide me over, I occupied my time writing long letters to Robin and Genevieve and reading. Everything I read during those early months in 1972 became text for the same subject: the age-old oppression of women by men. I took pages of notes from Eleanor Flexner's *Century of Struggle*, memorizing the names and biographies of the nineteenth-century feminists. In Charlotte Brontë's autobiographical *Villette*, which Genevieve recommended to me, I found a female sensibility painfully close to my own. When I reread Malraux's book on the 1929 Shanghai uprising, *Man's Fate*—also at Genevieve's prompting—I found myself identifying not with the terrorist Ch'en, as I had when I had read it in 1969, but with May Gisors, a left activist and wife of the hero. I couldn't help wondering what sort of book Malraux would have produced if May had chosen to identify with women instead of with the working class, with feminism over Marxism.

Robin sent me a copy of *The First Sex*, a newly published book by Elizabeth Gould Davis, a Sarasota librarian, and a work she told me had changed many of her ideas. Davis's reading of history fitted in closely with Robin's version of feminist revolution. She argued that ancient accounts of Atlantis and myths of a Golden Age were actually remembrances of the earliest civilizations: peaceful, technologically advanced gynocracies. Thousands of years ago, those gynocracies had been overrun by crude, male-dominated warrior tribes, and ever since, male-run society had continued to pollute the planet. Robin was excited by this thesis because she was beginning to believe that feminist revolution should aim not at mere equality between men and women but at outright women's rule—gynocracy —for an indefinite period. She urged me to read the Davis book and let her know what I thought.

What I thought—and confirmed after research in the St. John's College library, where I reread Hesiod, Suetonius, and Plato—was that Davis had most of her facts wrong and had grossly misinterpreted modern scholarship. Nevertheless, I found her book evocative and compelling. For the past months I had been living in a kind of gynocracy of my own with Robin as my chief adviser and other women as my only sources of intimacy and affection. I felt deeply nourished by this environment and wondered how many other women who lived now in relatively servile situations might be liberated in a world run by women. After so long a period of political inertness, Robin and the women's movement were stimulating me again into the role of an advocate, this time on behalf of radical (some would say separatist) feminism.

Through Stephanie I met one woman activist in Santa Fe who in her views and personality seemed to me a potential radical feminist. Her name was Elisa Chavez, and she worked as a nurse with a group that wanted to found a free clinic in the *barrio*. I went out of my way to please her, volunteering for clinic-associated errands and supporting her complaints against her male co-workers at a time when few in the Chicano movement were protesting sexism. Elisa—who had no idea I was anyone but Carla Weinstein, a friend of Stephanie's—kept urging me to come to meetings and public events that I tried to avoid for security reasons. One commitment I could not escape was attendance at a lecture by Joshua Horn, a British physician who had practiced medicine in mainland China. Elisa admired him greatly and pressed me so strongly to come and hear him that I feared a refusal might damage our friendship.

Stephanie and Polly accompanied me to the lecture at a Santa Fe church. Arriving a few minutes late, we seated ourselves quietly at the rear of the church. A man a few rows ahead of us happened to be facing the rear door as we sat down. His thick eyebrows shot up at the sight of us, and he whispered something to the woman next to him. I turned to Stephanie.

"That man is looking at you like his eyes are going to pop out of his head," she whispered. "Do you know him?"

I looked at his back. Broad shoulders, blue work shirt, long, dirty blond hair. He turned around again, and our eyes met. His face was concealed by a bushy blond beard and mustache. Whom did those gesticulating eyebrows, the half-insolent, half-pleading expression remind me of? The name in my head was Mark Rudd, but I pushed it aside.

"He looks sort of familiar," I admitted. "But he can't possibly be the person I've got in mind. Probably someone I knew in high school. You're sure you don't know him?"

"Positive. I've seen almost everyone in this room before, but not him."

I couldn't afford the risk of being greeted in public by my real name—and certainly not in front of Polly. I had never confided my identity or my situation to her, and if she became suspicious for any reason, I would be forced to leave the only safe hideout I had found in New Mexico. If this stranger was going to confront me, I would have to make sure that it happened on the street, well out of Polly's hearing. The moment the lecture was over, I would bolt from the hall.

Every ten minutes, it seemed, the man turned around to stare and gesture at me. I kept looking away. This could not be Rudd, who would feel as wary at meeting another fugitive as I did. He would not wiggle his eyebrows or whisper in so obvious a way to the person next to him. This man was a dangerous fool, someone to avoid if I possibly could. But leaving in the middle of the lecture would raise too many questions to answer later. Meanwhile, Horn droned on.

Suddenly the lights snapped on, ending a slide show, and Horn called for questions. Up in a flash and leaving Stephanie to cover my retreat, I slid from the table and fled outside.

I walked up and down the street, catching my breath and wondering if the stranger would follow me. The next person out the church door was Stephanie. Her words came in gasps.

"That guy jumped up from his seat the second he saw you were gone," she said. "I had to head him off at the landing. He was very polite. Said he was an old friend of yours and that he'd just like to talk to you. I told him you'd gone to the ladies' room. He asked me to bring you a message and find out if he could see you later."

"Did he say what his name was?"

"Tony."

My pulse went still. It had been no trick of my imagination. Somehow Rudd and I, after two years as fugitives, had ended up at the same lecture nearly a continent away from where we had last been together.

"Tell him I'll wait for him here," I said to Stephanie.

As he emerged from the church, I recognized him more from his off-balance stride than from his changed face. In a moment his arms were around me.

"My God, it's you, it's really you," he said. "When I saw you walk into that church, I thought my eyes were playing tricks on me. What the hell are you doing here?"

"What are *you*?"

"I sort of hesitated to come, to tell you the truth. We don't go to too many public events. But, Jesus, I'm glad I was at this one. Listen, I read your piece about Sam. It's great. We all loved it."

About his praise for my essay, I had mixed feelings. I couldn't read my eulogy of Sam now without cringing. But Rudd's use of the word "we" won me over. I could not let him go without finding out how the Weathermen were surviving. Except for sporadic news —a bombing in the Capitol in March claimed by the Weather Underground, a condolence note on Sam's death from one of my New York Weatherman contacts which Maude had passed onto me—I had heard nothing of them in two years, and my curiosity was more than casual.

"I really want to talk to you," Rudd said. "But I can't stay here. I'm with people who don't know who I am, and I've got to get back to meet them. And I may not be in town much longer."

"Can't we meet later tonight?"

"Yeah, that ought to work. Say, about midnight? At the plaza? You know where that is?"

"Yes."

"I'll be in a station wagon with New Mexico plates."

Polly was going to think it odd when I left the house at midnight Nothing in Santa Fe was open then. I decided to worry about that later.

* * *

I parked my Opel a block from the plaza and detoured some distance on foot, watching for loiterers. When I spotted a cruising white station wagon, I hid in the shadows until I recognized Rudd at the wheel and was sure that he was alone.

We drove to a park outside of town, where Rudd cut the engine and switched off the lights. Having come to the end of surprised exclamations at our encounter, neither of us knew what to say. We couldn't very well ask about mutual friends or what the other had been doing for the last two years. Finally I asked how long he had been in Santa Fe.

"Seven or eight months, I guess. But we're going to be leaving very soon."

"You're here with others from . . . the organization?"

"No. Just the woman I live with."

That Rudd lived with a woman who was not herself a fugitive was the second of the evening's surprises. I had concluded months ago—around the time my affair with Tim failed to work out as I hoped—that only a crazy like Lonnie would give up a normal life in order to live with someone who was underground. What magic did Rudd possess that had persuaded a woman to go into hiding with him?

"Is that someone you met since you went under?" I asked.

"No. She's a very old friend of mine."

I dimly remembered that reports of Rudd in the Columbia days had mentioned his girl friend, a Barnard student. Then I'd heard that Rudd had left her after he became famous. Could this be the same woman?

Rudd was saved from answering that question by the approach of a cop car. The lights flashed in our rearview mirror, and the car stopped a few feet behind us.

"Don't panic," Rudd said edgily. "What's your name? The name on your ID?"

"Carla Weinstein." So far I had only a library card, but it would do in a pinch.

"I'm Tony Schwartz."

He rolled down the window for the cop. His voice was only a shade too hearty.

"What can I do for you, Officer?"

The cop, seeing we were white and over the legal age, was apologetic. Something about a mugging in the park last night, a routine check. I turned my face half toward the window to keep him from getting a glimpse of me. When Rudd assured him we were on our way home, he sauntered back to his patrol car.

Rudd turned the ignition key. "I guess we'd better get back," he said.

He stopped at the plaza, next to the arcade. In the daytime this block was lined with peddlers selling turquoise and moccasins. Now, in the dark, it smelled of pine needles, and the old La Fonda Hotel loomed over us like a memory.

"Are you leaving very soon?" I pleaded. "I could meet you somewhere tomorrow or the next day. I'd really like to talk more."

"Why don't you meet me Saturday at the Pizza Hut on the Albuquerque highway? There's always a crowd there at lunchtime. Say, one o'clock? If I'm not there in an hour, then split."

As I walked back to my car, I kept thinking of how Rudd had reacted to the cop's approach, slipping on his false identity like a comfortable old shirt, assuming I would do the same. Tony Schwartz. I liked the name; unpretentious, Jewish, it suited him. Since leaving Pat, I had not known the pleasure of sharing danger with another fugitive. I hadn't realized until now how much I missed it.

Rudd's warning that he might be leaving town in a matter of days turned out to be mere camouflage. He and his lover, who called herself Flan, were well settled into their lives in Santa Fe, living in a small adobe six blocks from the house I shared with Polly. Rudd worked off the books for a local construction firm while Flan had a part-time secretarial job. They owned two huge dogs, took karate lessons four times a week at a local school where they knew most of the other students, and kept a small picture of Che Guevara in a gilt frame over their bed—the sole visible reminder of Rudd's past.

I gradually learned that while Rudd considered himself a part of "the organization," he was living in a kind of exile from it. He was vague about the reasons and bristled once when I referred to his having been "kicked out." He called it a "cooling-off period" and tried to imply that it was more a sabbatical than an expulsion. His defensiveness gave him away. Obviously he had gotten in some sort of trouble with the others which he didn't want to discuss with me.

For fear of exposure to Polly, Rudd never visited my house, but he, Flan, and I became friends anyway. We visited a ghost town outside Albuquerque, taking all three of our dogs. I was allowed to observe one of their karate classes (after swearing I would never repeat to anyone their involvement in the dojo, about which they were passionate). Rudd showed me a clipping about a new national organization of leftists which had given him hope for the future of the movement and which I guessed had been sent to him by some still-active member of the Weather Underground. I tried to explain to Rudd and Flan that I was now a radical feminist; but Rudd kept insisting genially that I was still "one of them," and Flan seemed to defer to his political judgment. We once had an argument over his reference to my San Diego c-r group as "low-level political work," a description I found insulting. On April 28 Rudd wanted me to go out with them to celebrate the anniversary of the Columbia uprising, but I refused, saying I no longer was pleased by the impact that event had had on my later life. But for the most part, we enjoyed each other's unexpected company and relished the rare opportunity to share lives as fugitives.

One day, when Rudd was at work and Flan had the afternoon off, she invited me to their house for lunch. Over cheese and avocado sandwiches on homemade bread, she startled me by confessing she was trying to get pregnant.

"But, Flan, what would you do with a baby if you got picked up?" I asked, thinking at once of Pat and Jenny.

She said that she and Tony (as she always called Rudd) had discussed the problem and believed they could manage. Their separation from the organization was due to end soon, perhaps as early as next month. When they were reunited with the others, they would have a support system to take care of the child should anything happen to them.

My stomach twisted with jealousy. A baby! What did I think of having a child? When I decided to go underground, I had envisioned my future as so filled with adventure that a child could only get in the way. Since then I had rigidly closed the door on the subject whenever it threatened to pop up. For I could not imagine that I would ever live with someone the way Rudd lived with Flan or have a community that would help me raise a child.

God, what a choice I had made! If I had gone to prison like Nate, I would be almost free by now, ready to start my life over as though the bombings hadn't happened. Or if I'd stayed in New Hampshire with Pat . . . but no, that would never have worked. If Dana and I had seen ahead to this that night we sat on a bench in Abingdon Square, would I still have followed her to California? Or would I have gone to prison? I could feel the pain distorting my face. Flan must be thinking I despised her. Managing a smile, I said what was expected.

"Flan, that's wonderful. I hope you won't have to wait much longer."

If I had an underground community, it consisted of Robin, Ken, and Blake, and certainly Robin treated me as a member of her family. In the spring of 1972, when she received an advance from her publisher for a completed manuscript of poems, she immediately proposed using the money to pay for a vacation for the four of us. Her plan was to take Blake and meet me in New Mexico, where we would spend a few days alone. We would then rent a car big enough for the four of us to travel comfortably and drive to Arizona, where we would pick up Kenneth at the airport. Together we would visit Grand Canyon, Bryce Canyon, and Zion Park, staying in motels and perhaps camping out for one or two nights with brand-new equipment Robin had bought for the trip. At the end Robin might return with me to New Mexico for a few more days alone while Ken and Blake went back to New York.

It was a very strange trip, beginning with Robin's arrival at the Albuquerque airport. In her compulsion for disguise she had costumed Blake as a girl in ruffled organdy and ribbons. At two and a half he was too young to be abashed by his gender change. In fact, he seemed quite giddy, both from excitement and from the Dramamine Robin had given him to counteract air sickness. He twirled around the Albuquerque airport, showing off his petticoats and alternating cries of "Mommy, Mommy"—as he was instructed to call Robin for the purpose of disguise—with "Robin, Robin," his usual way of addressing her.

A bit embarrassed at the money Robin was spending on the trip, I had tried to save on motel bills by asking Stephanie if she knew anyone who could put us up. She suggested Gareth and Jim, two gay male friends of hers who lived in a rural area outside Albuquerque. They had been told nothing more than that Robin's and my names were Donna and Carla and that we hoped to be left alone as much as possible.

On the second night of our stay, while Robin was putting Blake to sleep in our shared room, I wandered into the kitchen to find our hosts poring over a new copy of the *Ladder*, a lesbian literary magazine. The magazine featured an account of one of Robin's recent lectures with a full-page photo which Gareth waved in my face. "Doesn't Robin Morgan bear a remarkable resemblance to our friend Donna?" he demanded.

Until this point I had worried only that I might be recognized—not Robin. The situation posed no immediate threat to me, but since Robin had taken such pains with her disguise and her alias, I was as shaken as if I were really endangered. Unhappily I admitted that Donna was indeed Robin Morgan (I saw no way around that) and warned the two men never to repeat a word about her visit. They assured me, with much comradely winking and chuckling, that they would protect our secret. I returned to the bedroom as soon as I could and told Robin what had happened.

Robin was enraged. She thought I had been foolish to admit her identity when I could have continued to deny it, however unconvincingly, but she was even angrier at Gareth and Jim for having pressured a confession out of me. She stormed into the kitchen and declared that if they ever breathed a word about our visit, she would have them executed by a feminist militia. Robin's quick, articulate temper was one of her most characteristic traits, one which I envied; in similar circumstances, I usually cried. Gareth and Jim, as good-hearted as any people who ever put me up, took the outburst with good humor. Though they had no earthly reason to want to help us any further, they graciously agreed to let us use their names to rent a car and drive with Blake to the Page, Arizona, airport, to meet Kenneth. I felt very thankful.

Grateful for the privacy of the car after we left Gareth and Jim's, I reveled in the opportunity to talk with Robin on the long drive to Arizona. With Blake sleeping in the back seat, I poured out my life to her as the majestic scenery sped by, almost unnoticed. We were two hours late for our rendezvous with Kenneth, and though I liked him well enough, I wasn't happy to have my precious time alone with Robin come so quickly to an end.

The three of us made noble efforts to get along as we traveled from one dazzling site to the next, but with Blake demanding almost constant attention and Kenneth—from my point of view—a mostly intrusive presence, I couldn't help feeling frustrated. When

I finally confessed this to Robin, she responded by asking Kenneth to cut short his vacation and fly home with Blake that night.

Kenneth told me later that he never forgave me for initiating that suggestion. Although he himself had been openly bisexual for years, he saw the mutual attraction between Robin and me as a sign that I was diabolically determined to destroy his marriage. He thought I was unworthy of Robin's gifts and attentions and that I had placed her under a spell. I was mostly ignorant of his suspicions of me—possibly because Robin and I were not lovers. In spite of the erotic undercurrent between us, I remained afraid of repeating my unsatisfying experience with Pat, and Robin seemed even less eager for a homosexual involvement. Still, I thought of our relation as exclusive and passionate and implicitly sexual. Though we never had an affair, and though I would have been horrified to think of Robin's leaving her marriage or her public career for me, I didn't wonder at Kenneth's jealousy of us.

What I didn't understand for many years was that while Robin was cultivating an intimacy with me, she was also under pressure from left-wing lesbian/feminists (then a growing force in the women's movement) to produce lesbian credentials. She managed to boost her image both as a leftist and a militant feminist by resorting to public and private hints that she had a woman lover who was underground. This, of course, jeopardized my security. It also made me seem like a liar, or at least strangely reticent, when I finally met Robin's feminist acquaintances and innocently denied that we had been lovers. Robin had implied the contrary so often and in so many parts of the country that ten years later I still encounter women who think that we had an affair.

When I came home from my trip with Robin, Polly told me she was moving. Tired of eking out a living as a maid, she had accepted an offer from her parents to spend the summer caring for their house in Connecticut while they vacationed in the West. She asked if I wanted to move east with her. A greater treat than a free summer in the vicinity of my family and Robin I could not imagine, but I also realized that Polly was asking me mostly from politeness. I could not take advantage of her generosity without explaining the risk—especially if my family and friends were going to visit me in the Connecticut house. So I explained my situation and added that if she had no objection, I would be very grateful to accompany her.

I think Polly must have found it hard to take my fugitive status seriously. Or perhaps she was simply too kind to hold it against me. She put her arms around me and said, "Welcome," and assured me that it made no difference to her at all.

At the same time Rudd and Flan were making plans to rejoin the Weather Underground at some undisclosed location. In anticipation of this I had given them a note to pass on to Bernardine Dohrn, who in the past year appeared to have risen to sole leadership of the organization. I told Bernardine that although I'd changed my political views and become a feminist since the last time we had seen each other, I would still be interested in meeting with her and possibly with other Weatherwomen at a convenient time and place. Bernardine had sent back a warm message suggesting a meeting in San Francisco in early July. This sounded perfect: I could spend June in San Diego seeing friends from my c-r group and, after my meeting with Bernardine, drive east to join Polly in Connecticut.

I told Robin with great excitement about Polly's offer and about my planned meeting with Bernardine and perhaps other women in "the Beatles." While she was delighted to hear about the Connecticut opportunity and sent me some money which, together with a contribution from my parents, would pay for the trip, her letter was filled with admonishments about the other part of my news.

"I think it is a fantastic chance," she wrote, "for, well LOTS of things to happen, but it could also be an important chance for you to really raise your own banner very high, in a kind of test against the situation." She understood, she said, how much I wanted colleagues with whom I could let my hair down and that I might be unwilling to alienate them by coming on with too strong a feminist line. But the Weatherwomen, she felt, "seem daring enough to respect and respond to a direct 'Hound of Heaven' breathing-urgently-down-the-neck approach regarding feminism, as opposed to subtle hints and suede gloves." In any case, whether they could respect it or not, she had expectations of me. "What I'm whiffling around trying to say," she wrote, "is that you better damned not wimp out with them or I'll be really 'pissed off.' The least they can do is listen and the worst they can do is think you're crazy. Which you really do have the potential of becoming and better learn to be shiningly proud of."

"Hound of heaven," indeed. Much as I adored Robin, her presumptuousness could get on my nerves. What right did she have to suggest how I ought to act with people she didn't even know?

Yet I acknowledged the need for her warning. The temptation I felt to join the only white radical underground then functioning was a very strong one; it was the chief basis of my friendship with Rudd and Flan. How much more keenly I would experience the pull in the presence of Bernardine and other Weatherwomen, Robin might well have guessed better than I.

I reached the buffalo enclosure at Golden Gate Park twenty minutes early for my meeting with Bernardine. I was disguised only by a pair of sunglasses—and by the two years I had aged since any photo of me had appeared. I wondered if I would recognize Bernardine. Until recently she had been one of the FBI's Ten Most Wanted fugitives, and her face adorned the jackets of a number of books on the left. I expected to see her dramatically changed, since she had survived a hunt much more intense than the one for me.

I picked her out of the crowd at fifty yards. Her strong-jawed face was unmistakable. Hip-hugging jeans showed off her famous long legs, and she wore one of the low-cut blouses she had been known for in her days as a radical left emcee. The one difference was her hair: the color was startling, like copper set on fire by the July sun. How could she risk so conspicuous a shade? She caught the attention of everyone she passed.

When we were opposite each other, I said the first words that came to my lips. "I recognized you from the color of your hair."

She laughed—a confident, unapologetic laugh.

"I recognized you," she said, matching my tone, "from your dog."

We walked through the park and sat down on a grassy knoll.

"I brought something for you," said Bernardine. "A present from some of the other women."

She poured the contents of a leather pouch into my cupped hands. Beads, made of glass and wood, brilliant as Bernardine's hair, slid through my fingers. We picked them out of the grass.

"I'm so sorry they're not strung," said Bernardine. "There was hardly any time left when they realized they wanted to give you a gift. They admire you so much, you know. They were terribly excited when I told them I was going to see you."

How was I to reconcile Robin's fire-breathing image of these women with this childlike chaos of beads?

I was trying to think of ways to challenge her on feminist subjects. Instead, Bernardine, a born leader, subtly took the conversational lead from me. For most of the afternoon she told me what the Weathermen had been doing for the past two years. Virtually all the information she gave me had appeared already in their public statements, but Bernardine managed to make it seem new and intended for my ears alone.

She began by asking my forgiveness for the rude way the organization had treated me when I first arrived in San Francisco in 1970. They'd had a difficult time taking care of their own people, let alone outsiders, and under severe pressure had been inconsiderate of many dear friends. Since that time they had given up the idea that they could function as an underground without assistance from an overground movement. Having alienated many more moderate leftists, they worked hard to build bridges back to the movement. As a measure of how much they had changed their views from the revolutionary zeal of 1970, she admitted that some members of the organization were working in McGovern for President campaign offices.

"If McGovern can win the nomination and election," she said, "it's possible we won't even need an underground anymore. Some of our people are very excited at the idea of going home again."

I was astounded.

"You mean you think that McGovern would get the charges against you dropped?"

She shook her head. "Not that many members of our group are facing charges, at least not serious charges," she said. "A few are underground because they could be used to trace others. Some choose to live that way because it's most convenient for their work. In the past couple of years some have surfaced quietly, just by using their own names again and waiting to see if they're picked up."

"And no one has gone to jail?"

"A couple have received probation."

Although it was hard for me to reconcile this information with my picture of the Weather Underground as serious fugitives, it was true. With the exception of the charges against Cathy Wilkerson and Kathy Boudin for the explosion in the Wilkerson town house that killed three of their friends, and conspiracy charges against Bernardine and a dozen others that were dropped by 1974, the Weathermen were of little interest to prosecutors. They were working hard to stay together not so much from fear of the law as because of their belief that the idea of an underground had a powerful effect on people. I thought this was wrongheaded. I no longer believed, as

I had in 1970, that the country was in any way ready for a revolution, leftist or otherwise, and I couldn't imagine that enough people were still interested in joining an organized underground to make the idea work. But I was, whether I liked it or not, a fugitive, and I couldn't help being fascinated.

As the sun went down, Bernardine and I moved our conversation to a tiny Ukrainian restaurant. A waitress greeted Bernardine as a regular customer (I wondered how many San Franciscans knew her as the woman with the fiery hair) and brought us garlic soup. Bernardine asked how long I could stay in San Francisco.

I was staying with Grundoon in the apartment of two career women, friends of someone in my c-r group.

"I think I can manage another day or two," I said.

"Would you be interested in meeting with any other women? I'm thinking of one in particular who's especially interested in you."

I asked whom she meant.

"Cathy Wilkerson."

To some radicals, the blazing town house from which Cathy had disappeared represented the death of the movement. To me, Cathy Wilkerson represented survival.

"I would love to see her again," I said.

I was rewarded with a slow, dazzling smile.

The two Weatherwomen and I met for dinner in a downtown restaurant. Behind the nonprescription granny glasses Cathy wore as a disguise she had the same fragile intensity I remembered from Swarthmore. Her close friendship with Bernardine brought home again to me how isolated I was.

Two incidents reinforced the point. The first occurred when Cathy murmured to Bernardine that a man at the bar was staring at her.

"He's probably wondering if he's got the nerve to pick up three of us," Bernardine said lightly. But she took a pair of granny glasses identical to Cathy's from her purse and dangled them in her hand. Cathy nodded, and Bernardine put the glasses on. Those gestures riveted my attention, suggesting an intimacy it had taken years of underground life together to develop. How would it feel to have as a regular dinner companion someone so concerned with protecting me?

The second incident grew out of Cathy's admission that she knew I had once stayed with college friends in San Francisco. She too was involved with a friend from Swarthmore—Brian Stone, whose mother had lent me the money for my abortion. The two of them had carried on an intermittent affair ever since she had graduated. He was the person who had helped her most in her first year underground. They met now as often as they could in the apartments of friends who were safe from the Shoes—the Weather Underground code word for the FBI.

My first response to this news, as to the news that Rudd was living with a woman, was jealousy. Brian was thoughtful, bright, and attractive. He could go out with dozens of women who weren't fugitives. Why would he risk prison for Cathy—appealing as she was? And why had I failed to develop such a relationship myself? In the last year, I had given up even casual sex with strangers, let alone any attempt to become close to a man.

Then my radical feminism came rushing back to save me, whispering that Cathy was deluded to risk such an intimacy. She was in danger not only of capture whenever passion made her careless but also of precipitous rejection whenever Brian decided he was tired of living a lie. A woman might be willing to give up her overground life for a man, as Flan had for Rudd, but the reverse would never happen. And so, I told myself, I was better off celibate, which was what Robin always insisted as well.

On the second afternoon of my stay, Bernardine and I drove to the top of Mount Tamalpais. The view of San Francisco in its shroud of fog and of the sparkling mosaic of Sausalito was spectacular. Bernardine replaced her cotton pullover with a crocheted bikini top and offered me a blender drink of cantaloupe, eggs, and orange juice.

I wondered if Robin would think I had wimped out. Every time I tried to confront Bernardine on feminism she reacted like some Great Mother of the Underground, ready to hear the prayers of all fugitive faiths. We SDSers have lost our arrogance, she kept telling me. We don't think we have one right answer. We respect anyone who can survive underground, and we'll never ask you to compromise your beliefs, feminist or otherwise. You want to meet only with Weatherwomen? Fine. To call China a male supremacist state? To suggest that women in the Weather Underground ought to separate from the men? I may not agree with you, but I'm willing to listen. Frustrated in all my attempts either to start a fight or to win her over, I brought up Mark Rudd, who had given ample evidence of his sexism. She looked concerned.

"It's really too bad," she said, "that the person you ran into was Tony. A lot of our women feel the same way about him that you do. It's the main reason he was asked to take some time off.

"Feminism has become very important to us. Some of our women are lesbians and are active in the gay rights movement. A few are living in an all-women's collective. We also have contacts with feminists outside the organization. I'm not very educated about the women's movement because I see only fugitives. But some of our other women would love to meet with you and discuss what they're doing. Are you by any chance going to be on the East Coast soon?"

I told her I was heading east the next morning.

"Perhaps you'd like to meet these women then," she said. "One of them is Clare, who was your connection in New York before you went underground. She has profound love and respect for you. Since you last saw her, she's been living in the all-women's collective I mentioned and has gone through many changes.

"Another is a fugitive who isn't one of us but has drawn close to the organization recently. I've met her only briefly myself, but I like her very much. Perhaps you remember her; her name is Mary Moylan."

Moylan was one of the two women in the Catonsville 9, a group of Catholic radicals who set fire to draft card files in 1968. Four of the nine went underground following their conviction. Only Moylan survived as a fugitive more than a few months. She had sent a letter to *Rat* after the women's take-over congratulating us and declaring herself committed to "living and working exclusively with sisters."

I could see no harm in saying that I would love to meet them and in giving Bernardine the number in Connecticut where I could be reached.

On the morning of my departure Bernardine, Cathy, and I met for breakfast and farewells at a fish house on the San Francisco Bay. The Weatherwomen gave me the name and address of a woman through whom they could be reached, and Bernardine promised to write me in Connecticut.

As we walked along the rocks toward my car, Cathy dropped a few feet behind Bernardine and me. Bernardine's back was to the shore, and I faced her. She gazed directly into my eyes.

"I'm very sorry to be saying good-bye," she said. "But I'm sure there'll be more meetings. It's been wonderful to see you."

"It's been wonderful for me, too," I said. "I'm very glad to have gotten to know you."

"The word I want to use embarrasses me. But it keeps coming to mind. You're—well, you're extraordinary. Funny, it shouldn't really be a compliment. But it applies to you somehow. I feel very privileged that you've spent time with us."

To me, it was Bernardine who was extraordinary. I had been forced into my circumstances by chance and blind impulse and since then had muddled along, managing no more than my own survival. Bernardine had chosen her life, using her intelligence and leadership ability in the service of her ideas. She had managed to hold together a radical underground which, though small and shaky, was unique in United States history and had been an inspiration to others. Anyone could do what I had; Bernardine's accomplishments had required a gift for politics and hard work.

Later I came to wonder if she had been manipulating me with her graciousness and fine words. While she impressed me as sincerely interested in feminism, she was eventually to publish a long piece denouncing "the counterrevolutionary politics and direction of the Weather Underground" under her own leadership and confessing that in 1974 she and the others had "set out to destroy the women's movement." Her admitted hostility to femininism may have developed only after our meeting and may, in fact, have been influenced by my own subsequent acts. But it is also possible that she had been hypocritical with me from the beginning, flattering me in order to get what information she could. All I can say with certainty is that she impressed me deeply.

Polly's family's house in Connecticut had stone fireplaces, a three-car garage, furniture soft as whipped cream, a refrigerator that dispensed ice cubes at the touch of a switch, and more rooms than I could keep track of. A tribute to successful entrepreneurship (Polly's family owned a small business), it was an ironic and perfectly safe place for a fugitive to meet with family, friends, and fellows in the underground. Polly lived out of one of the downstairs rooms, working on a book on Southwest Indian myths. I lived upstairs, where I read Sylvia Plath and Doris Lessing and typed hundreds of drafts of a document called "Dear WeatherMan" which was meant to explain my disaffection with the male left to anyone who cared to read it. I couldn't manage to get past the first 200 words.

Clare and Mary Moylan came to visit me from their home in Boston. After my time with Bernardine and Cathy on the West Coast, my visit with them was like the remake of a classic film with inferior actors and a mutilated script. Clare, whom I had liked very much when we knew each other in New York, seemed to have remodeled her appearance to match Bernardine's as closely as possible. She used the same astonishing red henna on her hair, wore the same kind of low-cut blouses and dangling earrings, and even copied Bernardine's inflections and her habit of gazing directly into someone's eyes while talking. Clare was one of the Weather Underground leaders (the head of the entire East Coast wing, she told me) who was not technically a fugitive. When I wondered why she would choose to live underground, the health and self-confidence she had gained since our last meeting in New York gave me a clue. Perhaps she derived from her connection to Bernardine the same sort of strength I drew from Robin. That would explain her otherwise peculiar sacrifice as well as her strong resistance to my attack on the Weathermen's ideas.

Mary Moylan, like Clare and Bernardine, wore bell-bottoms and Indian jewelry that clashed oddly with her plain Irish looks. Because of her letters to the women's *Rat,* I expected to find in her an ally. Instead, she launched an offensive against the women's movement so virulent that Clare had to mediate between us. She failed to see what feminists meant by calling Madame Binh, chief negotiator for the North Vietnamese in Paris, a "female token" or by using the same term for Bernardine. She insisted that when the Weatherwomen opposed the Vietnam War by placing a bomb in a women's rest room in the Pentagon—as they had done last May—they weren't working on male-identified issues. They were acting on behalf of Vietnamese *women,* whose "beautiful, gentle humanity," as Moylan later wrote in a privately circulated paper "in the face of attempted genocide both awe & inspire us." She accused radical feminists of showing disrespect for other women when they criticized their choice of political issues.

Our argument was heated and lasted well into the night. When I look back on that night and on the rest of my meetings with the Weatherwoman, the individual points we debated seem less important than certain underlying issues. For what struck me most forcibly about the Weatherwomen I met in the summer of 1972 was not their ideas but their unanimity, preserved somehow across a continent and in spite of the difficulties of covert communication. The Weather Underground's half-facetious code name for itself was the Eggplant. The name seemed to suit the homely, vegetarian-style community these fugitives had managed to form. Nothing was more important to them than staying together. To ensure this, they paid loving attention to each other's most minute needs and allowed no question of political principle to drive them apart.

When my own dream of a revolutionary underground had died, I had embraced feminism and a commitment to Robin to sustain me. To preserve their underground, the Weatherwomen had to resist any such radical change in ideas. This difference was the basis of our clash and the grounds for our inevitable split a year later.

Robin came to Connecticut several times that summer and telephoned regularly. Because she was absorbed in her own problems, she didn't press me much on the subject of the Weatherwomen. Her publisher, Random House, was demanding that she drop from her manuscript a poem that pinned responsibility for the death of Sylvia Plath on Ted Hughes. At first Robin said she would rather not publish the book at all than back off from her attempt to bring Hughes to justice (at least on the page). When Random House called her bluff, she gave in and over the summer produced some six or eight new versions of the poem. While she relied on Kenneth, a highly accomplished poet, to help her maintain her literary standards through the legal revisions, I was to be the watchdog of her feminist purity. Once she asked me, drenched in tears, if I didn't secretly accuse her of selling her soul when she agreed to revise the poem. As is true of most of the dramatic scenes into which I was drawn with Robin, the poem, in retrospect, hardly seemed worth the anguish. At the time, I was touched by Robin's integrity and grateful for the chance to make a small contribution to her peace of mind.

Another new bond between us that summer grew from our shared admiration for the six-part BBC series about the life of Elizabeth I with Glenda Jackson in the title role, which Robin had raved about when it was shown in New York the previous winter. I watched it for the first time in summer reruns on Polly's family's color TV and was impressed by the tremendous intelligence Jackson brought to the role and by the intense, poignant solitude in which the historical Elizabeth seemed to have lived her life. It made me uneasy to discover that Robin's reverent attitude was for other reasons: not only for Jackson's gifts and for the queen's loneliness but for Elizabeth's unbridled power, her right to overrule Parliament and Privy Council, and her absolute prerogative of life and death over her subjects. Robin even invented a new slogan, a half-joking paraphrase of a radical left line about Vietnamese guerrillas—"Elizabeth R, Live Like Her"—and began cautiously to repeat it around the women's movement. This hint that she was begining to reject not only the sexism of leftist men but the very social democratic principles from which the movement had developed should have alarmed me more, but conscious of my heretical (in Robin's eyes) contacts with the Weather Underground and fearing a politically based conflict with her at so sensitive a time, I refrained from challenging her. And as always, Robin presented her views with such comical flair and with such an appearance of radical daring that it was hard to have any response but shared amusement.

In Connecticut I also saw my mother for the first time since New Hampshire. Because my father traveled often on business, it had been easy for him to meet me under an alias in almost any city in the country. We had stayed together in hotels in San Diego and Santa Fe and hiked on a trail in a New Mexico state park. My mother had fewer excuses to leave New York and was also more fearful of being apprehended when we were together. I managed to persuade her that the trip to Connecticut was completely safe. Influenced by my new feminist beliefs, I tried to get along with her better than I had in the past and started taking her side in quarrels with my father.

They had brought sad news to our meeting. My father's sister, to whom I felt a strong bond, although we had not seen each other in many years, had committed suicide a few months earlier. Sheila had eloped at sixteen with a man whose obnoxiousness was legendary in my family. Although her husband was a licensed accountant, he was unable to hold a job. At forty, my aunt earned a law degree at Columbia and went to work to support the two of them. Because of a quarrel between Sheila and my mother, I lost touch with her when I was still in high school, but I cherished the music encyclopedias and thesauruses she had given me. Perhaps because of that early sympathy, I always had an idea that she would have understood my arrest and bail jumping. And now she was dead—of an overdose of sleeping pills which had also killed her husband, who was said to have had cancer of the prostate at the time of the joint suicide.

Another death was also on my mind. Earlier in the year Patch and Lissa Dellinger, my closest friends from college, had lost their first-born child to sudden infant death syndrome. I had considered sending a condolence note to them through my parents, but it seemed so insufficient—and because of their connection to Dave Dellinger, I was afraid to contact them directly. Although I did eventually resume my contact with Patch and Lissa and express my sympathy as well as I could, I couldn't forgive myself my failure to be with them when my presence might have helped. It plagued me that fugitive life would always be like this—at my friends' and families' tragedies, my condolences would be meager and belated, my assistance withheld.

What if something happened to my parents? Where would I be and what could I do without risking capture? I had no answer.

At the end of the summer, with Polly's family due back any day, she proposed that we move to Denver and rent a house together. She was willing to fly on ahead of me and stay with friends until she found us a place to live. Meanwhile, I went to Boston for a visit I'd promised Mary Moylan and Clare.

The three of us met at an agreed-upon restaurant, but when it turned out to be around the corner from where my brother was living, Clare suggested that we go somewhere else.

"The Shoes keep a close watch on our families," Clare said. "The brother of one of us had a concussion when agents slammed him against a brick wall trying to get information—and he didn't even know anything." She suggested that we return to the apartment she and Mary shared and scrounge supper from their refrigerator.

I followed their car into a seedy section of town, where they stopped in front of a sagging tenement. The apartment was a third-floor walk-up in the rear of the building. Mary and Clare led the way up the stairs and let me precede them into a sparsely furnished living room. A woman was sitting in a rocking chair, her back to me. At the sound of footsteps she turned around. A small woman with a heart-shaped face, she wore denim cutoffs and an ironic smile.

"Hello, Jane," she said. "Don't you remember me?"

I turned and looked at Clare, whose mouth was open in astonishment. She and Mary exchanged glances with each other and with the woman in the chair.

"I don't know who you are," I admitted at last.

"I'm Kathy Boudin."

I had met her once before in the Greenwich Village town house owned by her father, an associate of Sandy Katz's, but I could never have recognized her. She had changed her appearance from stolid to elfin and looked ten years younger than her age, which was thirty. Known as one of the most intellectually gifted of the SDSers who founded Weatherman and from a solidly leftist background, she also belonged to Mary and Clare's all-women's collective. (It turned out that they were the only three members.) She had been dying to argue feminist politics with me since she first heard of my letter to Bernardine, and I came to wonder later if she had planned her seemingly accidental intrusion into the apartment.

My intention had been to spend a day and two nights with Mary and Clare, seeing if we could resolve the differences that had developed in Connecticut. Kathy's appearance forced a change in plans—since I was reluctant to say outright that I didn't wish to speak with her. Hoping to avoid a combined onslaught from the three of them, I suggested that we divide the next day into thirds so that I could spend a few hours with each of them alone.

This was a foolish idea, as it turned out. Arguing with Boudin was particularly tiring and not only because of her quick-wittedness. Unlike the other Weatherwomen, she was forthright in discussing her personal life. For the past year, she told me, she had been very much in love with a woman with whom she had just broken up. Contrary to my insistence that intimacies between women tended to be equal, she said that her experience of both dominance and submission with her lover had been as intense as in her affairs with men. She thought I was wrong to say that separating from men was the only way for women to achieve autonomy. Some women maintained their independence while living and working with men; others never achieved it even when they lived only with women. Through this entire conversation she kept her gaze focused on me so steadily that I was convinced she was trying either to hypnotize me or to get me to sleep with her. Or both.

The most trying part of being with the three Weatherwomen in Boston was maintaining the pretense that we liked one another and were friends. I was fond of Clare but did not find her stimulating. Boudin intimidated me, and Moylan irritated me. I kept trying to figure out why I had agreed to this visit. Sometimes I thought the reason was my wish to maintain a connection to the Weather Underground for whatever help the organization could give me. At other times I conceived of myself as a missionary for the feminist movement who had a duty to convert them. I certainly wasn't having a good time; the apartment was bleak and cramped, and we didn't go outside, having agreed that a group including three federally wanted fugitives was probably safest indoors. And I had almost nothing to eat since the Weatherwomen seemed to subsist contentedly on plain yogurt and cucumbers and had nothing else in the refrigerator.

Late at night Kathy returned to her own apartment, where she was supposed to have been all along, and Clare went with her. Mary and I rolled out sleeping bags. I was exhausted and ready for sleep when unexpectedly Mary began speaking of Robin Morgan—whose name I had, of course, assiduously avoided all through our conversations.

"It's a shame what's happened to that woman since she's become a feminist leader," Mary said. "I used to admire her so much. But the women's movement can be so vicious, and I'm afraid Robin's become a casualty."

The silence in the room seemed alive and beating in my ear.

"A close friend of mine went to a speech Robin gave in Chicago recently," Moylan continued. "It was a great speech—Robin's so talented, you know. My friend went to congratulate her, and they ended up at dinner with a few other women. At the restaurant, which was crowded, Robin drank a lot and I guess she lost control. She started talking in a very loud voice about the Eggplant, telling these outlandish lies.

"In one story, she said that Bernardine had come to a house Robin rented in Florida last winter, disheveled, strung out on dope, and clinging to the arm of some man. She begged Robin for a place to stay, and Robin harbored her. But when she kept acting in a self-destructive manner, Robin claims that she asked her to leave."

My stomach was heaving. Mary went on quietly, showing no recognition of the effect her story was having on me.

"Of course, the story is nonsense. I don't know if Robin ever harbored a fugitive, but she certainly never saw Bernardine—underground or overground. And that sort of talk in a crowded restaurant

—well, what if an undercover agent were at the next table? Robin's just bringing trouble on herself. And all because she has this weird need to discredit the Eggplant."

I told Mary her story couldn't possibly be true. I reminded her that I had known Robin at *Rat,* where she had never been observed to take a drink and was the soul of discretion. Not only the *Rat* women but other friends of mine had admired Robin's exceptional prudence. Moylan would not be budged from her tale. It was true, she said, that Robin was once an admirable woman, but the pressures of the feminist lecture circuit had robbed her of her mental health.

If I discounted the drunkenness and the loud talk, which struck me as utterly improbable, that still meant a stranger knew what no one except Robin, Ken, and I were supposed to: that a fugitive had visited the family in Florida. And how could Moylan have heard such a rumor unless Robin had talked?

Moylan, perhaps seeing that I had gone gray, apologized for upsetting me. I agreed that we should try to go to sleep.

I tossed all night, wide awake and feeling that I was falling off the edge of the world. The superficial plausibility of Moylan's account had plunged me into a crisis of doubt: about Robin's truthfulness, about the foundation of my friendship with her, about the very commitment to feminism on which my meeting with the Weatherwomen was supposedly predicated.

For until this moment, I had accepted Robin's long-held hostility toward the Weather Underground as a logical corollary to her feminism. And I had viewed my own attraction to Dohrn & Company as a humiliating weakness—as evidence that I still experienced some masochistic need for male approval. Moylan's story, though, had raised in me a deeply suppressed question about the nature of Robin's antipathy to the left. Was it possible that I was following her on a less-than-rational course? That she was inspiring me toward attitudes dangerous both to her and me? That my enormous faith in her was somehow misplaced, and was going to be used against me?

I wished nothing more than to hear that Moylan had invented the story. Lying a few feet away from me, she snored lightly. Nothing about her sleep suggested a troubled conscience.

By the morning I could no longer bear my uncertainty. In the hope of finally shaking a denial from Moylan, I admitted to her that I was the fugitive who had stayed with Robin in Florida—though I denied having seen her since—and begged Moylan to tell me more details. From whom had she heard the story? Moylan would not say. She simply repeated that it was true and suggested that I call Robin as soon as possible. If I was afraid to phone her directly, Mary could perhaps get word to her for me through her friend. I said that wouldn't be necessary.

After breakfast and hurried farewells to the Weatherwomen, I drove six hours to the house of my friend Lynn Gottlieb, who had invited me to San Diego and was now living in Syracuse. On my second night at Lynn's, Robin returned my call.

Gripping the receiver so hard it seemed to perspire into my hand, I told her everything Moylan had said. Robin's answer came immediately.

"It's not true," she said. "Not a single word of it."

I let my breath out.

"When you were last in Chicago?" I pressed.

"Let me think. I haven't spoken in Chicago—God, it was a whole year ago. That was the time I called you from the airport, after I heard about Sam."

"You mean, before you were in Florida?"

"No, wait. I was there in March, just before I saw you in Santa Fe. And I did have dinner on that trip with a couple of women. Oh, yes, I see what happened. This is amazing."

"What's amazing?"

"The story you heard is true. Except it's not about me. There was a woman at that dinner—one of those leftist groupies, I'm afraid—who claimed to have been visited by Peggy." (Peggy was the private code name Robin and I used for Bernardine.) "That was her description of Peggy that you heard repeated. And it was she who got very drunk—it's coming back to me now. The rest of us practically had to carry her out of the restaurant. How clever of her to turn around and blame the whole thing on me!"

I wanted so much to believe her. The last forty-eight hours had been a nightmare I longed to dissolve.

"She gave me a terrible time with that story," I said. "I kept trying to shake her, but I couldn't."

Robin began to sob out loud.

"Thank you, dear heart, for trusting me," she wept. "It's worth all the vilification to have one friend like you. I love you for believing in me. Thank you. Thank you."

The sound of her crying made me wretched.

"I had a horrible time with them," I repeated.

"I know. But it will be all right. Really it will."

Although I was relieved at first, questions kept returning to me over the next months. I tried hard to repress them. How could I doubt someone who had given me so much? My faith in Robin was the basis of my sanity; if I lost that, the void would be unbearable. Instead I turned my anger on the Weather Underground. I was never to know which woman had told me the truth.

XVI
Renunciation

By the time I arrived in Denver, Polly had found us an apartment in a transient working-class neighborhood. Like the others on the block, ours was a former one-family dwelling that had been divided into rental units as the neighborhood decayed. Upstairs Polly was already occupying the rear bedroom, leaving me the front room, which with its sloping eaves had a certain attic charm. She gave me her extra furniture: a mattress on a metal frame, an armchair in need of reupholstering, a card table to use as a desk. The room was, by my most careful count and not including the nights I had camped out, the forty-second I had occupied in three years.

A week of job hunting produced a string of rejections. I had no roots in the community and no written references, and I appeared overeducated for the positions I applied for. When the money my parents had given me in Connecticut ran out, I went to Kelly Girl, a temporary agency, where I was assigned at once to a secretarial position at Beth Jacob, an Orthodox Jewish high school for girls—probably because my alias, Weinstein, persuaded the employment counselor that I would get along better with the rabbi-principal than the applicants named González or Smith would. After a week or two I was able to persuade Rabbi Schwab, my boss, to hire me permanently.

The job didn't pay much and required sacrifices. I had to wear clothes suitable to a strict religious environment: no pants, sleeveless tops, or hems above the knee were permitted. I also had to split with my employer the $200 penalty fee required by Kelly

Girl for taking a permanent position. The job was worth it. Working in the Orthodox Jewish community of Denver where life revolved around *shul,* births, marriages, and deaths and where no one had ever heard of the Yippies, *Rat,* or the Weather Underground, I felt as safe as I could have anywhere. And although every tenet of Orthodox Judaism contradicted my feminist beliefs, I couldn't help warming to the energetic Rabbi Schwab, to the ascetic vice-principal, Rabbi Lauer, and to the students.

My stay with the Weatherwomen in Boston seemed to have happened far in the past, and as I looked forward to a mid-October visit from Robin, I wished we would never have to discuss the subject again. Unfortunately, in a moment of weakness, I had given Mary and Clare the address of a friend who would forward mail to me. Soon after I settled in Denver, a packet of letters arrived from the Weatherwomen dated September 13. They had written especially to remind me that it was the anniversary of Attica and had enclosed clippings that discussed the findings of the riot's official commission report, of which they were highly critical. By contrast, Clare told me, they had reread my introduction to Sam's letters and "loved it again—in some ways it stands as a *great* historical record of the period."

These letters, no doubt well meaning, were deeply upsetting to me. Even more than I wanted to forget the existence of the Weather Underground, I wanted to erase from the historical record the fact that I had ever written admiringly of Sam. And it was at the very least dense of the Weatherwomen, after all the emphasis I had placed on my newfound feminism, to write to me as though my chief identity were that of an Attica widow. Robin's imminent visit was a further reminder of how I had failed not only in my attempt to convince the Weatherwomen of feminist truths but even in my intention to keep from them the secret of my connection to her.

Robin arrived in Denver with gifts of clothes, books, and periodicals, with news clippings on feminist events and new poems of hers and Kenneth's to show me. She was in high spirits, and I kept postponing telling her of how I had betrayed her to Mary Moylan. By the end of the day, as we were taking a walk in a park near my house, I could no longer hold back the truth. I blurted out that I had confessed to the Weatherwomen my visit to Robin in Florida.

Robin stopped in the middle of the path. Her chin trembled as though she were suppressing a scream. I was prepared for her to explode at me. "I hate those women," she said at last. "God help me, but I hate them."

She blamed everything on the Weatherwomen, arguing that they had planned from the beginning to demolish me. Boudin's intrusion she saw as part of a plot to wear me down. Moylan's story had been saved for the end of the day when my resistance was lowest. The purpose of the entire visit had been only to weasel information from me. Now that they knew Robin and I were in touch, they had what they wanted. They would continue to worm their way into my confidence, gathering more and more details about my connections to the women's movement, not out of interest in feminism but for their own male-leftist ends. I ought to have resisted them, of course, but Robin couldn't blame me for what had happened. I had been a virtual hostage in their apartment, cut off from the outside world, half-starved—no wonder I had been broken.

It boiled down to this: according to Moylan, Robin was so bent on discrediting the male left that she would make up lies about fugitives, regardless of the risk. According to Robin, the Weather Underground was so eager to co-opt the women's movement that its members would spread lies about Robin. I could no longer handle the tension of trying to maintain relations with two such hostile forces. And if it came to a choice, the decision was easy. The Weatherwomen had given me nothing; Robin had given me a life.

"I guess what I have to do," I said to Robin, "is cut the Weatherwomen completely out of my existence. Maybe I should publish the piece I started last summer. You know—'Dear WeatherMan'?"

"Yes," said Robin absently. The emotion that had accumulated in her voice drained away like an audience leaving the theater. "You should," she added, "make it a piece to the Weather*women*."

I promised myself that by her next visit I would have a draft of something printable.

I rented a portable typewriter and set it up on the card table. Pulling out the attempted drafts of "Dear WeatherMan" I had written in Connecticut, I started fresh with Robin's suggested salutation, "Dear sisters in the Weather Underground." Beginning with a description of my meeting with Rudd in Santa Fe, I went on to describe how I now felt about Sam, using language that would ensure I would never again be addressed as a grief-stricken widow. Adrenaline flowed from me onto the page. The more I wrote, the angrier I grew. I was possessed through that fall and winter with my attempt to destroy every vestige of power the left still had over me, deliberately setting out to alienate my former associates as I had once set out to alienate the establishment world of my parents.

I exposed my private life with Sam in ways I had not dared do when I wrote the memoir of him: the slave/master games I'd allowed him to impose on me; the time he wrote "WASH ME" in black Magic Marker on the refrigerator; the affairs with Pat and Billie Banks; the sexist, cold letters he had sent me from Attica. I supplied as many details about the misogyny of men in the Weather Underground as I could, concentrating on Mark Rudd, whom I knew. I named only men in the piece, not women, and I gave no clues to disguise or location that could result in the apprehension of fugitives. For all the virulence of my attack, I had no wish to lead the police to the Weather Underground. But then to assure myself and Robin that I wasn't shrinking from the attack, I closed the open letter with the most violent, offensive words I could invent.

"And so, my sisters in Weatherman," I wrote, "you fast and organize and demonstrate for Attica. Don't send me news clippings about it, don't tell me how much those deaths moved you. I will mourn the loss of 42 male supremacists no longer."

To express so much anger without paying a price may be impossible. Just as the bombings resulted in the hardships of fugitive life and eventually imprisonment, the extreme hostility of my open letter earned me permanent enemies. I am sorry that I was understood by some to be praising Rockefeller's decision to send troops into the prison yard. I abhorred the violence of what happened at Attica, and I believed that the murders committed by the state were senseless and unjustified. But I was done with mourning a man who had contributed so much misery to my life. I no longer wanted to be identified with him and his cause, and I let that be known in the most unmistakable language, with little regard for the consequences.

"It is blank history you are rolling into your typewriter," Robin wrote me after seeing the draft of the open letter, "and your mind and spirit and fingers are shaping it. Oh my dearest friend." My other readers were less enthusiastic. Genevieve urged me to make the piece more constructive and give the Weatherwomen reasons to "come on over" to feminism. Polly, the only person in Denver to whom I could show my draft, said she couldn't imagine that many people were interested in my revelations about Sam and the men in the Weather Underground and that I should say more about what I believed as a feminist. I decided they were right. From January until April, on my free evenings and weekends, I worked on a second section of the piece, describing my ideology as it had evolved in the years I was underground.

"My first year underground was very hard," I wrote. "Expecting to die for the revolution in a matter of months, I was unprepared to find myself not only alive but living a rather unadventurous and secluded existence less than a year after disappearing. . . . I started to travel and for a few months just roamed almost aimlessly, from one community to another across the country.

"As I traveled, I slowly became aware that nothing was less relevant to the lives of most people in this country than the white left, with which I still identified myself. . . . As I moved around, I could see more clearly than ever the oppression of black, Chicano, Puerto Rican and Indian peoples. Yet at the same time I was learning concretely that women existed in well-defined subcultures within each white and Third World community. Finally, all my experiences kept reminding me of one fact of my own identity that I was continually trying to forget: *that I was a woman*. . . . I now began to think that if my politics were to be based on my own situation and not on someone else's perception of reality, I would have to deal with the fact that the rest of the world thought of me as a woman first of all, before it even listened to what I had to say."

After commenting on the widespread impact of the women's movement and attributing the growth of my own feminism entirely to my participation in a c-r group (rather than partly to my personal relationship with Robin, which, of course, could not be mentioned), I proposed a viewpoint diametrically opposed to that held by most feminist leaders. While Firestone and other viewed the task of the feminist movement as the abolition of gender-based distinctions, I proclaimed that biology was "the source and not the enemy of feminist revolution." I defined female biology as the capacity to bear and nurture children, which all women shared regardless of whether or not they were actually mothers, and claimed that this capacity gave rise to "those psychological qualities which have always been linked with women, both in ancient lore and modern behavioral science . . . empathy, intuitiveness, adaptability, awareness of growth as a process rather than as goal-ended, inventiveness, protective feelings toward others, and a capacity to respond emotionally as well as rationally."

I then projected the goal of feminist revolution as the establishment of matriarchy, "a society in which these [female qualities] are the qualities all human beings admire and strive to embody, a society in which the paradigm for all social relationships is that of a healthy and secure mother to her child." I closed the piece with a semireligious invocation to "the Mother," inspired by some of my recent reading about ancient goddess-worshipping cultures.

Among my friends, this second section of the piece was a smashing success. My c-r group, to whom I sent copies, responded with letters praising it. Genevieve, who was beginning a book on motherhood, wrote that my passages about female superiority and matriarchy were "central to our thought and deserve to be written in fire." Robin sent me a letter longer than the piece itself, suggesting revisions and assuring me that it would outlast *Das Kapital.* She suggested that I give the two sections together a title that would call attention to the theoretical content of the second part rather than the address to the Weatherwomen in the first. We settled on a phrase borrowed from the German anthropologist J. J. Bachofen, who had written a book about matriarchy called *Myth, Religion and Mother Right.* We then began making plans to get the essay published. It would be called "Mother Right: A New Feminist Theory."

Rereading "Mother Right" today, I have mixed reactions. The virulence of the first section is excessive, yet has a ring of conviction that becomes hollow in the second, theoretical part. While I continue to believe that biology has more to do with consciousness than many feminists like to admit, my advocacy of matriarchy as a governmental structure now seems wrongheaded or at least naïve. I also smile at my determination to set forth a revolutionary ideology that explains everything—sociology, economics, psychology, anthropology, and religion—in twelve pages. Why didn't I end the piece when I was on firmer ground, discussing my travels underground and the bond I felt with my c-r group? Those two points alone could have justified my turn to feminism.

The answer, I think, is that I still needed a system of thought that was both revolutionary and comprehensive. I couldn't tolerate any form of ambivalence or the idea that there was no solution to the horrors I saw in the world. This need had led me into the radical left in 1969 and into radical feminism in 1972. I also still needed one strong personality who would keep assuring me that my chosen system worked and that I was brave and right to follow it. Sam had filled that function when I was in the left, and now Robin had taken his place. The major difference was not gender (as Robin wanted me to think and as I believed for years) but something less obvious. For while Sam and leftist thinking had led me underground, Robin and her version of feminism were leading me back to my family, to the friendships I'd formed in college, and to the world of middle-class values I had violently rejected in 1969.

I didn't want to leave Denver or give up my job, but staying there after the piece was published was dangerous. *Time*, for example, which was used as the basis of a social studies course at Beth Jacob, had covered my case when I was arrested and went underground and might do so again, possibly with a photograph that would be recognized at the school. Robin urged me to take advantage of the offer of hospitality from two Wisconsin feminists, Chris and Emma, whom she had mentioned to me during our first underground meeting in San Diego. It was also important that the postmark on the envelopes containing my essay reveal nothing about my whereabouts, so Robin agreed that she would mail them herself from New York. To secure an indefinite leave of absence from the rabbis, I invented a dramatic story of a sudden family illness and at the end of April departed Denver by car for my new hideout in Madison.

Robin wanted to leave as little as possible to chance. She met me in Madison the day after my arrival and took home with her twenty copies of "Mother Right," which Emma had run off on her office machine and which we had already addressed to feminist and establishment publications. I then waited impatiently to see reports of my piece in the newspapers. Two weeks passed. The pieces seemed to have been dropped into a well.

For a time Robin and I thought she had made some mistake at the post office window and aroused the suspicion of postal clerks who had opened the envelopes and turned them over to the FBI. Now I think the problem had more to do with other events: the day I left Denver was the day Nixon announced the resignations of Haldeman, Ehrlichman, Kleindienst, and Dean, and Watergate news crowded items of less importance out of the news. Unable to accept that my months of effort had produced an essay too insignificant to merit even a small news item, let alone publication in full, I devised a new strategy. I made ten more copies of "Mother Right" and addressed them personally to journalists who had covered my case in 1969 and 1970. I then drove to Chicago to drop the copies in a safe mailbox.

On May 23, 1973, a story by Linda Charlton appeared in *The New York Times* under the headline FEMALE FUGITIVE BIDS WOMEN SHUN LEFTIST UNITS. One of my mug shots accompanied the piece. I thought I had changed too much in the three and a half years since the photo was taken to worry about recognition, but Robin had other ideas. She wanted me to hide out in Madison at least two more weeks to see if *Time* would pick up the story and jeopardize my return to Denver.

My stay in Madison stretched into six weeks and was more arduous than I anticipated. I was making weekly phone calls to the rabbis to invent new tales of the life-threatening illness that was supposedly keeping me in the East. Chris and Emma were also proving to be less than ideal hosts. They idolized Robin and had been enamored with the idea of helping a woman fugitive. But when harboring me turned into weeks of dreary waiting, limiting their space and social opportunities, they became restless—as almost anyone would—and I grew itchy to get out of their way.

At the end of May Robin called Madison to say that *off our backs*, a Washington-based feminist paper, had received "Mother Right" and was going to print it in its entirety. *It Ain't Me Babe*, an Iowa City paper, was planning to run excerpts. A few days later Robin called again in great excitement. She had just learned that *Ms.*, by far the largest of the feminist periodicals with a circulation of 200,000, was going to feature "Mother Right" uncut and, as I had requested, without an accompanying photo. I left Madison the next morning with more relief than joy.

Over the winter Polly had moved from our apartment to a place of her own on the north side of town. In midsummer I followed her there, moving into a three-and-a-half-room sunny apartment, the handsomest place I had been able to afford since going underground. My neighbors, born-again Christians eager for converts, gave me a dining-room table and chairs, and at garage sales I acquired a full-sized bed, a brocaded couch, and a desk with lots of cubbyholes. The stability I'd achieved by then is evident by my ownership now, eight years later, of some of the clothes and kitchen items I bought that year, the only mementos of my underground life I still have except for letters.

With the Beth Jacob students on vacation and Rabbi Schwab and his wife traveling in Israel for the summer, vice-principal Rabbi Lauer and I had the office to ourselves. With little to do except answer an occasional phone call, we passed most of our working hours in talk. The thirty-two-year-old rabbi encouraged my curiosity about the Hebrew language and the intricacies of talmudic law and listened to my feminist ideas with patience and even sympathy. Although our talk rarely turned to personal matters, his continual probing of my thoughts and his rare ability to listen sometimes overwhelmed me with a longing to confide in him. Of course, I didn't dare; a strictly law-abiding man, he would have been thrown into a fierce dilemma over whether to turn me in—a dilemma best avoided.

The appearance of the August *Ms.* was a high point of my time in Denver. Newly confident of my safety and aching to hear the response to my ideas, I began attending meetings of feminist organizations, where I described myself only as Carla Weinstein, a school secretary. I heard occasional mention of my piece, quite a lot of talk about matriarchy, and frequent mention of Robin's name as one of the most respected leaders in the radical wing of the movement. This sort of talk made me burst with pride and wish I could assert my real identity and boast of my friendship with Robin.

I became hooked on the Watergate hearings that summer and tuned them in every evening after work. My fascination was not so much with the jousting for power in the White House or with the unmasking of Nixon as with the drama of crime, retribution, and forgiveness played out before the Ervin committee. Robin, who loved displays of righteous indignation, adored Sam Ervin and Lowell Weicker. She and Kenneth were appalled at my own favorite character, Jeb Magruder, whose plea that he had been misled by his patriotic ideals and by his superiors was very moving to me. Contrition about an erroneous ideology and about crimes committed in its name had been my own dominant feeling for the last year and I identified strongly with the former Mitchell aide.

In August my mother came to stay with me, our first visit together without my father since I had gone underground. Competition and resentment between us went back too far to put them aside by an act of will. But when she commented approvingly at the sight of women construction workers on the highway, I felt a surge of empathy and love. Our time together was the happiest I could remember having with her. She had never read my *Ms.* piece (she said she was too frightened to see my name on the cover to look inside), but I sometimes thought of it as a sort of tribute to her, as if "Mother Right" were an abbreviation for "My mother was right." For wasn't my renunciation of the left a tacit admission that she had been perceptive all along about Sam?

In October 1973, with Beth Jacob on Succoth vacation, I flew east to spend a week with Robin and Ken and Blake in a cottage in upstate New York. At the end of the trip I met my parents for an overnight stay at an Albany motel where they had registered, as usual, under false names. On that night, October 20, Nixon fired Archibald Cox.

The papers the next morning were full of quotes from major figures in the Senate demanding Nixon's impeachment. Over breakfast my parents and I talked of nothing else. Nixon's hubris, possibly Nixon's madness; his isolation in the White House, stripped of all his advisers but Alexander Haig; the danger to the country if he continued in office. "Nixon will have to go," my mother said, "now that everyone knows what he is." I was notoriously poor at figuring out what "everyone" thought, but it seemed to me that again my mother was right.

As I flew back to Denver, alternately reading the newspapers and looking down at the ocean of clouds, a new thought sent the papers sliding from my lap. We had never expected this in 1969. We had talked of a fascist coup, of a communist revolution, of anarchy—never of impeachment. But what if this was the very change in climate we had been waiting for? Not as drastic, certainly far short of revolutionary, and yet an enormous shift in the winds. Chaos at the highest levels of government. A constitutional crisis. Could a radical fugitive returning now possibly fall through the cracks at the Justice Department, evading a prison sentence?

It was unquestionably worth trying.

Months passed before I was able to discuss my idea at any length with Robin and with my parents and finally arrange a meeting with Sandy Katz. During that time I lived an outwardly normal life, continuing to work for the rabbis and gradually to become involved in the Denver women's movement. But the longing to have done with my underground life grew in me steadily. In March 1974 I flew to New York to meet with Katz in an apartment arranged for us by Genevieve.

Sandy had lost some hair since I'd last seen him and appeared tired. As the movement faded, he had fewer political clients, and he seemed unsurprised that I was contemplating surrender.

He explained to me that I would have to face two felony counts, for the bombing conspiracy and bail jumping, each carrying a maximum penalty of five years. The bail-jumping charge would almost certainly be dropped in exchange for my voluntary surrender. The bombing charge was more difficult since I had already pleaded guilty. I would have to come before Judge Pollack again, whose disposition for harsh sentences had not lessened over the years. Still, the U.S. attorney's office might be persuaded to support a light sentence on the grounds that I had rehabilitated myself while underground. He guessed I would go to jail for a year, perhaps a year and a half.

I was disappointed. I had hoped to hear that I could withdraw the guilty plea completely and go to trial on the bombing charges. Sandy said that was out of the question.

Then for the first time in months I thought of Pat, who did not have the problem of a guilty plea on the record. I asked Sandy what would happen if we surrendered together. Would the U.S. attorney be encouraged to go more easily on us both?

"He might," Sandy said. "It couldn't hurt."

The gleam in his eye encouraged me.

"I'm not in direct contact with her," I added hastily. "But I might be able to find her. If so, I'll tell her to get in touch with you at your office?"

"That's fine."

"She'll use the code name Hill," I told him. In my mind, Pat had already agreed to my scenario.

A call from Denver to the last phone number I had for Pat revealed that she had left the area about six months ago. I then tried phoning the post office where she had maintained a box to see if she still picked up mail there.

The post office clerk recognized Pat's alias with alarming promptness. "Oh, no, she canceled her box a long time ago," she told me. "She's living in Vermont now."

I assumed this was a fiction Pat had left to cover her tracks.

"I don't suppose she left a forwarding address?"

"No, but I can tell you where she is. She works at the Good Earth health food store in Brattleboro."

I hung up, nonplussed. I wanted very much to find Pat, but I hoped for her sake that the post office clerk's story was wrong. If I could trace her this easily, then so could a hundred other people. I telephoned the Good Earth health food store and asked for Pat by her alias, Suzanne Davis.

"Shoshana!" someone yelled. In another moment she was on the phone. I didn't know whether to be glad or horrified.

"Suzanne, it's Ellen," I said, using the name by which she had last known me. "Do you have a minute?"

She sounded very surprised. "Well, maybe a minute. But I'll have to keep working while we talk."

"Is there some other place I can call you?"

"Not really. What's on your mind?"

As she rang up purchases with one hand and held the receiver with another, and as an operator periodically interrupted me to demand more coins, I tried to distill for her my last six months of reflection and planning. The idea that Watergate had created a climate in which our surrender might be received favorably was new to her. So was the notion that a fugitive might want to surrender for a reason other than despair. But she promised that she would call Sandy's office, using the agreed-upon alias, and would talk over the possibility with him.

Pat never called Sandy. A month after we spoke, a letter from her arrived in my post office box. She wrote that she had decided not to get in touch with him because she saw no particular advantage to ending her underground life. "It would remove certain hassles, create others, and basically leave me with the same tangle of underlying problems. . . . i do not view my present status vis a vis the Hospital or Health System [our code for the law and law enforcement] in general as being responsible for the aches and pains of my existence." As to Jenny, whom she had not seen in nearly five years, she said, "after all this time i cannot just have back what i lost. And whether i go in or stay out, i will, sometime in the future, make connections with her, and see what kind of relationship, if any, we can have." Finally, she seemed convinced that surrendering herself would mean a long prison sentence. Even if she could make a favorable deal in advance, "once they have their hands on your little body, there you are at their mercy. You can't turn around and say, 'But you promised . . .'" She did not understand, she said, why I was taking this step.

In the years of our separation we had moved far apart. I was not especially unhappy with my life in Denver. At the time of my correspondence with Pat over surrender, I was secure in my job, was teaching a course in women's history at a free university and had made tentative friendships with local feminists. I earned enough money to enjoy occasional visits with Robin and by taking some precautions was able to maintain regular contact with her and other former friends as well as with my parents. But once I glimpsed the opportunity to give up my subterfuges and resume my own identity, to live openly in New York if I chose, and to write and publish and work in the women's movement independently and without fear of discovery, my pleasures in Denver paled. Pat never shared these ambitions. Having made peace with the loss of Jenny and content to work the cash register in a health food store, she saw no reason to risk a change. She may well have been living in exactly the same way had she never been indicted for the bombings and fled New York to avoid arrest.

I asked Sandy to wait until I was safely out of Denver before he reminded the U.S. attorney's office of my existence. I then told the rabbis and Beth Jacob students that at the end of the school year I would be joining an archaeological excavation in Guatemala. I sold my furniture in a yard sale, transferred the ownership of my now-battered Opel to Polly, and in June 1974 left Denver with Grundoon and all the possessions I could stuff in the back seat of a driveaway car headed east.

In Pittsfield, Massachusetts, I rented a furnished room with a hot plate for $16 a week. I couldn't keep Grundoon with me, so I boarded her on a farm near Syracuse where Lynn Gottlieb occasionally checked on her for me. I missed my dog's company in Pittsfield, where I had little to do but think about the future and wait impatiently to hear how the negotiations for my surrender were proceeding.

One day in July my room telephone rang with a message from a lawyer—not Sandy, from whom I'd been expecting the call, but his associate Carol Lefcourt. She had news that she didn't want to discuss over the telephone. We agreed to meet in a town that was accessible to Pittsfield by bus and not far from Carol's weekend home.

The message I had waited for months to hear was delivered to me in the parking lot of a Burger King. Carol and Sandy had gone to the prosecutor's office together for an appointment with a highly placed official in the criminal division. When they were waiting to be shown into his office, Peter Teubner, the young assistant attorney with whom Sandy had first discussed the case, met them in the hall. He told them that his superior had refused the appointment as soon as he learned it concerned a fugitive. The department policy was "No deals." They would talk to me only after I had surrendered.

"What does that mean?" I pressed.

Carol twisted her hair.

"It means they're going to throw the book at you," she said. "They'll clap you in jail and start pressuring you to talk. If you don't—and maybe if you do—they'll hit you with years in prison. Maybe as much as ten years, though more likely four or five. You won't make bail, so whatever they decide to do, you're going to have to put up with it."

"What do you think I should do?"

"Go home and wait. At least another couple of years."

"I don't have a home," I said.

Carol's discomfort increased.

"I hate being the one to bring you this message," she said. "Sandy should have done it, but he's a coward. He was just too upset to talk to you."

I went back to Pittsfield that night in a state of numb despair. My eyes burned but would not shed tears. My throat was tight, but the scream wouldn't come. I didn't know how much I had wanted to put this life of aliases and furnished rooms and meeting my friends and family in motels behind me until now. I couldn't go back to Denver. Even if my job were waiting for me, to return to it now after having left so jubilantly would feel like defeat and make me miserable. And the idea of starting over again in Pittsfield or anywhere else seemed beyond me. My parents' money and the vacations and love I shared with Robin were no longer enough: I wanted a real life, in my own name, with my own history and with some sort of work more meaningful than keeping school files in order. And I wanted sexual intimacy again, and, yes, even marriage and children—if that wasn't too much stability to hope for.

Over the next few days, as I was reading *Daniel Deronda*, a bit of George Eliot's dialogue kept echoing in my mind. "If you determine to face these hardships and still try," the composer Herr Klesmer says to the heroine, speaking of her desire to become an actress, "you will have the dignity of a high purpose, even though you may have chosen unfortunately. You will have some merit, though you may win no prize. You have asked my judgment on your chances of winning. I don't pretend to speak absolutely; but measuring probabilities, my judgment is:—you will hardly achieve more than mediocrity."

After these harsh words, the heroine Gwendolen Harleth rejects the "dignity of a high purpose" in favor of marrying a wealthy but immoral suitor. I decided—and George Eliot had as much to do with my choice as anyone else—that I would take the high road. I was going to turn myself in and accept the consequences, no matter how much time I had to spend in jail.

Robin urged me not to give another thought to walking into the prosecutor's office until she'd had a chance to scout out a new lawyer for me. She insisted that somewhere someone had to have better connections than Sandy, and she would ask around until she found that person. Until then I was to sit tight, George Eliot or no.

Meanwhile, Patch and Lissa, who had been the most wonderfully faithful of friends ever since I'd come east, loaned me the use of their second car and invited me to spend a week with them at a house in Maine. On my way up, I realized I would be passing within a few miles of Brattleboro. It seemed to me that it wouldn't hurt to talk with Pat face to face. I telephoned her at the health food store, and she told me that she had only forty-five minutes for lunch but would spend it with me if I wanted.

It amazed me that Pat could work at a movement center like the Good Earth store without being detected. There on the main street of Brattleboro nearly every ex-radical from New York, Cambridge, and Berkeley must have passed her at one time or another. Pat herself, emerging from the crowded store in a sleeveless shirt and shorts, seemed more concerned with the possibility that she would be late returning from lunch.

We walked up the street to a grassy spot. Pat unwrapped a sandwich and offered me a bite.

"I understand you've changed your mind about going in," she said.

How did she know what had happened? Had Sandy talked?

"Tell me where you heard that," I said.

"Oh, just around. But the prosecutors told you they wouldn't make a deal."

"The only thing I've changed my mind about is the lawyer I'm going to use," I said. "Now I wish you'd tell me where you heard this."

Pat admitted then that after having written to me in April that she would never surrender, she had begun making inquiries. A male friend had persuaded her that Watergate might make a difference in the prosecutor's reception to a radical's surrender and that in any case it wouldn't hurt to ask. In other words, I thought furiously, when a man said to her precisely what I had said, she paid attention.

"Listen, Suzanne," I said. "You seem to be in no hurry to do this, and I am. I'll probably be making a second inquiry to the U.S. attorney's office this month or next. If you're trying to negotiate a deal at the same time, they'll use us against each other. Do us a favor: if you don't want to cooperate with me, then stay out of my way. I'll keep in touch with you and let you know as soon as I've turned myself in. Okay?"

She seemed frightened by my intensity.

"Sure," she said, attempting to laugh. "I'm so lazy and disorganized it will probably be a year before I get around to seeing a lawyer anyway."

As I drove recklessly away from Brattleboro, a dismal thought occurred to me. What if Pat's friend was suggesting that she turn evidence against me in exchange for her own acquittal? And what if she was annoyed enough over my memoir and now over "Mother Right"—which she hadn't mentioned—to do that?

I had to believe that, far apart as we had grown, she would spend many years in prison before she would dream of giving me up. Certainly that was the way I felt about her. My loyalty to Pat, in spite of our differences, was a moral bottom line.

The lawyer Robin found for me, Michael Armstrong, had been chief counsel for the Knapp Commission on police corruption in New York and had achieved local fame when the commission hearings were televised. He had further enhanced his reputation when Rockefeller appointed him to fill the term of a Queens prosecutor indicted in a kickback scandal. With his natural aplomb and Kennedyesque charm, Armstrong cultivated friendships with many celebrities, including Gloria Steinem, who suggested him to Robin as a lawyer with impressive establishment connections. Robin met and approved of him and then set up a meeting between us in the Albany bus terminal.

For the interview, my mother sent me a new red pants suit with a white jacket and a matching bag and shoes. I manicured my nails and combed my hair a dozen times and arrived at the bus terminal a full hour before Armstrong. He put me immediately at ease, entertaining me with anecdotes from his days on the Knapp Commission, cases he had won as a prosecutor, famous people he had known. He was not in the least pretentious or self-important, wearing his success so easily it seemed he'd been born to it—as perhaps he had.

He asked me surprisingly few questions. He didn't want to know where I was living or what I had been doing underground. That information might put him in a compromising position. He had already read my memoir of Sam and "Mother Right," which Robin had given him. He said he interpreted "Mother Right" as a renunciation of terrorism and asked me if that was accurate. I answered with an earnest speech about the male propensity for violence and how it had damaged women in the left. This was evasive, but Armstrong appeared satisfied.

He thought the best way to handle my case was to go over the usual heads directly to Paul Curran, now U.S. attorney for the

Southern District of New York. Curran was a personal friend of Armstrong's—they played tennis together on Saturdays. He might get Curran to wipe the guilty plea from the books and let me go to trial on the bail-jumping charge. Or maybe we should let the plea stand and argue for concurrent sentences. Ideas poured out of him like grass from a lawn mower. At some point in our meeting I realized he had made up his mind to represent me.

I wondered what had decided him. It wasn't money: he knew that I had none and that my legal difficulties had already imposed a tremendous hardship on my family. He agreed to take my case for a sum that, for a lawyer at the top of his profession, was a pittance. Nor had he made up his mind because of his acquaintance with Gloria or Robin's persuasive powers. He had come to Albany still undecided. I suppose that I touched him. He saw himself as a father figure helping a nice middle-class girl who had temporarily gone astray to return home to her family.

Mike's paternalism comforted me but didn't contribute to an open lawyer-client relationship. Where Sandy's cynical presumptions would have teased the truth out of me, Mike seemed to want to believe that I had never been deeply involved in criminal acts.

"In a way it's too bad you made such a public break with your radical pals," he said, referring to "Mother Right." "It doesn't give you much useful information to trade. I don't suppose, for example, that you know where Patty Hearst is?"

He chuckled. Since her February kidnapping the newspaper heiress had become the most famous fugitive in America.

"No," I answered. "All I know about Patty Hearst is what I read in the papers."

He asked me no more questions about the underground, and I volunteered nothing. As for my complicity in the bombing conspiracy, he saved the crucial question for the last five minutes when I was walking with him to his car.

"How about your own involvement?" he asked me then. "Any overt acts?"

My mind's eye saw a vision of myself in a white dress carrying a pocketbook full of explosives, riding the elevator to the fortieth floor of the Federal Building, leaving the bag in an electrical closet—and I intuited somehow that this benign and fatherly man did not want to know the truth.

"No," I said firmly. "No overt acts."

Astoundingly he never repeated the question.

On November 8, 1974, I called Mike Armstrong's office from a pay phone across the street from my Pittsfield rooming house.

"Curran's going to call off his dogs," he said genially. "How soon can you get here?"

My heart knocking against my ribs, I said I would need at least a week. I figured I would be going directly to a prison cell and I wanted to pack and say farewells first.

"You'd better get here sooner than that," Mike answered. "We don't want the FBI to think you're getting cold feet. And you don't have to worry about prison just yet. Curran's going to ask for bail."

Bail! Since my meeting with Carol Lefcourt, I hadn't allowed myself to think that I would be free in less than a year. Mike Armstrong seemed a miracle worker.

Warned by Mike that I should not go to their Forest Hills apartment until my surrender was formal, my parents had borrowed an apartment on the Upper East Side of Manhattan where I could stay. I arrived there on Monday—after returning Patch and Lissa's car to Boston—with the idea of surrendering on Tuesday morning. On Monday afternoon Mike called to say that one or two problems had developed and that I should come to his office to talk them over.

I was in a legal limbo during this period in New York, neither free nor in hiding and facing the risk that arrangements for my surrender could be jeopardized if the press got wind of it in advance. My mother, who had been afraid to be seen with me during most of the time I was underground, was now afraid to leave my side. Walking through New York with her, alert at every moment to the danger of being spotted, I was under more tension than I had been since my first few months as a fugitive. And while the deal for my surrender was not yet consummated, I was in no position to consider returning to fugitive life—not when the FBI knew I was already in New York and my mother had me under constant surveillance. The news of a possible hitch in plans was extremely alarming.

I met Mike in his office in the evening. While he continued to maintain that the problem wasn't serious, he looked worried. Judge Pollack, instead of rubber-stamping Curran's request that I be released on reasonable bail, had insisted that I first submit to interviews by FBI agents. Mike assumed that the FBI would have little interest in the details of an old bombing conspiracy but that they would want to know something about my underground life. Was there anything I could tell them that would attest to my upstanding character in the past few years? I hadn't by any chance worked for the Red Cross or lived in a convent?

When I said that I had worked for a year and a half at an Orthodox Jewish school for girls, Armstrong was ecstatic. He instructed me to call the rabbis first thing in the morning, reveal my identity to them, and ask them to call him at once, collect. If they would vouch for my good character during my employment, it would be a great help.

Now, he wanted to know, was there anything at all about which I wouldn't want to talk with the FBI? Of course, I wouldn't want to inform on my parents, who were technically guilty of harboring me, or to get innocent, well-meaning friends like Robin into trouble. The FBI wouldn't be interested in people like them anyway. They would want the names of the criminal types—the ones who had bombed buildings or assassinated cops. Was there anyone in that category I wouldn't be willing to talk about?

I didn't know how to answer him. Even if it were true that the FBI wouldn't prosecute friends like Lynn Gottlieb or Patch and Lissa, I still hated the idea of talking to the government about them. And of course, I couldn't talk about the leftists whose activities would interest the FBI—Greg and Robert and Maude and Pat and Dana, who had been so crucial in my first months underground. Finally, the FBI would know from "Mother Right" that I had some contact with the Weather Underground and would want to hear all about that.

Seeing how upset I was, Armstrong proposed to postpone the surrender until Thursday, November 14. In the meantime, he and I would spend some more time together, going over my underground life and figuring out where the problems lay.

Late that night, still in my legal limbo and watching carefully for spies, I took a cab to Robin and Ken's apartment. Robin and I stayed up all night, discussing the best way to handle the crisis.

My idea was that I should tell Mike the whole truth but explain that I couldn't give the FBI any information that would lead to the capture of fugitives or the prosecution of people for harboring me. Robin thought that was ridiculous. What I didn't want repeated to the FBI, she argued, I shouldn't tell Mike at all. Instead, I should invent a fiction to cover the few months I had lived with Pat and the even briefer period I had been with the Weather Underground. I could omit all mention of Pat and simply claim that during the time I was actually traveling with her I was with a male stranger I had picked up in California. As for the Weatherwomen, all I had to do was invent different cities for our meetings and say that I had never known their real names. It might sound implausible, but if I could persuade Mike that it was true, he would take care of the FBI for me.

This was perhaps the most deluded strategy on which Robin and I had ever collaborated. My own experience as a defendant had taught me how vital it was for a lawyer to be informed of all the dangers the client faced. To attempt to lie to the government without letting Mike know what I was doing would seriously jeopardize his ability to represent me, which was all the protection I had. Yet I accepted Robin's advice, naïvely confident in her wisdom.

When I repeated the story to Mike, he seemed to suspect that I was omitting vital information, but he was elated at having received glowing testimonials from the rabbis in Denver. Rabbi Schwab had even offered to fly to New York to testify in my behalf, which turned out to be unnecessary but which touched Mike—and me—very much. So the gaps in my story remained and plans for my surrender on Thursday proceeded.

In the company of my parents and my lawyer, I presented myself at the U.S. attorney's office at nine on the morning of November 14, 1974, four and a half years since the day I jumped bail. My parents were asked to wait in the hall. For the next eight hours I was interrogated intensively by Assistant U.S. Attorney David Cutner; the chief assistant, Silvio Mollo (a hard-liner who appeared furious that I was making bail by going over his head to Paul Curran); and two FBI agents. I stuck rigorously to the tale I had invented with Robin, reverting whenever I could to stories about my c-r group or Polly or the Denver rabbis and students, who were all completely safe from prosecution. I admitted to having met Mark Rudd in Santa

Fe (where I said I had arrived by chance), but I disguised the identities and locations involved in my other meetings with the Weather Underground. And I claimed that I had not heard a word from or about Pat since she disappeared from New York five years and two days ago. My interrogators took detailed notes, alternately blustered and cajoled, but finally seemed persuaded by my story. At tense moments Mike would pick up the testimonials the rabbis had provided and wave them in the prosecutor's face, as if to say, "How's a judge going to deny bail to a girl like this?"

At a little before 6:00 P.M. a U.S. marshal escorted me into Judge Pollack's courtroom. Except for my lawyer, government personnel, a UPI court reporter, and my parents sitting alone in the spectator section, the room was empty, but I could still see the ghosts of the frenzied scenes of 1970.

On Armstrong's recommendation, I entered a plea of guilty to bail jumping. I now stood convicted of two felonies carrying a maximum penalty of ten years.

"If I release you on bail tonight," the stony-faced judge said, peering down from the bench, "it will be in the custody of your parents and on the condition that you reside with them until sentencing. Do you agree?"

The right words came without my having to think about them. "Your Honor," I said, "it's been five years since I last saw my parents' home. I would consider it a privilege."

For the first time in my memory Judge Pollack smiled.

Within hours of being freed on bail, I was regretting having talked to the government at all. Refusal to cooperate with authority had been a basic principle of the left for years, and one that I shared. I had agreed to talk not so that I could lead the government to my former friends but to try to persuade my interrogators, and through them the judge, that I had lived a relatively upstanding life while underground and that I'd had only marginal contact with the rest of the radical left. Where necessary, I had denied and dissembled to protect those who had helped me and others who were still underground—including members of the Weather Underground who were not exactly friends of mine. Still, I had violated my conscience and was now punished by fear of the consequences.

One element of my story in particular was bothering me. I had explained my travels in my first eight months of underground life by saying that I arrived in San Francisco alone, met a man in a park, and eventually went east with him. I had also admitted to using the alias Ellen Davis Blake. Now I remembered that I had signed that alias on a lease to the house in Jaffrey. If through a diligent search of New Hampshire real estate agents, the FBI located the house and then showed pictures of Pat to our Jaffrey neighbors, they might conclude that she had lived there, too. And if they could trace her from Jaffrey through her next few homes to Brattleboro, both she and I would be in serious trouble.

As soon as I could get to a pay phone that night, I called her. I explained that I'd been subjected to interrogation and that although I had said nothing about her and had given no addresses, the FBI might now be able to locate the Jaffrey house. If it was at all likely that she could be traced to Brattleboro from that address, she ought to take cover for a couple of months.

She immediately began to berate me for talking to the FBI. I couldn't blame her. But yelling at me was beside the point. What was important was that she make plans to move.

She told me she would never leave Brattleboro.

I realized that she was happy in her community and didn't wish to move. Yet I could hardly believe that she meant it. I thought of the farmhouse in New York which we had left against our wishes because of Maude's fear. And of the many moves Pat had made in New England since we were together—apparently never bothering to change her alias or conceal her new address from former neighbors. I remembered moving on such slight provocations as the Republican convention's coming to San Diego. How could she expect to survive as a fugitive if she wouldn't change location when necessary? I tried to convince her that she was wrong, but I made no headway.

The following months were hellish. The FBI continued to interrogate me until my sentencing date of January 13, pursuing the flaws in my story. I kept repeating the same fictions over and over, dreading each day to hear the news that Pat had been picked up and my falsehoods discovered.

Meanwhile, rumors swept through the left that I had turned informant in order to win a light sentence. "Mother Right" had already earned me enemies, and newspaper reports of my cooperation fueled their hostility. *off our backs*, the feminist journal that had been the first to print "Mother Right," canceled an interview with me and published a hostile story about my surrender instead. Fred Cohn, Sandy Katz's partner, bragged to me that his wife was active in a group seeking to discredit me and that he himself counted me an enemy. Once on my way up the courthouse steps, heading for an interview with my probation officer, I was recognized by a woman demonstrating for prisoners' rights. "Jane Alpert, why are you ratting on all your friends?" she called. I stopped in my tracks, wanting to challenge her with the truth but became tongue-tied when I saw the anger that was contorting her face.

On January 13, 1975, Judge Pollack sentenced me to twenty-seven months in prison: eighteen months for the bombing conspiracy, nine months for bail jumping, to be served consecutively.

Was this a lighter sentence than I would have received had I not given the FBI some version of my underground life? It's hard to say. Other mitigating circumstances helped: my white middle-class origins, my college education, the support of my family, the recommendations of the Beth Jacob rabbis, letters from dozens of social service agencies asking that I be allowed to perform volunteer work for them for a period of years rather than go to jail. Still, I received approximately the same sentence as Nate had in 1970, when the bombings were fresher in the public's mind and the pressure on the judge to punish us was greater. When Cathy Wilkerson surrendered in 1980 and pleaded guilty to the explosion in the town house that had killed three of her friends, she received a sentence of one to three years—also about the same as mine. Other Weatherfugitives—like Rudd and Dohrn—received only probation when they finally surrendered, but the charges against them were rioting and other lesser offenses, not bombings.

On January 27, the date decreed by Pollack, my parents drove me to the gates of the State Correctional Institute at Muncy, Pennsylvania, a mostly women's prison that housed federal inmates under a contract with the federal government.

The bucolic setting of the prison concealed a hellhole of lunacy and brutality such as I had not believed existed outside movies. A crude form of nationalism was on the rise among the black inmates, about half the prison population. As a radical I was urged by the militant black prisoners to teach them to make a bomb. When I refused, they suspected I was a traitor. Condemned by them and by other black inmates for being white and educated, I was no more popular with the white inmates. They expected me to side with them against the blacks and were baffled and angry when I refused. As a matter of principle, I turned down an assignment in the administration building and was sent instead to the sadistically run prison kitchen. As much as I was allowed, I stayed alone in my room, keeping to a schedule of reading and writing and guarding my sanity like a caged bird.

On March 12, in the seventh week of my sentence, Pat Swinton was arrested at the Good Earth health food store in Brattleboro. True to her word, she had not budged from the day I called to warn her.

Mike Armstrong phoned the prison to tell me the news. I was very sad to hear of her capture and said if I could do anything to help her, I would. I would have been glad to repeat to the FBI what I had already said: that she had never been involved in the bombings and that I had not seen her since she disappeared.

The next day Mike called again. He said that when Pat Swinton appeared at her arraignment in federal court, her lawyer, Fred Cohn, announced that we had lived together when we were underground and that Pat had known since I surrendered that she would be picked up.

To the best of my knowledge, this was the first the government ever heard about Pat's and my shared history. In other words, Pat Swinton and Fred Cohn had informed on me. Aware that I had concealed information from the FBI, they provided evidence that I had lied and subjected me to possible felony charges for my false statements.

On March 20, eight days after her arrest, Pat went free on $200,000 bail provided by a wealthy relative. Shortly after her release she embarked on a speaking tour, the main point of which was to tell her audiences that my conversations with the FBI had led to her arrest.

That I had lied to the FBI to protect her; that she was living in a center of radical activity where she was likely to be arrested anyway; that she had repeatedly refused either to turn herself in or to move; that the first hard information that we had lived together came not from me but from Pat's lawyer, Fred Cohn—all this Pat knew but never admitted in public and perhaps never to herself. With the eager assistance of others in the left, including some former friends I had also protected from prosecution, she preached that I had given her up in exchange for a light sentence for myself and suggested that I might now become a prosecution witness at her trial.

That spring and summer Pat's denunciations of me penetrated the prison gates. Public reports that I had informed against a codefendant turned me into an obvious target for fellow prisoners' frustrations. I was repeatedly punished: knocked down, robbed of my contact lenses (which were ground up in the kitchen potato machine), threatened at knifepoint.

Robin organized a group of feminists called the Circle of Support for Jane Alpert that issued leaflets attempting to counter Pat's claims and argue my integrity to the women's movement. Most of those who joined the Circle had been led, like me, by the insights of the feminist movement to radically change their political beliefs and their personal lives. They saw me as someone who had been forced to pay an unusual public price for the views that they had been able to adopt more privately, though with no less emotional turmoil. Most of them didn't know me, yet they became my ardent defenders for the duration of my imprisonment, sending me warm personal letters and gifts, telling the other side of the story to the journalists covering Pat's case.

In August, U.S. Attorney Paul Curran called Mike to say that he had just received proof that I had lied to FBI agents about my contact with Pat Swinton and that he had a witness who would testify to the fact. If I refused to talk about her role in the bombings at her September trial, I would be charged not only with civil and criminal contempt but with making false statements to federal authorities, a felony. For each false statement I had made (I guessed there were hundreds), I could serve another five years in prison.

In September, in the eighth month of my sentence, I was put on the stand at Pat's trial. Granted immunity from further prosecution, I was ordered by Judge Pollack to tell what I knew of Pat's role in the bombings.

I looked across the courtroom at Pat, the first time I had seen her since I had tried to persuade her, more than a year ago, to turn herself in. Could she have thought, even for a moment, that I meant to testify against her?

I refused to answer the judge's questions.

Nate, who had been released from prison in 1972 and was now enrolled in college as a condition of his parole, also refused to testify. He was sent to jail in civil contempt for five days, the duration of the trial.

George Demmerle took the stand, but although he had once known Pat well, he failed to identify her at the defense table. Was he reluctant to put a fourth person behind bars because of a five-year-old bombing conspiracy or did he have some remorse over the undercover role he had played? Or was he simply dumber than we had imagined?

The government's surprise witness was Lonnie.

Having learned of my surrender and Pat's arrest through newspaper reports, he had gone to the FBI on his own and volunteered a complete account of his travels with us. In a series of interviews with FBI agents in Cincinnati (where he was living with his parents) and New York, he had furnished a colorful, detailed, and astoundingly accurate story—which he repeated under oath on the witness stand.

Lonnie's knowledge of the bombing conspiracy was hearsay and fragmentary. He could not help Cutner convict Pat for a crime that had occurred nearly a year before he met her. He knew, however, much more than enough to put me away for the lies I had told in an attempt to protect Pat.

Pat was acquitted of all charges. She raised her arms in a boxer's salute, hugged her lawyer, and raced outside to a press conference, where she told a *Post* reporter that she felt sorry for Lonnie, whose hesitant answers and terrified demeanor made it clear that he was an unwilling witness. As for me, she said that although I had refused to testify in the end, I was still an informant who had led to her arrest. Later she charged me with perpetuating racist stereotypes about prisoners by claiming that my life was in danger.

In May 1976, a few months before the end of my sentence, both Nate and I were indicted for criminal contempt, a charge carrying a sentence at the discretion of the judge. I was released from prison in September 1976 (I had a standard seven months cut from my sentence for good behavior) but went back in November 1977 to serve an additional four months for the contempt charge. All told, I spent two years in prison. Perhaps the government decided this was punishment enough; I was not indicted for lying to the FBI.

Pat returned to a lavish welcome at her Brattleboro commune. She changed her name legally to Shoshana, the last name she had used as a fugitive. For the next year or so newspapers reported her occasional speeches or mentioned her in connection with antinuclear protests. At the time I was sentenced for criminal contempt, I received letters from some of her associates, apologizing for their former accusations and expressing regret at my sentence. Pat and I were never in touch. In early 1979 I heard that she had left Brattleboro and was taking acting classes in New York City.

My split with Pat was extremely painful, but more so was the break with Robin that followed my release from prison. The first crack in our friendship appeared in late 1974, in the weeks before my sentencing, when I wanted to confess to Mike Armstrong that I had lied to him and to cut off any further conversations with the FBI. Robin, strongly seconded by Kenneth, berated my weakness and insisted that I keep repeating the fictitious story—advice that was, in the end, disastrous.

She supported me loyally when I was under attack in prison, but it was difficult to maintain our friendship during the incarceration. Her visits gradually diminished in length and frequency, and she appeared preoccupied by other matters. Many inmates had similar experiences in the visiting room, and despite my fears, I believed Robin's assurances that we would resume our intimacy once I was free. When I was first released, we performed the rituals of close friendship: I baby-sat for Blake and taught him Latin; Robin helped me write a book proposal; I gave parties after her joint poetry readings with Kenneth; she introduced me to her friends. But under the surface the affection I'd come to count on was absent.

I think perhaps that Robin had been more attached to what she perceived as the romance of fugitive life—hardly romantic to me—than in the more mundane possibilities of my postprison identity. No longer an adventure, I turned into an encumbrance—and while I had paid my debt to society, it seemed that my debt to Robin remained outstanding. She became increasingly disappointed and exasperated until the inevitable hurtful end: two years after my release, she summoned me to a family conference at her home, where I was told by Kenneth, Blake, and Robin in turn that I was destructive to the family and was to be banished from their lives. So Robin disposed of me, finally, with a gesture as extravagant as the one she had used to adopt me, flying 1,200 miles into my obscure San Diego hideout to recruit me into feminism.

Some of the connections I severed in the course of my surrender will never be mended: the misunderstanding went too deep; the bitterness does not recede. For others, I still have hope.

In March 1980 I wrote Nathan Yarrow care of his lawyer. We had last seen each other in September 1975 at Pat's trial, when I was in custody. He had thrown his arms around me, but the marshals chased him away. At my sentencing for the contempt charge in 1977 I learned from Nate's lawyer that he was living and working somewhere in the South, was married and that his wife had just given birth to a baby girl. I felt nervous at renewing so charged an acquaintance, but I told myself the worst he could do was fail to answer my letter.

His answer was warm and immediate. Enclosed with it was a snapshot of his three-year-old daughter. A few weeks later we managed to arrange a visit in New York.

Nate looked wonderful. He had lost the skeletal gauntness of his early twenties and grown strong and healthy. His corduroy pants and flannel shirt were well pressed, and a new down jacket took the place of the torn army fatigues he used to wear. I was oddly relieved to see a pair of scuffed army boots on his feet, proving, like an old scar, that he was still the same Nathan.

As we tramped through the scenes of our shared past, Nate told me his story. When he went to prison in 1970, his contact with everyone he had known in the left abruptly stopped. This was his choice, partly because he wanted to use the solitude of prison to rethink his political beliefs and partly because he feared that any communication with his friends would be used by the government against him and them. After a few months in prison his main struggle became maintaining his sanity. He learned to fast and meditate and, through a book by Baba Ram Dass given him by another prisoner, became interested in Buddhism. In time religious commitment subsumed his old political beliefs. He was paroled in the fall of 1972, after he had renewed his relationship with his parents and agreed to reenroll at the university he'd dropped out of in 1966.

At the time Nate received his subpoena to testify at Pat's trial, he had completely shed his leftist identity. He was living with a woman he had met at the university whom he loved and with whom he was planning to raise a family. Holding down a job he liked as manager of a small business, he now conceived of his life more in religious than political terms. He had made the decision not to testify against Pat—subjecting himself to a four-month prison term—for personal rather than political reasons, something he said Pat was unable to understand.

His feelings about Sam resembled my own. He told me that while we were living on the Lower East Side, he had heroicized Sam. Once they were in prison together, he began to see how fragile his idol was. Nate was in the second year of his sentence when he learned of Sam's death at Attica. For many days he was unable to react at all, but at last he realized that he had been furious at Sam ever since he learned that Sam had talked to Demmerle against his express request. Discovering the depth of his anger at Sam after so much time had come as a shock.

Through our long walk and a spaghetti dinner we got along better and better. Yet all day I waited for his criticism. I was expecting him to tear apart "Mother Right" and to demand an explanation of why I had talked to the FBI when I surrendered. The challenges never came. The closest we came to an argument was late in the evening when I made light of a meditation practice he was describing.

"I expected better of you," he snapped. Then he broke into a laugh that brought the past flooding back to me, a rainbow glimmering through the clouds of his face. "I'm sorry," he said, "I didn't mean that. No opinion you could have of my beliefs could make me love you less."

And I realized that Nate didn't care how I had chosen to renounce the past or what mistakes I had made in the process. Ten and a half years since the night FBI agents broke into my apartment and carted us off to jail, after drastic changes in our systems of belief and with many differences remaining, we were still friends. It seemed miraculous.

An hour after Nate's plane departed, walking through the streets of Queens, I found myself drenched in tears. They were as much from joy as from the sadness of separation.

Certainly personal rage and pain, more than politics, had led me to break violently with my parents in adolescence, to bomb buildings, and later to reject the left with all the hostility I could muster. In the past few years I had gained some inner peace and self-control. My surrender had helped. So had writing the book and professional counseling, my family's steadfastness and Ed's undemanding love. And in some way I can't explain, when Nate, vibrant and beautiful after all that happened, offered me his friendship, I felt from him something I can only call forgiveness. I had taken one more step. My surrender had helped. So had writing the book and professional counseling, my family's steadfastness and the affection and respect of friends. And in some way I can't explain, when Nate, vibrant and beautiful after all that happened, offered me his friendship, I felt from him something I can only call forgiveness. I had taken one more step.

Author's afterword to the Citadel Underground edition

When the original edition of *Growing Up Underground* went out of print five years ago, my sadness was tinged with relief. Its publication in 1981 had stirred such denunciation and rage that I wondered whether some sort of virus had slipped, without my knowing it, from the typewriter into the manuscript. Was it possible that the book was not the open act of atonement I intended, but rather an expression of a subconscious will to provoke—a continuation of the extreme and violent acts that were its subject?

Yet I was heartened to hear, over the years, from readers who had been deeply moved. Many were contemporaries who had kept secret their own stories of risk, rebellion, and narrow escape. Many more were so young that they had only the vaguest firsthand impressions of the Vietnam War era. They, in particular, were grateful for the book as a cautionary tale. They told me that it helped them understand how the charged political atmosphere of the late 1960s drove many of my generation over the edge—and that by describing that edge in familiar and recognizable detail, it illuminated.

The unexpected and gracious invitation of Citadel Underground to put the book back in print has evoked in me feelings as mixed as those with which I faced its disappearance. These days, I rarely discuss my past—not from embarrassment, but because it seems so bizarre in the context of my everyday life. For thirteen years, I have lived in the same rented New York City apartment. I get up, get dressed, and go to work with the rest of the world. I campaign for progressive public officials. I write letters to Congress to support the right to abortion, wilderness preservation, funding for public housing, nuclear disarmament. I think a lot about mortality.

Growing up is a continuous process, and I have changed as much since I first wrote the book as I did in the decade it concerns. The temptation to rewrite my ten-year-old prose is great. If I were to start again with the Prologue, the events would be the same, but the narrative voice would be more guarded. The portraits of individuals would be more nuanced. The whole would be less a recitation of facts, and more of a judgment, of myself and others.

But to keep faith both with readers and with a younger self who, for better or worse, risked unvarnished truth, I have left the book as it was. This is a verbatim reprint of the original edition, with the sole exception of a few paragraphs at the end that referred to my life in 1980, and for which this afterword takes the place.

CITADEL UNDERGROUND provides a voice to writers whose ideas and styles veer from convention. The series is dedicated to bringing back into print lost classics and to publishing new works that explore pathbreaking and iconoclastic personal, social, literary, musical, consciousness, political, dramatic and rhetorical styles.

For more information, please write to

CITADEL UNDERGROUND
Carol Publishing Group
600 Madison Avenue
New York, New York 10022

Citadel Underground Board of Advisors (CUBA)